T0224801

Beginning Salesforce DX

Versatile and Resilient Salesforce Application Development

Ivan Harris

Apress®

Beginning Salesforce DX: Versatile and Resilient Salesforce Application Development

Ivan Harris
FROME, UK

ISBN-13 (pbk): 978-1-4842-8113-0 ISBN-13 (electronic): 978-1-4842-8114-7
https://doi.org/10.1007/978-1-4842-8114-7

Managing Director, Apress Media LLC: Welmoed Spahr
Acquisitions Editor: Susan McDermott
Development Editor: Laura Berendson
Coordinating Editor: Jessica Vakili

Distributed to the book trade worldwide by Springer Science+Business Media New York, 1 New York Plaza, New York, NY 10004. Phone 1-800-SPRINGER, fax (201) 348-4505, e-mail orders-ny@springer-sbm.com, or visit www.springeronline.com. Apress Media, LLC is a California LLC and the sole member (owner) is Springer Science + Business Media Finance Inc (SSBM Finance Inc). SSBM Finance Inc is a **Delaware** corporation.

For information on translations, please e-mail booktranslations@springernature.com; for reprint, paperback, or audio rights, please e-mail bookpermissions@springernature.com.

Apress titles may be purchased in bulk for academic, corporate, or promotional use. eBook versions and licenses are also available for most titles. For more information, reference our Print and eBook Bulk Sales web page at http://www.apress.com/bulk-sales.

Any source code or other supplementary material referenced by the author in this book is available to readers on the Github repository: https://github.com/Apress/Beginning-Salesforce-DX. For more detailed information, please visit http://www.apress.com/source-code.

Printed on acid-free paper

To my wife Rosie, and my son Hugo.

Table of Contents

About the Author

After graduating from Lancaster University with a degree in Electrical and Electronic Engineering, **Ivan Harris** spent the first 15 years of his career in the aerospace and defense industry, designing, writing, and testing safety-critical embedded software.

During the second half of his career, he held several C-level technology and product leadership roles, helping B2B software companies bring innovative new solutions to market. Domains included game software development tools, information management and security, mobile network optimization, mobile network renewable energy, public cloud application development, and artificial intelligence.

More recently, Ivan has focused on creating products that are built on, or that integrate with, Salesforce. He has launched five Salesforce AppExchange apps, including his own, and an AI platform that integrates with Service Cloud to provide customer service automation.

Ivan then joined Salesforce as a Senior Program Architect in Australia, working with some of their largest and most complex multicloud customers on enterprise transformation projects to help accelerate their time to value.

In September 2022, Ivan joined Provar Testing as their Chief Technology Officer in the UK. Provar provides an end-to-end test automation solution designed especially for Salesforce.

Ivan enjoys running, walking his two dogs, supporting his local rugby union team, and listening to his extensive vinyl collection in his spare time.

About the Technical Reviewer

Ramzi Akremi is an Associate Director in Accenture's Salesforce Business Group, responsible for software engineering and DevOps.

He has more than 20 years of CRM delivery experience and more than 12 years on Salesforce and has directly impacted roughly 300,000+ users worldwide.

During these 12 years, Ramzi has formed and led the large teams behind some of the most significant Salesforce deployments.

His aim for the last years has been to create, apply, and evangelize an open source asset-based (DX@Scale), engineering-led approach to deliver Salesforce solutions at scale. The impacts of such an approach are stellar: continuous delivery on Salesforce is finally possible, with systems that are resilient to change, leading to continuous value delivered to his customers and a high level of engagement within the teams.

When Ramzi is not working, he enjoys family time, playing the guitar, having passionate conversations about software engineering, and imagining how he can help people "play a game they can win."

About the Technical Reviewer

Foreword

In 2011, Marc Andreessen famously wrote that "software is eating the world,"[1] and over a decade later, this trend continues with no sign of slowing down. The demand for Salesforce developers has followed a similar upward trajectory, but the mechanics of Salesforce development have changed beyond recognition in that time.

Apex development was originally carried out through the online Salesforce application, initially via a rudimentary editor available from setup, and later using the Developer Console, which could never quite decide if it wanted to be a simple editor or an IDE. Local development was made possible through the Force.com IDE plugin for Eclipse. Deployments required direct interaction with the Metadata API or figuring out how to express logic in XML build files for the Ant migration tool to process. For those of us that had come from an enterprise Java or C# environment, the tools felt distinctly subpar.

This changed in late 2017 when the new Salesforce Developer Experience, or Salesforce DX, became generally available. The source of truth pivoted from the code that was present in a Salesforce org to source control. Features could now be developed in isolation and easily incorporated into production systems, continuous integration went from being a challenge to a requirement, and DevOps became something we did rather than something we explained wasn't really possible with the existing tooling.

The Salesforce product set was also expanding during this time, through acquisitions and internal development, and the Salesforce Developer Experience began to go wide as well as deep. Building custom user interfaces now requires modern JavaScript skills and is no longer possible through the online Salesforce application. The Salesforce CLI has rebuilt with multicloud capabilities, allowing deployment at the project level of not only Salesforce platform metadata but Marketing Cloud, Heroku, MuleSoft, and more. The tooling has become more powerful, but also more complex and with a bigger learning curve.

[1] `https://a16z.com/2011/08/20/why-software-is-eating-the-world/`

To truly harness the power of the Salesforce Developer Experience, developers need a deep understanding of the available tools and how to use them effectively – this book is a key companion in that learning journey.

Salesforce development isn't just about pro-code however – the platform has always been highly configurable, and significant investment in Salesforce Flow has seen it become one of the leading low-code enterprise application development platforms. Salesforce DevOps Center introduces point and click change management best practice to low-code development environments but is again underpinned by the Salesforce Developer Experience. Low-code developers looking to reduce their reliance on pro-coders to handle issues like merge conflicts, invalid metadata, and deployment errors also need an understanding of the tools and processes involved, which they can gain from this book.

With a wealth of experience of Salesforce development from both the systems integration and independent software vendor perspective, Ivan Harris provides guidance for all roles involved in Salesforce application development to allow them to make the most of the sophisticated tools and processes that we now have at our disposal.

Keir Bowden
CTO, BrightGen
Salesforce MVP and CTA

CHAPTER 1

Introduction

As of April 2022, Salesforce, Inc. ranked #1[1] for customer relationship management (CRM) applications with a market share of 23.8%, which is larger than the combined market share of the next four highest ranking businesses. In this context, the CRM market includes Sales Force Productivity and Management, Marketing Campaign Management, Customer Service, Contact Center, Advertising, and Digital Commerce Applications. Salesforce has over 150,000 customers using its Salesforce products.

Salesforce was founded in 1999 and completely disrupted the existing CRM market as a pioneer of the Software as a Service (SaaS) subscription model. Prior to SaaS, customers made a one-off payment for a lifetime, or perpetual, product license. They could also purchase a yearly support contract to receive minor version updates and limited technical support. Major version upgrades usually required an additional upgrade fee. The customer bore the financial and operational burden of establishing and managing an on-premise data center, forecasting and budgeting for compute capacity, building the security infrastructure, and deploying, updating, and patching software products. With the advent of the SaaS model, customers subscribe to use a product on a pay-as-you-go basis. The product is cloud hosted and typically accessed via a browser or a mobile application, although in some cases "thin clients" are used. The SaaS vendor takes responsibility for managing the product and the cloud infrastructure that it runs on, including feature releases, bug fixing, operating system patching, security, and provisioning enough compute capacity to ensure that every customer in the multitenant environment enjoys a responsive experience.

As businesses often have their own unique requirements, Salesforce products are customizable to meet their specific needs. When a customization isn't sufficient, applications can be built on the Salesforce Platform, the same platform that powers Salesforce's own products. To develop applications and customizations that extend the

[1] www.salesforce.com/campaign/worlds-number-one-CRM/

I. Harris, *Beginning Salesforce DX*, https://doi.org/10.1007/978-1-4842-8114-7_1

core capabilities of its products, Salesforce provides no-code, low-code, and pro-code development tools. Examples of each development tool model are as follows:

- **No-Code Development**: Lightning App Builder, which utilizes a point-and-click, drag-and-drop user interface to create Lightning pages from prebuilt components.
- **Low-Code Development**: For this model, a little programming knowledge is needed, such as an understanding of formulae and logical statements, to write validation rules and formula fields.
- **Pro-Code Development**: Includes writing Apex classes, Apex triggers, Visualforce pages, and Lightning web components.

For no-code and low-code development, system administrators typically use the Setup area in a Salesforce product. For pro-code development, Salesforce provides developers with tools such as the Developer Console, Ant Migration Tool, the Salesforce User Interface Code Editor, and Workbench. In the past, Salesforce also provided the Force.com IDE for Eclipse, which has now been retired.

Salesforce is renowned for its relentless innovation, in its pursuit to deliver increasing value to its customers and partners, which extends to its development tools. Salesforce Developer Experience, more commonly known as "Salesforce DX" or "SFDX," is the latest generation of development tools that became generally available with the release of Salesforce's Winter '18 update in October 2017. Salesforce DX introduces new tools and new ways of working that transform how administrators and developers develop and deploy Salesforce applications and customizations in today's fast-paced, demanding, and complex business environments, including

- **Salesforce DX Projects**: A new local filing system folder structure that stores source format files, configuration files, and other project-related files to support development with Salesforce DX tools
- **Source Format**: A more granular alternative to Metadata API format files that simplifies source code control and collaborative development and reduces the time taken to synchronize changes between Salesforce DX projects and scratch orgs
- **Scratch Orgs**: Short-lived orgs that can be created and destroyed as and when required during the development lifecycle

- **Salesforce CLI**: A suite of commands that can be executed from the command line to interact with scratch orgs and non-scratch orgs such as sandboxes and production orgs
- **Salesforce Extensions for Visual Studio Code**: An extension pack that adds support for Salesforce DX development to the free Visual Studio Code integrated development environment
- **Source-Driven Development**: A switch to the version control system, rather than a production org, being the source of truth
- **Package Development Model**: Modular, versioned development using unlocked packages and managed packages, which are containers for functionally related metadata components that make up an application or customization

Salesforce DX is evolving rapidly, with new features being added all the time. The Salesforce DX team has said that in the future some of those features will be instrumental in attracting administrators to the toolset. That said, it's fair to say that today, Salesforce DX is aimed squarely at development teams. Therefore, this book is focused on application and customization development, and it will be of interest to developers who are members of two types of teams:

1. **Internal Development Team**: This team consists of in-house developers and/or third-party consultancies developing applications and customizations for a single customer.
2. **AppExchange Partner Development Team**: This team develops applications for listing on the Salesforce AppExchange enterprise marketplace, which currently lists over 5000 prebuilt solutions.[2]

You may be a developer embarking on a fresh project and you want to use Salesforce DX from the get-go, or perhaps you have an existing application or customization that you are thinking of transitioning to Salesforce DX. Either way, this book, which is laid out in the following two parts, will take you from a novice to a proficient Salesforce DX practitioner:

[2] https://appexchange.salesforce.com/appxContentListingDetail?listingId=aON3A00000FvKly

1. **Part I - Preparing for Salesforce DX**: In this part, you set up your development environment, and you will be introduced to the core concepts of Salesforce DX, equipping you with the tools and foundational knowledge to dive into SFDX in Part II.
2. **Part II - Working with Salesforce DX**: We transition from theory into practice in this part, where you will explore the core concepts of Salesforce DX in more detail using hands-on examples.

By the end of the book, you will be armed with the tools and the key skills needed to put Salesforce DX at the heart of your development lifecycle. Whether you work in a team undertaking internal development of company-specific applications and customizations, or you work in an AppExchange Partner team developing packaged solutions for Salesforce AppExchange, you can apply the skills that you have learned to radically improve your development practices. You will also be ready to explore more advanced Salesforce DX topics at your own pace.

If you are ready to improve team collaboration, increase quality, shorten development cycles, and enhance feature traceability, read on!

Chapter Summary

This chapter introduced Salesforce.com, Inc., how it pioneered the enterprise SaaS subscription model, and why it opened its products and platform for application and customization development. We saw that development can now be undertaken using the Salesforce DX toolset and new ways of working, which is the subject of this book. We also learned how the two parts of the book will take you from novice to proficient SFDX practitioner.

In the next chapter, which is the first in Part I of the book, we'll set up your development environment so that you have the toolkit needed to develop applications and customizations using Salesforce DX.

PART I

Preparing for Salesforce DX

In this part of the book, we will prepare you to start developing applications and customizations using Salesforce DX. We'll start by setting up your development environment. We will then provide a high-level overview of Salesforce DX, introducing the core concepts and how they work together. By the end of Part I, you will be equipped with the toolkit and foundational knowledge needed to transition to Part II, where we will get hands-on and dive deeper into the Salesforce DX concepts.

CHAPTER 2

Environment Setup

The only tool that you need in order to develop applications or customizations using Salesforce DX is the Salesforce CLI, a command-line interface for executing Salesforce DX commands. Having said that, to improve productivity, an integrated development environment (IDE) is preferred. There are several IDEs to choose from, including Illuminated Cloud (a plug-in for the IntelliJ IDEA IDE), The Welkin Suite, and others. In this book, we are going to standardize on using Visual Studio Code with the Salesforce Extensions for Visual Studio Code; the extension pack is published by Salesforce, and both the extension pack and Visual Studio Code are free. To set up our complete desktop development environment, we will walk through the installation of the following tools:

- **Salesforce CLI**: A command-line interface, or "CLI," that you use to execute commands to support the full application or customization development lifecycle.
- **Java Development Kit**: The Java Platform, Standard Edition Development Kit, or "JDK," is a prerequisite for some of the features in the Salesforce Extensions for Visual Studio Code pack.
- **Visual Studio Code**: A free and open source integrated development environment, or "IDE," that is available for Windows, Linux, and macOS, also known as "VS Code."
- **Salesforce Extensions for Visual Studio Code**: Adds support for working with Salesforce DX projects and the Salesforce CLI to the Visual Studio Code IDE.

Note We will set up additional tools when they are required by a chapter; for example, the Git setup is included in Chapter 9, "Version Control."

I. Harris, *Beginning Salesforce DX*, https://doi.org/10.1007/978-1-4842-8114-7_2

For more advanced topics on setting up Salesforce DX and the Salesforce Extensions for Visual Studio Code, please refer to the following resources:

- **Salesforce DX Setup Guide**: `https://developer.salesforce.com/docs/atlas.en-us.sfdx_setup.meta/sfdx_setup/sfdx_setup_intro.htm`
- **Salesforce Extensions for Visual Studio Code**: `https://developer.salesforce.com/tools/vscode`

If you already have a Salesforce DX development environment setup, you can skip to Chapter 3, "Concepts Overview"; otherwise, let's proceed to set up the first tool, the Salesforce CLI.

Installing the Salesforce CLI

The Salesforce CLI, short for "command-line interface," executes commands that are entered on a terminal application's command line. The CLI commands are used during Salesforce DX application or customization development and can be entered manually or by automation tools such as scripts and DevOps systems. We will dive into the Salesforce CLI in Chapter 4, "Salesforce CLI."

To install the Salesforce CLI, visit the following page:

- `https://developer.salesforce.com/docs/atlas.en-us.sfdx_setup.meta/sfdx_setup`

Click the **Install the Salesforce CLI** menu item in the left-hand navigation bar to expand its submenu, then click your operating system and follow the instructions.

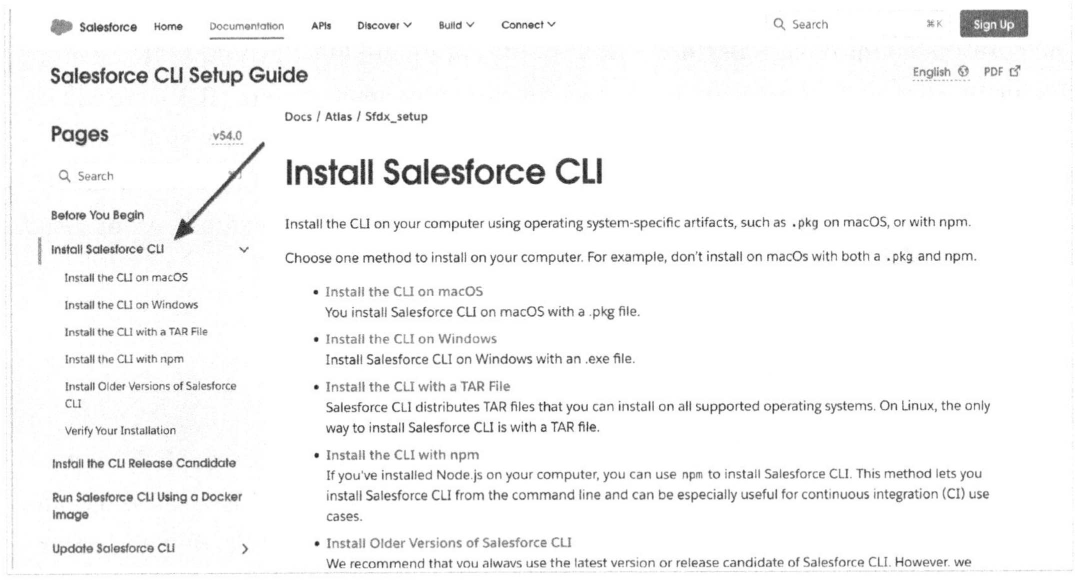

Figure 2-1. *Salesforce CLI installation screen*

After the installation has completed, and every time you use the CLI thereafter, it is good practice to check that you have the latest version installed. To do so, open a terminal application and enter the following command:

```
$ sfdx update
```

Note The preceding `sfdx update` command assumes that you followed the instructions in the **Install the CLI on macOS** installation steps. If you installed the CLI using the steps in the **Install the CLI with npm** section, updates are performed using the command `npm update --global sfdx-cli`.

To display the installed CLI version number, enter the following command:

```
$ sfdx --version
```

which will display the following.

Listing 2-1. Salesforce CLI version information

```
sfdx-cli/7.148.3 darwin-x64 node-v17.3.0
```

With the Salesforce CLI installed, you could go right ahead and develop applications and customizations using Salesforce DX from the command line. If you want to be more productive though, you need an integrated development environment (IDE). We will be standardizing on Visual Studio Code, with the Salesforce Extensions for Visual Studio Code, as our IDE in this book. Before installing the IDE, you need to install the Java Development Kit, which is a prerequisite for some of the Salesforce Extensions for Visual Studio Code features.

Installing the Java Development Kit

Version 8 or 11 of the Java Platform, Standard Edition Development Kit, or "JDK," is a prerequisite for some of the features in the Salesforce Extensions for Visual Studio Code. To find out if you already have the JDK installed, open a terminal application and enter the following command:

```
$ java --version
```

If the JDK is installed, you should see an output similar to the following, which shows that version 11.0.15 is installed.

Listing 2-2. Java version information

```
java 11.0.15 2022-04-19 LTS
Java(TM) SE Runtime Environment 18.9 (build 11.0.15+8-LTS-149)
Java HotSpot(TM) 64-Bit Server VM 18.9 (build 11.0.15+8-LTS-149,
mixed mode)
```

To install the latest release of version 8 or 11 of the JDK, visit one of the following pages:

- **Version 8**: `www.oracle.com/java/technologies/javase-jdk8-downloads.html`
- **Version 11**: `www.oracle.com/java/technologies/javase-jdk11-downloads.html`

An Oracle account is required before you can download Java. If you don't already have one, it's free and easy to set one up by clicking the **View Accounts** link at the top of the page.

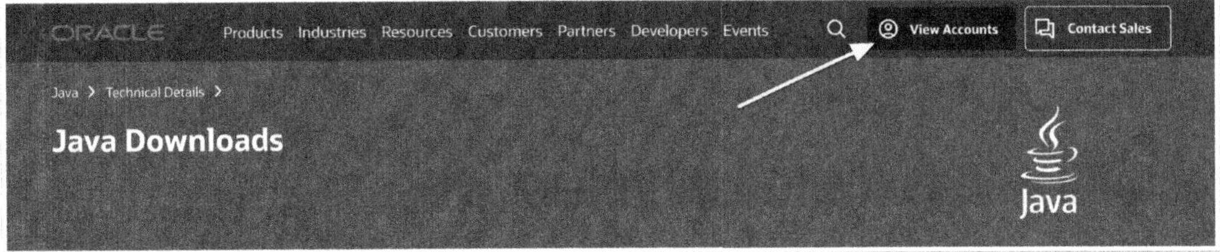

Figure 2-2. *Create Oracle account link*

Log in to your Oracle account, then scroll down the page where you have the option to download the JDK for your operating system.

Java SE Development Kit 11.0.15

Java SE subscribers will receive JDK 11 updates until at least **September of 2026**.

These downloads can be used for development, personal use, or to run Oracle licensed products. Use for other purposes, including production or commercial use, requires a Java SE subscription or another Oracle license.

JDK 11 software is licensed under the Oracle Technology Network License Agreement for Oracle Java SE.

JDK 11.0.15 checksum

Linux **macOS** **Solaris** **Windows**

Product/file description	File size	Download
x64 DMG Installer	154.92 MB	jdk-11.0.15_osx-x64_bin.dmg
x64 Compressed Archive	155.43 MB	jdk-11.0.15_osx-x64_bin.tar.gz

Figure 2-3. *JDK downloads*

Follow the instructions to complete the installation for your operating system. Please ensure that you always have the latest release installed by regularly checking your version number. Unfortunately, there is no command-line update option for the JDK, so you will have to follow the preceding steps to install a newer version.

Note Oracle announced that, effective January 2019, Java SE 8 public updates will no longer be available for "Business, Commercial, or Production use" without a commercial license. OpenJDK can be considered as an alternative; more information can be found here: `https://openjdk.java.net/install/`.

Up next, we will install Visual Studio Code before installing the Salesforce Extensions for Visual Studio Code.

Installing Visual Studio Code

Visual Studio Code, or "VS Code," is a lightweight, extensible, and open source IDE created by Microsoft that is free for both personal and commercial uses.

To install VS Code for macOS, Windows, or Linux, visit

- `https://code.visualstudio.com/`

  and click the **Download** button.

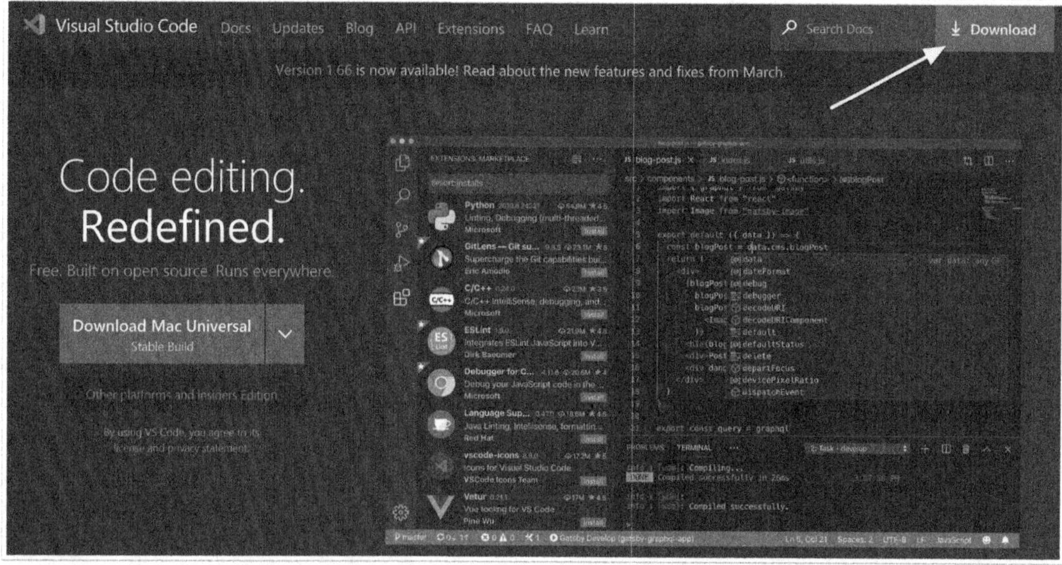

Figure 2-4. *Visual Studio Code home page*

On the next screen, click your operating system.

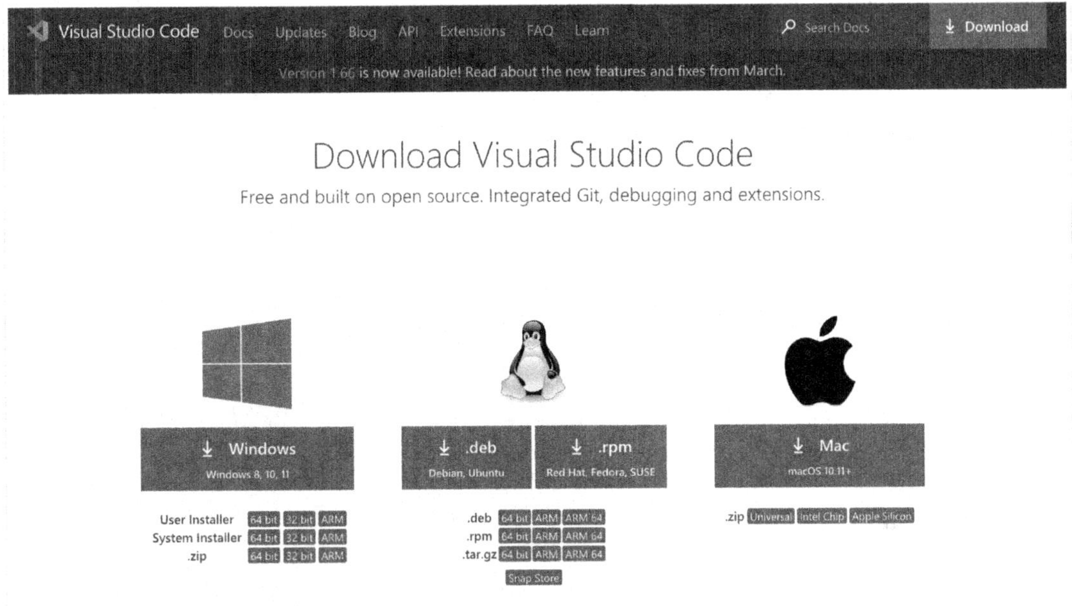

Figure 2-5. *Visual Studio Code operating system download screen*

The download will commence, and the Getting Started screen will be displayed. Click **SETUP** in the left-hand navigation pane.

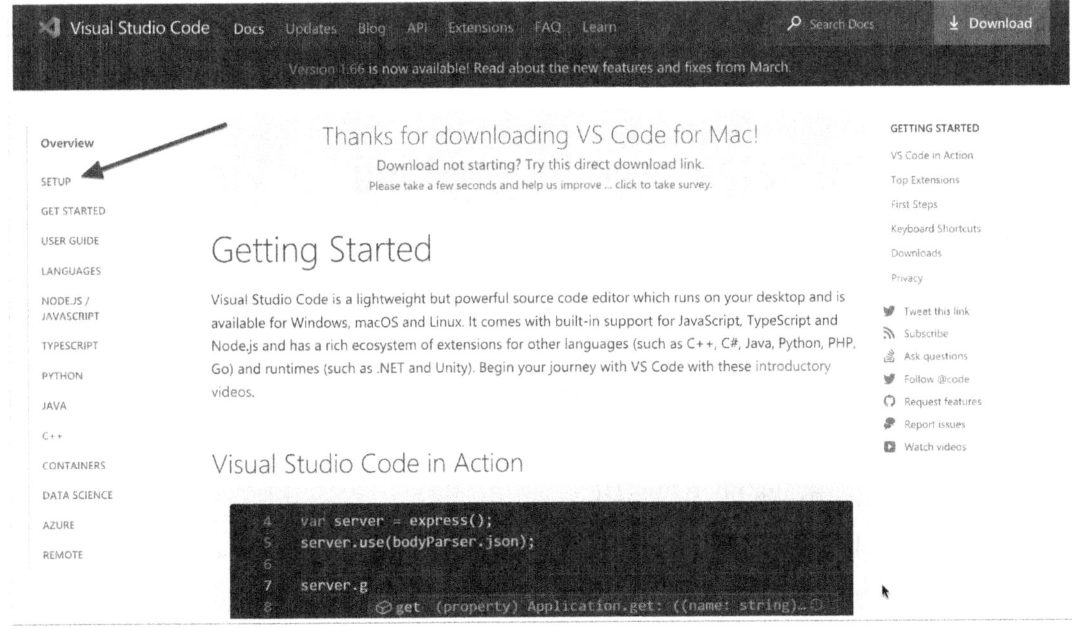

Figure 2-6. *Visual Studio Code Getting Started screen*

Setup instructions vary by operating system. Click your operating system that's listed below **SETUP** and follow the instructions. Once installation is complete, make sure that you regularly check for system updates by opening VS Code and clicking the **Code** menu and the **Check for Updates...** menu command.

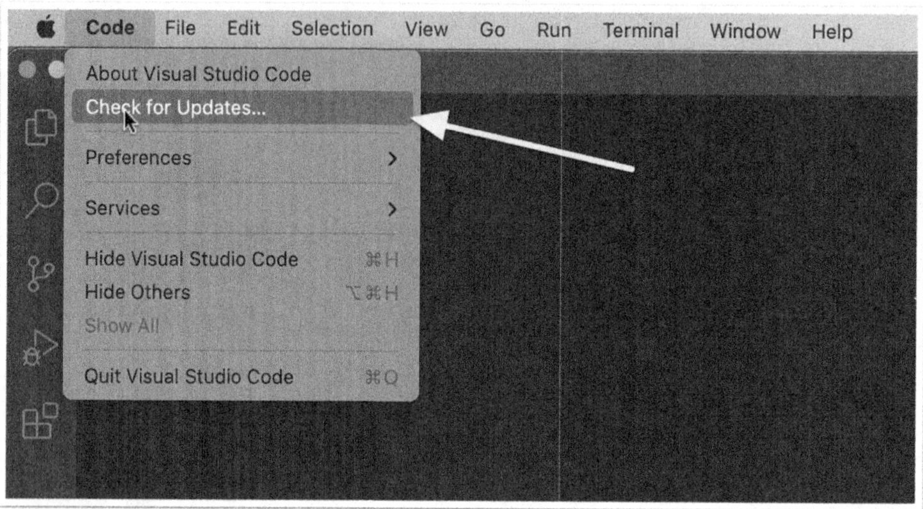

Figure 2-7. *Visual Studio Code check for updates*

With the JDK and VS Code set up, you can now set up the Salesforce Extensions for Visual Studio Code.

Installing the Salesforce Extensions for Visual Studio Code

The Salesforce Extensions for Visual Studio Code is a pack that contains a collection of extensions that are added to VS Code to support developing Salesforce applications and customizations using Salesforce DX. The following extensions are included in the pack:

- **Salesforce CLI**: Connects VS Code to the CLI to make the CLI commands available in the IDE.
- **Apex**: Adds development support, including syntax highlighting, code completion, and refactoring, for Apex code.

- **Apex Interactive Debugger**: Allows you to debug Apex code from within VS Code.
- **Apex Replay Debugger**: Debug logs can be used to simulate an interactive debugging session.
- **Lightning Web Components**: Adds development support for Lightning web component bundles.
- **Aura Components**: Adds development support for Aura component bundles.
- **Visualforce**: Adds development support for Visualforce pages and components.
- **SOQL**: A SOQL Query Builder for creating queries using an intuitive user interface.
- **Salesforce Lightning Design System (SLDS) Validator**: Adds code completion, syntax validation, and syntax highlighting when working with the SLDS.

The Salesforce Extensions for Visual Studio Code can be found by visiting this page:

- `https://marketplace.visualstudio.com/items?itemName=salesforce.salesforcedx-vscode`

Perform the following steps:

1. Click the **Install** button.
2. If a window pops open reminding you to install Visual Studio Code first, click the **Continue** button.

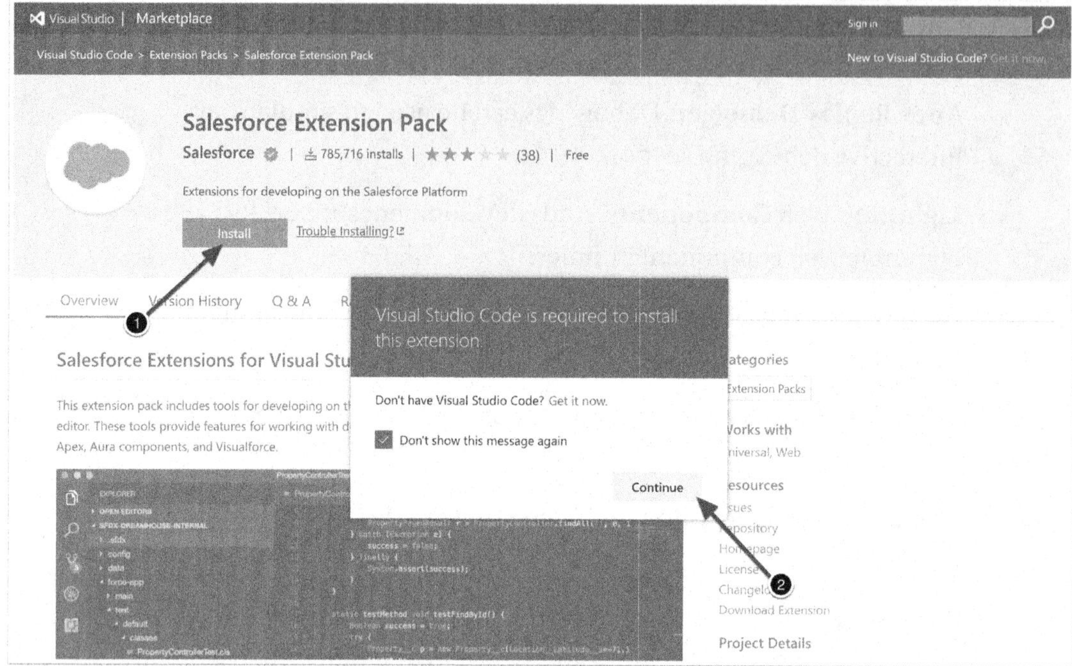

Figure 2-8. *Salesforce Extensions for Visual Studio Code home screen*

A window will pop up asking to open Visual Studio Code. Click the **Open Visual Studio Code** button. Visual Studio Code will open with the Salesforce Extension Pack installation page open in a tab. Click the **Install** button.

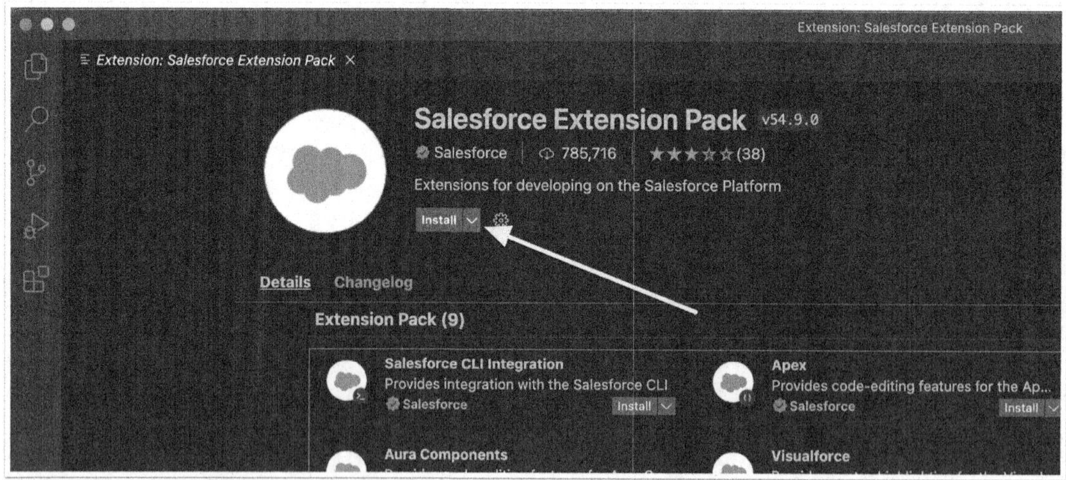

Figure 2-9. *Salesforce Extensions for Visual Studio Code installation screen*

When the installation is complete, close and reopen VS Code to enable the extensions that were added.

That completes the setup of your desktop development environment. We'll now summarize what was performed in this chapter.

Chapter Summary

In this chapter, we installed a complete desktop-based development environment for Salesforce DX, including the Salesforce CLI, the Java Development Kit, Visual Studio Code, and the Salesforce Extensions for Visual Studio Code.

Salesforce DX encompasses many concepts, which are difficult to explain in isolation. The next chapter will provide a high-level overview of all the core concepts, which will make it easier to follow the later chapters where we dive into more detail.

CHAPTER 3

Concepts Overview

When Salesforce DX was launched, it introduced multiple new tools and ways of working, which I have collectively called "concepts," all designed to work smoothly together, including

- Salesforce CLI
- Visual Studio Code
- Salesforce DX projects
- Source format metadata
- Scratch orgs
- Unlocked packages
- Second-generation managed packages (2GP)
- Dev Hub
- Namespaces

Although these concepts will be covered in a lot more detail in Part II of the book, I'll introduce them now so that we have a high-level understanding of each and how they fit into the Salesforce DX landscape. Don't worry if the introduction leaves you with more questions than answers; by the end of the chapter, you will have a good foundational understanding of Salesforce DX, so that you are well prepared to explore the concepts in more detail later.

The first concept that we'll look at is the Salesforce CLI.

I. Harris, *Beginning Salesforce DX*, https://doi.org/10.1007/978-1-4842-8114-7_3

Salesforce CLI

The Salesforce command-line interface, or "CLI" for short, allows users to execute Salesforce DX commands using the command line in a terminal application. Most operating systems include a terminal application, and third-party applications are also available; for example, these are the default terminal applications by operating system:

- **macOS**: Terminal.
- **Windows**: Windows Console.
- **Linux**: Examples include GNOME Terminal, Xterm, and Konsole.

Visual Studio Code, the integrated development environment that you installed in the previous chapter and we'll be introducing next, includes the built-in integrated terminal that can be used to execute commands, so you don't need to switch between VS Code and a terminal application.

Assuming that you have followed the Salesforce CLI setup instructions in Chapter 2, "Environment Setup," open your operating system's terminal application and enter the following command on the command line:

```
$ sfdx force --help
```

This displays the help information for the `force` namespace. We will examine the structure of a CLI command in Chapter 4, "Salesforce CLI." The output in the macOS Terminal application looks like this.

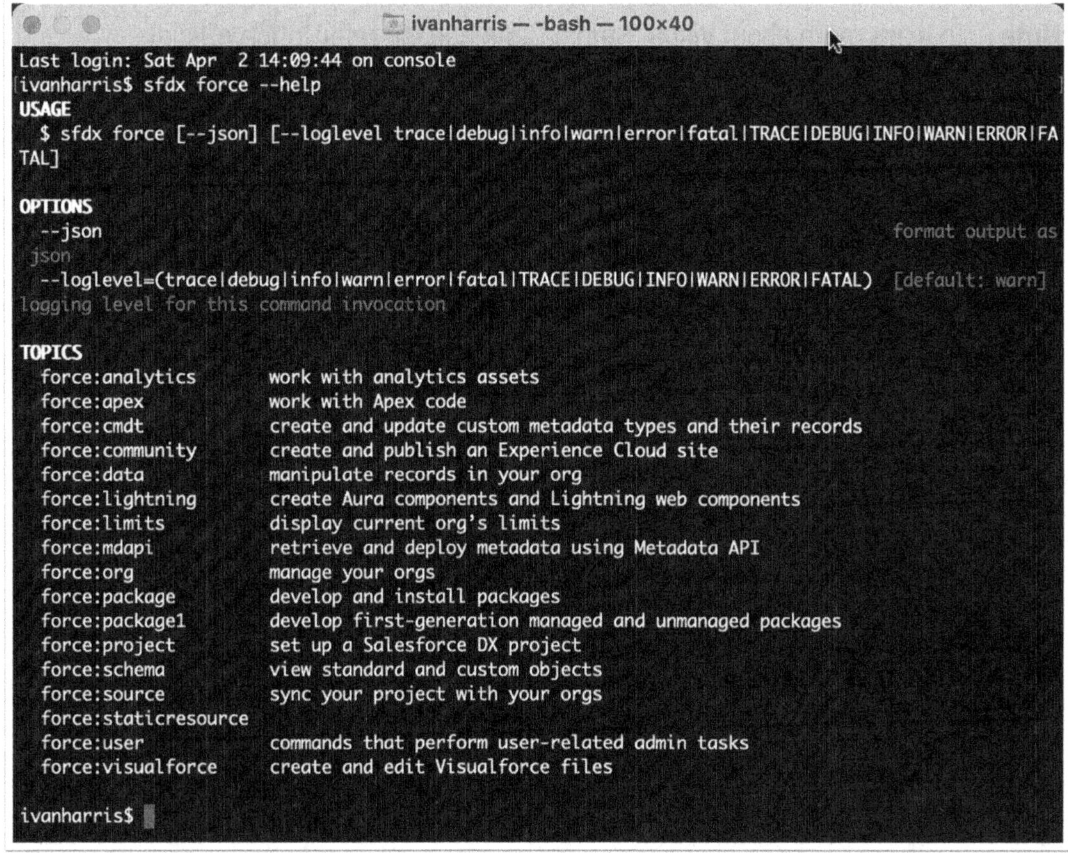

***Figure 3-1.** macOS Terminal application executing a Salesforce CLI command*

Most examples in the book will show how to execute a CLI command using the Visual Studio Code integrated terminal and the Visual Studio Code Command Palette. Let's introduce Visual Studio Code next, which covers both methods.

Visual Studio Code

In Chapter 2, "Environment Setup," you set up Visual Studio Code, also known as "VS Code," and installed the Salesforce Extensions for Visual Studio Code, giving you an integrated development environment, or "IDE," that's tailored to Salesforce DX development. We will now discover where to find VS Code's frequently referred to features.

Note To learn more about Visual Studio Code, please refer to the official documentation: `https://code.visualstudio.com/docs`. For the Salesforce Extensions for Visual Studio Code, the documentation can be found here: `https://developer.salesforce.com/tools/vscode`.

We'll be looking at Salesforce DX projects in more detail in Chapter 6, "Projects"; that said, I have created a new project so that we can explore the VS Code user interface. We can see the project's directory structure in VS Code's Side Bar (1), which is where you access files that are stored in the project.

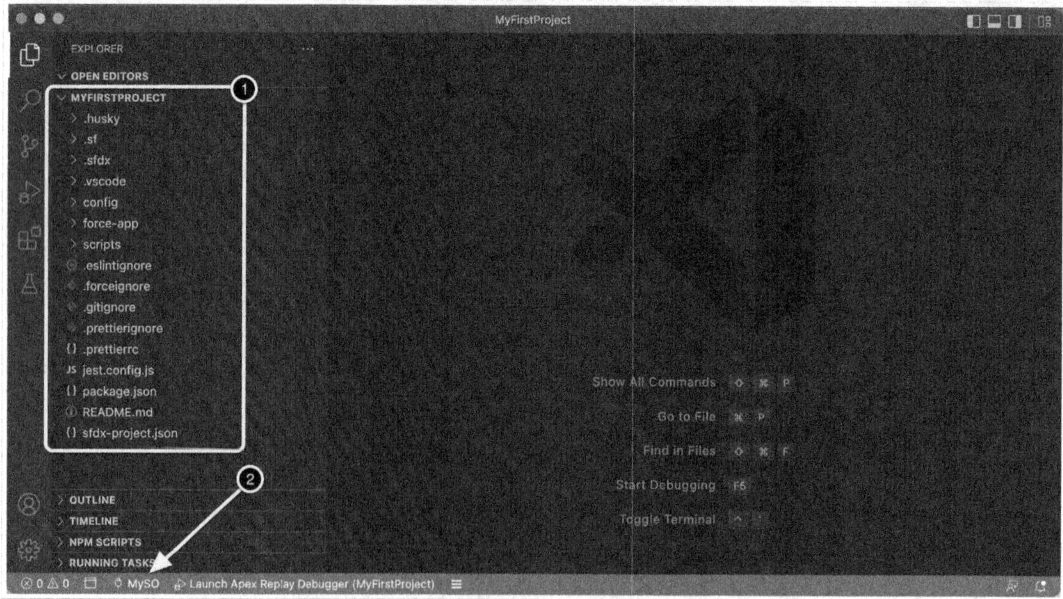

***Figure 3-2.** Visual Studio Code with a Salesforce DX project open*

The Status Bar shows that `MySO` has been set as the username for the default org (2), meaning that any org-related commands executed from VS Code's integrated terminal, context menus, or Command Palette will be executed against this org by default.

To open VS Code's integrated terminal to issue Salesforce CLI commands via a command line, click the **Terminal ➤ New Terminal** menu item, which opens the terminal inside the VS Code user interface at the Salesforce DX project's root directory. This means that you don't need to open your operating system's terminal application and navigate to the project directory before executing any CLI commands for the project. As an example, running the `force:org:list` CLI command from the terminal window's command line will display the following output.

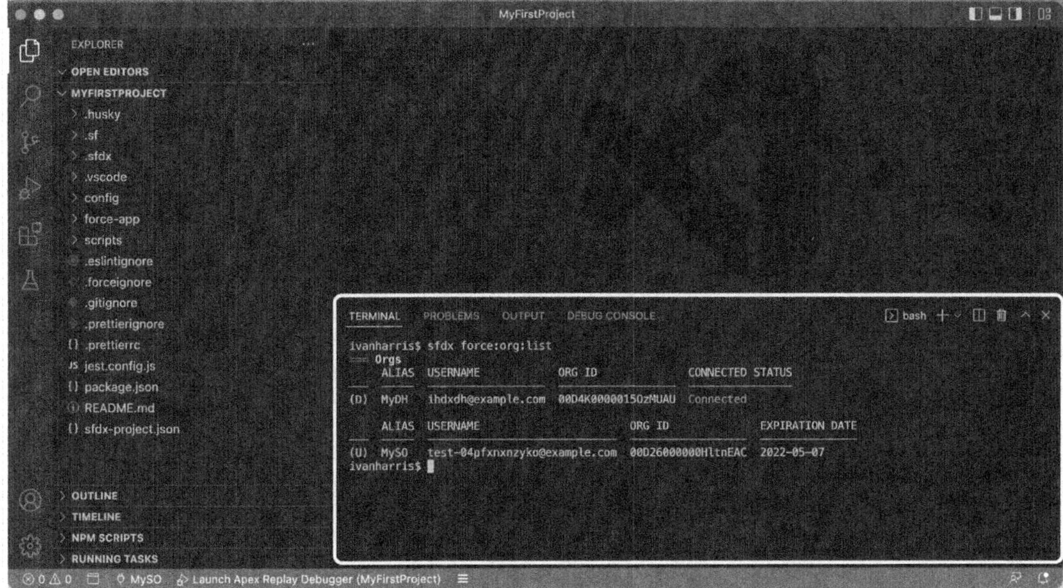

Figure 3-3. *Visual Studio Code's integrated terminal*

As you become familiar with the Salesforce CLI commands and VS Code, you may want to use the Salesforce DX context menu items and the Command Palette commands that have been added to VS Code by the Salesforce Extensions for Visual Studio Code.

Note Many of the context menu and Command Palette commands require an org with a default username. In the preceding figure, we can see that the VS Code Status Bar shows `MySO` as the default username. This can be set using the command line, as we will discover in Chapter 7, "Orgs."

Open the VS Code Command Palette using one of the following methods:

- **Key Combination**: **Ctrl+Shift+P** (Windows and Linux) or **Cmd+Shift+P** (MacOS).
- **Application Menu**: **View ➤ Command Palette...**.

- **Manage Icon**: Click the **Manage icon**, which looks like a gear, at the bottom of the VS Code Activity Bar and click the **Command Palette...** menu item.

Filter the commands in the Command Palette by entering SFDX, then scroll up and down to see the complete list of Salesforce DX commands that can be executed using the Command Palette.

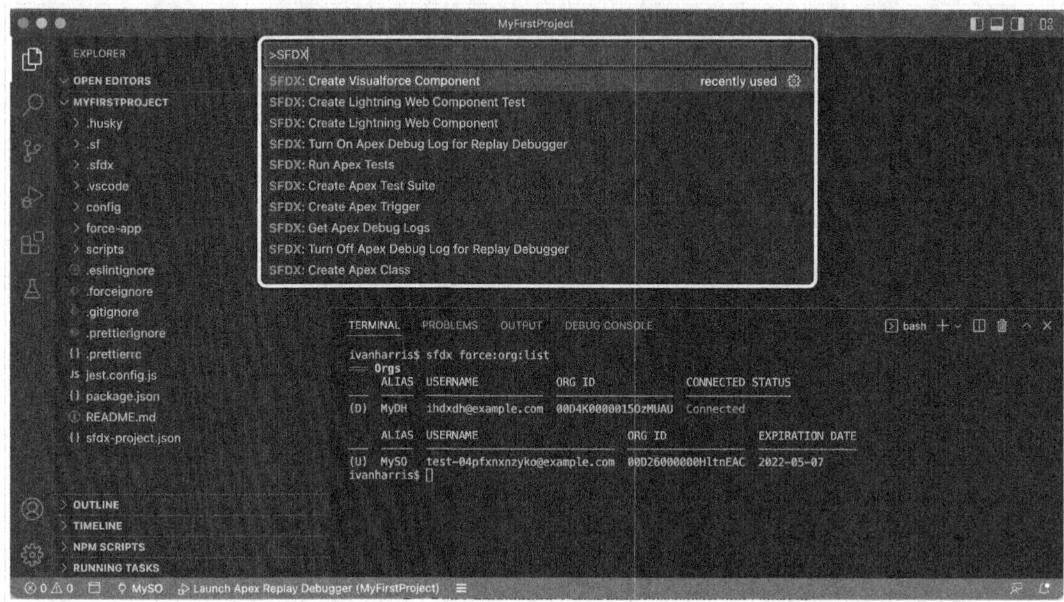

Figure 3-4. *Visual Studio Code Command Palette*

Selecting the command **SFDX: Display Org Details for Default Org** will open VS Code's output window, which will display the command output as follows.

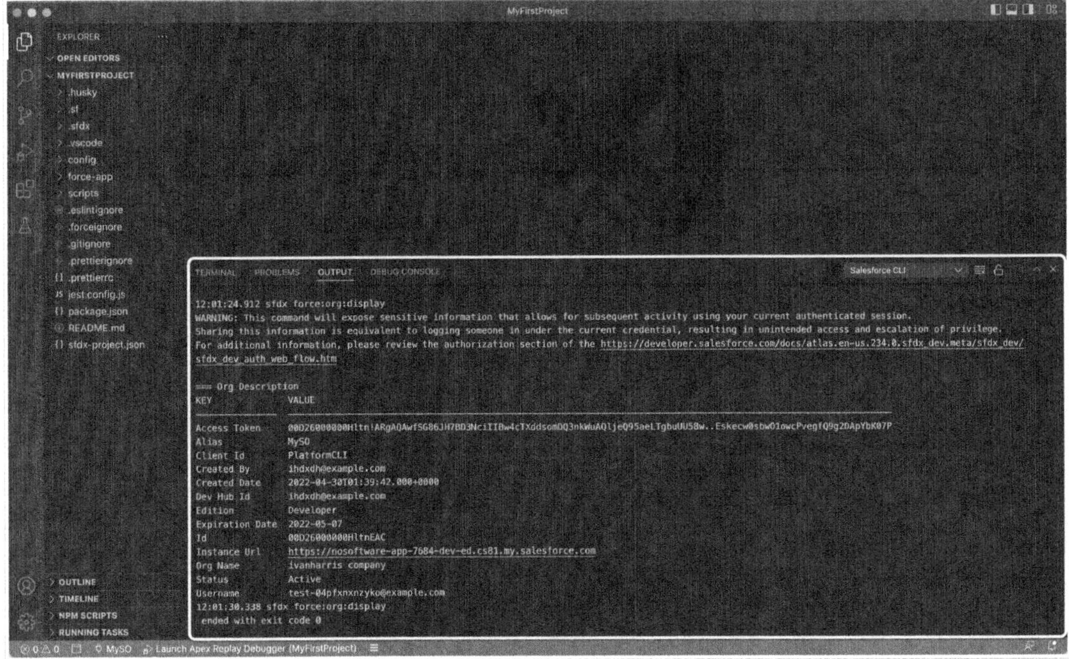

***Figure 3-5.** Visual Studio Code Command Palette output*

To see an example of a Salesforce DX context menu, you can expand the `force-app/main/default` directory hierarchy in the Explorer view and right-click the `classes` directory. This will display the context menu for that directory, which includes several **SFDX:** commands.

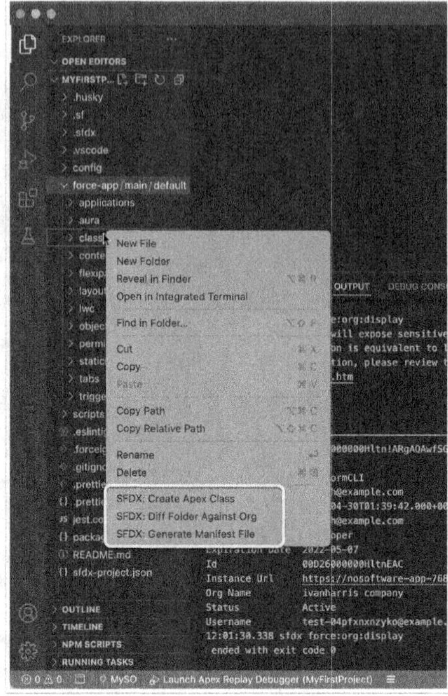

Figure 3-6. *Visual Studio Code context menu*

Visual Studio Code with the Salesforce Extensions for Visual Studio Code installed works with Salesforce DX projects, which we introduce next.

Salesforce DX Projects

Salesforce DX introduced a new project structure to store all the assets related to a customization or application that is being developed, whether it's a customization for a production org, an internal custom application, or an application for AppExchange. The project structure consists of a directory hierarchy to store files that are accessible from your development environment. The files are project assets that include, among other things:

- **Project Configuration Files**: Various files that govern how the Salesforce CLI should work with the Salesforce DX project and orgs; examples are the project configuration file and scratch org definition file.

- **Tool Configuration Files**: Files to modify the behavior of tools such as VS Code, Git, ESLint, and Prettier.
- **Metadata**: The components that an application or customization consists of, such as custom objects, Apex classes, and approval processes, in source format or Metadata API format.
- **Test Data**: Data used to conduct end-to-end tests.
- **Scripts**: Shell scripts to automate the execution of multiple CLI commands.

The following listing illustrates the Salesforce DX project directory structure immediately after a new project has been created.

Listing 3-1. Salesforce DX project directory structure

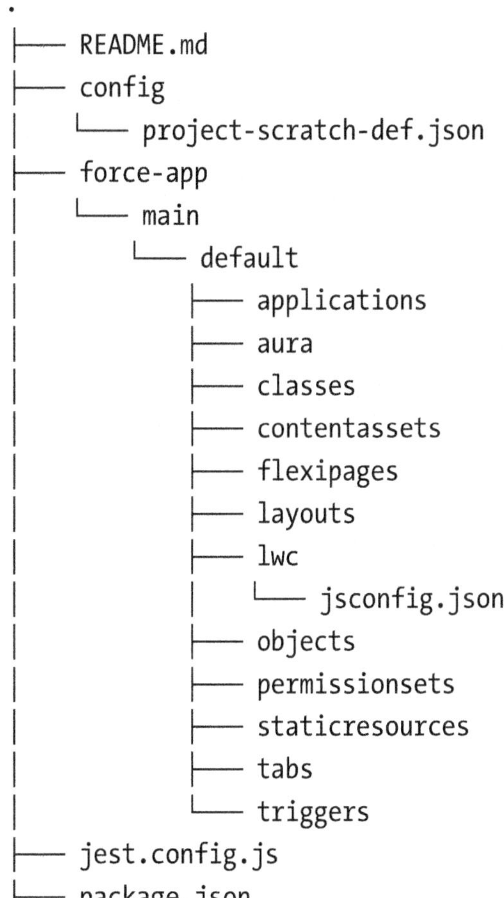

```
.
├── README.md
├── config
│   └── project-scratch-def.json
├── force-app
│   └── main
│       └── default
│           ├── applications
│           ├── aura
│           ├── classes
│           ├── contentassets
│           ├── flexipages
│           ├── layouts
│           ├── lwc
│           │   └── jsconfig.json
│           ├── objects
│           ├── permissionsets
│           ├── staticresources
│           ├── tabs
│           └── triggers
├── jest.config.js
├── package.json
```

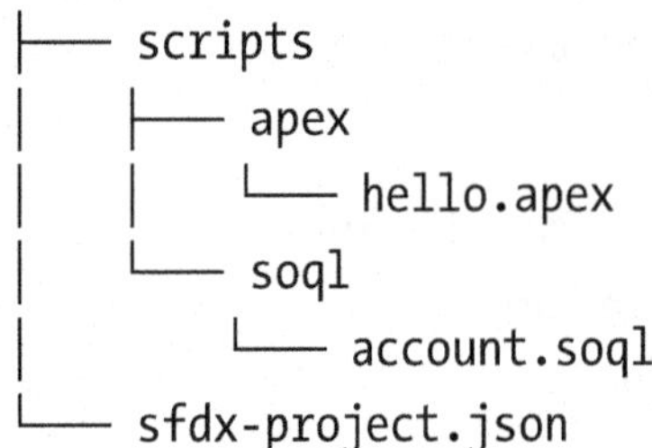

We won't explore the structure any further here as we'll look at the directories and files in more detail in Chapter 6, "Projects"; suffice to say, this scaffolding is created for you automatically when you create a new project.

The next section will look at the new metadata source format and how it supports a faster and more collaborative way of working.

Source Format Metadata

Salesforce metadata is everything in your Salesforce org that's not data records. The Salesforce metadata describes how the data records, such as Contacts, are stored, processed, and displayed. Example metadata types include custom objects, Apex classes, Visualforce pages, Lightning component bundles, and approval processes.

Prior to Salesforce DX introducing the new source format, the Metadata API format was used to store metadata in a local filing system, and the Metadata API was used to deploy metadata to and retrieve metadata from an org when change sets were not being used. The metadata source format is more granular than the Metadata API format. For example, here is the Metadata API format file for a custom object that has a single custom field.

Listing 3-2. Metadata API format custom object

```
objects
└── Example_Object__c.object
```

And here is the same custom object in source format.

Listing 3-3. Source format custom object

```
objects
└── Example_Object__c
    ├── Example_Object__c.object-meta.xml
    └── fields
        └── Example_Field__c.field-meta.xml
```

As you can see, the custom field has its own metadata XML file, rather than being bundled in with the custom object. The more granular file structure speeds up synchronization of changes between a local Salesforce DX project and a source-tracked org, which includes scratch orgs or Developer sandboxes and Developer Pro sandboxes that have source tracking enabled. It also simplifies collaborative development as developers can work on separate, smaller files. We will return to metadata in Chapter 8, "Metadata."

We've just heard that source format metadata can be synchronized between a Salesforce DX project and a source-tracked org, such as a scratch org. Let's look at scratch orgs next.

Scratch Orgs

Salesforce DX introduced a new org type, scratch orgs, that can be created when needed and destroyed when no longer required. Scratch orgs are short-lived, remaining active for between 1 and 30 days, with 7 days being the default. When a scratch org is created, it can be configured as a particular edition (Developer, Enterprise, Group, or Professional), with specific features and settings enabled. This allows scratch orgs to mirror the configuration of a production org, making them an alternative to Developer and Developer Pro sandboxes when developing internal customizations and custom applications. When developing AppExchange apps, scratch orgs are an alternative to Developer Edition orgs that can be configured with the edition, features, and settings that an app depends on.

Unlike Developer Edition orgs, Partial Copy sandboxes, Full Copy sandboxes, and production orgs, scratch orgs are source-tracked.

Note It's also possible to enable Developer and Developer Pro sandboxes to be source-tracked, which will be covered in Chapter 5, "Dev Hub."

Salesforce DX tracks changes between source format metadata in a local Salesforce DX project and a scratch org and synchronizes changed metadata between the two. As we saw in the previous section, the more granular structure of source format metadata makes synchronizing a very efficient process.

We will explore scratch orgs, plus the other org types that Salesforce DX supports, in Chapter 7, "Orgs." For now, we will turn our attention to unlocked packages.

Unlocked and 2GP Packages

Salesforce AppExchange Partner development teams have been developing managed packages for some time, which are used to deploy applications consisting of many metadata components to production orgs as a single container. Internal development teams have to date used change sets or the Metadata API to deploy customizations and applications to production orgs. Salesforce DX supports two new package types to improve on these deployment options - unlocked packages and second-generation managed packages (2GP).

Second-generation managed packages are a reimagining of the first-generation managed packages used by development teams creating applications for distribution via Salesforce's AppExchange enterprise marketplace. Second-generation managed packages are developed entirely using the Salesforce CLI and leverage scratch orgs rather than Developer Edition orgs and avoid the packaging org with its manual package creation steps. Furthermore, 2GPs can be split into multiple dependent packages rather than using a single, monolithic managed package.

Unlocked packages enable internal development teams to bundle the metadata components that make up a customization or application for deployment as one or more versioned containers. Unlike managed packages though, unlocked packages do not obfuscate the metadata components that they contain, allowing them to be modified after deployment.

Chapter 13, "Package Development," will dive into unlocked packages and second-generation managed packages in more detail.

Next in line is an introduction to the Salesforce DX concept of a Dev Hub.

Dev Hub

A Developer Hub, or "Dev Hub", is a Salesforce org with the Dev Hub feature enabled. A Dev Hub is needed when creating and managing scratch orgs and packages using the Salesforce CLI. When the Dev Hub feature is enabled in a Salesforce org, the Active Scratch Orgs and Scratch Orgs Info apps become available in the org, which show information about scratch orgs that have been created using the Dev Hub. We explore the subject in more detail in Chapter 5, "Dev Hub."

When the Dev Hub feature is enabled in a Salesforce org, the Namespace Registries app also becomes available, which allows namespaces to be linked to the Dev Hub so that namespaced scratch orgs can be created. Namespaces are the subject of the next section.

Namespaces

Namespaces are not a new concept; however, how they are used with Salesforce DX is new. Namespaces, which are unique identifiers across all Salesforce orgs, are used with second-generation managed packages, and can optionally be used with unlocked packages, to avoid naming conflicts for deployed metadata components. A namespace can be associated with a Salesforce DX project that's being used to develop a package. The namespace is then incorporated into the package when a package version is built. As mentioned in the previous section about Dev Hubs, the namespace will also be added to any created scratch orgs. This allows packages to be tested before the metadata components are built into a package version. We will revisit namespaces in Chapter 13, "Package Development."

Chapter Summary

In this chapter, we had a high-level overview of the core Salesforce DX concepts. We deliberately avoided going into too much detail; instead, we gained the foundational knowledge to set the scene for the chapters to follow in Part II and noted the chapter where we will dive deeper into a topic.

With your development environment set up and this foundational knowledge, it's time to get practical with the Salesforce DX concepts, starting with a detailed look at the Salesforce CLI, which is the first chapter in Part II of the book.

PART II

Working with Salesforce DX

In Part I, we set the stage for developing applications and customizations using Salesforce DX. You set up your development environment and completed an overview of Salesforce DX. In Part II, we're going to transition from theory to practice. We'll build on Part I's foundational knowledge and explore the Salesforce DX concepts in more detail, where we will encounter the most frequently used Salesforce CLI commands. By the end of Part II, you'll have all the skills needed to build applications and customizations that can be deployed using unpackaged metadata, unlocked packages, and second-generation managed packages (2GP).

CHAPTER 4

Salesforce CLI

In Part I, you set up your Salesforce DX development environment and took a high-level tour of the core Salesforce DX concepts to put everything into context. In this chapter, you will start building on that foundation and learn a lot more about the Salesforce CLI. Two resources that are well worth bookmarking to help you on your journey from a Salesforce DX novice to a seasoned practitioner are as follows:

- **Salesforce DX Developer Guide**: `https://developer.salesforce.com/docs/atlas.en-us.sfdx_dev.meta/sfdx_dev/sfdx_dev_intro.htm`
- **Salesforce CLI Command Reference**: `https://developer.salesforce.com/docs/atlas.en-us.sfdx_cli_reference.meta/sfdx_cli_reference/cli_reference.htm`

The Salesforce CLI is the command-line interface that's at the heart of Salesforce DX. Using the CLI, you can perform tasks such as creating and destroying scratch orgs; authorizing non-scratch orgs; exporting, importing, and manipulating test data; developing and installing managed and unlocked packages; creating Salesforce DX projects; and migrating metadata components between your Salesforce DX project and source-tracked and non-source-tracked orgs. The CLI can also be integrated with your preferred application development tools, such as continuous integration and continuous deployment systems like Jenkins or CircleCI, or integrated development environments like Visual Studio Code.

We'll start your Salesforce CLI deep dive by exploring the structure of a CLI command.

I. Harris, *Beginning Salesforce DX*, https://doi.org/10.1007/978-1-4842-8114-7_4

Anatomy of a CLI Command

Understanding the CLI command structure aligns us on a common language when discussing commands while also making it more intuitive when you start navigating up and down the hierarchy of command topics. A CLI command has the following structure:

```
$ sfdx <namespace>:<command> [parameters] [arguments]
...or...
$ sfdx <namespace>:<topic>:<command> [parameters] [arguments]
...or...
$ sfdx <namespace>:<topic>:<subtopic>:<command> [parameters] [arguments]
```

The elements that make up a command are as follows:

- `sfdx`: The command-line application that executes a CLI command.
- `<namespace>`: The highest-level topic, which groups together all related topics, subtopics, and commands. Example Salesforce CLI namespaces are `alias`, `auth`, `config`, and `force`, among others.
- `<topic>`: A grouping of related subtopics and commands.
- `<subtopic>`: Topics can be further divided into subtopics that group together related commands.
- `<command>`: The command to be executed.
- `[parameters]`: A command can be passed parameters, also known as options in the CLI command-line help. Some parameters require a value, such as `--sobjecttype=Contact`, where `Contact` is the value, while others don't, such as `--json`. Parameters that require a value can use either a space or an equals sign to separate the parameter name and its value.
- `[arguments]`: A command can also be passed arguments consisting of a `Value` (known as an arg) or a `Name=Value` pair (known as a vararg).

Note Parameters have a long name and often have a short name as well. For example, the long name `--sobjecttype` has a corresponding short name of `-s`. The long name is preceded by a double hyphen, whereas the short name is preceded by a single hyphen. When describing command-line parameters, both will be shown like this: `--sobjecttype|-s`.

Here are some commands at different levels of the `sfdx` `<namespace>:<topic>:<subtopic>` hierarchy, using a mixture of long names and short names for the command parameters and an argument in the final example:

```
$ sfdx commands
$ sfdx config:list --json
$ sfdx force:org:open -u MySO
$ sfdx force:data:record:create \
    --sobjecttype Case \
    --targetusername MySO \
    --values \
      "Subject='Generator fuel gauge is inaccurate'"
$ sfdx force:user:create \
    -a=MyUser \
    username=someone@example.com
```

The first example shows the command `commands`, which doesn't require a namespace, being executed by the `sfdx` application. The second executes the `list` command in the `config` namespace. The third illustrates the `open` command being executed, which is part of the `org` topic in the `force` namespace. The fourth command shows the use of a subtopic, where `record` is a subtopic of the `data` topic. The final example shows a `Name=Value` argument, in this case `username=someone@example.com`.

It's useful understanding the general structure of a CLI command; but this knowledge needs to be supplemented with knowing the namespaces, topics, and subtopics that are available, what their commands are, and the parameters and arguments that a command supports. This information is available via command-line help; next, we'll now learn how to access command-line help and what the format of the help information is.

Command-Line Help

If you ever need to explore the namespaces, topics, and subtopics that are available, to view the structure of a Salesforce CLI command, or to remind yourself what parameters and arguments can be passed to a command, the CLI includes a useful library of help information. Help can be viewed by passing the parameter `--help`, or its short name variant `-h`, at any level of the `sfdx <namespace>:<topic>:<subtopic>` hierarchy on the command line.

Note Help information is also available in the online Salesforce CLI Command Reference, which can be found here: `https://developer.salesforce.com/docs/atlas.en-us.sfdx_cli_reference.meta/sfdx_cli_reference/cli_reference.htm`.

To illustrate the format of command-line help, let's view the output from the `sfdx force --help` command, which provides help for the `force` namespace.

Listing 4-1. sfdx force --help output

```
USAGE
  $ sfdx force [--json] ↩
      [--loglevel trace|debug|info|warn|error|fatal|TRACE|DEBUG|INFO|WARN|
      ERROR|FATAL]

OPTIONS
  --json format output as json
  --loglevel=(trace|debug|info|warn|error|fatal|TRACE|DEBUG|INFO|WARN|
  ERROR|FATAL) [default: warn] logging level for this command invocation

TOPICS
  force:analytics      work with analytics assets
  force:apex           work with Apex code
  force:cmdt           create and update custom metadata types and
                       their records
  force:community      create and publish an Experience Cloud site
```

```
force:data              manipulate records in your org
force:lightning         create Aura components and Lightning web components
force:limits            display current org's limits
force:mdapi             retrieve and deploy metadata using Metadata API
force:org               manage your orgs
force:package           develop and install packages
force:package1          develop first-generation managed and unmanaged
                        packages
force:project           set up a Salesforce DX project
force:schema            view standard and custom objects
force:source            sync your project with your orgs
force:staticresource
force:user              commands that perform user-related admin tasks
force:visualforce       create and edit Visualforce files
```

The sections in the command-line help offer the following information:

- `USAGE`: Shows how to invoke the command. Parameters or arguments that are optional are surrounded by square brackets.
- `OPTIONS`: Explains each of the parameters that can be passed to the command. `--json` is an example of a parameter that takes no value, while `--loglevel` is an example of a parameter that takes a value. If a parameter has a default value, it will be stated in the description to the right of the parameter.
- `TOPICS`: Lists the topics that are grouped by this `force` namespace.

Other sections that you will encounter in command-line help output are as follows:

- `VERSION`: This section displays the CLI version number, and it only appears in the help for the `sfdx` application.
- `COMMANDS`: If the `sfdx` application, namespace, topic, or subtopic has commands that can be executed, they are listed in this section. It is possible to have a mix of commands and namespaces/topics/subtopics depending on the level in the hierarchy.
- `DESCRIPTION`: Help for a command includes this section, which provides an overview of the command's purpose and some examples of how to invoke the command.

The `sfdx <namespace>:<topic>:<subtopic>` hierarchy begins with the `sfdx` application, which can provide help about itself, access its namespaces, and has its own commands that can be executed. Let's learn more about this application next.

The sfdx Application

`sfdx` is the command-line application that executes Salesforce CLI commands. To view help information for the `sfdx` application, execute the command `sfdx help` or pass the parameter `sfdx --help`, and you will see the following.

Listing 4-2. sfdx --help output

```
Salesforce CLI

VERSION
  sfdx-cli/7.148.3 darwin-x64 node-v17.3.0

USAGE
  $ sfdx [COMMAND]

TOPICS
  alias    manage username aliases
  auth     authorize an org for use with the Salesforce CLI
  config   configure the Salesforce CLI
  force    tools for the Salesforce developer
  info     access cli info from the command line
  plugins  add/remove/create CLI plug-ins

COMMANDS
  autocomplete  display autocomplete installation instructions
  commands      list all the commands
  help          display help for sfdx
  plugins       list installed plugins
  update        update the sfdx CLI
  which         show which plugin a command is in
```

You will observe that the `sfdx` application currently has access to six built-in namespaces, also known as top-level topics. These are the namespaces that are created when installing the Salesforce CLI. The CLI team will probably add more namespaces in the future, and a number of topics have been promoted to namespaces since the CLI was released, including the `force:auth` and `force:config` topics that became `auth` and `config` namespaces, respectively. New namespaces can also be added by installing third-party plug-ins. The six built-in namespaces that are present at the time of writing this book are as follows:

- `alias`: Manages user-friendly aliases for orgs, which can be used instead of the lengthier and harder to remember usernames.
- `auth`: Authorize an org that is not a scratch org, such as a Developer Edition org, sandbox, or production org, for use with the Salesforce CLI.
- `config`: Use this namespace to manage configuration variables used by the CLI commands in the `force` namespace, such as the default scratch org and default Dev Hub usernames. We will cover this namespace in the next section, "Controlling the CLI."
- `force`: This is the largest namespace, which contains all the topics, subtopics, and commands that are used to develop applications and customizations for the Salesforce Platform. The bulk of this book is devoted to this namespace, so we will be diving into a lot more detail in due course.
- `info`: Displays information about the CLI, which is currently the release notes for the latest version by default or a specific version if specified.
- `plugins`: Plug-ins implement and extend the CLI's functionality. The CLI comes with its own plug-ins, and new plug-ins can be developed by third parties to extend the CLI's functionality. The `plugins` namespace is used to manage the plug-in lifecycle, including creating, installing, updating, and deleting a plug-in. Developing plug-ins is beyond the scope of this book, so we won't be exploring the `plugins` namespace in more detail.

Most of the commands that we will explore in this book are in the `force` namespace.

In addition to the namespaces that the `sfdx` application has access to, it has commands that it can execute itself, which are as follows:

- `autocomplete`: This command displays instructions for configuring Bash and Zsh shells once the command autocomplete plug-in has been installed.
- `commands`: Outputs a complete list of commands supported by the `sfdx` application and all namespaces, topics, and subtopics. This command has several parameters to determine how much information is displayed and in what format. Explore the parameters by executing `sfdx commands --help`.
- `help`: Displays the help information shown in the previous listing.
- `plugins`: Lists all the installed CLI plug-ins.
- `update`: Updates the CLI to the latest version. As mentioned in Chapter 2, "Environment Setup," it's best practice to run this command frequently to ensure that you are on the latest version.
- `which`: Reports which plug-in a CLI command is implemented in. For example, run `sfdx which force:data:soql:query` and you will see that this command is in the `@salesforce/plugin-data` plug-in.

In summary, the `sfdx` application executes CLI commands, it has access to six built-in namespaces, and it can execute six commands that do not require a namespace. The built-in namespaces will likely grow over time, and installing third-party plug-ins can add new namespaces.

In the next section, we will explore the ways that configuration parameters can be used to define default command parameters and to modify the behavior of the `force` namespace commands that are executed by the `sfdx` application.

Controlling the CLI

Each Salesforce CLI command in the `force` namespace takes inputs from a variety of sources that determine how the command will function. Some inputs are configuration settings that modify a command's default behavior, such as changing a command's default output format from human readable to JSON. Other inputs are data values that the command operates on to achieve its purpose. We learned about the structure of a CLI command in the section "Anatomy of a CLI Command." Let's use that knowledge to step through an example command and describe its inputs. You'll be learning about the `force:user:create` command in Chapter 10, "Test Users," later in the book; for now, just focus on the parameters and arguments that we will be explaining.

```
$ sfdx force:user:create \
    --setalias=MyUser \
    --definitionfile=./config/user-def.json \
    --targetusername=MySO \
    --apiversion=55.0 \
    --json \
    --loglevel=debug \
    username=someone@example.com
```

The command-line parameters and arguments that are passed to the command are as follows:

- `--setalias|-a`: This parameter is an example of passing a data value to the command for it to act on. In this case, the command will create an alias `MyUser` that can be used to reference the user in other CLI commands, rather than using their username. [Optional]
- `--definitionfile|-f`: Another parameter that passes a data value to the command. The value in this instance is the path to a file that contains additional parameters to use when creating a user, including initial field values for the User record. [Optional]
- `--targetusername|-u`: The data value for this parameter tells the command which scratch org the user should be created in. The scratch org username or alias can be passed as a value. A default target org username or alias can be set using an environment variable or runtime configuration value, as we shall see later in this section. This is an example of a command taking inputs from a variety of sources. [Optional]

- `--apiversion`: This is the first parameter that is a configuration setting that modifies the default command behavior. By default, the CLI assumes that the Dev Hub is on the same API version as the CLI. If you are using a different CLI version than the Dev Hub, the value passed to this parameter should be set to the Dev Hub version. A default API version can also be specified using an environment variable or a runtime configuration value. [Optional]
- `--json`: Another configuration setting parameter, in this case one that doesn't take a value. The default command behavior is to send its output to the terminal application in human-readable format. Use this parameter to instruct the command to output in JSON format. An environment variable, but not a runtime configuration value, can also be used to set JSON as the default output format. [Optional]
- `--loglevel`: This configuration setting parameter changes the level of detail in log messages that are written to the `sfdx.log` log file. The default command behavior is to use a log level of `warn`; the value passed to this parameter can set the log level to `fatal`, `error`, `warn`, `info`, `debug`, or `trace`. [Optional]
- `username=someone@example.com`: The final input to the command is an example of an argument being used to pass a data value for the command to act on. This argument is used to set initial field values in the newly created User record. The `Name=Value` pair can also be passed to the command using the user definition file that is a value for the `--definitionfile` that you saw earlier. [Optional]

This walk-through has revealed that a CLI command can take inputs in the form of configuration settings and data values. Moreover, these inputs can come from command-line parameters and arguments, file parameters, environment variables, and runtime configuration values. We also saw that in some cases the same configuration setting or data value can come from multiple inputs, in which case, which input takes priority? Consider the following input sources; we'll discuss their relative priority in a moment:

1. **Command-Line Parameters and Arguments**: Parameters and arguments that are passed to a command on the command line. Examples in the `force:user:create` command walk-through earlier are `--json`, `--targetusername=MySO`, and

username=someone@example.com. We'll be seeing many examples of CLI commands using command-line parameters and arguments as we progress through the book.

2. **File Parameters**: Some CLI commands accept files that include additional parameters, such as the user definition file that was passed to the preceding command using the --definitionfile|-f parameter.

3. **Environment Variables**: Environment variables can be used to store default configuration settings and default data values. For example, the SFDX_LOG_LEVEL environment variable defines the log level for log messages that are written to the sfdx.log log file.

4. **Runtime Configuration Values**: Runtime configuration values can also be used for setting default configuration settings and data values. There are two types of configuration values: global and local. Global values are visible to all projects in your development environment, whereas local values are only visible to a single project. Local values have priority over global values.

As we saw when walking through the force:user:create command, the different methods for providing inputs to a CLI command are not mutually exclusive; for example, it's possible to set the configuration setting or default data value using a runtime configuration value, plus an environment variable, and also by passing a command-line parameter. When this occurs, the command needs to determine which input takes priority. Fortunately, input priorities are well defined; the preceding list is in priority order, with the highest priority at the top (command-line parameters and arguments) and the lowest priority at the bottom (runtime configuration values).

Command-line parameters and arguments trump all other input sources as they are the highest priority. Because these inputs are typed into the command line along with the command to be executed, there's never any ambiguity about where the command received its input from. That said, there are some configuration settings that do not have a command-line parameter or argument equivalent, so other input sources must be used. Furthermore, updating the command-line parameters and arguments for a large number of commands in scripts or DevOps tools can be laborious and error prone. So, there's always a trade-off between the less ambiguous command-line parameters and arguments and the other input sources that offer more convenience, but with increased ambiguity.

Note Ambiguous means that when the same input is set using file parameters, environment variables, and runtime configuration values, it's not obvious which source provided the input without inspecting each.

We'll now explore each input source in reverse priority order, which means starting with runtime configuration values.

Runtime Configuration Values

When executing Salesforce CLI commands in the `force` namespace, you can use runtime configuration values to either override a command's default behavior or provide default data values. Suppose that you want the CLI commands to use the Metadata REST API rather than the default Metadata SOAP API. Or you want to avoid entering the same target org username for a series of CLI commands, to reduce typing effort and potential typing errors. Both are good candidates for leveraging configuration values.

The `config` namespace is used to manage runtime configuration values. The values that can be managed are listed as follows along with their environment variable and command-line parameter equivalents if they exist. Remember that runtime configuration values are lowest priority, followed by environment variables, then file parameters and command-line parameters and arguments have the highest priority.

- `apiVersion`: The API version of the Dev Hub and CLI is usually the same; if you want to use a different CLI version, such as a prerelease version, set this to the API version of the Dev Hub.
  - **Environment Variable**: `SFDX_API_VERSION`
  - **Command-Line Parameter**: `--apiversion`
- `customOrgMetadataTemplates`: When the Salesforce CLI is used to create new metadata types, it uses predefined templates to provide the default content. These templates can be overridden to provide your own default content using this runtime configuration value.
  - **Environment Variable**: `SFDX_CUSTOM_ORG_METADATA_TEMPLATES`
  - **Command-Line Parameter**: None; however, you can set the `customOrgMetadataTemplates` parameter in the `./sfdx/sfdx-config.json` file.

- defaultusername: The default target org username that will be used when executing a CLI command.
  - **Environment Variable**: SFDX_DEFAULTUSERNAME
  - **Command-Line Parameter**: --targetusername | -u
- defaultdevhubusername: The default Dev Hub username that will be used when executing CLI commands that require a Dev Hub to operate.
  - **Environment Variable**: SFDX_DEFAULTDEVHUBUSERNAME
  - **Command-Line Parameter**: --targetdevhubusername | -v
- disableTelemetry: By default, information is sent to Salesforce about CLI usage and performance. Set this to true if you would prefer not to send the data.
  - **Environment Variable**: SFDX_DISABLE_TELEMETRY
  - **Command-Line Parameter**: None
- instanceUrl: The instance URL used by the auth commands when authorizing non-scratch orgs such as Developer Edition orgs, sandboxes, and production orgs. Set this configuration variable to your default, such as https://login.salesforce.com, https://test.salesforce.com, or https://<mydomain>.my.salesforce.com.
  - **Environment Variable**: SFDX_INSTANCE_URL
  - **Command-Line Parameter**: --instanceurl|-r
- maxQueryLimit: Overrides the default number of records that a CLI command can return. The default is 10,000 records.
  - **Environment Variable**: SFDX_MAX_QUERY_LIMIT
  - **Command-Line Parameter**: None

- `restDeploy`: By default, the CLI uses the Metadata SOAP API for deployments. Set to true to use the Metadata REST API.
  - **Environment Variable**: `SFDX_REST_DEPLOY`
  - **Command-Line Parameter**: None

The `config` namespace commands that are used to manage runtime configuration values are as follows:

- **`config:get`**: Reads a configuration variable
- **`config:list`**: Lists all configuration variables
- **`config:set`**: Sets a configuration variable
- **`config:unset`**: Clears a configuration variable

We'll now run through each of these commands, starting with the `list` command.

Listing Runtime Configuration Values

To list the currently set runtime configuration values, simply execute the following command:

```
$ sfdx config:list
```

The command will output the following.

Listing 4-3. Runtime configuration values listing

```
=== List Config
Name                     Value    Location
______________________   _____    _______
defaultdevhubusername    MyDH     Global
defaultusername          MySO     Local
```

The `config:list` command can take the following parameters:

- `--json, --loglevel`: For parameter descriptions, please refer to the discussion on global parameters in the section "Command-Line Parameters and Arguments" later in this chapter.

> **Note** To list all runtime configuration values using the Visual Studio Code Command Palette, execute the command **SFDX: List All Config Variables**.

The previous listing shows that two configuration values have been set, namely, the default Dev Hub username (`defaultdevhubusername`) and the default target org username (`defaultusername`). We will set, get, and unset another configuration value in a moment.

The `Value` column shows the value that has been assigned to the configuration value. The reason that the Dev Hub and default target org usernames don't look like username email addresses, such as `someone@example.com`, is that these configuration values can be assigned either a username or an alias. `MyDH` and `MySO` are both aliases; we'll be exploring aliases in Chapter 7, "Orgs."

The `Location` column will show whether a configuration value is global or local. A location of `Global` means that the configuration value is visible to all Salesforce DX projects created in your development environment, whereas `Local` means that the configuration value is only visible to a specific Salesforce DX project. Local configuration values override global ones, so it is possible to have both a global and a local value of the same name. The location is defined when setting a runtime configuration value, as we will see in the next section.

We'll now show how a runtime configuration value can be set.

Setting a Runtime Configuration Value

To illustrate how to set a runtime configuration value, we will set the default instance URL. The instance URL is used by commands in the `auth` namespace when authenticating an org that is not a scratch org, such as a Developer Edition org, sandbox, or production org. Let's assume that in your production org, you have set My Domain to `mydom`, that your sandbox instance is `cs1`, and that you most often use the `auth` commands to authenticate a sandbox called `uat`. The URL for this sandbox would be

```
https://mydom--uat.CS1.my.salesforce.com
```

The following command sets the `instanceUrl` runtime configuration value to the sandbox URL. The value is set by passing a `Name=Value` pair argument; in this example, `instanceUrl` is the name, and `https://mydom--uat.cs1.my.salesforce.com` is the value.

```
$ sfdx config:set \
    instanceUrl=https://mydom--uat.cs1.my.salesforce.com \
    --global
```

The command output confirms that the runtime configuration value has been set.

Listing 4-4. Successfully setting a runtime configuration value

```
=== Set Config
Name             Value                                       Success
───────────────  ─────                                       ───────
instanceUrl      https://mydom--uat.cs1.my.salesforce.com    true
```

The parameters that can be passed to this command are as follows:

- `--global|-g`: Sets a runtime configuration value that is global and therefore visible to all projects. If the parameter is not present, the value is set as local and therefore only visible to the project where it was set from. [Optional] [Default: `local`]
- `--json, --loglevel`: For parameter descriptions, please refer to the discussion on global parameters in the section "Command-Line Parameters and Arguments" later in this chapter.

Note To set a local configuration value, you must execute the `config:set` command from a directory within a Salesforce DX project hierarchy; otherwise, you will get an error. Global configuration values can be set from any directory in your development environment.

Execute the `config:list` CLI command again to see the `instanceURL` configuration value alongside the existing values.

Listing 4-5. Updated runtime configuration value listing

```
=== List Config
Name                   Value                                   Location
─────────────────────  ───────                                 ────────
defaultdevhubusername  MyDH                                    Global
defaultusername        MySO                                    Local
instanceUrl            https://mydom--uat.cs1.my.salesforce.com Global
```

Rather than listing all the configuration values, as we did earlier, you can read a subset of named values, as we shall see next.

Reading Runtime Configuration Values

The `config:list` command lists all of the currently set global and local runtime configuration values. If you're only interested in reading specific values, as part of a script, for instance, use the `config:get` command with the names of the values as arguments separated by spaces, as follows:

```
$ sfdx config:get defaultusername instanceUrl
```

The output from the command should resemble the following.

Listing 4-6. Output from reading named runtime configuration values

```
=== Get Config
Name             Value                                 Success
───────────────  ───────                               ─────────
defaultusername  MySO                                  true
instanceUrl      https://mydom–uat.my.salesforce.com   true
```

Although we only passed command-line arguments to the command, the following parameters are also available to use:

- `--json`, `--loglevel`, `--verbose`: For parameter descriptions, please refer to the discussion on global parameters in the section "Command-Line Parameters and Arguments" later in this chapter.

Note To output whether the configuration value is global or local, pass the `--verbose` parameter to the command.

When you no longer need a runtime configuration value, it can be cleared. We'll round off our exploration of a configuration value's lifecycle by doing that next.

Clearing a Runtime Configuration Value

When you have finished using a runtime configuration value, you can clear it by executing the following command, which is passed the name of the runtime configuration value as an argument:

```
$ sfdx config:unset instanceUrl --global
```

The command will confirm that the value has been cleared with this output.

Listing 4-7. Successfully clearing a runtime configuration value

```
=== Unset Config
Name                Success
────────────────    ─────────
instanceUrl         true
```

This command can have the following parameters passed to it:

- `--global|-g`: Indicates whether a global or local runtime configuration value should be unset. [Optional] [Default: `local`]
- `--json, --loglevel`: For parameter descriptions, please refer to the discussion on global parameters in the section "Command-Line Parameters and Arguments" later in this chapter.

Make sure that you unset the configuration value with the intended global or remote location. In the preceding example, we set a global configuration value, so to unset it we must also specify that we are clearing a global configuration value.

You now have a good understanding of how to use the `config` namespace to manage runtime configuration values, which define configuration settings and default data values for the `force` namespace commands. Next up are environment variables, which are higher priority than runtime configuration values and therefore override them when an equivalent environment variable is set. Environment variables also include additional variables that have no runtime configuration value equivalent.

Environment Variables

Environment variables are one of the four ways that inputs can be supplied to CLI commands in the `force` namespace, the other methods being runtime configuration values, file parameters, and command-line parameters and arguments.

We saw in the previous section on runtime configuration values that each of the configuration values has an equivalent environment variable, giving us the choice of using either to provide the same input to CLI commands. Environment variables have a higher priority and therefore override the equivalent runtime configuration value. As the complete list of environment variables is quite extensive, totaling almost 40 at the time of writing, we won't list the purpose of each one here. The previous section described some common variables, and the full list of environment variables can be found in the Salesforce DX Developer Guide. Instead, we will focus on how to set environment variables.

Note Please search for "Environment Variables" in the Salesforce DX Developer Guide for a complete list of variables. The section can be found here: `https://developer.salesforce.com/docs/atlas.en-us.sfdx_setup.meta/sfdx_setup/sfdx_dev_cli_env_variables.htm`.

There are three ways to set an environment variable:

- For a single command
- For all commands in a single terminal application session, using temporary environment variables
- For all commands across all terminal application sessions, using persistent environment variables

Note The following examples use the Bash shell on macOS. Please refer to the documentation for your shell of choice and use its corresponding instructions.

To set an environment variable as an input to a single CLI command, set the variable before the command on the same command line. For example, enter the following two commands in the same terminal application session to display the command outputs in JSON format:

```
$ SFDX_CONTENT_TYPE=JSON sfdx force
$ SFDX_CONTENT_TYPE=JSON sfdx force:org:list
```

Use the `export` command to set an environment variable via the command line to modify all the CLI commands that are executed in the same terminal application session thereafter. Executing the following commands generates the same JSON output as the preceding two commands while only setting the environment variable once. The `unset` command clears the environment variable; otherwise, the environment variable remains until the terminal application session ends.

```
$ export SFDX_CONTENT_TYPE=JSON
$ sfdx force
$ sfdx force:org:list
$ unset SFDX_CONTENT_TYPE
```

For an environment variable to persist between terminal application sessions, add the variable to a shell configuration file by following these instructions:

- Open a terminal application.
- From the terminal application's command line, execute the command `echo $HOME` to find the current user's home directory.
- Edit the file `<HOME>/.bash_profile` file using a text editor, where `<HOME>` is the user's home directory from the previous step.
- Add the line `export SFDX_CONTENT_TYPE=JSON`, then save and close the file.
- Close and reopen your terminal application.

- Enter the command echo `$SFDX_CONTENT_TYPE`; the output should be `JSON`.
- Execute the CLI command `sfdx force` and observe that the output is in JSON format.

So far, of the four ways that CLI commands can take configuration settings and data value inputs, we have covered runtime configuration values and environment variables. The next method that we'll look at is file parameters, before moving on to command-line parameters and arguments.

File Parameters

Some CLI commands in the `force` namespace take their inputs from configuration and definition files that contain multiple file parameters. We'll be covering the various types of definition and configuration files used by Salesforce DX in future chapters; in particular, project configuration files appear in Chapter 6, "Projects"; scratch org definition files are explored in Chapter 7, "Orgs"; and we'll look at user definition files in Chapter 10, "Test Users." The key thing to remember is that file parameters override runtime configuration values and environment variables, but they are lower priority than command-line parameters and arguments. Although we won't be explaining the files in detail yet, here are a few examples that illustrate the relative priority of file parameters and how overrides work.

In the section on runtime configuration values, we came across the `instanceUrl` value and its environment variable equivalent `SFDX_INSTANCE_URL`, which tells commands in the `auth` namespace what URL to use when accessing an org, such as `https://test.salesforce.com` for sandboxes. Both the runtime configuration value and the environment variable can be overridden when the Salesforce DX project configuration file contains the `sfdcLoginUrl` file parameter, as highlighted in the following listing.

Listing 4-8. sfdcLoginUrl file parameter

```
{
  "packageDirectories": [
    {
      "path": "force-app",
```

```
      "default": true
    }
  ],
  "namespace": "",
  "sfdcLoginUrl": "https://test.salesforce.com",
  "sourceApiVersion": "54.0"
}
```

The project configuration file is not passed to a CLI command using a command-line parameter, as it contains project-wide values. Most other configuration and definition files serve a more command-specific purpose and are therefore passed to CLI commands using command-line parameters. A case in point is the scratch org definition file that you will be seeing a lot of while working with Salesforce DX. The file determines the features and settings that will be present when a scratch org is created and is passed to the `force:org:create` command using the `--definitionfile|-f` command-line parameter, such as in the following:

```
$ sfdx force:org:create \
    -a MySO \
    -f ./config/project-scratch-def.json
```

Although the scratch org definition file can contain many file parameters that define the shape of the scratch org to be created, it only has a single required parameter, `edition`, which states the edition of scratch org that should be created (Developer, Enterprise, Group, or Professional), and is highlighted in the following.

Listing 4-9. Scratch org definition file edition parameter

```
{
  "edition": "Developer"
}
```

The final way that inputs can be provided to CLI commands is using command-line parameters and arguments, which we'll discuss next.

Command-Line Parameters and Arguments

Of the four ways that inputs can be supplied to CLI commands, command-line parameters and arguments are the highest priority and therefore override the three other methods: file parameters, environment variables, and runtime configuration values.

In the section "Anatomy of a CLI Command" earlier, we explained that the structure of a CLI command includes command-line parameters and arguments. As a reminder, this is the structure of a command:

```
$ sfdx <namespace>:<topic>:<subtopic>:<command> ↩
    [parameters] [arguments]
```

We also learned that some parameters take values, while others do not, and that arguments can be just a value or a `Name=Value` pair. This example shows a command taking an argument that is just a value (`defaultusername`) as an input:

```
$ sfdx config:get defaultusername
```

whereas this example includes a parameter that takes a value (`-f ./config/project-scratch-def.json`), a parameter that doesn't take a value (`--json`), and a `Name=Value` pair argument (`edition=Enterprise`):

```
$ sfdx force:org:create \
    -f ./config/project-scratch-def.json \
    edition=Enterprise \
    --json
```

In the second example, the `edition=Enterprise` argument overrides the `"edition": "Developer"` parameter in the scratch org definition file that we saw in the previous section, which causes an Enterprise Edition scratch org to be created rather than a Developer Edition scratch org. This demonstrates a command-line argument overriding a file parameter.

As with file parameters, environment variables, and runtime configuration values, some command-line parameters and arguments are configuration settings that determine the command's behavior, `--json`, for example, while others are data values for the command to act on, such as `edition=Enterprise`.

Many command-line parameters and arguments are specific to the CLI command being executed. We'll be encountering these as we work through the book when describing those commands. There are, however, a few command-line parameters that serve the same purpose regardless of the command that they are passed to. These are known as global parameters, or flags. For example, all commands can take the `--json` parameter that changes the command output format to JSON. Rather than describing each global parameter every time we discuss a CLI command, we'll describe them once here:

- `--json`: Changes the command output to JSON format, which is particularly useful when scripting multiple commands, where the output of one command needs to be parsed for parameter values to pass to another command.
- `--loglevel`: Sets the logging level for the CLI commands, which determines the granularity of the logging messages written to the `sfdx.log` log file.
- `--apiversion`: Normally, the API version used by the CLI and the Dev Hub are the same. If they need to be different, for example, because you are experimenting with a prerelease version of the CLI against a GA version of the Dev Hub, set this parameter to the API version used by the Dev Hub.
- `--perflog`: When present, writes API performance information to the `apiPerformanceLog.json` log file. Note that the `--json` parameter must also be present for API performance information to be emitted.
- `--concise`: Passed to some commands to request more succinct output.
- `--quiet`: Used by some commands to suppress any command output.
- `--verbose`: Some commands that take this parameter support a more expansive output with additional information.

Note Not all commands take all of these parameters; however, when they do take any of the parameters, they serve the same purpose regardless of the command that they are passed to.

The last three parameters, `--concise`, `--quiet`, and `--verbose`, determine the level of detail in a command's output and are therefore fairly self-explanatory. The `--apiversion` parameter is only used if the API that the CLI is using is different than the Dev Hub API version, which usually happens when you are experimenting with a prerelease version of the CLI, and there's not much more that can be said about that. Unfortunately, there is no documentation about the `--perflog` parameter; perhaps it's for Salesforce support use, or there might be a performance profiling feature in the future. This leaves the `--json` and `--loglevel` parameters, which deserve some further explanation. We'll start with the `--json` parameter.

JSON Formatted Command Output

The default output format for the CLI commands is a useful, human-readable format; sometimes, though, we want the output to be read by computers, for example, when scripting the CLI or when calling the CLI from continuous integration/continuous delivery systems. Fortunately, all the `force` namespace commands accept the `--json` global parameter to change the format of the command's output to JSON. This data-interchange format is not only human readable, but, more importantly, it's easy for computers to read and write.

Note If you are new to JSON, `www.json.org/` is a good place to start familiarizing yourself with it.

Here's an example. If you enter the command `sfdx force`, the output is a nice rendition of the Salesforce cloud logo and some useful links to further information. You can also see the API version, which is highlighted in bold.

Listing 4-10. sfdx force human-readable output

```
                 DX DX DX
             DX DX DX DX DX DX            DX DX DX
          DX DX DX      DX DX DX    DX DX DX DX DX DX
        DX DX              DX DX DX DX DX     DX DX DX
       DX DX                 DX DX DX             DX DX    DX DX DX
      DX DX                    DX DX                 DX DX DX DX DX DX DX
     DX DX                                           DX DX DX       DX DX DX
     DX DX                                             DX             DX DX DX
      DX DX                                                               DX DX
      DX DX                                                                DX DX
       DX DX                                                               DX DX
     DX DX                                                                  DX DX
   DX DX                                                                    DX DX
 DX DX                                                                      DX DX
DX DX                                                                      DX DX
DX DX                                                                     DX DX
DX DX                                                                    DX DX
 DX DX                                                    DX           DX DX
 DX DX                                                  DX DX DX DX DX DX
  DX DX                                                 DX DX DX DX DX
    DX DX DX   DX DX                     DX            DX DX
       DX DX DX DX DX                   DX DX DX DX DX DX
          DX DX  DX DX                  DX DX DX DX DX
                  DX DX              DX DX
                    DX DX DX     DX DX DX
                      DX DX DX DX DX DX                     v54.0
                          DX DX DX

* Salesforce CLI Release Notes: https://github.com/forcedotcom/cli/tree/
main/releasenotes
* Salesforce DX Setup Guide: https://sfdc.co/sfdx_setup_guide
* Salesforce DX Developer Guide: https://sfdc.co/sfdx_dev_guide
* Salesforce CLI Command Reference: https://sfdc.co/sfdx_cli_reference
```

```
* Salesforce Extensions for VS Code: ↩
    https://marketplace.visualstudio.com/items?itemName=salesforce.
    salesforcedx-vscode
```

If you just needed the API version, perhaps because your script is designed to work with a specific version, how do you extract just the API version number "54.0" from the output? The first step is to format the output as JSON by passing the `--json` command-line parameter to the command, like this: `sfdx force --json`. The resulting output changes to the following.

Listing 4-11. sfdx force JSON output

```
{
  "status": 0,
  "result": {
    "apiVersion": "54.0"
  }
}
```

The output isn't as interesting, and it lacks the help links, but it does include the API version number. Although we won't be covering scripting and automation in this book, here's an example of how you would use the jq command-line JSP processor to extract just the API version number:

```
$ sfdx force --json | jq -r .result.apiVersion
```

```
The command will simply output a number, the API version.
```

Listing 4-12. API version number output

```
54.0
```

This value can then be used as an input to subsequent script commands. The second global parameter that deserves further explanation is the `--loglevel` parameter.

CLI Logging

If an issue arises when executing a CLI command, a high-level error is written to the `stdout` stream, which is sent to the terminal application. This error on its own may not be enough information to determine the cause of an issue, so more detailed information is needed. Errors are also written to the `stderr` stream, which sends log messages to a log file with the path `<HOME>/.sfdx/sfdx.log`, where `<HOME>` is the user's home directory. A big difference between the `stdout` and `stderr` streams is that the level of detail in the log messages written to `stderr`, and therefore to the `sfdx.log` log file, can be varied by passing the `--loglevel` command-line parameter to a command.

Note To get the value for `<HOME>`, enter `echo $HOME` on a terminal application's command line.

The `--loglevel` command-line parameter takes a log level value, which can be one of the following:

- `fatal`
- `error`
- `warn` [default]
- `info`
- `debug`
- `trace`

The `fatal` level outputs the least information, the `trace` level outputs the most, and the levels are cumulative; in other words, setting the logging level to `info` means that all `fatal`, `error`, and `warn` level information is also logged. For example, the following command opens a scratch org with the alias `MySO` and sets the log level to `debug`:

```
$ sfdx force:org:open \
    --targetusername=MySO \
    --loglevel=debug
```

The logging information can then be viewed by opening the `sfdx.log` file using your preferred text editor.

Note To make it easier to view what has been written to the log file, delete the log file before running the command. That said, please don't delete any other files in the same directory, as these are used internally by the CLI.

Using the `--loglevel` command-line parameter changes the log level for an individual command. To change the log level for multiple commands, you can either pass the `--loglevel` parameter to each command or you can set the environment variable `SFDX_LOG_LEVEL` to the desired log level. The environment variable's log level will then be used for all commands, unless overridden using the `--loglevel` command-line parameter for an individual command.

Most development environments provide multiple ways to perform a task; using Visual Studio Code, the Salesforce Extensions for Visual Studio Code and the Salesforce CLI are no different. In the next section, we will look at four ways that a Salesforce CLI command can be executed.

Salesforce CLI Command Execution

A Salesforce CLI command can be executed using four different methods:

- Using a terminal application
- Using the Visual Studio Code integrated terminal
- Using the Visual Studio Code Command Palette
- Using a Visual Studio Code context menu

Note Please refer to the section "Visual Studio Code" in Chapter 3, "Concepts Overview," for screenshots of the VS Code integrated terminal, Command Palette, and context menu.

At this stage, don't worry about the specifics of the commands that we will be using, as we'll be covering them in detail later in the book; simply know that these command execution methods exist and how to perform them.

We will first create a Salesforce DX project called `SalesforceDXCLI` using the terminal application method.

Using a Terminal Application

To create a Salesforce DX project using a terminal application, launch the terminal application and change directory to where you would like to create the project. Then execute the following command:

```
$ sfdx force:project:create \
    --projectname SalesforceDXCLI
```

The output from this command will resemble the following.

Listing 4-13. Output from the force:project:create command

```
target dir = /Users/ivanharris/Documents/Book/Code
   create SalesforceDXCLI/config/project-scratch-def.json
   create SalesforceDXCLI/README.md
   create SalesforceDXCLI/sfdx-project.json
   create SalesforceDXCLI/.husky/pre-commit
   create SalesforceDXCLI/.vscode/extensions.json
   create SalesforceDXCLI/.vscode/launch.json
   create SalesforceDXCLI/.vscode/settings.json
   create SalesforceDXCLI/force-app/main/default/lwc/.eslintrc.json
   create SalesforceDXCLI/force-app/main/default/aura/.eslintrc.json
   create SalesforceDXCLI/scripts/soql/account.soql
   create SalesforceDXCLI/scripts/apex/hello.apex
   create SalesforceDXCLI/.eslintignore
   create SalesforceDXCLI/.forceignore
   create SalesforceDXCLI/.gitignore
   create SalesforceDXCLI/.prettierignore
   create SalesforceDXCLI/.prettierrc
   create SalesforceDXCLI/jest.config.js
   create SalesforceDXCLI/package.json
```

The command has created a project root directory called `SalesforceDXCLI` with a directory hierarchy below it. We will be delving into this structure further in Chapter 6, "Projects." To open this project in VS Code, launch VS Code, click the **File ➤ Open Folder...** menu item, navigate to the `SalesforceDXCLI` directory that you have just created, and click the **Open** button.

Delete the `SalesforceDXCLI` directory so that the next section can show how to create the same project using VS Code's integrated terminal.

Using the Visual Studio Code Integrated Terminal

To use VS Code's integrated terminal to create the same project that we created using the terminal application, follow these steps:

1. Launch Visual Studio Code if it is not already launched.
2. Open the integrated terminal by clicking the **Terminal ➤ New Terminal** menu item.
3. In the integrated terminal, change directory to where you want to create the project.
4. Enter `sfdx force:project:create --projectname SalesforceDXCLI` on the command line.

This will create the same directory structure that was created when executing the command from the terminal application's command line. To open the project in VS Code, perform the following:

1. Click the **File ➤ Open Folder...** menu item.
2. Browse to the `SalesforceDXCLI` root directory.
3. Click the **Open** button.

Note If you didn't delete the existing `SalesforceDXCLI` project before creating this project of the same name, the newly created project's files will have overwritten the existing ones.

Next, we will create the same project using VS Code's Command Palette. Close the folder in VS Code using the **File ➤ Close Folder** command and delete the existing `SalesforceDXCLI` project first.

Using the Visual Studio Code Command Palette

The final way that we will create a Salesforce DX project is to use VS Code's Command Palette. To create the same project as in the previous sections, do the following:

1. Launch Visual Studio Code if it is not already launched.
2. Open the Command Palette by clicking the **View ➤ Command Palette...** menu item.
3. Select the **SFDX: Create Project** command.
4. Hit **return** to select the default `standard` project template.
5. Enter `SalesforceDXCLI` as the project name and hit **return**.
6. In the directory browser dialog, select the directory where you would like to create the project.
7. Click the **Create Project** button.

Note In step 3, if the **SFDX: Create Project** command is not visible, start typing the command until it appears in the list.

VS Code will then open the project, so there is no need to separately open the project as you did when using the terminal application and VS Code's integrated terminal.

In the next section, we will create an Apex class using a VS Code context menu. This time, don't delete the `SalesforceDXCLI` project as we will be reusing it.

Using a Visual Studio Code Context Menu

To show how to execute CLI commands using a context menu, we will create an Apex class by performing the following steps:

1. Launch Visual Studio Code if it is not already launched.
2. Open the `SalesforceDXCLI` project that you created in the previous section.
3. Click the `force-app` directory in the Explorer view in VS Code's Side Bar to expand the `force-app/main/default` directory hierarchy.

4. Right-click the `classes` directory to display the context menu for that directory.
5. Click the **SFDX: Create Apex Class** menu item.
6. The Command Palette will open, enter `CLICmdEx` for the class name, and hit **return**.
7. Hit return again to select the default directory for the files that will be created.

This will create the files `CLICmdEx.cls` and `CLICmdEx.cls-meta.xml` in the directory `force-app/main/default/classes` including skeleton code and metadata XML.

Given that there are four methods for executing a Salesforce CLI command, which should you use? We'll cover the pros and cons of each next.

Which Command Execution Method?

Of the four Salesforce CLI command execution methods outlined earlier, which should be used and when? The first choice is between using a terminal application vs. the three Visual Studio Code methods, namely, the integrated terminal, Command Palette, and context menus. Everything that can be done with a terminal application can also be done with VS Code's integrated terminal, so there's little merit in using the terminal application once you have started to use Visual Studio Code; not to mention, working with the integrated terminal reduces application switching as you remain within the VS Code application.

Once the decision has been made to go all-in with Visual Studio Code, when do you use the integrated terminal's command line rather than the Command Palette or context menus? Firstly, not all commands have been implemented, as yet, in the Command Palette and context menus, so the integrated terminal must be used for those commands. Secondly, in order to simplify the Command Palette and context menus, only the most frequently used command parameters have been implemented. To use the remaining parameters, the command must be executed in the integrated terminal, which presents a good trade-off between ease of use and power use.

The final choice between the Command Palette and context menus comes down to scope, or context. The context menu commands are shortcuts to Command Palette commands when the command can be applied to a narrow context, such as a directory, a file, or some highlighted text rather than the whole project. An example is deploying source to a target org. Executing the command from the Command Palette applies to all metadata components, whereas executing the command from a file's context menu will apply to just that component.

In summary, work within the Visual Studio Code app as much as possible and familiarize yourself with executing Salesforce CLI commands from the integrated terminal's command line, as all commands and parameters are available there. As you become comfortable with the commands, start using the Command Palette and context menus for ease of use when the commands support the parameters that you need.

Let's wrap up by summarizing what we have learned in this chapter.

Chapter Summary

In this chapter, you familiarized yourself with the Salesforce CLI command structure and how to get help from the command line. We also discovered how to control CLI commands using configuration settings and data values that are provided by command-line parameters and arguments, file parameters, environment variables, and runtime configuration values. We then looked at global parameters and showed how to use them to change a command's output format to JSON and how to vary the level of a command's logging detail. Finally, we looked at the various ways that a Salesforce CLI command can be executed from a terminal application and Visual Studio Code.

To use the commands in the `force:org` topic, a Dev Hub is needed. The next chapter shows how to create a trial Dev Hub org, enable the Dev Hub feature, add Dev Hub users, and how to authorize the Dev Hub org using the Salesforce CLI.

CHAPTER 5

Dev Hub

The Salesforce CLI connects to a Developer Hub, or "Dev Hub," to create and manage scratch orgs. Normally, you would enable and use a Dev Hub in a production org, or in a partner business org if you are a Salesforce AppExchange Partner. If you want to use one of these orgs for your Dev Hub, please jump to the section "Enabling the Dev Hub," which is after the next section. If you would prefer to experiment with Salesforce DX without touching an existing org, create a free trial org that has a Dev Hub enabled by following the instructions in the next section.

Note A Developer Edition trial org can be used as a Dev Hub. The benefit is that a Developer Edition org does not expire; the downside is that it only allows 3 active scratch orgs, and only 6 can be created each day. The trial Dev Hub org that we will use allows 20 active scratch orgs and for 40 to be created daily. More about these limits in the "API Limits" section later in the chapter.

Creating a Trial Dev Hub Org

To enable a Dev Hub in a separate org, rather than using your production or partner business org, you can create a 30-day trial org here:

- `https://developer.salesforce.com/promotions/orgs/dx-signup`

Fill in your details and click the **Sign me up** button.

I. Harris, *Beginning Salesforce DX*, https://doi.org/10.1007/978-1-4842-8114-7_5

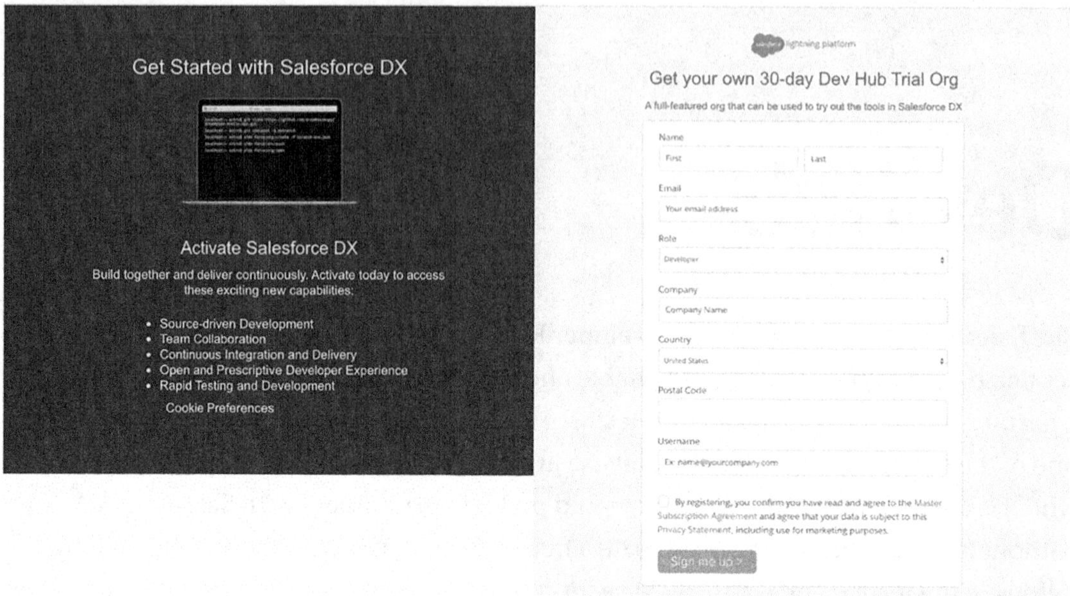

Figure 5-1. *Dev Hub trial org sign-up screen*

You will receive a verification email. Click the **Verify Account** button in the email and enter a password on the screen that opens in a browser. Make a note of this password and the username that you used when signing up, as you will need them when authorizing the org with the Salesforce CLI later. You now have your own trial Dev Hub org, and the Getting Started screen that opens has a few useful links that you can peruse at your leisure.

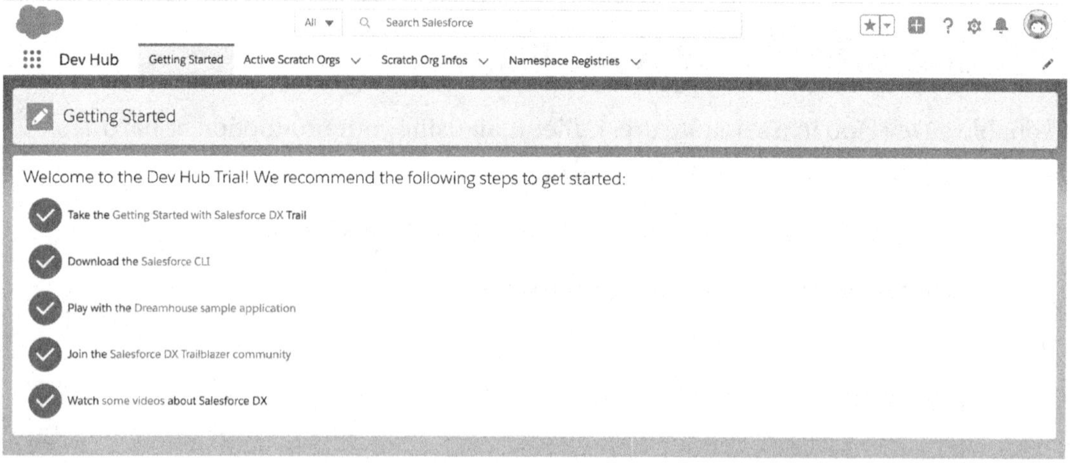

Figure 5-2. *Dev Hub Getting Started screen*

Now that you have a Dev Hub org, you are ready to enable the Dev Hub.

Enabling the Dev Hub

To enable the Dev Hub in your org, navigate to **Setup ➤ Development ➤ Dev Hub** and toggle the **Enable Dev Hub** setting to **Enabled.**

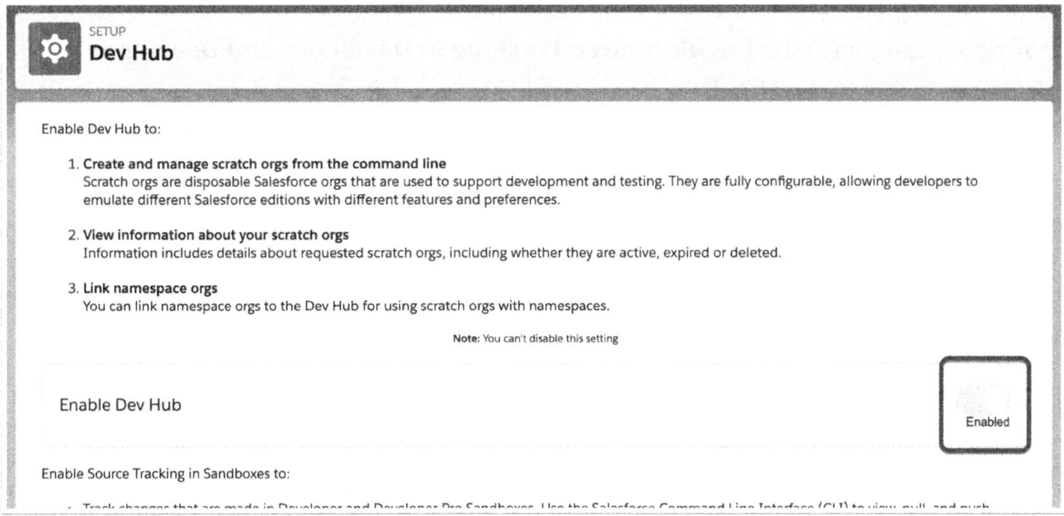

Figure 5-3. *Enable Dev Hub settings*

Note The Dev Hub will already be enabled if you signed up for a trial Dev Hub org.

In Chapter 8, "Metadata," we will explore source tracking, which can be used with scratch orgs, Developer sandboxes, and Developer Pro sandboxes. Source tracking is enabled by default in scratch orgs; however, support in sandboxes must be explicitly enabled, which we will do in the next section.

Enable Source Tracking for Sandboxes

In Chapter 3, "Concepts Overview," we learned that Salesforce DX introduced Salesforce DX projects, source format metadata, and scratch orgs. These three features support synchronization of metadata changes between scratch orgs and a local Salesforce DX project. In the Salesforce Spring '21 Release, Salesforce extended source tracking support to sandboxes. To enable the feature in the org where your Dev Hub is enabled, navigate to **Setup ➤ Development ➤ Dev Hub** if you are not currently on that page, then scroll down and toggle the **Enable Source Tracking in Developer and Developer Pro Sandboxes** setting to **Enabled.**

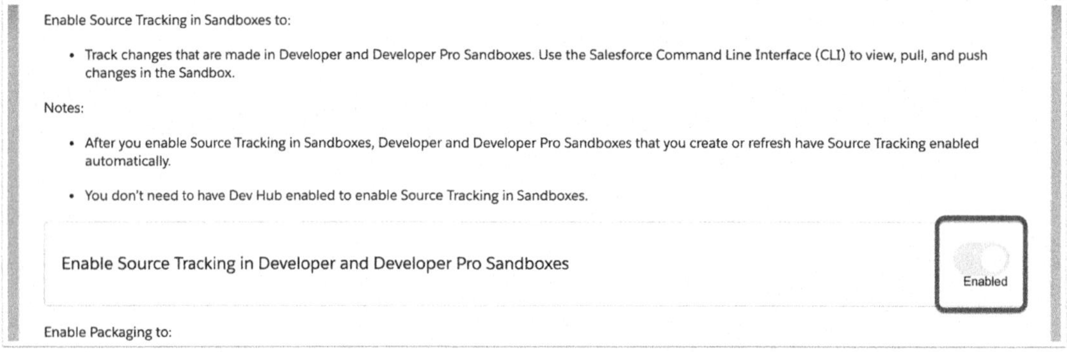

Enable Source Tracking in Sandboxes to:
• Track changes that are made in Developer and Developer Pro Sandboxes. Use the Salesforce Command Line Interface (CLI) to view, pull, and push changes in the Sandbox.
Notes:
• After you enable Source Tracking in Sandboxes, Developer and Developer Pro Sandboxes that you create or refresh have Source Tracking enabled automatically.
• You don't need to have Dev Hub enabled to enable Source Tracking in Sandboxes.
Enable Source Tracking in Developer and Developer Pro Sandboxes
Enabled
Enable Packaging to:

Figure 5-4. *Enable source tracking for sandboxes*

Note Source tracking only applies to Developer and Developer Pro sandboxes; it does not apply to Partial Copy and Full Copy sandboxes.

Salesforce DX supports two new package types, unlocked packages and second-generation managed packages (2GP). We'll enable support for these package types next as we will be covering them later in the book.

Enabling Unlocked Packages and Second-Generation Managed Packages

To use the new unlocked package and second-generation managed package (2GP) types, which Salesforce DX has introduced for deploying applications and customizations, we need to enable support for them. We'll be using both new package types later in the book. Navigate to **Setup ➤ Development ➤ Dev Hub** if you are not currently on that page, then scroll down and toggle the **Enable Unlocked Packages and Second-Generation Managed Packages** setting to **Enabled**.

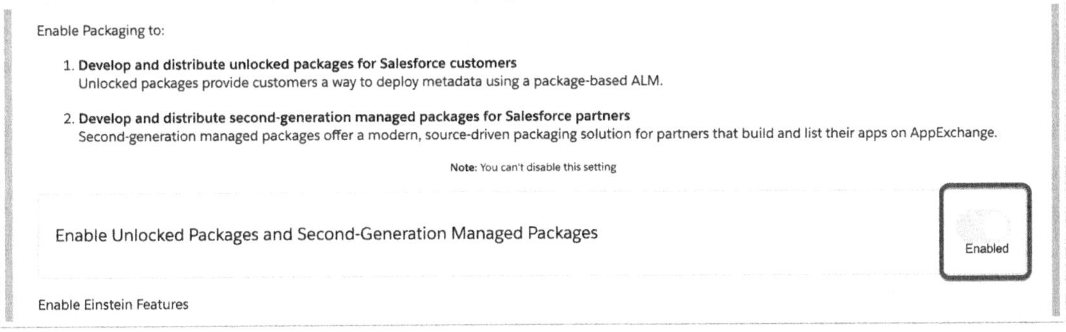

Figure 5-5. *Enable Packaging settings*

Salesforce Einstein has separate terms and conditions that must be accepted to enable Einstein in an org. The Dev Hub has a handy feature that means you only need to do this once, regardless of how many scratch orgs you create. We'll do this next.

Enabling Einstein Features

To enable Einstein in an org, you must accept some Einstein-specific terms and conditions. When developing Einstein applications or customizations using Salesforce DX, it would be very inconvenient to perform these manual steps every time you create a scratch org. Fortunately, you can do it once in the Dev Hub, so that every scratch org that is created using the Dev Hub will have the terms and conditions accepted by default. Navigate to **Setup ➤ Development ➤ Dev Hub**, if you are not currently on that page, scroll down, and toggle the **Enable Einstein Features** setting to **Enabled**.

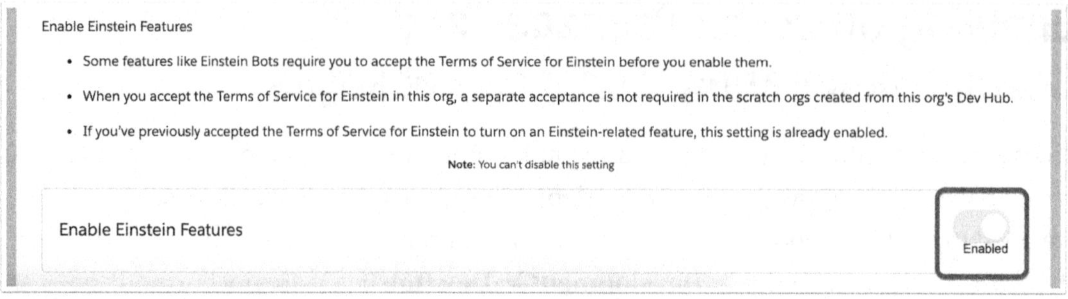

Enable Einstein Features
• Some features like Einstein Bots require you to accept the Terms of Service for Einstein before you enable them.
• When you accept the Terms of Service for Einstein in this org, a separate acceptance is not required in the scratch orgs created from this org's Dev Hub.
• If you've previously accepted the Terms of Service for Einstein to turn on an Einstein-related feature, this setting is already enabled.
Note: You can't disable this setting
Enable Einstein Features
Enabled

Figure 5-6. *Enable Einstein Features*

A Try Einstein dialog will open. Check the **I'm authorized by my company to accept these terms** checkbox and click the **Try Einstein** button.

Although you are installing these tools while logged in as a system administrator, in the following section we will see how to add additional users who are not system administrators so that they can access the Dev Hub org to create and manage scratch orgs.

Adding Salesforce DX Users

Later, in Chapter 7, "Orgs," you will see that to create a scratch org using the Salesforce CLI, the user must specify which Dev Hub to use, and that the user needs to authenticate the org where the Dev Hub is enabled; therefore, the user must have an account setup in that org. Additionally, the user needs some permissions to access the following Salesforce DX objects in the org:

- ScratchOrgInfo
- ActiveScratchOrg
- NamespaceRegistry

Users with the System Administrator profile can create scratch orgs using a Dev Hub by default, as they already have the permissions required to access the Salesforce DX objects in the org where the Dev Hub is enabled. But not all users need, or should have, the privileged level of system access that system administrators enjoy. You can give users Dev Hub access with more restricted permissions than a system administrator if they are assigned one of the following licenses:

- Salesforce
- Salesforce Platform
- Developer
- Salesforce Limited Access - Free

Note All AppExchange partners are allocated 100 Salesforce Limited Access – Free licenses.

The Developer license comes with a Developer profile and a Developer permission set. To give users access to the Dev Hub when they are assigned the Developer license, simply assign the Developer profile and the Developer permission set to the user. This will give the user the necessary permissions to access the Salesforce DX objects needed to create and manage scratch orgs. By the way, this also allows them to work with namespaces and second-generation managed packages; more on these later!

For users who are assigned the Salesforce, Salesforce Platform, and Salesforce Limited Access - Free licenses, create a new permission set that gives access to the Dev Hub objects and assign the permission set to the users. To create the permission set, complete these steps:

1. Log in to the org where the Dev Hub is enabled. This will be your production org, partner business org, or the trial Dev Hub org that you created earlier.
2. Navigate to **Setup ➤ Users ➤ Permission Sets**.
3. Click the **New** button.
4. In the Permission Set Create page, enter the following field values:
   a. **Label**: Salesforce DX User
   b. **API Name**: Salesforce_DX_User
   c. **License**: Select `--None--` if you want to assign the permission set to users with different licenses; otherwise, select the license that is assigned to the users who require Dev Hub access.
5. Click the **Save** button.

6. The Salesforce DX User permission set will open. Scroll down to the Apps section and click the **Object Settings** link.
7. Scroll down and click the **Scratch Org Infos** link.
8. Click the **Edit** button.
9. In the Object Permissions section, check the **Read**, **Create**, **Edit**, and **Delete** checkboxes.
10. Click the **Save** button.
11. Perform steps 7–10 for the following objects and settings:
    a. **Active Scratch Orgs**: **Read**, **Edit**, and **Delete**
    b. **Namespace Registries**: **Read**

If you now navigate to **Setup ➤ Users ➤ Permission Sets**, click the **Salesforce DX User** permission set and then click the **Object Settings** link in the Apps section; the settings for the Salesforce DX objects should look like this.

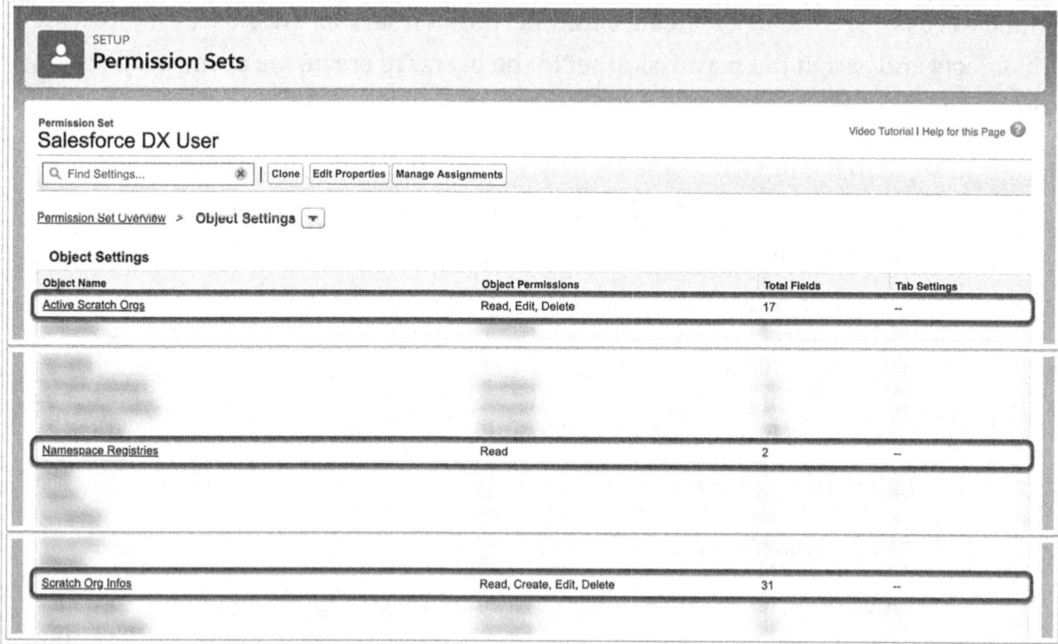

Figure 5-7. *Salesforce DX User permission set*

The permission set can now be assigned to any users that need Dev Hub access who have the required licenses assigned.

Later in the book, we will be exploring managed packages, including second-generation managed packages, where users will need additional permissions. You can either create a new permission set or modify the existing Salesforce DX User permission set to add the new permissions. To add the second-generation managed package permissions to the Salesforce DX User permission set, follow these instructions:

1. Log in to the Dev Hub org.
2. Navigate to **Setup ➤ Users ➤ Permission Sets**.
3. Click the **Salesforce DX User** permission set link.
4. Scroll down to the System section and click the **System Permissions** link.
5. Click the **Edit** button.
6. Scroll down and find the **Create and Update Second-Generation Packages** permission and check the checkbox.
7. Click the **Save** button.
8. If a Permission Changes Confirmation dialog opens, review the changes, which should show that you have enabled a single System Permission called Create and Update Second-Generation Packages. If this is the case, click the **Save** button; otherwise, click the **Cancel** button and correct your changes.

The System Permissions will be displayed, and the Create and Update Second-Generation Packages permission should be checked, as in the following screenshot.

***Figure 5-8.** Create and Update Second-Generation Packages permission*

By this point, you have enabled the Dev Hub in an org and given access to users. The final step needed to use a Dev Hub, is to authorize the org with the Salesforce CLI.

Authorizing a Dev Hub Org

The Salesforce CLI commands in the `force:org` topic use a Dev Hub that is authorized by the CLI to create and manage scratch orgs. Under most circumstances, you will only need a single Dev Hub; that said, there are occasions when you will need multiple Dev Hubs, such as when you want to experiment using a separate Dev Hub rather than using your production one. In this section, we will see how to set up the following configurations:

- A default Dev Hub org with a global scope so that it can be used with multiple Salesforce DX projects.
- A default Dev Hub org with a local scope that can only be used with a single Salesforce DX project.
- Two default Dev Hub orgs, one with global scope and one with local scope, so either can be used.

Note We will be learning more about Salesforce DX projects in Chapter 6, "Projects," and we'll be covering commands in the `auth` namespace in Chapter 7, "Orgs." We therefore won't be describing the commands and parameters in depth here.

The preceding configuration examples mention a default Dev Hub org. Defaults are useful so that you don't have to name the org in every `force:org` command. For example, in the following two `force:org:create` commands, the first command names a target Dev Hub org, whereas the second one doesn't as it assumes that a default has been set up:

```
$ sfdx force:org:create \
    --setalias MySO \
    --setdefaultusername \
    --targetdevhubusername MyDH
```

```
$ sfdx force:org:create \
    --setalias MySO \
    --setdefaultusername
```

If you run the second command without a default Dev Hub org, you will get the following error.

Listing 5-1. Dev Hub org required error

```
ERROR running force:org:create:  This command requires a dev hub org
username set either with a flag or by default in the config.
```

We'll now authorize a global scope Dev Hub org and set it as a default.

Authorizing a Global Scope Dev Hub Org

To authorize a Dev Hub org so that it can be used by multiple Salesforce DX projects, launch a terminal application and change to a directory that is not part of a Salesforce DX project. Then execute the following command to start the Dev Hub org authorization process:

```
$ sfdx auth:web:login \
    --setalias MyGlobalDH \
    --setdefaultdevhubusername \
    --instanceurl https://login.salesforce.com
```

Note Although you could use the Visual Studio Code integrated terminal to execute the preceding command, we can't use the VS Code Command Palette to authorize a Dev Hub org that has a global scope, as the Command Palette command assumes that a project configuration file is present with the `sfdcLoginUrl` file parameter defined. The preceding command is stand-alone, as we provided the login URL as a command-line parameter.

When the command is executed, it opens a Salesforce login screen. Enter the username and password of the Dev Hub org that you set up earlier in the chapter. An Allow Access screen will appear; click the **Allow** button to grant the Salesforce CLI access to the Dev Hub org.

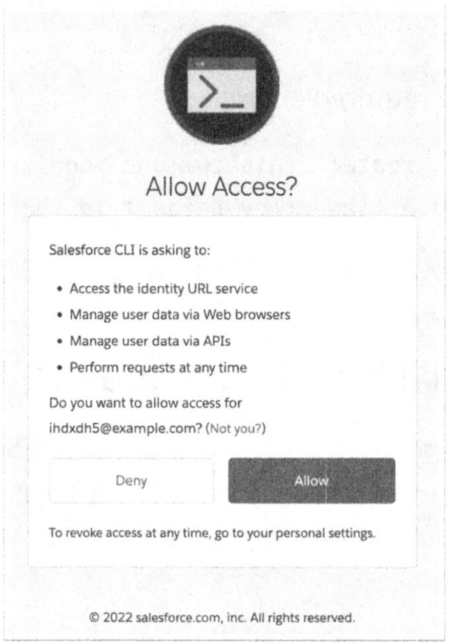

Figure 5-9. *Allow the CLI access to the Dev Hub screen*

Note The Allow Access screen only appears the first time that you authorize a Dev Hub org, even if you log out and log back in again.

This authorization process uses the OAuth 2.0 web server flow, which utilizes a global connected app called Salesforce CLI, which is included with all non-scratch and scratch orgs. It allows the Salesforce CLI to authorize the Dev Hub and connect to it thereafter. If you want more secure settings than the default connected app provides, you can create your own connected app and authorize using it by passing its consumer key to the `auth:web:login` command with the `--clientid|-i` parameter.

Return to the terminal application and enter the following command, which lists all authorized orgs and scratch orgs:

```
$ sfdx force:org:list
```

The output shows the newly authorized Dev Hub org. The (D) signifies that this org is the default Dev Hub org.

Listing 5-2. Registered Dev Hub org with global scope

```
=== Orgs
     ALIAS       USERNAME              ORG ID              CONNECTED STATUS
──── ─────────── ───────────────────── ─────────────────── ────────────────
(D)  MyGlobalDH  ihdxdh5@example.com   00D5i000002NfhIEAS  Connected
```

To see the scope of the Dev Hub org, execute the following command that you came across in Chapter 4, "Salesforce CLI":

```
$ sfdx config:get defaultdevhubusername --verbose
```

This results in the following output, showing the defaultdevhubusername runtime configuration value.

Listing 5-3. Global scope Dev Hub org runtime configuration value

```
=== Get Config
Name                   Value       Success  Location
────────────────────── ─────────── ──────── ────────
defaultdevhubusername  MyGlobalDH  true     Global
```

Two things are of note: (1) the value passed to the --setalias|-a parameter when we executed the auth:web:login command has been assigned to the defaultdevhubusername runtime configuration value, and (2) because the authorization was done outside of any Salesforce DX projects, its location, or scope, has been set to Global. Because runtime configuration values are used to store the default Dev Hub org, this is the reason that there can be a global scope and a local scope default at the same time.

Before we look at a local scope default Dev Hub org, reset back to initial conditions by executing the following two commands in the terminal application:

```
$ sfdx auth:logout --targetusername MyGlobalDH
```

```
$ sfdx config:unset defaultdevhubusername --global
```

The first command logs out of the Dev Hub org and removes it from the list of authorized orgs, while the second clears the `defaultdevhubusername` runtime configuration value. Re-run the `force:org:list` and the `config:get defaultdevhubusername --verbose` commands to confirm this.

We'll now move on to authorizing a default Dev Hug org with a local scope.

Authorizing a Local Scope Dev Hub Org

In this section, we will authorize a default Dev Hub with a local scope, so that it's only visible to a single project, which needs a Salesforce DX project. In the terminal application, change to a directory where you want to create a new Salesforce DX project, then create the project using the following command:

```
$ sfdx force:project:create \
    --projectname SalesforceDXDevHub
```

Next, change to the root directory of the new project and execute the following command:

```
$ sfdx auth:web:login \
    --setalias MyDH \
    --setdefaultdevhubusername
```

This time, the `--instanceurl|-r` parameter is not necessary as the `sfdcLoginUrl` parameter in the project configuration file is used, although you can of course override the file parameter with the command-line parameter.

When the login screen opens in a browser, enter the username and password for your second Dev Hub org, and click the **Allow** button in the Allow Access screen, to grant the Salesforce CLI access to the Dev Hub org. Run the `force:org:list` command to view the newly authorized Dev Hub org.

Listing 5-4. Registered Dev Hub org with local scope

```
=== Orgs
       ALIAS  USERNAME              ORG ID                 CONNECTED STATUS
─────  ─────  ────────────────────  ─────────────────────  ──────────────────
(D)    MyDH   ihdxdh@example.com    00D4K0000015OzMUAU     Connected
```

Then run the config:get defaultdevhubusername --verbose command to confirm its local scope.

Listing 5-5. Local scope Dev Hub org runtime configuration value

```
=== Get Config
 Name                   Value  Success    Location
 ─────────────────────  ─────  ─────────  ───────────
 defaultdevhubusername  MyDH   true       Local
```

Again, the Salesforce CLI has set the `defaultdevhubusername` runtime configuration value, and because the `auth:web:login` command was executed from within a Salesforce DX project directory, it has automatically set the scope to `Local`. This authorized Dev Hub org is only the default for this project. To confirm this, change to a directory that's not part of a Salesforce DX project, and re-run the `force:org:list` and `config:get defaultdevhubusername --verbose` commands. The following outputs show that no default Dev Hub org has been authorized.

Listing 5-6. Local scope default Dev Hub org viewed from outside a Salesforce DX project

```
=== Orgs
 ALIAS  USERNAME              ORG ID                 CONNECTED STATUS
 ─────  ────────────────────  ─────────────────────  ──────────────────
 MyDH   ihdxdh@example.com    00D4K0000015OzMUAU     Connected
```

Listing 5-7. Local scope Dev Hub org runtime configuration value viewed from outside a Salesforce DX project

```
=== Get Config

 Name                      Value         Success       Location
 ───────────────────────── ───────────── ───────────── ─────────────
 defaultdevhubusername     undefined     true          undefined
```

Note that in the first listing, the (D) annotation is no longer present for the local scope Dev Hub org. You can also see in the second listing that the runtime configuration value is not set as Value and Location are set to undefined.

We will now see that a global and local default Dev Hub org can be set up and how this configuration can be used.

Authorizing a Global and Local Scope Dev Hub Org

To illustrate both a global and local scope Dev Hub org coexisting, ensure that you still have the local scope Dev Hub org set up as per the previous section. Also, make sure that you are not in a directory that is part of a Salesforce DX project. Then reauthorize the global scope Dev Hub org as you did in the earlier section called "Authorizing a Global Scope Dev Hub Org." As a reminder, here is the command to execute:

```
$ sfdx auth:web:login \
    --setalias MyGlobalDH \
    --setdefaultdevhubusername \
    --instanceurl https://login.salesforce.com
```

Now run the force:org:list and config:get defaultdevhubusername --verbose commands again.

Listing 5-8. Registered Dev Hub orgs with default global and nondefault local scopes

```
=== Orgs
      ALIAS       USERNAME             ORG ID              CONNECTED STATUS
 ──── ─────────── ──────────────────── ─────────────────── ────────────────
      MyDH        ihdxdh@example.com   00D4K0000015OzMUAU  Connected
 (D)  MyGlobalDH  ihdxdh5@example.com  00D5i000002NfhIEAS  Connected
```

Listing 5-9. A global scope Dev Hub org runtime configuration value hiding a local scope Dev Hub org

```
=== Get Config

 Name                     Value              Success  Location
 ───────────────────────  ────────────────   ───────  ───────
 defaultdevhubusername    MyGlobalDH         true     Global
```

The first listing shows both authorized Dev Hub orgs with the global scope being the one that is now set as the default. The second listing shows that the `defaultdevhubusername` runtime configuration value is currently set to the Dev Hub org with the global scope.

Now change back to the root directory of the `SalesforceDXDevHub` Salesforce DX project that you created in the section "Authorizing a Local Scope Dev Hub Org." Then run the `force:org:list` and `config:get defaultdevhubusername --verbose` commands once more.

Listing 5-10. Registered Dev Hub orgs with nondefault global and default local scopes

```
=== Orgs
     ALIAS       USERNAME              ORG ID              CONNECTED STATUS
───  ──────────  ────────────────────  ──────────────────  ─────────────────
(D)  MyDH        ihdxdh@example.com    00D4K0000015OzMUAU  Connected
     MyGlobalDH  ihdxdh5@example.com   00D5i000002NfhIEAS  Connected
```

Listing 5-11. A local scope Dev Hub org runtime configuration value hiding a global scope Dev Hub org

```
=== Get Config

 Name                    Value  Success  Location
 ──────────────────────  ─────  ───────  ────────
 defaultdevhubusername   MyDH   true     Local
```

You can see that the Dev Hub org with the local scope is now the default.

With both global and local scope Dev Hub orgs set up, the global scope Dev Hub org will always be visible to a Salesforce DX project unless you have set up a default Dev Hub org with a local scope. So, in most circumstances, such as when you want to work with a Dev Hub that is enabled in a production org, you don't need to authorize a Dev Hub org when you create a new project. However, should you wish to use a different org for a specific project, you can authorize another Dev Hub org and set it as the default with local scope.

Note As we discussed in Chapter 4, "Salesforce CLI," there are actually three ways to tell a CLI command what Dev Hub org to use (in highest to lowest priority order): (1) using the `--targetdevhubusername|-d` command-line parameter, (2) using the `SFDX_DEFAULTDEVHUBUSERNAME` environment variable, and (3) using the `defaultdevhubusername` runtime configuration value. As such, any of these methods can be used to specify a different Dev Hub org for a specific project as a local runtime configuration value overrides a global one, both local and global runtime configuration values can be overridden by an environment variable, and, finally, a command-line parameter overrides them all.

You'll be using a Dev Hub to create scratch orgs, which you will learn more about in Chapter 7, "Orgs." As with most resources in the Salesforce Platform, there are limits to how many scratch orgs you can create and have active at any one time. In the next section, we will find out what those limits are.

API Limits

The Salesforce Platform is a multitenanted environment, and to ensure fair access to the available resources for all tenants, Salesforce sets resource usage limits. The same is true for scratch orgs. Salesforce limits the number of scratch orgs that can be created in a day and how many scratch orgs can be active at any one time. Those limits relate to the org where the Dev Hub is enabled and vary depending on the org edition and partner status.

The following table shows the scratch org limits by org edition, which are correct at the time of writing.

Table 5-1. Salesforce org edition scratch org limits

Org Edition	Active Scratch Orgs	Daily Scratch Orgs
Developer Edition	3	6
Dev Hub Trial	20	40
Enterprise Edition	40	80
Unlimited Edition	100	200
Performance Edition	100	200

Note To see the latest scratch org limits, please search for "Supported Scratch Org Editions and Allocations" in the Salesforce DX Developer Guide here: `https://developer.salesforce.com/docs/atlas.en-us.sfdx_dev.meta/sfdx_dev/sfdx_dev_intro.htm`.

To view the scratch org limits for a Dev Hub org, open a terminal application and execute the following CLI command:

```
$ sfdx force:limits:api:display \
    --targetusername MyDH
```

This command's parameters are

- `--targetusername|-u`: The username or alias of the org to execute the command against, in this case the Dev Hub org. [Optional]
- `--apiversion, --json, --loglevel`: Please refer to the discussion on global parameters in the section "Command-Line Parameters and Arguments" in Chapter 4, "Salesforce CLI."

The output should resemble the following, where the scratch org limits are highlighted in bold.

Listing 5-12. Dev Hub scratch org limits

```
Name                                          Remaining     Max
─────────────────────────────────────────── ──────────── ────────────
ActiveScratchOrgs                             3             3
AnalyticsExternalDataSizeMB                   40960         40960
BOZosCalloutHourlyLimit                       20000         20000
ConcurrentAsyncGetReportInstances             200           200
ConcurrentEinsteinDataInsightsStoryCreation   5             5
ConcurrentEinsteinDiscoveryStoryCreation      2             2
ConcurrentSyncReportRuns                      20            20
DailyAnalyticsDataflowJobExecutions           60            60
DailyAnalyticsUploadedFilesSizeMB             51200         51200
DailyApiRequests                              14973         15000
DailyAsyncApexExecutions                      250000        250000
DailyBulkApiBatches                           15000         15000
DailyBulkV2QueryFileStorageMB                 976562        976562
DailyBulkV2QueryJobs                          10000         10000
DailyDurableGenericStreamingApiEvents         10000         10000
DailyDurableStreamingApiEvents                10000         10000
DailyEinsteinDataInsightsStoryCreation        1000          1000
DailyEinsteinDiscoveryPredictAPICalls         50000         50000
DailyEinsteinDiscoveryPredictionsByCDC        500000        500000
DailyEinsteinDiscoveryStoryCreation           100           100
DailyFunctionsApiCallLimit                    50000         50000
DailyGenericStreamingApiEvents                10000         10000
DailyScratchOrgs                              6             6
DailyStandardVolumePlatformEvents             10000         10000
DailyStreamingApiEvents                       10000         10000
DailyWorkflowEmails                           1890          1890
DataStorageMB                                 5             5
DurableStreamingApiConcurrentClients          20            20
FileStorageMB                                 20            20
HourlyAsyncReportRuns                         1200          1200
HourlyDashboardRefreshes                      200           200
HourlyDashboardResults                        5000          5000
```

```
HourlyDashboardStatuses                        999999999     999999999
HourlyLongTermIdMapping                        100000        100000
HourlyManagedContentPublicRequests             50000         50000
HourlyODataCallout                             1000          1000
HourlyPublishedPlatformEvents                  50000         50000
HourlyPublishedStandardVolumePlatformEvents 1000          1000
HourlyShortTermIdMapping                       100000        100000
HourlySyncReportRuns                           500           500
HourlyTimeBasedWorkflow                        50            50
MassEmail                                      10            10
MonthlyEinsteinDiscoveryStoryCreation          500           500
MonthlyPlatformEventsUsageEntitlement          0             0
Package2VersionCreates                         6             6
Package2VersionCreatesWithoutValidation        500           500
PermissionSets                                 1500          1500
PrivateConnectOutboundCalloutHourlyLimitMB  0             0
SingleEmail                                    15            15
StreamingApiConcurrentClients                  20            20
```

You can see that the limits confirm that this Dev Hub was created using a Developer Edition trial org.

If you are a Salesforce AppExchange partner, the scratch org limits depend on your partner tier as per the following table.

Table 5-2. *Salesforce AppExchange partner tier scratch org limits*

Partner Tier	Active Scratch Orgs	Daily Scratch Orgs
Summit Tier	300	600
Crest Tier	150	300
Ridge Tier	80	160
Base Tier	40	80
Partner Trials	20	40

Note To see the latest scratch org limits for AppExchange Partners, please search for "Scratch Org Allocations for Partners" in the Salesforce ISVforce Guide here: `https://developer.salesforce.com/docs/atlas.en-us.packagingGuide.meta/packagingGuide/packaging_intro.htm`.

Chapter Summary

This chapter introduced the Developer Hub, or "Dev Hub," which is used by the Salesforce CLI commands in the `force:org` topic to create and manage scratch orgs. We saw how to create a trial Dev Hub org and how to enable the Dev Hub in nontrial orgs. Then we explored how to add additional users to the Dev Hub org so that they can create and manage their own scratch orgs. After learning how to authorize a Dev Hub org using the CLI, we discovered how to determine the number of scratch orgs that can be created in a day and how many can be active at any time.

Now that you have a Dev Hub enabled, the next task to complete before you can use it to create scratch orgs is to create a Salesforce DX project, which is the subject of the next chapter.

CHAPTER 6

Projects

In Chapter 3, "Concepts Overview," we saw that Salesforce DX has introduced a new project directory structure, which stores project assets such as configuration files, metadata, test data, and scripts. In this section, we'll explore the project structure and project creation in more detail.

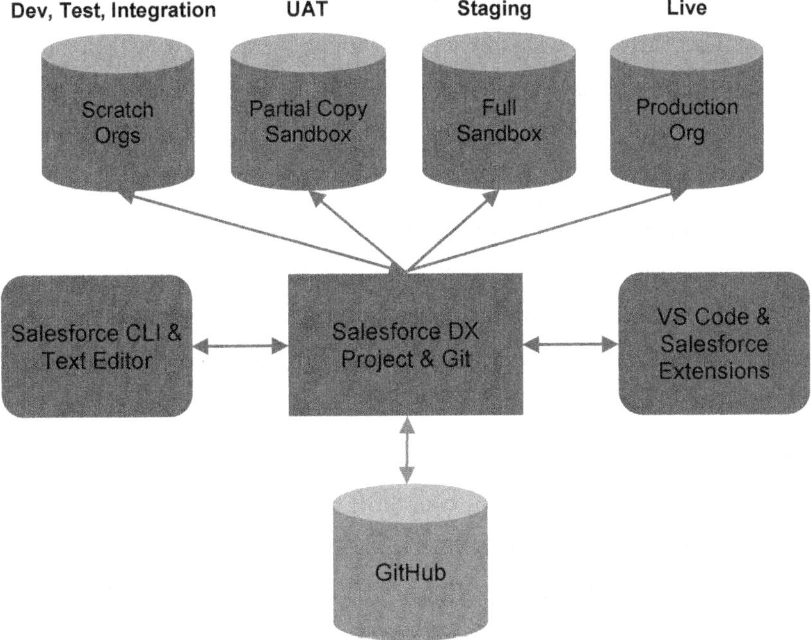

Figure 6-1. *Salesforce DX project and system interaction*

I. Harris, *Beginning Salesforce DX*, https://doi.org/10.1007/978-1-4842-8114-7_6

During the application or customization development lifecycle, a Salesforce DX project sits at the heart of, and interacts with, the systems illustrated earlier and described as follows:

- **Development Environment**: Whether you are using the Salesforce CLI and a text editor or an integrated development environment such as Visual Studio Code, you are interacting with the Salesforce DX project to store metadata in source format and/or Metadata API format; migrating metadata components between the Salesforce DX projects and orgs; defining the configuration of scratch orgs, users, and sandboxes; executing scripts; and much more.
- **Version Control System**: In this book, we use the Git version control system and the GitHub repository hosting and collaboration service. The Salesforce DX project is a local Git repository that can be synchronized with a centralized, remote repository hosted by GitHub. The GitHub repository is the source of truth that multiple developers can collaborate on.
- **Salesforce Orgs**: Metadata components can be synchronized between the Salesforce DX project, source-tracked orgs, and non-source-tracked orgs. Scratch orgs can be created and destroyed when needed, and non-scratch orgs can be authorized for simplified interaction.

Note One of the design concepts of Salesforce DX is that it allows you to use your preferred software development tools. Therefore, the Salesforce CLI and Salesforce DX projects are open by nature, and there are an increasing number of tools that integrate with Salesforce DX, such as continuous integration and continuous delivery systems (CI/CD).

Before we dive into the Salesforce DX project directory and file structure, let's introduce the key commands that we will have a look at in this chapter.

This Chapter's Commands

This chapter introduces the following Salesforce CLI commands from the `force:project` topic:

- **`force:project:create`**: Creates a Salesforce DX project

Before we explore the `force:project:create` command further, let's examine the Salesforce DX directory structure and files in more detail.

Project Directories and Files

When a Salesforce DX project is created, the Salesforce CLI builds the scaffolding, or framework, of a directory structure and some templated configuration files.

Listing 6-1. Salesforce DX project directory structure

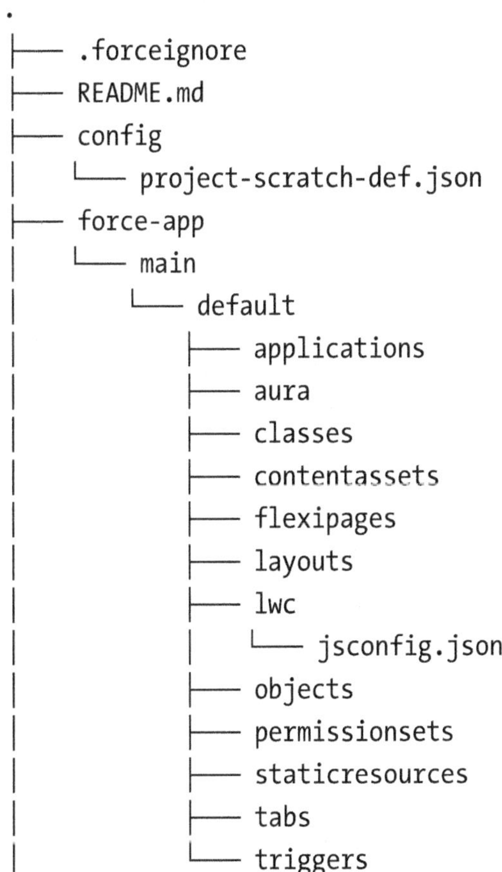

```
.
├── .forceignore
├── README.md
├── config
│   └── project-scratch-def.json
├── force-app
│   └── main
│       └── default
│           ├── applications
│           ├── aura
│           ├── classes
│           ├── contentassets
│           ├── flexipages
│           ├── layouts
│           ├── lwc
│           │   └── jsconfig.json
│           ├── objects
│           ├── permissionsets
│           ├── staticresources
│           ├── tabs
│           └── triggers
│
```

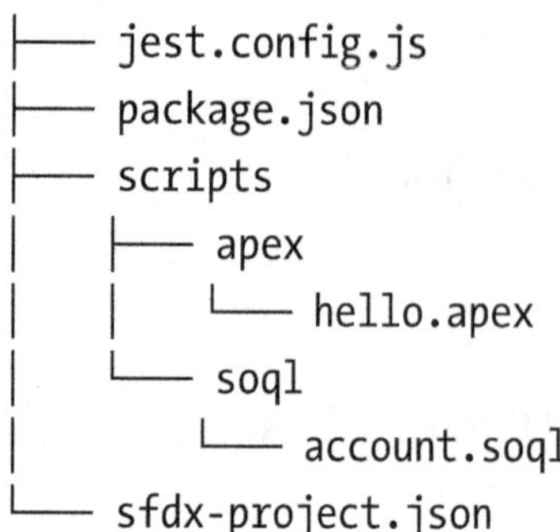

> **Note** When the project is created, several hidden directories and files beginning with "." are also added, which are used internally by tools such as Salesforce DX, VS Code, Git version control system, ESLint static code analysis, and the Prettier code formatter.

Working from the top of the listing, here is the purpose of each directory and file:

- `.forceignore`: Contains entries that prevent selected metadata components from being synchronized between source-tracked orgs (scratch orgs and Developer and Developer Pro sandboxes with source tracking enabled) and a Salesforce DX project and from being converted from source format to Metadata API format. The file is used by the `force:source` commands.
- `README.md`: A high-level guide to app deployment using Salesforce Extensions for VS Code and Salesforce CLI. When the project is added to a GitHub repository, this file becomes the repository's `README.md`. The contents are normally replaced with information about the project's application or customization.
- `config`: This directory contains the scratch org definition file, `project-scratch-def.json`, which defines the edition, features, and settings that a newly created scratch org must have. I like to store other configuration files here, such as a user definition file.

- `force-app`: The package directory where metadata in source format is stored. There can be multiple package directories, each containing functionally related metadata components. When developing unlocked packages and second-generation managed packages, each package directory becomes a separate package. The package directory hierarchy includes placeholder directories for common metadata types.
- `jest.config.js`: A configuration file for Jest, a JavaScript testing framework that is used for unit testing Lightning web components.
- `package.json`: A Node.js project manifest for setting up ESLint to highlight coding errors and bad practices while editing Lightning web components and Aura components.
- `scripts`: Placeholder directory for scripts. It includes sample anonymous Apex and a SOQL scripts that can be executed by selecting and executing the text from VS Code.
- `sfdx-project.json`: Project configuration file. The presence of this file in the root directory indicates that this directory hierarchy is a Salesforce DX project. The file contains project-wide parameters such as the list of package directories, the namespace to use when creating packages and scratch orgs, and the login URL to use when authenticating non-scratch orgs.

We'll be exploring most of these directories and files as we progress through the book, although, later in this chapter, we will dig into the `sfdx-project.json` project configuration file further.

Before doing that, we shall see how to create a new Salesforce DX project.

Creating a Salesforce DX Project

To create a Salesforce DX project, open a terminal application and navigate to the directory where you would like to create the project. Then execute this command:

```
$ sfdx force:project:create \
    --projectname SalesforceDXProjects
```

In this example, we used the only required parameter; here is the complete list of available parameters:

- `--outputdir|-d`: The directory where the project directory structure will be created. The default is `.`, which specifies the directory where the command is executed from. [Optional]
- `-- projectname|-n`: The name of the project. A project directory will be created using this name. [Required]
- `--defaultpackagedir|-p`: The name of the default package directory that metadata in source format is read from and written to when syncing with orgs. A directory of this name will be created in the project's root directory, and the project configuration file, `sfdx-project.json`, will indicate that this directory is the default package directory. [Optional] [Default: `force-app`]
- `--namespace|-s`: A Dev Hub can have multiple namespaces linked to it, but a project can only be associated with a single namespace. This parameter tells the CLI which namespace to use when creating unlocked packages, second-generation managed packages, and scratch orgs. [Optional]
- `--template|-t`: Three different types of project scaffolding can be created using the template `standard`, `empty`, or `analytics`, which determines what directories and files are added. `empty` creates a minimum viable directory and file structure, including the project configuration file and scratch org definition file. `standard` template adds configuration files for tools such as Git, ESLint, and VS Code. It also adds empty directories for metadata in source format. `analytics` is similar to `standard`, except that the only empty source format directory created is for the `waveTemplates` metadata type, and the scratch org definition file includes the `DevelopmentWave` feature to allow CRM Analytics development in a scratch org. [Optional] [Default: `standard`]
- `--manifest|-x`: Instructs the CLI to add a `manifest` directory containing a `package.xml` manifest file that can be used with the Metadata API. The manifest file includes common metadata types. [Optional]

- `--json, --loglevel`: Please refer to the discussion on global parameters in the section "Command-Line Parameters and Arguments" in Chapter 4, "Salesforce CLI."

Note To create a project using the Visual Studio Code Command Palette, execute the command **SFDX: Create Project**.

The output from this command will resemble the following.

Listing 6-2. Output from the force:project:create command

```
target dir = /Users/ivanharris/Documents/Book/Code
   create SalesforceDXProjects/config/project-scratch-def.json
   create SalesforceDXProjects/README.md
   create SalesforceDXProjects/sfdx-project.json
   create SalesforceDXProjects/.husky/pre-commit
   create SalesforceDXProjects/.vscode/extensions.json
   create SalesforceDXProjects/.vscode/launch.json
   create SalesforceDXProjects/.vscode/settings.json
   create SalesforceDXProjects/force-app/main/default/lwc/.eslintrc.json
   create SalesforceDXProjects/force-app/main/default/aura/.eslintrc.json
   create SalesforceDXProjects/scripts/soql/account.soql
   create SalesforceDXProjects/scripts/apex/hello.apex
   create SalesforceDXProjects/.eslintignore
   create SalesforceDXProjects/.forceignore
   create SalesforceDXProjects/.gitignore
   create SalesforceDXProjects/.prettierignore
   create SalesforceDXProjects/.prettierrc
   create SalesforceDXProjects/jest.config.js
   create SalesforceDXProjects/package.json
```

To open this project in VS Code, launch VS Code, click the **File ➤ Open Folder...** menu item, navigate to the `SalesforceDXProjects` directory that the `force:project:create` command just created, and click the **Open** button.

Let's now take a closer look at the `sfdx-project.json` project configuration file.

Configuring Salesforce DX Projects

The project configuration file, `sfdx-project.json`, is added to the root directory of a Salesforce DX project when it is created. It contains project configuration settings such as the project namespace and the API version that the metadata is compatible with. The default contents are as follows.

Listing 6-3. Default Salesforce DX project configuration file

```
{
  "packageDirectories": [
    {
      "path": "force-app",
      "default": true
    }
  ],
  "name": "SalesforceDXProjects",
  "namespace": "",
  "sfdcLoginUrl": "https://login.salesforce.com",
  "sourceApiVersion": "54.0"
}
```

The value for the `path` parameter defaults to `force-app`, unless a value is passed to the `--defaultpackagedir|-p` command-line parameter when executing the `force:project:create` command. Likewise, the `namespace` parameter value defaults to an empty string unless a value is passed to the `--namespace|-s` command-line parameter. The complete list of project configuration file parameters is as follows:

- `name`: The Salesforce DX project name. [Optional]
- `namespace`: A Dev Hub can have multiple namespaces linked to it, and a project can only be associated with a single namespace. This parameter tells the CLI which namespace to use when creating unlocked packages, second-generation managed packages, and scratch orgs. [Optional]
- `oauthLocalPort`: The `localhost` port to be used for the callback URL after a connected app's OAuth authorization. [Optional]

- packageAliases: Aliases that can be used to refer to packages and package versions rather than their IDs . [Optional]
- packageDirectories: This array of JSON objects lists the directories that will store metadata in source format. The CLI synchronizes the metadata components between these directories and orgs. There must be at least one default directory, which is used if a specific directory is not passed to a CLI command. Each directory typically contains functionally related metadata components that map to separate packages if second-generation managed packages are being developed. [Required]
- plugins: Used by plug-in developers to add and configure plug-ins. [Optional]
- pushPackageDirectoriesSequentially: Determines whether metadata components in multiple package directories are pushed as a single or multiple, sequential transactions when using the force:source:push command. Useful if there are dependencies between the package directories. [Optional] [Default: false]

  Allowed values are as follows:

  - false: Push the metadata components for all package directories in a single transaction regardless of the directory order in the project configuration file.
  - true: Push the metadata components for each package directory in their own transaction and in the order that the package directories are listed in the project configuration file.
- sfdcLoginUrl: The default URL used by the commands in the auth namespace, such as when authenticating a non-scratch org, for example, https://login.salesforce.com, https://test.salesforce.com, or https://<mydomain>.my.salesforce.com for production orgs, sandboxes, and production orgs with My Domain enabled, respectively. This file parameter overrides the SFDX_INSTANCE_URL environment variable and can in turn be overridden by the --instanceurl | -r command-line parameter. [Optional]

- `sourceApiVersion`: The Salesforce Platform API version that the metadata is compatible with. The value determines what metadata components are synchronized with orgs or converted using the `force:source` commands. [Optional]

Note There are additional project configuration file parameters that are used when working with unlocked packages and second-generation managed packages that are not included in the preceding list. We will be encountering some of them when we get to Chapter 13, "Package Development."

To close the chapter out, we'll finish by summarizing our learnings.

Chapter Summary

In this chapter, we looked at the structure of a Salesforce DX project and the files that are added when the project is created. We then saw how to create a project, and we wrapped up the chapter by examining the parameters in the project configuration file and their purpose.

In the next chapter, we will explore how Salesforce DX interacts with different org types, including scratch orgs, the new org type that was introduced by Salesforce DX.

CHAPTER 7

Orgs

Generally, there are two types of teams that develop applications and customizations for the Salesforce Platform, and before Salesforce DX arrived on the scene, the orgs that the two teams used were often different:

- **Internal Development Team**: This team develops applications and customizations for a single Salesforce customer's org. The team might be in-house, a third-party consultancy, or a mix of the two. The orgs used for development, test, integration, UAT, and staging are typically Developer, Developer Pro, Partial Copy, and Full Copy sandboxes. Metadata components are moved between the orgs using change sets or the Metadata API.
- **AppExchange Partner Development Team**: This team develops applications for listing on the Salesforce AppExchange enterprise marketplace. They use Developer Edition orgs during their application development lifecycle rather than sandboxes. As partners, Salesforce provides them with a partner business org, which includes an Environment Hub that is used to manage their development orgs. Metadata components are moved between orgs using the Metadata API.

Salesforce DX introduced scratch orgs, a new type of org that is an alternative to the Developer sandboxes, Developer Pro sandboxes, and Developer Edition orgs that are used by these development teams. Scratch orgs are transient orgs that exist for between 1 and 30 days (7 by default), created when needed and disposed of when no longer required. This makes them ideal for iterative development as you can spin up a fresh scratch org and push your application or customization to it for further development or testing. For internal developers, scratch orgs can be configured to include the same features and settings that are present in a production org. For AppExchange Partner developers, the features and settings that an app depends on can be configured in the scratch orgs.

I. Harris, *Beginning Salesforce DX*, https://doi.org/10.1007/978-1-4842-8114-7_7

Note It is still recommended that internal development teams use a Partial Copy sandbox for UAT and a Full Copy sandbox for staging prior to a production org deployment. AppExchange Partner developers tend to create beta versions of their managed package for prerelease testing.

Scratch orgs are always source-tracked, while Developer Edition orgs, Partial Copy sandboxes, Full Copy sandboxes, and production orgs are always non-source-tracked. Developer sandboxes and Developer Pro sandboxes are non-source-tracked by default and can be enabled for source tracking as described in Chapter 5, "Dev Hub." With source-tracked orgs, the Salesforce CLI keeps track of changes between the source format metadata components in your Salesforce DX project and the metadata components in a source-tracked org. Those changes, and only those changes, can be synchronized to keep the local Salesforce DX project and a source-tracked org in lockstep. As source format is much more granular than the Metadata API format, and only changed metadata is synchronized, the process is much faster. When using Metadata API format with source-tracked or non-source-tracked orgs, we need to tell the CLI what metadata components to deploy or retrieve, and as change tracking isn't available, all the requested metadata components will be deployed or retrieved, overwriting the same components in the org or the Salesforce DX project, respectively.

Source format metadata files, Metadata API format metadata files, and source tracking will be discussed further in Chapter 8, "Metadata," which follows this chapter. In this chapter, we will investigate how the Salesforce CLI is used to manage the lifecycle of scratch orgs and non-scratch orgs. Non-scratch orgs include Developer Edition orgs, all sandbox types (whether they are enabled for source tracking or not), and production orgs. We'll start by outlining the Salesforce CLI commands that will be introduced.

This Chapter's Commands

This chapter introduces the following Salesforce CLI commands from the `force:org` topic for working with scratch orgs and non-scratch orgs:

- **`force:org:clone`**: Clone a sandbox using a sandbox definition file.
- **`force:org:create`**: Create a scratch org using a scratch org definition file or a sandbox using a sandbox definition file.

- **force:org:delete**: Delete a scratch org or sandbox.
- **force:org:display**: Display details of an active scratch org or an authorized non-scratch org.
- **force:org:list**: List all active scratch orgs and authorized non-scratch orgs.
- **force:org:open**: Open an active scratch org or an authorized non-scratch org in a browser.
- **force:org:status**: Display the status of a sandbox create or clone operation.

We'll also be using the following commands from the **auth** namespace to authorize and log out of non-scratch orgs:

- **auth:web:login**: Authorize a non-scratch org using a browser.
- **auth:logout**: Log out of an authorized non-scratch org.

Before we start looking at scratch org management, we need to create a new Salesforce DX project for this chapter.

This Chapter's Project

To prepare a fresh Salesforce DX project for the chapter, follow the instructions in Chapter 6, "Projects," and create a project called `SalesforceDXOrgs` using the default `standard` template. As we will be working with scratch orgs, please ensure that you have a default Dev Hub org authorized with an alias of `MyDH` as described in Chapter 5, "Dev Hub."

With a Salesforce DX project in place, let's explore how to manage scratch orgs.

Managing Scratch Orgs

To manage the lifecycle of a scratch org from creation to deletion, we will be using the following commands:

- **force:org:create**: Create a scratch org using a scratch org definition file.
- **force:org:list**: List all active scratch orgs.

- **force:org:display**: Display an active scratch org's details.
- **force:org:open**: Open an active scratch org.
- **force:org:delete**: Delete a scratch org.

We'll start by creating a scratch org.

Creating Scratch Orgs

When creating a new scratch org using the Salesforce CLI, it becomes an active scratch org until its duration expires, after which it is automatically deactivated, although it is not automatically deleted.

Open the SalesforceDXOrgs Salesforce DX project in Visual Studio Code and run the following command in its integrated terminal to create a scratch org with the alias MySO:

```
$ sfdx force:org:create \
    --setalias MySO \
    --definitionfile ./config/project-scratch-def.json \
    --setdefaultusername
```

The parameters that are available for this command are as follows:

- --setalias|-a: Sets an alias for the new org that can be used instead of its username. Used for scratch org and sandbox creation. [Optional]
- --noancestors|-c: Prevents package ancestors that are defined in the project configuration file from being automatically added to a scratch org. This parameter is used when developing second-generation packages. Used for scratch org creation only. [Optional]
- --durationdays|-d: Sets the duration of a scratch org in days, with a range of 1 to 30 days. Used for scratch org creation only. [Optional] [Default: 7]

- `--definitionfile|-f`: The path to either a scratch org definition file or a sandbox definition file that contains file parameters used to configure a new scratch org or sandbox, respectively. Used for scratch org and sandbox creation. [Optional: Either a definition file is passed using this parameter, or `Name=Value` pair arguments must be provided for at least the required file parameters.]
- `--clientid|-i`: By default, the `force:org:create` command connects to a Dev Hub org using the connected app that was used when the Dev Hub org was authorized, which is either the global connected app called `Salesforce CLI` that's included with all orgs or a custom connected app. If you want to use a different connected app than the default, pass its consumer key to this parameter. Used for scratch org creation only. [Optional]
- `--nonamespace|-n`: The package configuration file can define a namespace to be used when creating scratch orgs, unlocked packages, and managed packages. Passing this parameter overrides the file parameter to create a scratch org with no namespace. This is useful when developing a package and you want to install it in a scratch org without a namespace for testing purposes. Used for scratch org creation only. [Optional]
- `--setdefaultusername|-s`: Marks the created org as having the default username. Used for scratch org and sandbox creation. [Optional]
- `--type|-t`: States what type of org to create, which can be `scratch` or `sandbox`. Used for scratch org and sandbox creation. [Optional] [Default: `scratch`]
- `--targetusername|-u`: Use this parameter when creating a sandbox. Pass the username or alias of a production org with spare sandbox licenses. Used for sandbox creation only. [Optional]
- `--targetdevhubusername|-v`: The username or alias of the Dev Hub org to use for creating the scratch org. Used for scratch org creation only. [Optional]

- `--wait|-w`: The amount of time in minutes that the `force:org:create` command will wait for the org to be created before timing out. Used for scratch org and sandbox creation. [Optional] [Default: 6]
- `--apiversion, --json, --loglevel`: Please refer to the discussion on global parameters in the section "Command-Line Parameters and Arguments" in Chapter 4, "Salesforce CLI."

Note To create a scratch org using the Visual Studio Code Command Palette, execute the command **SFDX: Create a Default Scratch Org...**.

When the command completes, it displays the new scratch org's Id and username.

Listing 7-1. New scratch org Id and username

```
Successfully created scratch org: 00D2z0000000vShEAI, ↩
  username: test-maectzkjtu6f@example.com
```

If you execute the `force:org:list` command, you will see that you now have an authorized Dev Hub and the active scratch org that you just created, where `(U)` signifies that this scratch org has the default username.

Listing 7-2. New active scratch org listing

```
=== Orgs
     ALIAS  USERNAME              ORG ID              CONNECTED STATUS
───  ─────  ────────────────────  ──────────────────  ────────────────
(D)  MyDH   ihdxdh@example.com    00D4K0000015OzMUAU  Connected
     ALIAS  USERNAME                       ORG ID              EXPIRATION DATE
───  ─────  ─────────────────────────────  ──────────────────  ───────────────
(U)  MySO   test-maectzkjtu6f@example.com  00D2z0000000vShEAI 2022-06-07
```

When the scratch org was created, a user with a username of the format `test-<unique_identifier>@example.com` was also created. The user is assigned the System Administrator profile and can be seen in the previous listing. We will see later in Chapter 10, "Test Users," that additional users can be added to the scratch org.

Note that to the left of the Visual Studio Code Status Bar, the default username is shown.

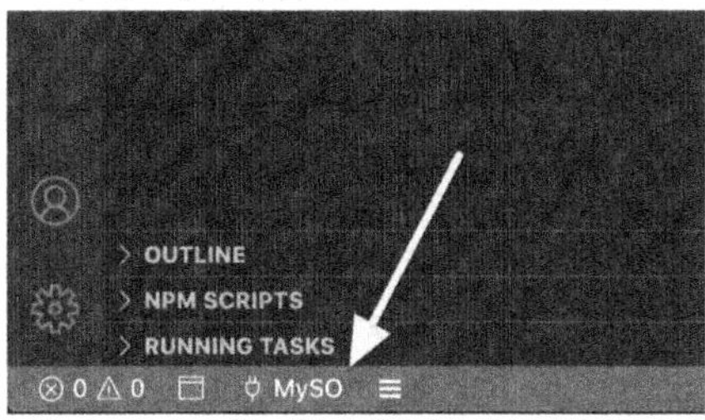

Figure 7-1. *Default org username in Visual Studio Code*

We've already encountered the `force:org:list` command a few times, albeit without any parameters. In the next section, we'll explore the parameters that can be passed to the command.

Listing Authorized Orgs and Active Scratch Orgs

As we've seen in the previous sections, to list authorized non-scratch orgs and active scratch orgs, you use the following command:

```
$ sfdx force:org:list
```

So far, we haven't explored the parameters that are available for this command, which are as follows:

- `--noprompt | -p`: When deleting expired scratch orgs using the `--clean` parameter, this parameter suppresses the deletion confirmation prompt. Applies to scratch orgs only. [Optional]
- `--all`: By default, the `force:org:list` command only shows active scratch orgs. To show expired scratch orgs, those marked for deletion and those with an unknown status, pass this parameter. Applies to scratch orgs only. [Optional]
- `--clean`: Deletes all non-active scratch orgs. To see non-active scratch orgs, run `force:org:list --all` first. Applies to scratch orgs only. [Optional]

- `--skipconnectionstatus`: The output from the `force:org:list` command includes a `Connected Status` column for non-scratch orgs (see Listing 7-2). By default, the `force:org:list` command checks that the CLI can still access each authorized non-scratch org using OAuth. To speed up the command's execution time, pass this parameter to skip the connection status check. Applies to non-scratch orgs only. [Optional]
- `--json, --loglevel, --verbose`: Please refer to the discussion on global parameters in the section "Command-Line Parameters and Arguments" in Chapter 4, "Salesforce CLI."

To see these parameters in practice, we'll first illustrate the `--all`, `--clean`, and `--noprompt|-p` parameters and then the `--skipconnectionstatus` parameter.

In the previous section, we ran the `force:org:list` command without the `--all` parameter, which resulted in the following output.

Listing 7-3. Active scratch org listing without the --all parameter

```
=== Orgs
     ALIAS  USERNAME             ORG ID              CONNECTED STATUS
───  ─────  ───────────────────  ──────────────────  ────────────────
(D)  MyDH   ihdxdh@example.com   00D4K0000015OzMUAU  Connected

     ALIAS  USERNAME                         ORG ID              EXPIRATION DATE
───  ─────  ───────────────────────────────  ──────────────────  ───────────────
(U)  MySO   test-maectzkjtu6f@example.com   00D2z0000000vShEAI  2022-06-07
```

However, if you include the `--all` parameter, scratch orgs that are no longer active and yet to be deleted are shown.

Listing 7-4. Active scratch org listing with the --all parameter

```
=== Orgs
    ALIAS  USERNAME                          ORG ID              CONNECTED STATUS
─── ─────  ────────────────────────────────  ──────────────────  ────────────────
(D) MyDH   ihdxdh@example.com                00D4K0000015OzMUAU  Connected
```

```
    ALIAS  USERNAME                         ORG ID              STATUS   EXPIRATION DATE
──  ─────  ───────────────────────────────  ──────────────────  ───────  ───────────────
(U) MySO   test-maectzkjtu6f@example.com    00D2z0000000vShEAI  Active   2022-06-07
    MySO1  test-lyxzufll455h@example.com    00D8E000000EqurUAC  Expired  2022-06-04
```

To delete non-active scratch orgs, run one of the following commands:

```
$ sfdx force:org:list --clean
```

```
$ sfdx force:org:list --clean --noprompt
```

The first command will prompt you with `Found (1) org configurations to delete. Are you sure (yes/no)?`, whereas the second will delete the scratch org without the confirmation prompt. If you re-run the `sfdx force:org:list --all` command, you will see that the expired scratch org has now been deleted.

Note To delete non-active scratch orgs using the Visual Studio Code Command Palette, execute the command **SFDX: Remove Deleted and Expired Orgs**.

Now we will take a look at the `--skipconnectionstatus` parameter. By default, the `force:org:list` command checks that the CLI can still connect to each authorized non-scratch org using OAuth. This check adds extra processing time to the command; however, there are some scenarios, such as when using scripts or continuous integration/continuous delivery systems, where you will want the command to run as quickly as possible. In these circumstances, it is highly likely that the orgs are still connected as they will have been authorized very recently, such as at the start of a script, in which case, skipping the connection status check will speed up command execution.

What does the `force:org:list` command look like when the connection status check fails? When a non-scratch org is authorized, the OAuth 2.0 web server flow uses either the global connected app called Salesforce CLI that is present in all orgs or a custom connected app if you have created one. To illustrate a connection status failure, I blocked connections in the Salesforce CLI connected app for the non-scratch org that has the alias `MyNS`, which led to the OAuth error in this listing.

Listing 7-5. Connected status OAuth error

```
=== Orgs
     ALIAS   USERNAME              ORG ID              CONNECTED STATUS
───  ──────  ────────────────────  ──────────────────  ──────────────────────────
(D)  MyDH    ihdxdh@example.com    00D4K0000015OzMUAU  Connected
     MyNS    ihDXns1@example.com   00D1r000002BEbSEAW  RefreshTokenAuthError

     ALIAS   USERNAME                             ORG ID              EXPIRATION DATE
───  ──────  ───────────────────────────────      ──────────────────  ───────────────
(U)  MySO    test-maectzkjtu6f@example.com        00D2z0000000vShEAI  2022-06-07
```

Now, if you run the command `sfdx force:org:list --skipconnectionstatus`, you will see the following output.

Listing 7-6. Org listing with connection status check skipped

```
=== Orgs
     ALIAS   USERNAME              ORG ID
───  ──────  ────────────          ──────────────────
(D)  MyDH    ihdxdh@example.com    00D4K0000015OzMUAU
     MyNS    ihDXns1@example.com   00D1r000002BEbSEAW

     ALIAS   USERNAME                       ORG ID              EXPIRATION DATE
───  ──────  ────────────────────────────   ──────────────────  ───────────────
(U)  MySO    test-maectzkjtu6f@example.com  00D2z0000000vShEAI  2022-06-07
```

Next up, let's see how to get more information about an authorized non-scratch org or an active scratch org.

Displaying Detailed Org Information

The `force:org:list` command displays summary information about all authorized non-scratch orgs and active scratch orgs. Use the following command to display more detailed information about an org, in this case the `MySO` scratch org that has the default username:

```
$ sfdx force:org:display
```

The parameters that are available for this command, which apply to both scratch orgs and non-scratch orgs, are as follows:

- `--targetusername|-u`: The username or alias of the non-scratch or scratch org that you want to display detail information for, which overrides the default username. [Optional]
- `--apiversion, --json, --loglevel, --verbose`: Please refer to the discussion on global parameters in the section "Command-Line Parameters and Arguments" in Chapter 4, "Salesforce CLI."

Note To display detailed org information using the Visual Studio Code Command Palette, execute the command **SFDX: Display Org Details for Default Org** for the org with the default username, or **SFDX: Display Org Details...**, which allows you to choose an org.

Because `MySO` is a scratch org, the command will display the following information.

Listing 7-7. Detailed scratch org information

```
=== Org Description
KEY                     VALUE
───────────────────     ───────────
Access Token            00D2z00000...
Alias                   MySO
Client Id               PlatformCLI
Created By              ihdxdh@example.com
Created Date            2022-05-31T00:25:22.000+0000
Dev Hub Id              ihdxdh@example.com
Edition                 Developer
Expiration Date         2022-06-07
Id                      00D2z0000000vShEAI
Instance Url            https://app-dream-901-dev-ed.cs119.my.salesforce.com
Org Name                ivanharris company
Status                  Active
Username                test-maectzkjtu6f@example.com
```

The following keys are displayed:

- `Access Token`: The OAuth access token that the Salesforce CLI uses to make API requests to the connected org. Displayed for both non-scratch orgs and scratch orgs.
- `Alias`: The alias for the org, which can be used instead of the `Username`, which is described below. Displayed for both non-scratch orgs and scratch orgs.
- `Client Id`: If the default global connected app called Salesforce CLI is being used for the org connection, `PlatformCLI` will be displayed here. If you created and used a custom connected app to authorize a non-scratch org or connect to a scratch org, its consumer key would be displayed here. Displayed for both non-scratch orgs and scratch orgs.
- `Created By`: The username of the Dev Hub user that created the scratch org. Displayed for scratch orgs only.
- `Created Date`: The date and time that the scratch org was created. Displayed for scratch orgs only.
- `Dev Hub Id`: Rather than being the org Id for the org where the Dev Hub is enabled, as you would expect from the name, this value is the same as the `Created By` value. Displayed for scratch orgs only.
- `Edition`: The scratch org edition, which can be a Developer, Enterprise, Group, or Professional Edition org. Displayed for scratch orgs only.
- `Expiration Date`: The date that the scratch org will expire and be deactivated. Displayed for scratch orgs only.
- `Id`: The org's Id. Displayed for both non-scratch orgs and scratch orgs.
- `Instance Url`: The URL to the login page for the Salesforce instance that the org is hosted on. Displayed for both non-scratch orgs and scratch orgs.
- `Org Name`: The name that has been assigned to the org. This listing shows the default name that is in the autogenerated project configuration file. Displayed for scratch orgs only.

- `Status`: The status of the scratch org such as `active`, `expired`, or `unknown`. Displayed for scratch orgs only.
- `Username`: The username of the user that was specified when executing the `force:org:display` command, either via the `--targetusername|-u` parameter or the default username. Displayed for both non-scratch orgs and scratch orgs.

Several of the key/value pairs described earlier are only displayed for scratch orgs. Here's a listing for a non-scratch org for comparison, in this case the Dev Hub org that I'm using for the book.

Listing 7-8. Detailed non-scratch org information

```
== Org Description
KEY                  VALUE
──────────────────── ──────────────────
Access Token         00D2600000…
Alias                MyDH
Client Id            PlatformCLI
Id                   00D4K0000015OzMUAU
Instance Url         https://ihdx-dev-ed.my.salesforce.com
Username             ihdxdh@example.com
```

Now that you can create a scratch org and display its detailed information, it's time to open a scratch org in a browser.

Opening Scratch Orgs

As with non-scratch orgs, such as Developer Edition orgs, sandboxes, and production orgs, a scratch org's user interface is browser based. Although you can log in to a scratch org by typing its login URL into a browser's address bar, it is more common and convenient to open the scratch org in a browser using the Salesforce CLI or via Visual Studio Code. Opening an active scratch org that has a default username is as simple as executing the following command:

```
$ sfdx force:org:open
```

This command's parameters, which apply to scratch orgs and non-scratch orgs, are as follows:

- `--browser|-b`: The browser that the org should be opened in, which can override the default browser. [Optional]

  Allowed values are as follows:

  - `chrome`: Opens the org in a Google Chrome browser
  - `edge`: Opens the org in a Microsoft Edge browser
  - `firefox`: Opens the org in a Mozilla Firefox browser
- `--path|-p`: The URL path, excluding the domain, of the page to display when the org is opened. For example, passing `-p lightning/o/Task/list` will open the Tasks list view. [Optional]
- `--urlonly|-r`: Displays information about the org to be opened but doesn't actually open the org. Information displayed includes the org Id, username, and full URL path. [Optional]
- `--targetusername|-u`: The username or alias of the org to open, which overrides the default username. [Optional]
- `--apiversion, --json, --loglevel`: Please refer to the discussion on global parameters in the section "Command-Line Parameters and Arguments" in Chapter 4, "Salesforce CLI."

Note To open the org with the default username using the Visual Studio Code Command Palette, execute the command **SFDX: Open Default Org**.

The org with the default username can also be opened from the Visual Studio Code Status Bar by clicking the window icon, which is right next to the default username.

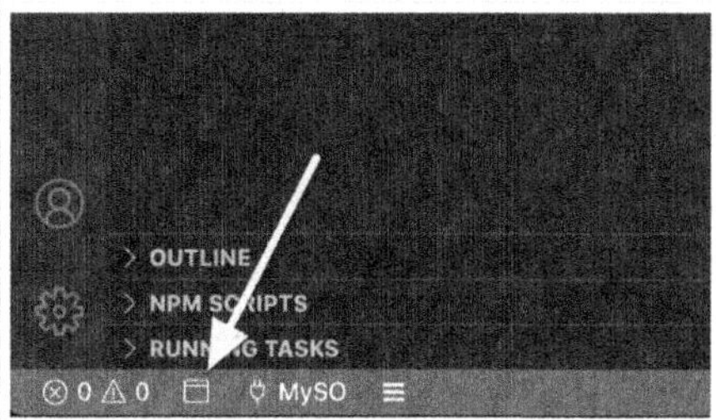

Figure 7-2. *Opening a default org in Visual Studio Code*

When opening any org for the first time, always click the **Allow** button in the Show notifications dialog that pops up.

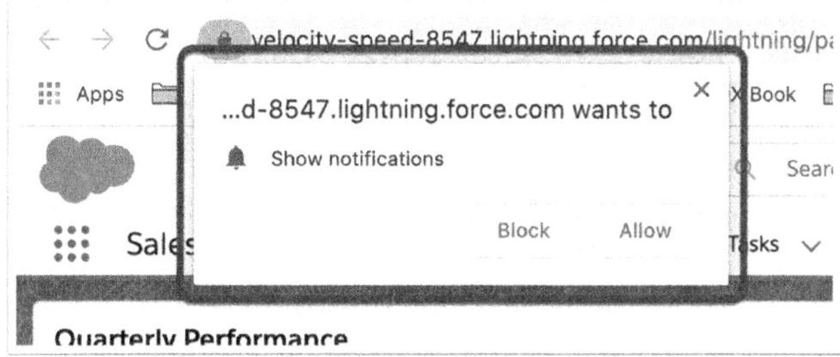

Figure 7-3. *Show notifications pop-up*

Although a scratch org will deactivate at the end of its duration, you can deactivate and delete an org earlier should you wish. We'll cover this last scratch org management command next.

Deleting Scratch Orgs

We learned in Chapter 5, "Dev Hub," that there is a limit to the number of scratch orgs that can be created each day and the number that can be active at any one time. This is one of the reasons that you will want to delete scratch orgs that are no longer being used. Another reason is to revert to initial conditions while reusing an alias by deleting a scratch org and spinning up a fresh one with the same alias. To delete a scratch org, execute the following Salesforce CLI command:

```
$ sfdx force:org:delete
```

This command's parameters can only be used with scratch orgs and sandboxes, not other types of non-scratch orgs such as Developer Edition orgs. The parameters are as follows:

- `--noprompt|-p`: Suppresses the `Enqueue scratch org with name: <username> for deletion? Are you sure (y/n)?` confirmation prompt that is displayed when attempting to delete a scratch org or sandbox. [Optional]
- `--targetusername|-u`: The username or alias of the scratch org or sandbox that you want to delete, which overrides the default username. [Optional]
- `--targetdevhubusername|-v`: The username or alias of the Dev Hub org to use to delete the scratch org, which overrides the default username. The same Dev Hub org must be used to delete the org that was used to create it. [Optional]
- `--apiversion, --json, --loglevel`: Please refer to the discussion on global parameters in the section "Command-Line Parameters and Arguments" in Chapter 4, "Salesforce CLI."

Note To delete the scratch org or sandbox with the default username using the Visual Studio Code Command Palette, execute the command **SFDX: Delete Default Org**. To delete a nondefault org, execute the Command Palette command **SFDX: Delete Org...** and provide the username or alias of the org to delete. To delete expired scratch orgs and those marked for deletion, execute the command **SFDX: Remove Deleted and Expired Orgs**.

The command marks an org for deletion, which may not happen immediately, especially if many orgs are being deleted. Executing this command without any parameters will mark the `MySO` scratch org for deletion as it is the org with the default username. After the command has been executed, running the `force:org:list` command will confirm that the scratch org is no longer active.

Listing 7-9. Org list with no active scratch orgs

```
=== Orgs
       ALIAS    USERNAME             ORG ID              CONNECTED STATUS
────   ───────  ────────             ─────────────       ─────────────────
(D)    MyDH     ihdxdh@example.com   00D4K0000015OzMUAU  Connected

No active scratch orgs found. Specify --all to see all scratch orgs
```

That completes the scratch org management lifecycle, from creation to deletion. We are now going to return to, and dig deeper into, scratch org creation and how to configure a scratch org as a specific edition with defined features and settings.

Configuring Scratch Orgs

Internal development teams developing customizations and applications for a single customer's production org are familiar with using sandboxes in their development cycle. Sandboxes automatically mirror the production org that they are created from. AppExchange Partner development teams who develop apps for listing on AppExchange set up their long-living Developer Edition orgs to include the features and settings that their app depends on. Both teams can now use scratch orgs instead and configure them to be a particular edition with the features and settings that they need.

When a scratch org is created, its configuration is defined using a scratch org definition file. This configuration file is incredibly powerful as it defines the shape of a scratch org to be created, for instance, the org edition type, add-on features to be included, and settings to be applied. Using a configuration file ensures that every time you create a new scratch org, it will consistently have the same configuration. The file can also be shared with other team members via a version control system so that everyone is developing and testing using the same org configuration.

A newly created project has a default scratch org definition file added automatically, which we will see next.

Scratch Org Definition File

When a Salesforce DX project is created using the `force:project:create` CLI command, a scratch org definition file called `project-scratch-def.json` is automatically added to the project's `config` directory.

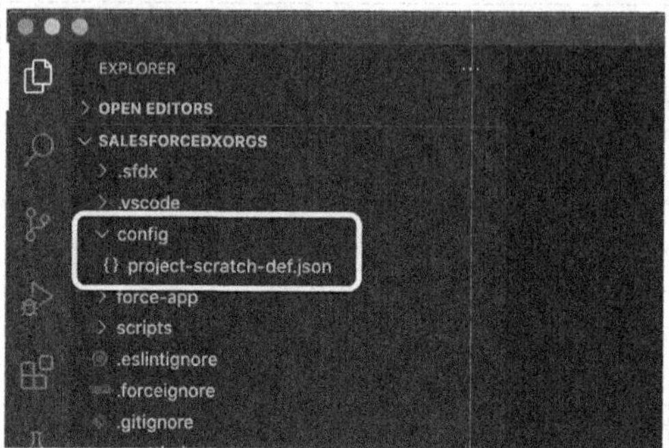

Figure 7-4. *Scratch org definition file location*

The default contents of the scratch org definition file depend on which template was specified using the `--template|-t` parameter when the project was created. The template options are `empty`, `standard`, or `analytics`, with `standard` being the default. When the `empty` template is specified, any scratch orgs created using the file will have the same features and settings as the requested edition, but no additional features or settings will be added.

Listing 7-10. Scratch org definition file for the empty template

```
{
  "orgName": "ivanharris company",
  "edition": "Developer",
  "features": []
}
```

When the `standard` template is used, some additional settings are automatically included.

Listing 7-11. Scratch org definition file for the standard template

```
{
  "orgName": "ivanharris company",
  "edition": "Developer",
  "features": ["EnableSetPasswordInApi"],
  "settings": {
    "lightningExperienceSettings": {
      "enableS1DesktopEnabled": true
    },
    "mobileSettings": {
      "enableS1EncryptedStoragePref2": false
    }
  }
}
```

The settings configure the following in the scratch org when it is created:

- `lightningExperienceSettings->` `enableS1DesktopEnabled`: Ensures that Lightning Experience is enabled in the scratch org.
- `mobileSettings->` `enableS1EncryptedStoragePref2`: Determines if the Salesforce mobile web uses browser caching to improve performance. The default scratch org definition file disables this setting so that any user interface changes won't be hidden by caching.

Finally, if the `analytics` template is used, the same settings are present as with the `standard` template; however, the `DevelopmentWave` feature is added.

Listing 7-12. Scratch org definition file for the analytics template

```
{
  "orgName": "ivanharris company",
  "edition": "Developer",
  "features": ["DevelopmentWave", "EnableSetPasswordInApi"],
```

```
  "settings": {
    "lightningExperienceSettings": {
      "enableS1DesktopEnabled": true
    },
    "mobileSettings": {
      "enableS1EncryptedStoragePref2": false
    }
  }
}
```

The DevelopmentWave feature ensures that the appropriate licenses, permission set licenses, and analytics features are added to the scratch org to allow CRM Analytics development.

The three file parameters in the scratch org definition file that we will now explore further, and which can be seen in Listing 7-12, are as follows:

- `edition`: States if the scratch org should be created as a Developer, Enterprise, Group, or Professional Edition org. All the out-of-the-box functionality for the specified edition will be included in the scratch org.
- `features`: Lists the functionality that doesn't come out of the box with the specified edition that should be added to the scratch org. Often, these mirror the separately licensed features that you have added to your production org.
- `settings`: Provides additional settings for the org edition and features to tailor the setup. These settings can also be found in the Setup area of your scratch org, where you can manually change the settings if you wish.

Note For the complete set of scratch org definition file parameters, please refer to the Salesforce DX Developer Guide: `https://developer.salesforce.com/docs/atlas.en-us.sfdx_dev.meta/sfdx_dev/sfdx_dev_scratch_orgs_def_file.htm`.

The first parameter that we'll dig into is the `edition` parameter.

Scratch Org Edition

The edition file parameter in the scratch org definition file instructs the Salesforce CLI to create a scratch org as a Developer, Enterprise, Group, or Professional Edition org. I personally prefer not to create Developer Edition scratch orgs as they include many features and settings by default. I prefer to explicitly add the features and settings that I need to one of the other scratch org editions. This ensures that a dependency is not inadvertently created on a feature or setting that might not be configured in a production org.

To modify the edition in the scratch org definition file, perform the following steps:

1. Launch Visual Studio Code.
2. Open the Salesforce DX project called SalesforceDXOrgs that you created at the start of the chapter.
3. Open the scratch org definition file config/project-scratch-def.json.
4. Set the orgName value to Salesforce DX Orgs.
5. Set the edition value to Enterprise.
6. Remove any features or settings.
7. Save the file.

The resulting file should look like this.

Listing 7-13. Scratch org definition file with the edition updated

```
{
  "orgName": "Salesforce DX Orgs",
  "edition": "Enterprise"

}
```

We will validate the changes by creating a new scratch org. If a scratch org with the default alias MySO is still active, delete it first by executing the CLI command force:org:delete in the VS Code integrated terminal. Then create a new scratch org using the same MySO alias:

```
$ sfdx force:org:create \
    --setalias MySO \
    --definitionfile ./config/project-scratch-def.json \
    --setdefaultusername
```

To validate that the scratch org definition file changes have been implemented in the scratch org, perform the following steps:

- Open the new scratch org using the CLI command `force:org:open`.
- Click **Allow** in the Show notifications dialog that pops up.
- Navigate to **Setup ➤ Company Settings ➤ Company Information**.
- Observe that the Organization Name is set to `Salesforce DX Orgs` and that the Organization Edition is set to `Enterprise Edition` as shown in the following.

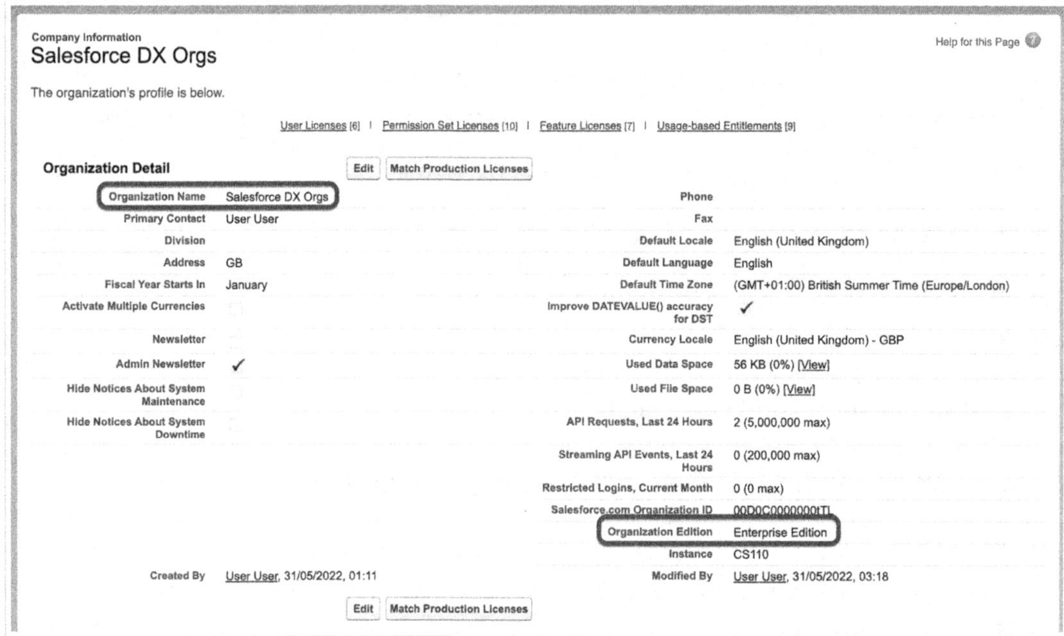

Figure 7-5. *Scratch org Company Information showing Organization Name and Edition*

The next section will explain how to add features and settings to your scratch org definition file.

Scratch Org Features and Settings

The `features` file parameter in the scratch org definition file defines the features that will be added when a scratch org is created. The `settings` parameter specifies the initial settings for a feature or for the org. It's worth bookmarking the following resources in the Salesforce DX Developer Guide and the Metadata API Developer Guide when working with scratch org definition files:

1. **Scratch Org Definition Configuration Values**: `https://developer.salesforce.com/docs/atlas.en-us.sfdx_dev.meta/sfdx_dev/sfdx_dev_scratch_orgs_def_file_config_values.htm`, for the list of features that can be added to a scratch org

2. **Scratch Org Settings**: `https://developer.salesforce.com/docs/atlas.en-us.sfdx_dev.meta/sfdx_dev/sfdx_dev_scratch_orgs_settings.htm`, for an introduction to settings, although as you will soon see, you will make more use of the next resource

3. **Metadata API Settings**: `https://developer.salesforce.com/docs/atlas.en-us.api_meta.meta/api_meta/meta_settings.htm`, for the settings that can be applied to a feature

Why do we need the Metadata API Settings? The opening paragraph of the Scratch Org Settings section in the Salesforce DX Developer Guide (resource #2) makes this very important statement:

> *In Winter '19 and later, scratch org settings are the format for defining org preferences in the scratch org definition. Because you can use all Metadata API settings, they are the most comprehensive way to configure a scratch org. If a setting is supported in Metadata API, it's supported in scratch orgs. Settings provide you with fine-grained control because you can define values for all fields for a setting, rather than just enabling or disabling it.*

It then provides a link to the Metadata API Developer Guide (resource #3). Given that the scratch org definition file supports identical settings as the Metadata API, there seems little point in Salesforce duplicating and maintaining the same information!

To become familiar with navigating the resources, let's work through adding the Chat service channel to a scratch org. The first step is to look up the feature in the Scratch Org Features page of the Salesforce DX Developer Guide (resource #1). The page looks like this.

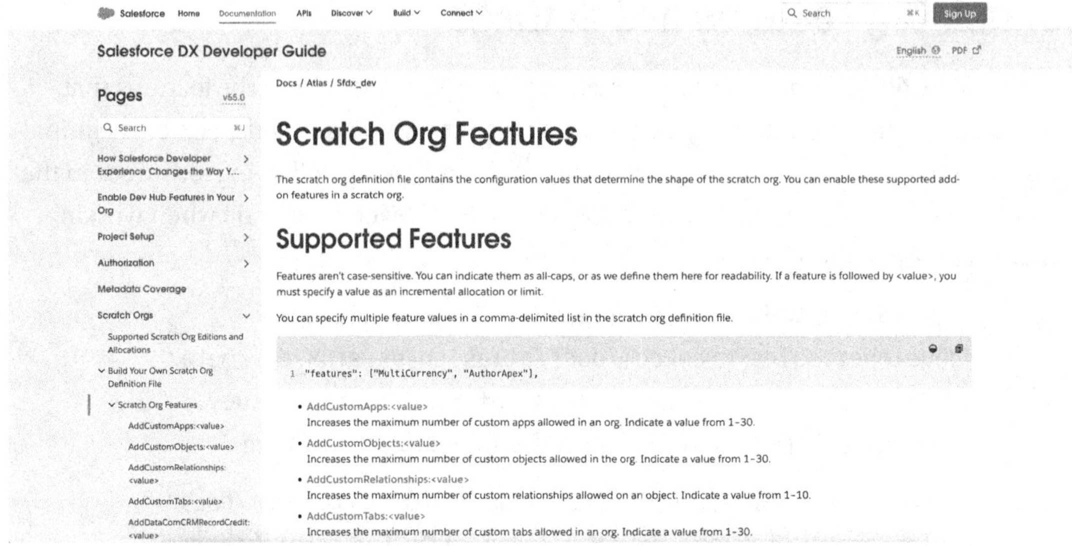

***Figure 7-6.** Scratch Org Features page*

The page lists all the features that can be added to a scratch org definition file. Scrolling down, the LiveAgent entry can be found, which looks as follows.

- LightningServiceConsole
  Assigns the Lightning Service Console License to your scratch org so you can use the Lightning Service Console and access features that help manage cases faster.
- LiveAgent
  Enables Chat for Service Cloud. Use web-based chat to quickly connect customers to agents for real-time support.
- LiveMessage
  Enables Messaging for Service Cloud. Use Messaging to quickly support customers using apps such as SMS text messaging and Facebook Messenger.

***Figure 7-7.** LiveAgent feature entry*

You now have the correct name for the feature. Next, you need to view the available settings for the feature. If you go to the Scratch Org Settings page of the Salesforce DX Developer Guide (resource #2), it looks like this.

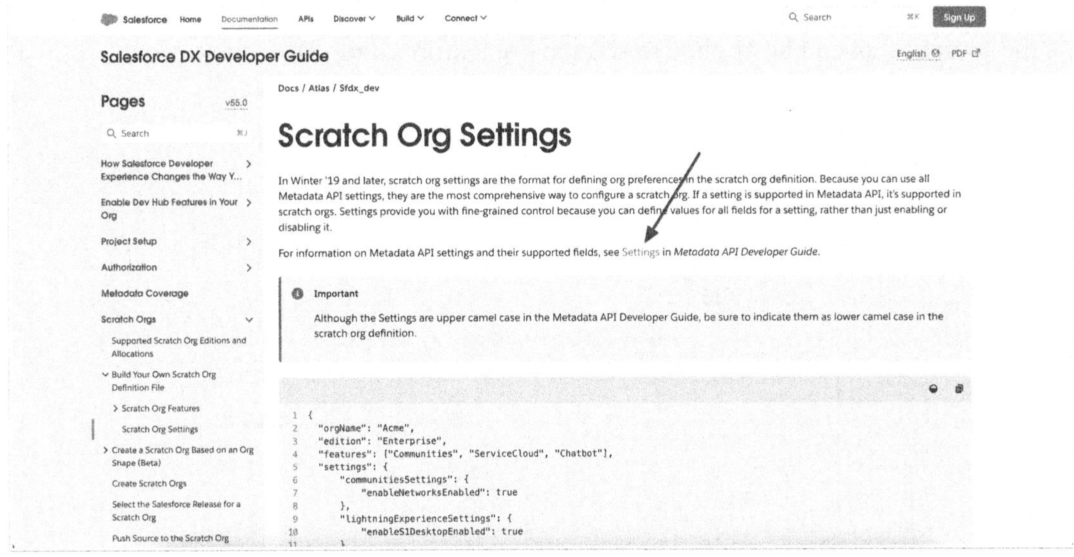

Figure 7-8. *Scratch Org Settings page*

You will notice immediately that the page doesn't contain much content. Instead, it refers you to the settings page of the Metadata API Developer Guide (resource #3). As noted earlier, the scratch org settings use all the Metadata API settings. Navigate to the Metadata API settings page by clicking the **Settings** link that the arrow points to in the preceding screenshot.

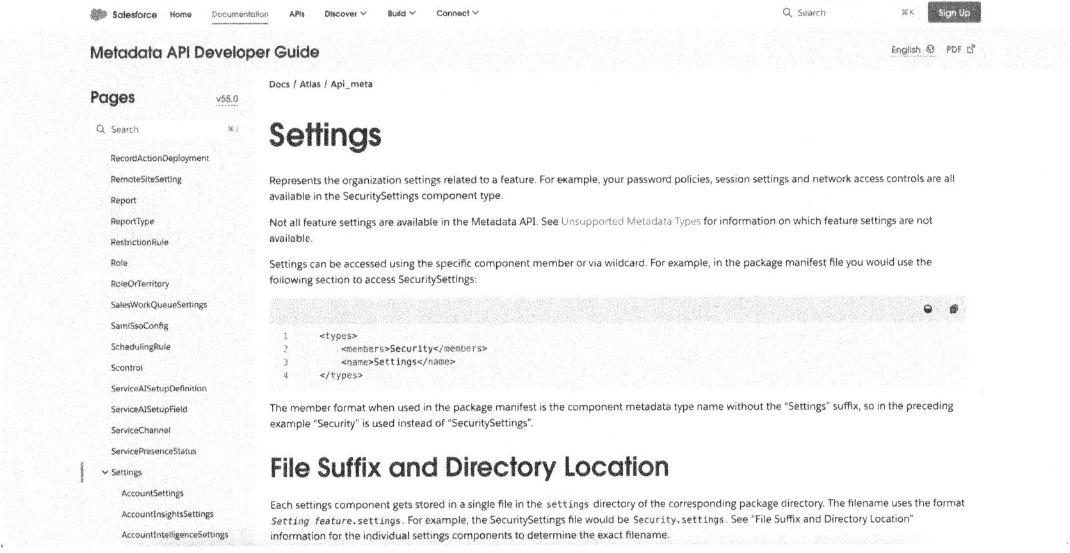

Figure 7-9. *Metadata API Settings page*

The Settings node is selected in the left-hand navigation tree, and under the node are the settings that can be applied to scratch org features added to a scratch org definition file.

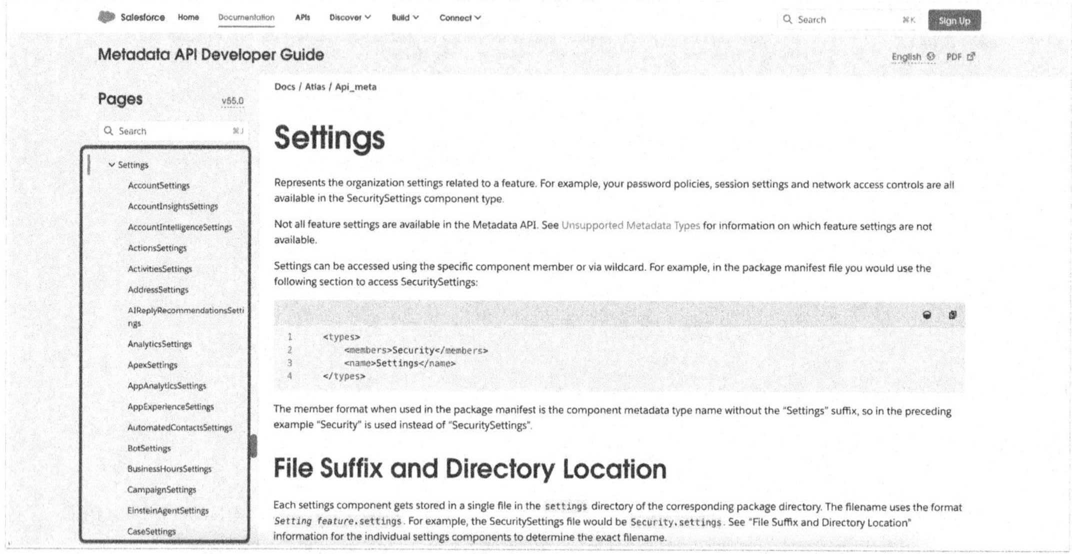

Figure 7-10. *Metadata API Settings page*

The naming convention for the settings is to simply append "Settings" to the feature name. Scroll down the settings and click the **LiveAgentSettings** node, which will display the available settings for the LiveAgent feature as follows.

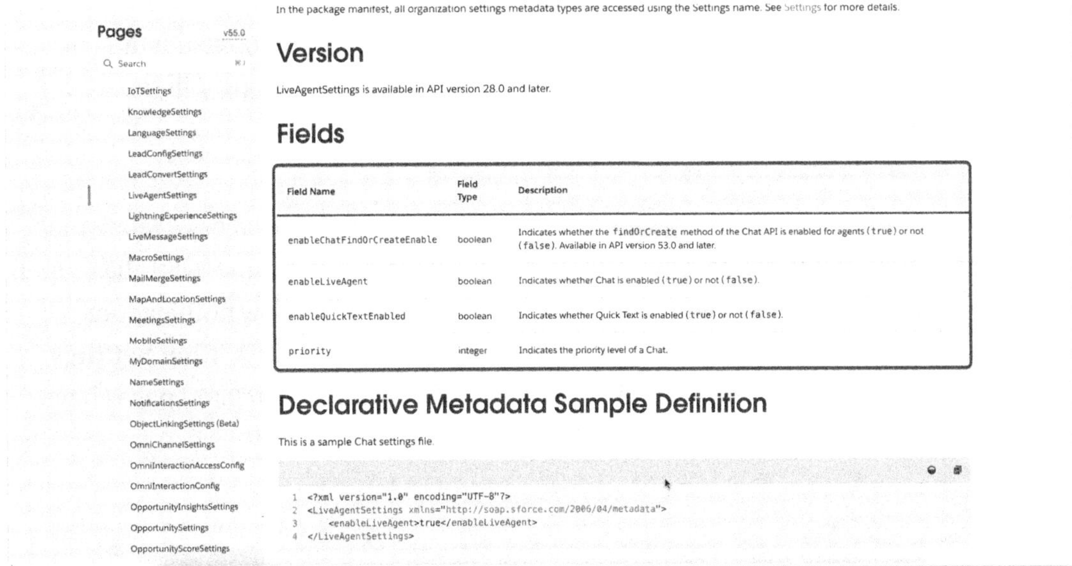

***Figure 7-11.** LiveAgentSettings page*

You can see `enableLiveAgent` in the table, which is the setting needed to enable Chat. In Visual Studio Code, edit the scratch org definition file and add this setting and the `LiveAgent` feature, so that it resembles the following listing.

Listing 7-14. Enabling the LiveAgent feature using the enableLiveAgent setting

```
{
  "orgName": "Salesforce DX Orgs",
  "edition": "Enterprise",
  "features": [
    "LiveAgent"
  ],
  "settings": {
    "liveAgentSettings": {
      "enableLiveAgent": true
    }
  }
}
```

Note The setting name in the Metadata API begins with an uppercase letter, while the same setting name in the scratch org definition file begins with a lowercase letter.

Now confirm that these changes are implemented in a new scratch org. Delete the existing `MySO` scratch org and recreate another scratch org with the same `MySO` alias. Open the new scratch org (don't forget to click the **Allow** button in the Show notifications dialog) and navigate to **Setup ➤ Feature Settings ➤ Service ➤ Chat ➤ Chat Settings** where you will see that Chat is enabled (1) and that additional Chat-related pages have been added to the Setup tree (2).

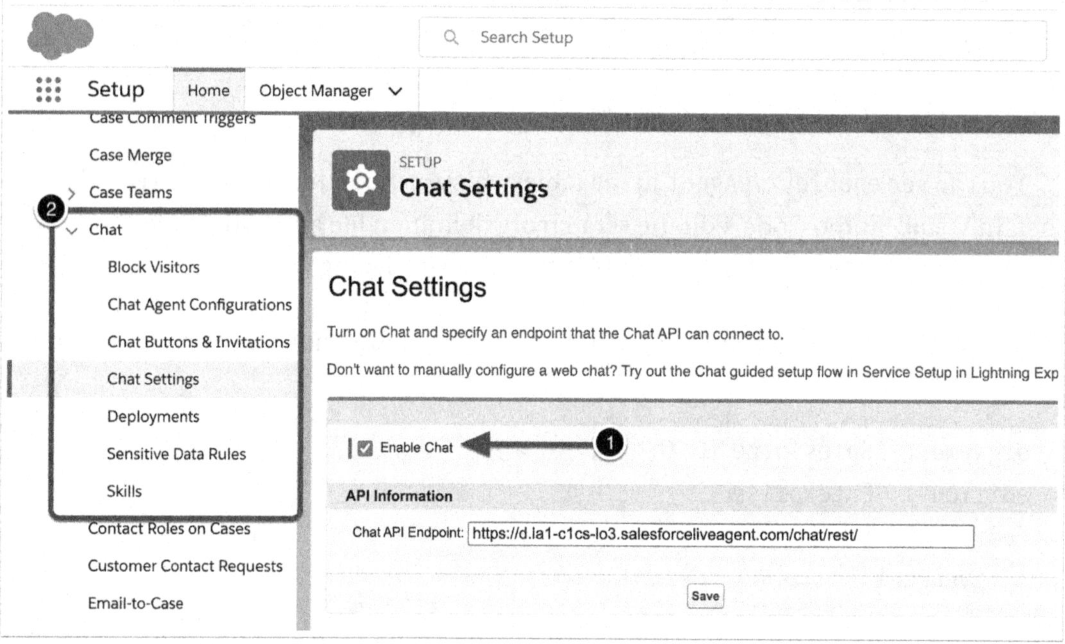

Figure 7-12. *Chat enabled in a scratch org*

So far, we have learned how to create scratch orgs and configure them using a scratch org definition file. With the definition file, we can define a scratch org to be a specific edition. Normally, when a non-scratch org is created, it includes some sample data. By default, a scratch org has no sample data, and we will discover how to include some in the next section.

Adding Sample Data

By default, when a scratch org is created it doesn't include any sample data. To confirm this, launch Visual Studio Code and open this chapter's `SalesforceDXOrgs` project. From the integrated terminal, use the `force:org:open` CLI command to open the scratch org with the alias `MySO`. Then launch the Sales app from the App Launcher (⠿) and open the Accounts tab. You will observe that no sample data has been included yet.

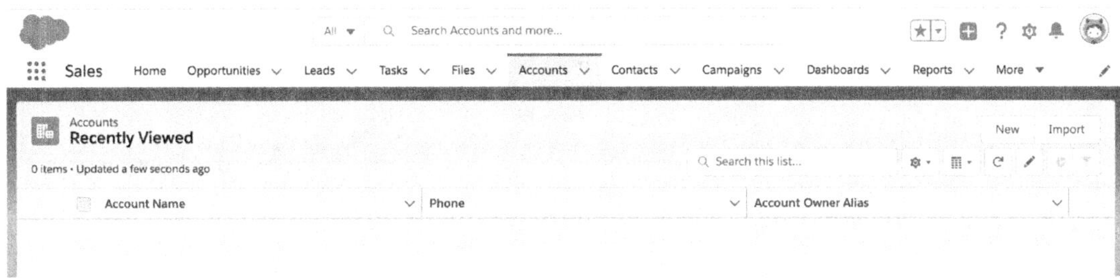

Figure 7-13. *Newly created scratch org with no sample data*

As an example, to add sample data for the standard objects that you are used to seeing in Enterprise Edition orgs, set the `hasSampleData` parameter to `true` in the scratch org definition file as follows.

Listing 7-15. Including standard sample data when a scratch org is created

```
{
  "orgName": "Salesforce DX Orgs",
  "edition": "Enterprise",
  "hasSampleData": true,
  "features": [
    "LiveAgent"
  ],
  "settings": {
    "liveAgentSettings": {
      "enableLiveAgent": true
    }
  }
}
```

Delete the scratch org with the alias `MySO` and create a fresh one using the same alias. Open the new scratch org and navigate to the Accounts tab in the Sales app again. This time, you will see that sample data has been included.

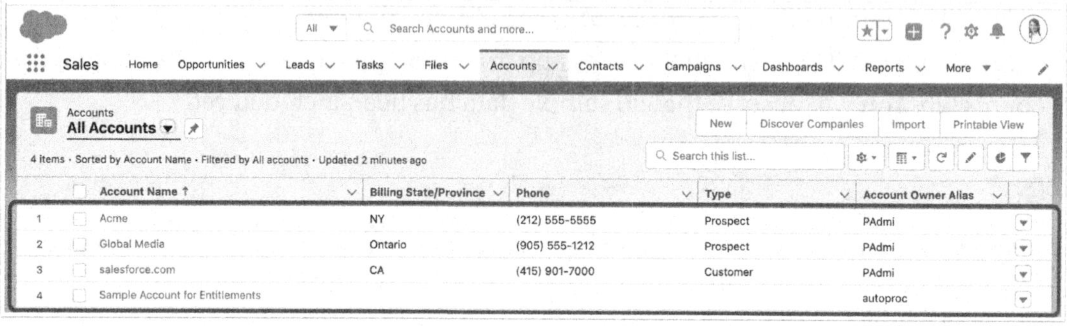

Figure 7-14. *Newly created scratch org with sample data*

Although the `hasSampleData` parameter is useful for adding sample data for standard objects in a scratch org, to perform end-to-end testing of a customization or application you will want to load custom test data; Chapter 11, "Test Data," will show how this is done.

We know by now that to manage scratch orgs, the Salesforce CLI must connect to a Dev Hub. We will now see how to view information about scratch orgs that the Dev Hub has created from within the Dev Hub org.

Viewing Scratch Orgs from a Dev Hub Org

As an individual developer, information about active scratch orgs that you have created can be retrieved using the Salesforce CLI, as we saw earlier. If you need to see information about all the active scratch orgs across a team, or if you want to see the history of scratch orgs that have ever been created, you can use the Dev Hub org to view this information.

When a Dev Hub is enabled in an org, the following standard objects become available:

- **Active Scratch Org**: This standard object has the API name ActiveScratchOrg. Its records can be viewed by selecting the Active Scratch Orgs item from the App Launcher.

- **Scratch Org Info**: This standard object has the API name ScratchOrgInfo. Its records can be viewed by selecting the Scratch Org Infos item from the App Launcher.

The Active Scratch Orgs item displays records for currently active scratch orgs, whereas the Scratch Org Infos item displays information about all scratch orgs that have been created, including currently active scratch orgs and deleted scratch orgs.

To view the Scratch Orgs Info item, follow these steps:

- Launch Visual Studio Code if it's not already launched.
- Open this chapter's `SalesforceDXOrgs` project.
- From the integrated terminal, execute the command `force:org:open --targetusername MyDH` to open the Dev Hub org.
- Click the App Launcher icon (⁝⁝⁝), click the **View All** link, and click the **Scratch Org Infos** item link.

The Scratch Org Infos tab will open, which will show the history of scratch orgs that have been created and deleted during this chapter, including the active scratch org that was created in the previous section.

Scratch Org Infos
Recently Viewed
11 items • Updated a few seconds ago

	Number	Org Name	Edition	Status	Created Date	Expiration Date
1	00000158	Salesforce DX Orgs	Service Enterprise	Active	12/06/2022, 00:58	18/06/2022
2	00000157	Salesforce DX Orgs	Service Enterprise	Deleted	31/05/2022, 03:51	07/06/2022
3	00000156	Salesforce DX Orgs	Service Enterprise	Deleted	31/05/2022, 03:47	07/06/2022
4	00000155	Salesforce DX Orgs	Service Enterprise	Deleted	31/05/2022, 03:18	07/06/2022
5	00000154	ivanharris company	Developer	Deleted	31/05/2022, 01:25	07/06/2022
6	00000153	ivanharris company	Developer	Deleted	30/04/2022, 02:39	07/05/2022
7	00000152	ivanharris company	Developer	Deleted	02/04/2022, 02:54	09/04/2022
8	00000151	ivanharris company	Developer	Deleted	19/03/2022, 03:14	26/03/2022
9	00000150	ivanharris company	Developer	Deleted	16/03/2022, 02:20	23/03/2022
10	00000149	ivanharris company	Developer	Deleted	12/03/2022, 01:32	19/03/2022
11	00000148	ivanharris company	Developer	Deleted	07/03/2022, 01:36	14/03/2022

Figure 7-15. *Scratch Org Infos list view*

Clicking the active scratch org displays its detail view, including the list of features that we enabled, in this case LiveAgent.

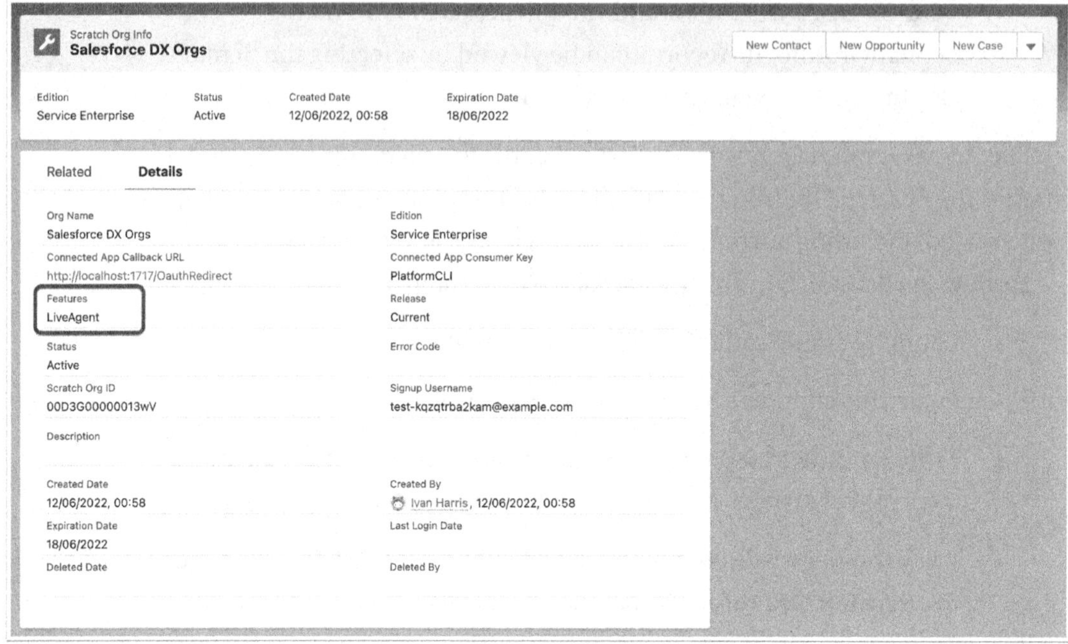

Figure 7-16. *Scratch Org Infos detail view*

To view the Active Scratch Orgs item, follow the preceding steps, but this time select the Active Scratch Orgs item from the App Launcher. This will display the Active Scratch Orgs list view.

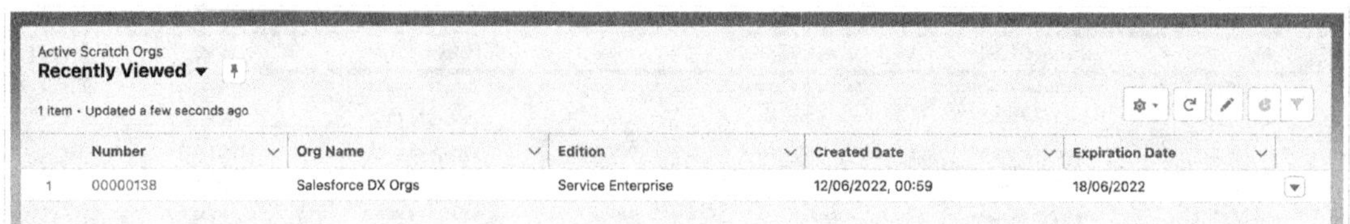

Figure 7-17. *Active Scratch Orgs list view*

The list view shows the active scratch org that we saw in the Scratch Org Infos earlier. Clicking it displays its detail view.

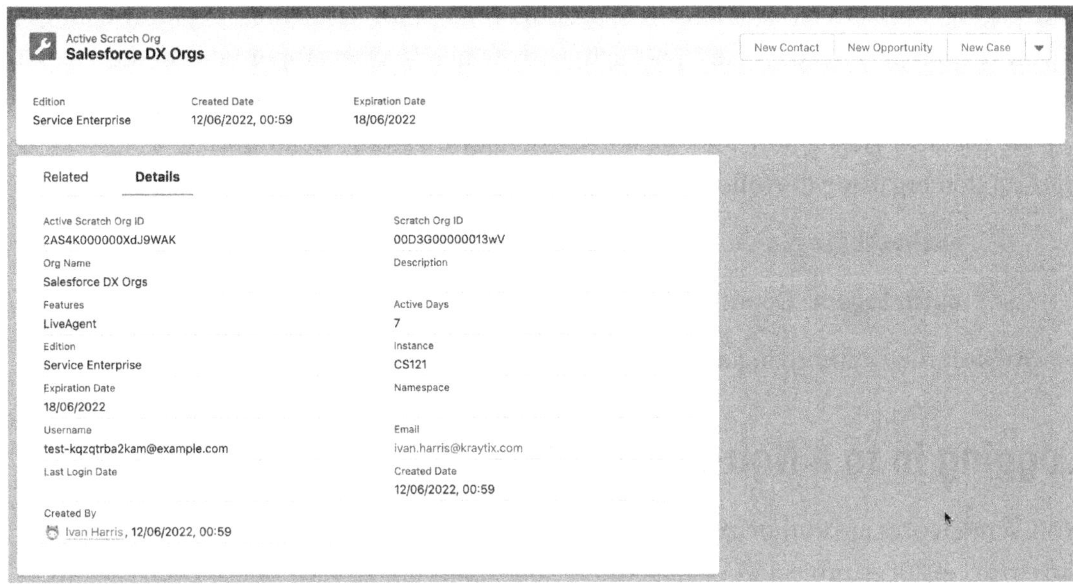

Figure 7-18. *Active Scratch Orgs detail view*

The Active Scratch Orgs detail view shows similar, although not identical, information as the Scratch Org Infos detail view.

Using the Dev Hub org to access scratch org information can be particularly useful for team-wide management of finite scratch org resources. Like other sObjects, the Active Scratch Org and Scratch Org Info standard objects can be customized, and applications can be built around them, for example, to limit per user scratch org creation, to generate high usage notifications that warn of limits being reached, and to automatically delete unused scratch orgs.

Scratch orgs support a new way of working for internal and AppExchange Partner development teams. That said, Salesforce DX can also connect to non-scratch orgs, which include Developer Edition orgs, sandboxes, and production orgs, using authorization.

Authorizing Non-scratch Orgs

Scratch orgs can replace Developer and Developer Pro sandboxes for internal development teams and Developer Edition orgs for AppExchange Partner teams. However, there are occasions when non-scratch orgs need to be used. Internal developers, for example, should still use Partial Copy and Full Copy sandboxes for UAT and staging, respectively, and of course production orgs for deployments. AppExchange Partner developers need to use a packaging org, which is a Developer Edition org configured with a namespace, to create first-generation managed packages.

We will now look at how the Salesforce CLI authorizes and deauthorizes a non-scratch org using the following commands:

- **`auth:web:login`**: Authorize a non-scratch org.
- **`auth:logout`**: Deauthorize a non-scratch org.

We'll start by authorizing a non-scratch org using a browser.

Logging In to a Non-scratch Org

Non-scratch orgs are authorized by logging in to them via a web browser. Open the `SalesforceDXOrgs` project in Visual Studio Code if it is not already open. Then execute the following command in the integrated terminal to authorize a Developer Edition org and give it the alias `MyDEOrg`.

Note Go to `https://developer.salesforce.com/signup` to sign up for a new Developer Edition org and make a note of its username and password as this will be needed when logging in to the org via a browser.

```
$ sfdx auth:web:login \
    --setalias MyDEOrg
```

The parameters that can be used with this command are as follows:

- `--setalias|-a`: Sets an alias for the authorized org that can be used instead of its username. [Optional]
- `--setdefaultdevhubusername|-d`: If the non-scratch org to be authorized has the Dev Hub feature enabled, this parameter will mark the Dev Hub org as the default for managing scratch orgs. [Optional]

- `--clientid|-i`: All orgs contain a global connected app called Salesforce CLI that is used by default for OAuth authorization purposes. If you create a custom connected app, to include increased security, for example, the value for this parameter is the connected app's consumer key. [Optional]
- `--instanceurl|-r`: The login URL of the instance that the non-scratch org is hosted on, for example, `https://login.salesforce.com`, `https://test.salesforce.com` or `https://<mydomain>.my.salesforce.com` for production orgs, sandboxes, and production orgs with My Domain enabled, respectively. This command-line parameter overrides the `sfdcLoginUrl` file parameter in the project configuration file. [Optional]
- `--setdefaultusername|-s`: Sets the username provided in the login credentials as the default username. All CLI commands that require a username will use this by default to run commands against the authorized org. [Optional]
- `--json, --loglevel`: Please refer to the discussion on global parameters in the section "Command-Line Parameters and Arguments" in Chapter 4, "Salesforce CLI."

Note To authorize an org and set it as the default username using the Visual Studio Code Command Palette, execute the command **SFDX: Authorize an Org**. To authorize an org and set it as the default Dev Hub org, execute the command **SFDX: Authorize a Dev Hub**.

The `auth:web:login` command initiates an OAuth web server flow authorization that uses the global connected app called `Salesforce CLI`, which is present in every org. The Salesforce login page opens in a browser where the non-scratch org login credentials are entered.

Figure 7-19. *Salesforce login screen*

The user is then asked to allow the CLI access to the org's resources.

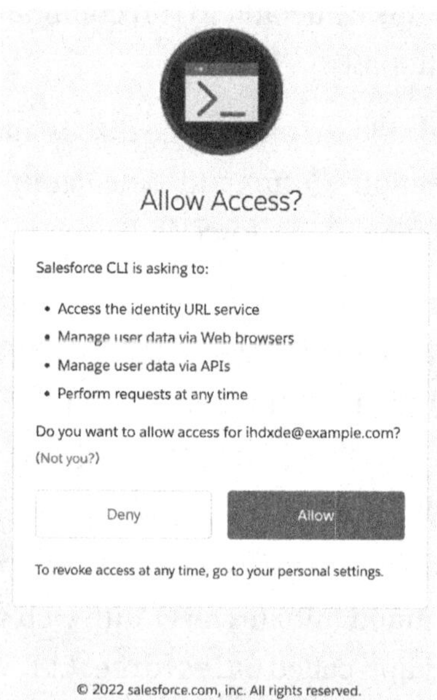

Figure 7-20. *Allow the CLI access to org resources screen*

After clicking the **Allow** button, the org opens in the browser. You can now log out of the org as the authorization process is complete. Returning to the Visual Studio Code integrated terminal, run the CLI command `force:org:list` to see the newly authorized org.

Listing 7-16. Newly authorized Developer Edition org

```
=== Orgs
      ALIAS        USERNAME             ORG ID              CONNECTED STATUS
────  ──────────  ──────               ───────────         ────────────────
      MyDEOrg      ihdxde@example.com   00D4K000004iaUvUAI  Connected
(D)   MyDH         ihdxdh@example.com   00D4K0000015OzMUAU  Connected

      ALIAS    USERNAME                       ORG ID               EXPIRATION DATE
────  ──────   ────────────────────────       ──────────────       ───────────────
(U)   MySO     test-kqzqtrba2kam@example.com  00D3G00000013wVUAQ   2022-06-18
```

You can now use the `force:org:display` and `force:org:open` CLI commands to view detailed org information and open the non-scratch org, respectively. Notice that with the `force:org:open` command, you no longer need to log in to the org using your credentials.

Once a non-scratch org has been authorized, it can be deauthorized by logging out of the org using the CLI.

Logging Out of a Non-scratch Org

To deauthorize a non-scratch org, log out of it using the following Salesforce CLI command, which in this instance will log out of the Developer Edition org with the alias `MyDEOrg` that we just created. As the org doesn't have the default username, we must name it.

```
$ sfdx auth:logout \
    --targetusername MyDEOrg
```

Here are all the parameters that can be used with this command:

- `--all|-a`: Logs out of all scratch orgs and non-scratch orgs. Note: This removes scratch orgs from the CLI's list, but it does not delete them. Use the Active Scratch Orgs page (accessed via the App Launcher) in the Dev Hub org to delete these scratch orgs; otherwise, they will count against your active scratch orgs limit. [Optional]
- `--noprompt|-p`: Bypasses the `Are you sure you want to log out from these org(s)?` confirmation prompt. [Optional]

- `--targetusername|-u`: The username or alias of the target org to delete. [Optional]
- `--apiversion, --json, --loglevel`: Please refer to the discussion on global parameters in the section "Command-Line Parameters and Arguments" in Chapter 4, "Salesforce CLI."

Note To log out of all scratch and non-scratch orgs using the Visual Studio Code Command Palette, execute the command **SFDX: Log Out from All Authorized Orgs**. To log out of the default org, whether it's a scratch org or non-scratch org, execute the command **SFDX: Log Out from Default Org**.

After executing the command, list all orgs using the `force:org:list` command, which confirms that the org is no longer in the list of authorized orgs.

Listing 7-17. Org list confirming Developer Edition org deletion

```
=== Orgs
     ALIAS  USERNAME             ORG ID              CONNECTED STATUS
───  ─────  ───────────────────  ──────────────────  ────────────────
(D)  MyDH   ihdxdh@example.com   00D4K0000015OzMUAU  Connected
     ALIAS  USERNAME                         ORG                 EXPIRATION DATE
───  ─────  ───────────────────────────────  ──────────────────  ───────────────
(U)  MySO   test-kqzqtrba2kam@example.com    00D3G00000013wVUAQ  2022-06-18
```

One type of non-scratch org, sandboxes, can also be created using the Salesforce CLI, which we will look at next.

Managing Sandboxes

Although scratch orgs can be used instead of Developer and Developer Pro sandboxes when developing internal customizations and custom applications, it is still recommended that Partial Copy and Full Copy sandboxes are used for UAT and staging. Those sandboxes can be created from a production org's Setup area and authorized using the `auth:web:login` command that we saw earlier, so that they are easy to work with using the Salesforce CLI. For example, when a sandbox has been authorized, metadata components can be deployed from a Salesforce DX project to the sandbox.

The Salesforce CLI includes several commands for working with sandboxes. We'll explore the following commands in this section:

- **force:org:create**: Create a sandbox using a sandbox definition file.
- **force:org:clone**: Clone a sandbox using a sandbox definition file.
- **force:org:status**: Display the status of a sandbox create or clone operation.
- **force:org:delete**: Delete a sandbox.

Note, the following commands perform the same function when working with authorized sandboxes as when working with other org types. We encountered these commands in the "Managing Scratch Orgs" section earlier in the chapter, so we won't repeat the command and parameter descriptions here.

- **force:org:list**: List all authorized sandboxes.
- **force:org:display**: Display detailed information about an authorized sandbox.
- **force:org:open**: Open an authorized sandbox in a browser.

Let's start by creating a sandbox using the Salesforce CLI.

Creating Sandboxes

We've seen that when working with scratch orgs, a Dev Hub is needed to manage the scratch org lifecycle. To work with sandboxes, a production org with spare sandbox licenses is needed instead. That said, if your Dev Hub is enabled in your production org, you can use the same org for managing scratch orgs and sandboxes.

The first thing that we need to do is authorize a production org using the `auth:web:login` command that we used earlier in the chapter. We'll give this org the alias `MyProdOrg`. Open the `SalesforceDXOrgs` project in Visual Studio Code, if it is not already open, and execute the following command in the integrated terminal:

```
$ sfdx auth:web:login \
    --setalias MyProdOrg
```

After logging in to the production org in the browser that opens, run the `force:org:list` command in the integrated terminal to confirm that the production org has been authorized.

Listing 7-18. Authorized production org

```
=== Orgs
      ALIAS      USERNAME                  ORG ID              CONNECTED STATUS
───── ────────── ───────────────────────── ─────────────────── ────────────────
(D)   MyDH       ihdxdh@example.com        00D4K0000015OzMUAU  Connected
      MyProdOrg  ivan.harris@███                  ██████████  Connected

      ALIAS  USERNAME                      ORG ID              EXPIRATION DATE
───── ────── ───────────────────────────── ─────────────────── ───────────────
(U)   MySO   test-kqzqtrba2kam@example.com 00D3G0000013wVUAQ   2022-06-18
```

Open the production org with the `force:org:open -u MyProdOrg` command if it is not already open. Navigate to **Setup ➤ Environments ➤ Sandboxes** to view the existing sandboxes (1) and confirm that the org has at least one sandbox license available (2).

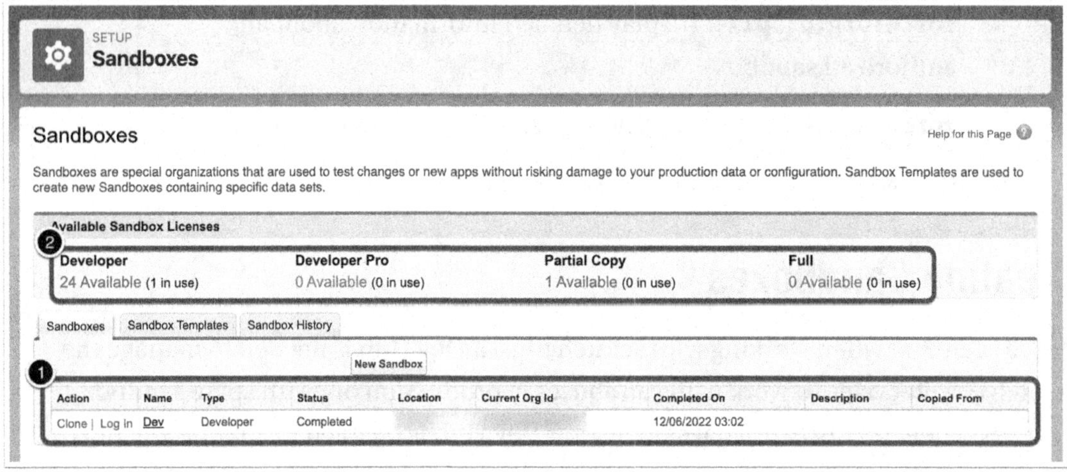

Figure 7-21. *Current sandboxes and licenses*

We will return to the sandbox page in the production org after we have programmatically created a sandbox using the Salesforce CLI.

When creating scratch orgs, a scratch org definition file is needed, and when creating a sandbox, a sandbox definition file is needed. The filename can be anything you like, and it can be stored in any directory within a Salesforce DX project. We'll call our sandbox definition file `sbx-uat-def.json` and store it in the `config` directory, where the scratch org definition file is also stored. Note, I have included a sandbox name in the filename; although this isn't mandatory, it's possible to have multiple sandbox definition files, so this helps with identification.

Create and save the following sandbox definition file using the filename and directory location mentioned earlier.

Listing 7-19. UAT sandbox definition file

```
{
    "sandboxName": "UAT",
    "licenseType": "Developer"
}
```

This will create a `Developer` sandbox type called `UAT`. Other sandbox types that can be created are `Developer_Pro`, `Partial`, and `Full`.

Note To see the complete set of supported sandbox definition file parameters, please refer to the Create a Sandbox Definition File page in the Salesforce DX Developer Guide here: `https://developer.salesforce.com/docs/atlas.en-us.sfdx_dev.meta/sfdx_dev/sfdx_dev_sandbox_definition.htm`.

To create the sandbox, execute the following command:

```
$ sfdx force:org:create \
    --setalias MyUATSbx \
    --definitionfile ./config/sbx-uat-def.json \
    --type sandbox \
    --targetusername MyProdOrg \
    --wait 60
```

The `force:org:create` command's parameters were described in the section "Creating Scratch Orgs" earlier in the chapter. The differences between creating a scratch org and creating a sandbox org are as follows:

- `--definitionfile|-f`: Points to a sandbox definition file rather than a scratch org definition file. [Optional: Either a definition file is passed using this parameter, or `Name=Value` pair arguments must be provided for at least the required file parameters.]

- `--type|-t`: As the default for this parameter is `scratch`, `sandbox` needs to be specified to create a sandbox. [Required]
- `--targetusername|-u`: The username or alias of a production org with spare sandbox licenses, which overrides the default username. [Optional]

The default for the `--wait|-w` parameter is 6 minutes. By specifying a longer time, in this case 60 minutes, the command will operate synchronously and will return when the command has completed or the wait period expires, whichever is the sooner. While the command is executing, an update is provided every 30 seconds.

Listing 7-20. Synchronous sandbox creation status updates

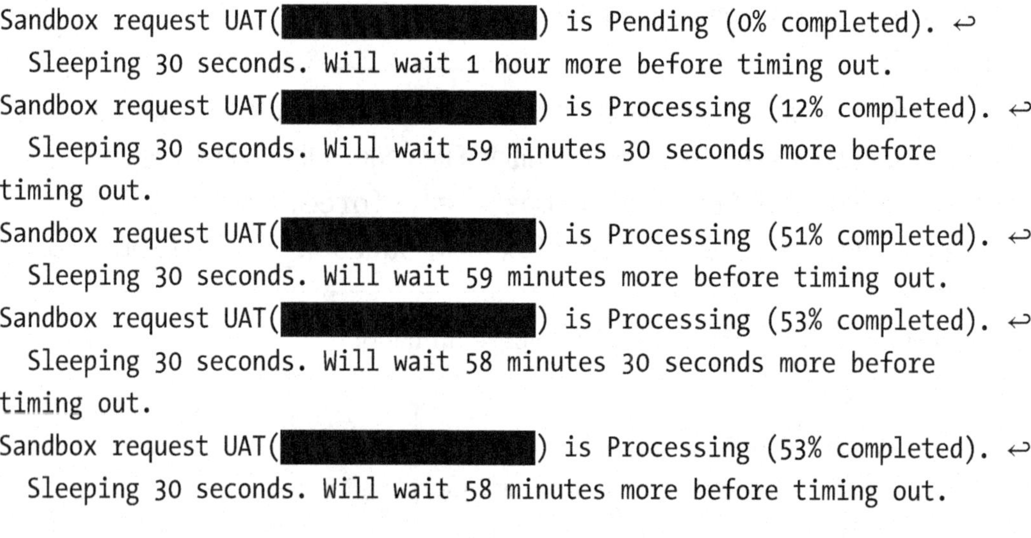

```
Sandbox request UAT([illegible]) is Pending (0% completed). ↩
  Sleeping 30 seconds. Will wait 1 hour more before timing out.
Sandbox request UAT([illegible]) is Processing (12% completed). ↩
  Sleeping 30 seconds. Will wait 59 minutes 30 seconds more before
timing out.
Sandbox request UAT([illegible]) is Processing (51% completed). ↩
  Sleeping 30 seconds. Will wait 59 minutes more before timing out.
Sandbox request UAT([illegible]) is Processing (53% completed). ↩
  Sleeping 30 seconds. Will wait 58 minutes 30 seconds more before
timing out.
Sandbox request UAT([illegible]) is Processing (53% completed). ↩
  Sleeping 30 seconds. Will wait 58 minutes more before timing out.
```

If you switch back to the sandbox page in the production org, you will see that the sandbox is in the process of being created.

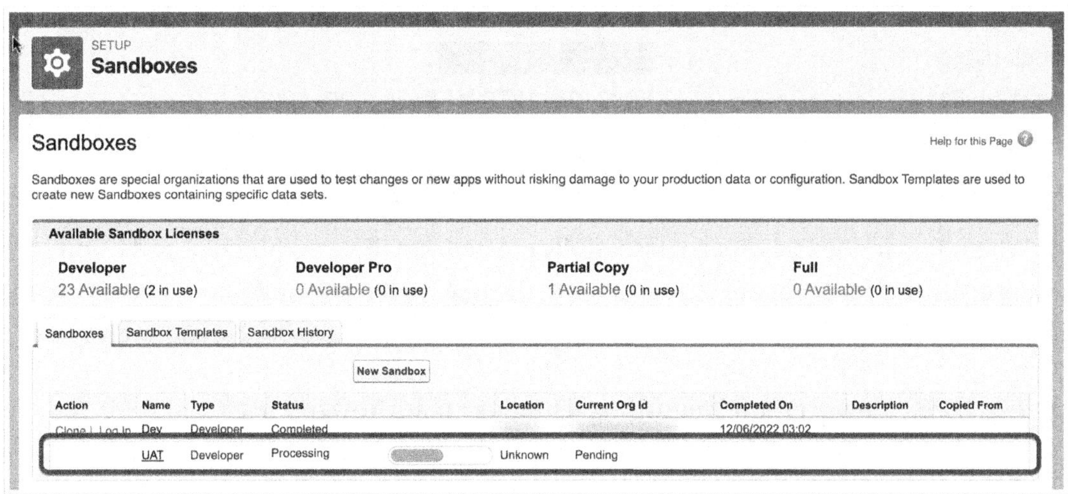

Figure 7-22. *Production org UAT sandbox creation in progress*

When the command completes, it outputs some information about the newly created sandbox.

Listing 7-21. Synchronous sandbox creation completed

```
Sandbox request UAT(                  ) is Processing (86% completed). ↩
  Sleeping 30 seconds. Will wait 27 minutes 30 seconds more before
timing out.
Sandbox request UAT(                  ) is Processing (94% completed). ↩
  Sleeping 30 seconds. Will wait 27 minutes more before timing out.
Sandbox UAT(                  ) is ready for use.
=== Sandbox Org Creation Status
Name                         Value
────────────────             ───────

Id
SandboxName                  UAT
Status                       Completed
CopyProgress                 100
Description
LicenseType                  DEVELOPER
SandboxInfoId
```

```
SourceId
SandboxOrg                     ███████████
Created Date                   2022-06-12T03:58:05.000+0000
ApexClassId
Authorized Sandbox Username    ivan.harris@███████████
```

When the sandbox has been successfully created, it will be authorized, and if you now execute the `force:org:list` command, the newly created sandbox will be shown in the list of authorized orgs.

Listing 7-22. Newly created sandbox listed as an authorized org

```
=== Orgs
     ALIAS      USERNAME                 ORG ID              CONNECTED STATUS
──── ───────── ──────────────           ───────────         ──────────────
(D)  MyDH       ihdxdh@example.com       00D4K0000015OzMUAU  Connected
     MyProdOrg  ivan.harris@████████     ████████████████    Connected
     MyUATSbx   ivan.harris@███████████  ████████████████    Connected

     ALIAS USERNAME                      ORG ID              EXPIRATION DATE
──── ───── ──────────────                ───────────         ──────────────
(U)  MySO  test-kqzqtrba2kam@example.com 00D3G00000013wVUAQ  2022-06-18
```

And the sandbox page in the production org will also show that the sandbox has been created.

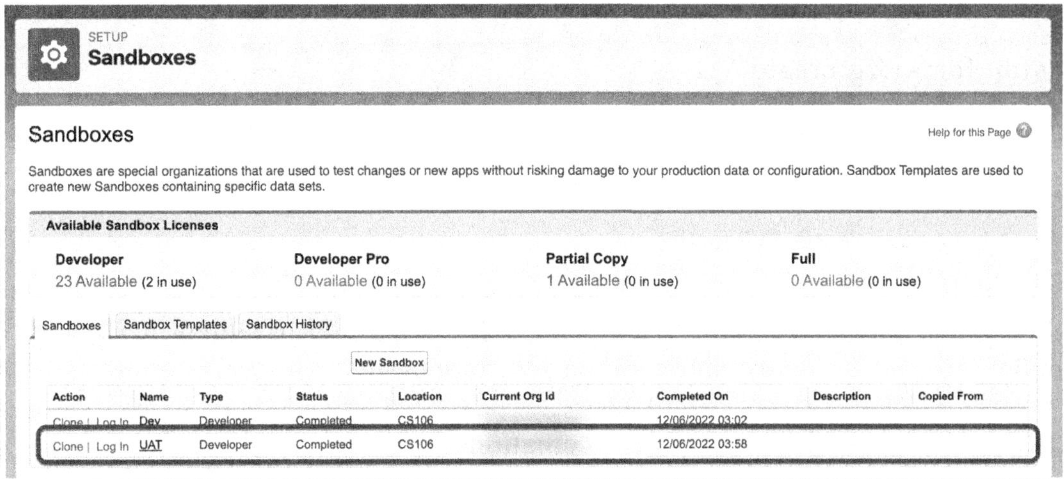

Figure 7-23. *Production org with newly created UAT sandbox*

In addition to creating sandboxes synchronously, sandboxes can also be created asynchronously.

Checking Sandbox Creation Status

In the preceding example, the sandbox took just under 27 minutes to be created synchronously. To avoid waiting that long for the command to return control to the integrated terminal, the wait time can be set to a lower value, with a minimum of 2 minutes, to execute the command asynchronously.

Create another sandbox definition file with the following contents, this time called `sbx-staging-def.json`, and again save it in the `config` directory.

Listing 7-23. Staging sandbox definition file

```
{
    "sandboxName": "Staging",
    "licenseType": "Developer"
}
```

Now execute the following command to create the sandbox asynchronously:

```
$ sfdx force:org:create \
    --setalias MyStagingSbx \
    --definitionfile ./config/sbx-staging-def.json \
    --type sandbox \
    --targetusername MyProdOrg \
    --wait 2
```

The command returns after two minutes, displays the following output, and continues to perform the sandbox creation asynchronously.

Listing 7-24. Asynchronous sandbox creation timed out

```
Sandbox request Staging(██████████████████) is Pending (0% completed). ↩
  Sleeping 30 seconds. Will wait 2 minutes more before timing out.
Sandbox request Staging(██████████████████) is Processing (26%
completed). ↩
  Sleeping 30 seconds. Will wait 1 minute 30 seconds more before
timing out.
Sandbox request Staging(██████████████████) is Processing (56%
completed). ↩
  Sleeping 30 seconds. Will wait 1 minute more before timing out.
Sandbox request Staging(██████████████████) is Processing (74%
completed). ↩
  Sleeping 30 seconds. Will wait 30 seconds more before timing out.
ERROR running force:org:create:  Sandbox status is Processing; ↩
  timed out waiting for completion.
```

The following command can then be used to resume observing the status output, just as if you had set a longer wait period with the `force:org:create` command:

```
$ sfdx force:org:status \
    --setalias MyStagingSbx \
    --sandboxname Staging \
    --targetusername MyProdOrg \
    --wait 60
```

The complete list of parameters for this command is as follows:

- `--setalias|-a`: When the sandbox creation is complete and it is authorized, this will be the alias that will be assigned. Note: Even if an alias was included with the original `force:org:create` command, the CLI does not remember that alias if the create command timed out before completion, so it needs to be set with this status command; otherwise, the org will not have an alias. [Optional]
- `--sandboxname|-n`: The name of the sandbox whose creation status is to be checked. This is the name assigned to the `sandboxName` file parameter in the sandbox definition file, which is the name of the sandbox that will appear in the sandbox page of the production org. To be clear, this parameter does not take a username or alias. [Required]
- `--setdefaultusername|-s`: Pass this parameter if the sandbox is to be the default org. [Optional]
- `--targetusername|-u`: The username or the alias of the production org that is being used to create the sandbox. [Optional]
- `--wait|-w`: The amount of time in minutes to wait for the command to complete. The command will return sooner if it completes before the wait period. If the wait period expires before the sandbox has been created, run the `force:org:status` command again. [Optional] [Default: 6]
- `--apiversion, --json, --loglevel`: Please refer to the discussion on global parameters in the section "Command-Line Parameters and Arguments" in Chapter 4, "Salesforce CLI."

When the command completes, it displays the sandbox creation completion status as in the following listing.

Listing 7-25. Asynchronous sandbox creation completion

```
Sandbox request Staging(███████████████) is Activating (95%
completed). ↩
  Sleeping 30 seconds. Will wait 57 minutes 30 seconds more before
timing out.
Sandbox request Staging(███████████████) is Activating (95%
completed). ↩
  Sleeping 30 seconds. Will wait 57 minutes more before timing out.
Sandbox request Staging(███████████████) is Activating (95%
completed). ↩
  Sleeping 30 seconds. Will wait 56 minutes 30 seconds more before
timing out.
Sandbox Staging(███████████████) is ready for use.
=== Sandbox Org Status
Name                        Value
_______________             ____________________

Id                          ███████████████
SandboxName                 Staging
Status                      Completed
CopyProgress                100
Description
LicenseType                 DEVELOPER
SandboxInfoId               ███████████████
SourceId
SandboxOrg                  ████████████
Created Date                2022-06-12T03:23:19.000+0000
ApexClassId
Authorized Sandbox Username ivan.harris@███████████████
```

As soon as the sandbox creation has completed, it will be authorized, as can be seen by executing the `force:org:list` command again.

Listing 7-26. Authorized staging sandbox

```
=== Orgs
    ALIAS        USERNAME                     ORG ID               CONNECTED STATUS
─── ──────────── ──────────                   ──────────────────   ────────────────
(D) MyDH         ihdxdh@example.com           00D4K0000015OzMUAU   Connected
    MyProdOrg    ivan.harris@                                      Connected
    MyStagingSbx ivan.harris@                                      Connected
    MyUATSbx     ivan.harris@                                      Connected

    ALIAS   USERNAME                        ORG ID               EXPIRATION DATE
─── ─────── ────────────────────            ──────────────────   ───────────────
(U) MySO    test-kqzqtrba2kam@example.com   00D3G00000013wVUAQ   2022-06-18
```

The new sandbox is also visible in the production org's sandbox page.

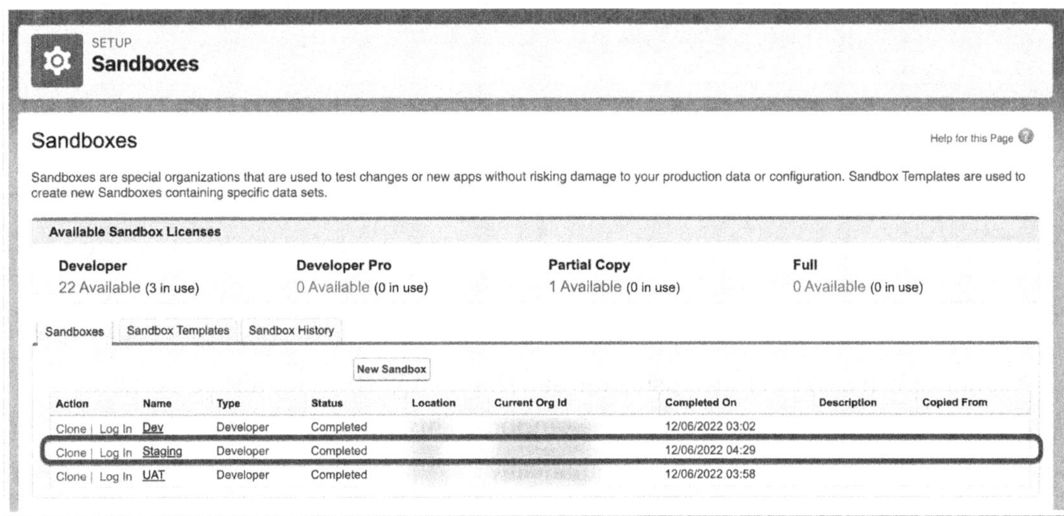

Figure 7-24. *Production org with newly created staging sandbox*

In the next section, we will see how sandboxes can also be cloned.

Cloning Sandboxes

Cloning a sandbox creates a copy of a sandbox including its license type, data, and metadata components. This is a quicker and more convenient method than creating a new sandbox and then deploying customization or application metadata components when you want to create a pool of identical sandboxes.

Cloning can be performed from a production org's Setup area, as can be seen in the following.

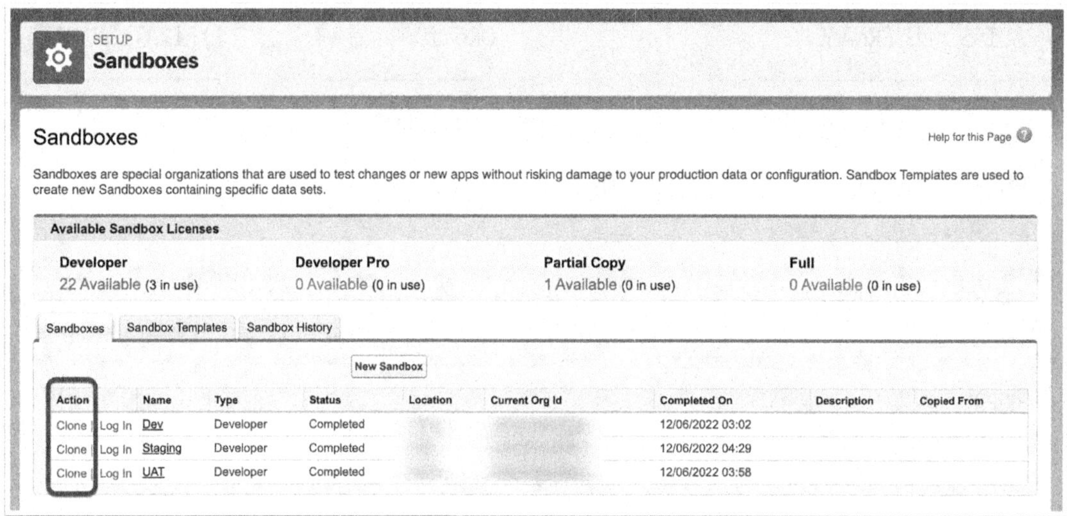

Figure 7-25. *Clone a sandbox option in a production org*

A sandbox can also be cloned using the Salesforce CLI, which requires a sandbox definition file, the same as when creating a sandbox. This time, the `licenseType` parameter is not required as the sandbox clone automatically has the same license type as the source sandbox. This time, we need to include the `sandboxName` for the sandbox clone and the `sourceSandboxName` of the sandbox to be cloned. Create a file called `sbx-sit-def.json` with the following contents and save it in the Salesforce DX project's `config` directory.

Listing 7-27. SIT sandbox definition file for cloning

```
{
    "sandboxName": "SIT",
    "sourceSandboxName": "UAT"
}
```

Now execute the following command to start the cloning process:

```
$ sfdx force:org:clone \
    --setalias MySITSbx \
    --definitionfile ./config/sbx-sit-def.json \
    --type sandbox \
    --targetusername MyProdOrg \
    --wait 60
```

The complete list of parameters for this command is as follows:

- `--setalias|-a`: When the sandbox cloning process is complete and it is authorized, this will be the alias that will be assigned. [Optional]
- `--definitionfile|-f`: Path to the sandbox definition file. [Optional: Either a definition file is passed using this parameter, or `Name=Value` pair arguments must be provided for at least the required file parameters.]
- `--setdefaultusername|-s`: Pass this parameter if the sandbox clone is to be the default org. [Optional]
- `--type|-t`: This must be set to `sandbox`. [Required]
- `--targetusername|-u`: The username or the alias of the production org that is being used to clone the sandbox. [Optional]
- `--wait|-w`: The amount of time in minutes to wait for the command to complete. The command will return sooner if it completes before the wait period. If the wait period expires before the sandbox has been created, run the `force:org:status` command. [Optional] [Default: 6]
- `--apiversion, --json, --loglevel`: Please refer to the discussion on global parameters in the section "Command-Line Parameters and Arguments" in Chapter 4, "Salesforce CLI."

The `-wait|-w` parameter and use of the `force:org:status` command to check the sandbox cloning status behaves exactly the same way as when creating a sandbox with the `force:org:create` command. When the cloning process is complete, run `force:org:list` to view the newly cloned sandbox.

Listing 7-28. Sandbox clone in the authorized org list

```
=== Orgs
     ALIAS        USERNAME                        ORG ID              CONNECTED STATUS
───  ──────────── ─────────────                   ──────────────────  ─────────────────
(D)  MyDH         ihdxdh@example.com              00D4K0000015OzMUAU  Connected
     MyProdOrg    ivan.harris@                                        Connected
     MySITSbx     ivan.harris@                                        Connected
     MyStagingSbx ivan.harris@                                        Connected
     MyUATSbx     ivan.harris@                                        Connected

    ALIAS USERNAME                      ORG ID              EXPIRATION DATE
─── ───── ──────────────                ──────────────────  ───────────────
(U) MySO  test-kqzqtrba2kam@example.com 00D3G00000013wVUAQ  2022-06-18
```

Viewing the sandboxes in the production org's Setup area shows the newly created sandbox clone as well.

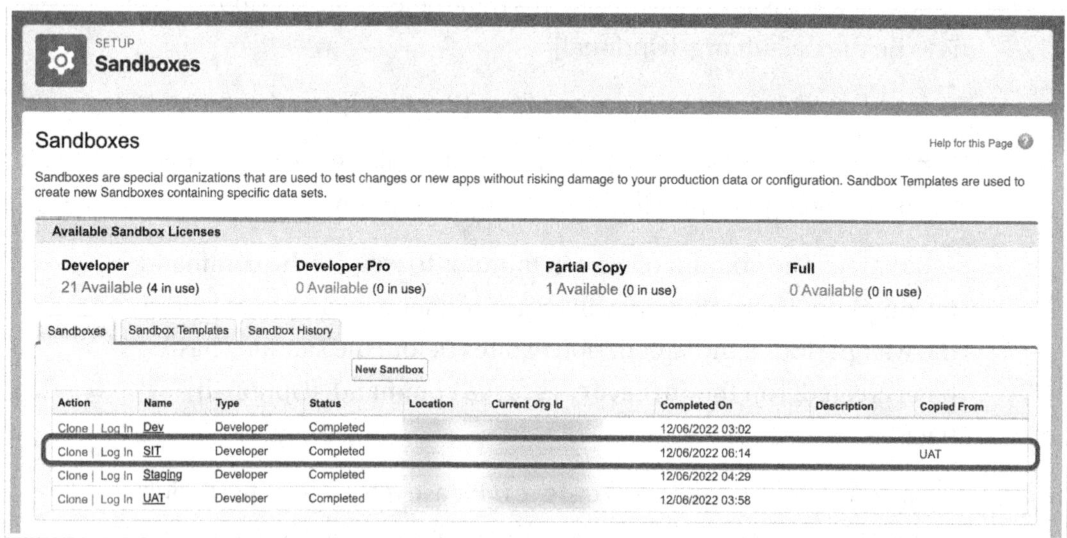

Figure 7-26. *Sandbox clone in a production org*

To complete the lifecycle management of sandboxes using the Salesforce CLI, we'll cover off deleting a sandbox next.

Deleting Sandboxes

Sandboxes are another limited resource in production orgs and should be deleted when no longer required. Sandboxes cannot be deleted until their refresh interval has expired, so you will have to wait to delete the sandboxes that you have just created. The refresh interval depends on the sandbox license type, as illustrated in the following table.

Table 7-1. *Sandbox refresh intervals*

Sandbox Type	Interval
Developer	1 day
Developer Pro	1 day
Partial Copy	5 days
Full Copy	29 days

If you try to delete a sandbox using the Salesforce CLI before its refresh interval has expired, you will get the following error.

Listing 7-29. Sandbox deletion before refresh interval expiration error

```
ERROR running force:org:delete:  Cannot complete this operation. You can
refresh or delete sandboxes only after the refresh interval for their
license type has elapsed. : SandboxApi
```

Furthermore, if sandboxes are accidentally deleted, customers have up to 48 hours to ask Salesforce to restore the sandbox. During that time, you cannot create a new sandbox or a sandbox clone with the same name as a sandbox that has been marked for deletion. For example, you will receive the following error if you try to clone a sandbox and the new sandbox name is the same as a sandbox that has been deleted in the past 48 hours.

Listing 7-30. Sandbox deletion before previous sandbox deleted error

```
ERROR running force:org:clone:  The name you specified is assigned to a
sandbox that's being deleted. You can reuse the name after the deletion
process finishes.
```

To delete the first sandbox that we created once its refresh interval has expired, use the following command:

```
$ sfdx force:org:delete \
    --targetusername MyUATSbx
```

The command parameters were detailed in the section "Deleting Scratch Orgs" earlier in the chapter, so we won't list them again here.

Listing the orgs using `force:org:list` will confirm that the sandbox has been removed from the list of authorized orgs, and the production org's Setup area will also show that the sandbox has been deleted.

That completes the sandbox management lifecycle from creation to deletion. Let's summarize what we covered in this chapter.

Chapter Summary

In this chapter, we explored the types of Salesforce orgs that Salesforce DX supports including scratch orgs and non-scratch orgs such as Developer Edition, sandbox, and production orgs. We learned how to manage the lifecycle of scratch orgs and sandboxes from creation to deletion. We also discovered how to authorize non-scratch orgs so that the Salesforce CLI can connect and interact with them. We spent some time focusing on how to configure scratch orgs so that they contain the features and settings that we need when they are created, which makes them a powerful alternative to Developer and Developer Pro sandboxes for internal development teams and to Developer Edition orgs for AppExchange Partner development teams.

Now that we can successfully manage orgs, the next chapter will introduce how metadata components are exchanged between a local Salesforce DX project and scratch and non-scratch orgs.

CHAPTER 8

Metadata

According to the Merriam-Webster online dictionary, metadata is "data that provides information about other data."[1] The simplest way to think about Salesforce metadata is that it's everything in your Salesforce org that's not data records. The Salesforce metadata describes how the data records are stored, processed, and displayed. Example metadata types include custom objects, Apex classes, Visualforce pages, Lightning component bundles, and approval processes.

Note Metadata components are instances of metadata types. For example, `CustomObject` is a metadata type, and the custom object `Example_Object__c` is a metadata component that is an instance of the `CustomObject` metadata type. To view a complete list of metadata types, please refer to the Metadata API Developer Guide at `https://developer.salesforce.com/docs/atlas.en-us.api_meta.meta/api_meta/meta_intro.htm`.

In Chapter 3, "Concepts Overview," we learned that Salesforce DX introduced the new source format for metadata components that are stored in a Salesforce DX project's local filing system. In this chapter, we will explore the difference between source format and the legacy Metadata API format files, how to synchronize metadata components between a local Salesforce DX project and source-tracked or non-source-tracked orgs, and how to convert between source format and Metadata API format files.

[1] "Metadata." *Merriam-Webster.com Dictionary*, Merriam-Webster, `www.merriam-webster.com/dictionary/metadata`. Accessed 24 Jul. 2022.

I. Harris, *Beginning Salesforce DX*, https://doi.org/10.1007/978-1-4842-8114-7_8

This Chapter's Commands

In this chapter, we will encounter the following `force:source` topic commands for working with metadata components that are stored locally as source format files in a Salesforce DX project:

- **`force:source:convert`**: Convert metadata that is stored in a local Salesforce DX project from source format to Metadata API format.
- **`force:source:deploy`**: Deploy source format metadata that is stored in a local Salesforce DX project to a source-tracked or non-source-tracked org.
- **`force:source:deploy:cancel`**: Cancel an asynchronous deployment that was initiated with a `force:source:deploy` command.
- **`force:source:deploy:report`**: Report on the status of an asynchronous deployment that was initiated with a `force:source:deploy` command.
- **`force:source:pull`**: Pull metadata from a source-tracked org and store it in source format in a local Salesforce DX project.
- **`force:source:push`**: Push a local Salesforce DX project's source format metadata to a source-tracked org.
- **`force:source:retrieve`**: Retrieve metadata from a source-tracked or non-source-tracked org and store it in source format in a local Salesforce DX project.
- **`force:source:status`**: Display the differences between a local Salesforce DX project's source format metadata and the metadata components in a source-tracked org.

We will also cover the following commands from the `force:mdapi` topic that are used when working with metadata components stored in Metadata API format files:

- **`force:mdapi:convert`**: Convert metadata that is stored in a local Salesforce DX project from Metadata API format to source format.
- **`force:mdapi:retrieve`**: Retrieve metadata from a source-tracked or non-source-tracked org and store it in Metadata API format in a local Salesforce DX project.

- **force:mdapi:retrieve:report**: Report on the status of an asynchronous retrieval that was initiated with a `force:mdapi:retrieve` command.
- **force:mdapi:deploy**: Deploy metadata that is stored in Metadata API format in the local Salesforce DX project to a source-tracked or non-source-tracked org.
- **force:mdapi:deploy:report**: Report on the status of an asynchronous deployment that was initiated with a `force:mdapi:deploy` command.
- **force:mdapi:deploy:cancel**: Cancel an asynchronous deployment that was initiated with a `force:mdapi:deploy` command.

Note For a complete list of the `force:source` and `force:mdapi` topic commands, please check out the Salesforce CLI Command Reference: `https://developer.salesforce.com/docs/atlas.en-us.sfdx_cli_reference.meta/sfdx_cli_reference/cli_reference.htm`. In this chapter, we will focus on the synchronization of metadata components and conversion of their file types.

Before exploring metadata in more detail, let's create a new Salesforce DX project for the chapter.

This Chapter's Project

As usual, we will create a fresh Salesforce DX project for this chapter. Please follow the instructions in Chapter 6, "Projects," and name the project `SalesforceDXMD` using the default standard template. We will be working with scratch orgs, so also ensure that you have a default Dev Hub org authorized with an alias of `MyDH` as described in Chapter 5, "Dev Hub."

The first thing that we will do is to review the difference between the new source file format and the legacy Metadata API file format used to store metadata components in a local Salesforce DX project.

Source Format vs. Metadata API Format

Before the advent of Salesforce DX, tools such as the Ant Migration Tool, Workbench, or Visual Studio Code could be used to retrieve metadata components from, and deploy metadata components to, a Salesforce org using the Metadata API. The metadata components retrieved from an org were stored in the local filing system using the Metadata API file format. The Metadata API format files can then be managed using a version control system to track metadata component changes. This is known as the "org development model" where the version control system is the source of truth, which is an alternative to the "change set development model" where the production org is the source of truth.

The challenges with Metadata API format files include

- The files can grow to become very large, which slows down retrieve and deploy operations.
- Complex components are bundled into a single file, making it difficult for teams to collaborate on the component.
- Changes are not tracked, so metadata components are overwritten whether they have changed or not, which can result in unintentional behaviors.

A custom object is an example of a complex metadata component that includes custom fields, validation rules, list views, and much more. Suppose you have a custom object called `Example_Object__c` that has a single custom field called `Example_Field__c`. When the custom object is stored in Metadata API format, a single file is created in a Salesforce DX project directory.

Listing 8-1. Metadata API format custom object

```
objects
└── Example_Object__c.object
```

If the contents of the file are inspected, we can see in the following file snippet that the custom field is bundled in the file along with the custom object elements.

Listing 8-2. Metadata API format custom object XML file

```
<enableSharing>true</enableSharing>
<enableStreamingApi>true</enableStreamingApi>
<externalSharingModel>Private</externalSharingModel>
<fields>
    <fullName>Example_Field__c</fullName>
    <externalId>false</externalId>
    <label>Example Field</label>
    <length>50</length>
    <required>false</required>
    <trackTrending>false</trackTrending>
    <type>Text</type>
    <unique>false</unique>
</fields>
<label>Example Object</label>
<nameField>
    <label>Example Object Name</label>
    <type>Text</type>
</nameField>
```

Salesforce DX introduced the new source format for storing metadata components in a local Salesforce DX project, which breaks complex components into separate files. Here is the same custom object stored in source format rather than Metadata API format.

Listing 8-3. Source format custom object

```
objects
└── Example_Object__c
    ├── Example_Object__c.object-meta.xml
    └── fields
        └── Example_Field__c.field-meta.xml
```

Rather than a single file containing both the custom object and the custom field, a separate file is used for the custom field. Looking at the custom field file, the same elements are present that were present in the Metadata API format file for the custom object.

Listing 8-4. Source format custom field XML file

```
<?xml version="1.0" encoding="UTF-8"?>
<CustomField xmlns="http://soap.sforce.com/2006/04/metadata">
    <fullName>Example_Field__c</fullName>
    <externalId>false</externalId>
    <label>Example Field</label>
    <length>50</length>
    <required>false</required>
    <trackTrending>false</trackTrending>
    <type>Text</type>
    <unique>false</unique>
</CustomField>
```

Breaking the metadata into separate, more granular files simplifies collaborative development as developers can work on smaller, discrete files that reduce the complexity of merging large, monolithic files. When source format metadata files are used with source-tracked orgs, the combination of source tracking and a more granular file structure results in much faster synchronization of changed metadata components between a local filing system and a source-tracked org.

In the "This Chapter's Commands" section earlier in the chapter, we saw that there are several different commands for synchronizing metadata components stored in a local Salesforce DX project in source format or Metadata API format with source-tracked and non-source-tracked orgs. With these many permutations, which commands should you use and when? We'll cover this next.

Metadata Synchronization Options

When choosing whether to use the `force:source` or `force:mdapi` topic commands to synchronize metadata components between a local Salesforce DX project and a Salesforce org, we must consider the local metadata file format and the type of org that we want to synchronize with. The local metadata file format can be source format or Metadata API format, and the org type can be source-tracked or non-source-tracked.

Note In Chapter 7, "Orgs," we saw that scratch orgs are always source-tracked orgs, while Developer Edition orgs, Partial Copy sandboxes, Full sandboxes, and production orgs are always non-source-tracked orgs. We also learned that Developer sandboxes and Developer Pro sandboxes are non-source-tracked by default and that source tracking can be enabled for them as described in Chapter 5, "Dev Hub."

As a refresher, here are the commands from the `force:source` and `force:mdapi` topics that can be used for metadata synchronization:

- **`force:source:pull`**: Pull metadata components from a source-tracked org and store them in a local Salesforce DX project in source format. Uses source tracking to synchronize the metadata components stored in the local Salesforce DX project with new, deleted, or changed components in the source-tracked org.
- **`force:source:push`**: Push metadata components that are stored in source format in the local Salesforce DX project to a source-tracked org. Uses source tracking to synchronize the metadata components in the source-tracked org with new, deleted, or changed components stored in the local Salesforce DX project.
- **`force:source:retrieve`**: Retrieve metadata components from a source-tracked or non-source-tracked org and store them in source format in the local Salesforce DX project. Does not use source tracking; therefore, retrieved components will overwrite locally stored source format files without merging any changes.
- **`force:source:deploy`**: Deploy metadata components that are stored in source format in the local Salesforce DX project to a source-tracked or non-source-tracked org. Does not use source tracking; therefore, deployed components will overwrite components in the source-tracked or non-source-tracked org without merging any changes.
- **`force:mdapi:retrieve`**: Retrieve metadata components in the form of a compressed zip archive from a source-tracked or non-source-tracked org and store the archive in a local Salesforce DX project.

Uncompress the zip archive to access the metadata components that are stored in Metadata API format. The retrieved metadata zip archive will overwrite an existing archive in the retrieve target directory without merging any new, deleted, or changed metadata components.

- **`force:mdapi:deploy`**: Deploy metadata components in the form of a zip archive, or a deployment directory containing components, that are stored in a local Salesforce DX project to a source-tracked or non-source-tracked org. The zip archive includes compressed metadata components in Metadata API format. When using a deployment directory, the components are compressed into a zip archive for you. The deployed metadata components will overwrite any components in the source-tracked or non-source-tracked org without merging any new, deleted, or changed metadata components.

That's a lot of options! However, the options can be reduced when following these leading practices:

1. Individual developers should avoid using Developer Edition orgs for their personal development. Use source-tracked orgs such as scratch orgs or source tracking–enabled Developer sandboxes and Developer Pro sandboxes instead.
2. Use source format for storing metadata components in a local Salesforce DX project. This allows changes to be tracked when using source-tracked orgs, speeds up exchanging metadata with source-tracked orgs, and offers more granular metadata, which simplifies collaboration.
3. Save source format metadata components in a version control system to eliminate the need to convert between source format and Metadata API format files.
4. Once metadata is in source format, use the `force:source` commands to push/pull metadata changes to/from source-tracked orgs and to deploy/retrieve metadata to/from non-source-tracked orgs. This maintains source format as the file format of record regardless of the org type.

This table summarizes which commands to use with different org types once leading practice has been adopted.

***Table 8-1.** Preferred commands for exchanging metadata with orgs*

Org Type	Track Changes?	Push or Deploy?	Pull or Retrieve?
Scratch	Y	`force:source:push`	`force:source:pull`
Developer sandbox[1]	Y	`force:source:push`	`force:source:pull`
Developer Pro sandbox[1]	Y	`force:source:push`	`force:source:pull`
Partial Copy sandbox	N	`force:source:deploy`	`force:source:retrieve`
Full sandbox	N	`force:source:deploy`	`force:source:retrieve`
Developer Edition	N	`force:source:deploy`	`force:source:retrieve`
Production	N	`force:source:deploy`	`force:source:retrieve`

1. Assumes that source tracking has been enabled; if not, use the `force:source:deploy` and `force:source:retrieve` commands.

In summary, always use the `force:source` topic commands and use `force:source:push/pull` when working with source-tracked orgs and `force:source:deploy/retrieve` with non-source-tracked orgs. Only use the `force:mdapi` commands until you have migrated to source format files.

Armed with this understanding of metadata component file formats and synchronization command leading practices, we are now ready to start synchronizing metadata, starting with source-tracked orgs and source format metadata files.

Synchronizing Source Format Metadata with Source-Tracked Orgs

Salesforce DX supports synchronization of new, deleted, and changed metadata components between source format files stored in a local Salesforce DX project and a source-tracked Salesforce org.

Salesforce DX features and tools that we have encountered so far come together to implement synchronization, which creates a highly productive, iterative environment for developing applications and customizations for the Salesforce Platform. Those features include Salesforce DX projects, source format metadata files, the Salesforce CLI, and source-tracked orgs. Salesforce DX projects provide the directory and folder hierarchy to store metadata components in source format in the local filing system. The granular source format metadata files, the `force:source:pull` and `force:source:push` CLI commands, and source-tracked orgs all ensure that only changed metadata components are synchronized between a local Salesforce DX project and a source-tracked org.

To illustrate the synchronization process, we will be using the following CLI commands:

- **`force:source:pull`**: Pull metadata from a source-tracked org and store it in source format in a local Salesforce DX project.
- **`force:source:push`**: Push a local Salesforce DX project's source format metadata to a source-tracked org.
- **`force:source:status`**: Display the differences between a local Salesforce DX project's source format metadata and the metadata components in a source-tracked org.

We'll start by pulling some metadata components from a source-tracked org to a local Salesforce DX project.

Pulling Source Format Metadata from Source-Tracked Orgs

Using the `force:source:pull` Salesforce CLI command, we can pull new and changed metadata components from a source-tracked org to a local Salesforce DX project. Any metadata components that have been deleted in the source-tracked org will also be deleted from the local Salesforce DX project. The command stores the metadata components in source format, and as the CLI keeps track of changes, only changed metadata is pulled, and we do not have to tell the CLI what components to pull.

To have metadata components to pull from a source-tracked org, we first need to create some. Use the following steps to create a custom object with a custom field in a fresh scratch org.

1. Launch Visual Studio Code if it's not already launched.
2. Open this chapter's `SalesforceDXMD` project.

3. If you have an existing scratch org with the alias `MySO`, either delete it or rename the alias.

4. Create a fresh scratch org, assign it the alias `MySO`, and set it as the default username.

5. Open the newly created scratch org and click the **Allow** button in the Show notifications pop-up that appears.

6. Navigate to **Setup ➤ Objects and Fields ➤ Object Manager**.

7. Click the **Create** action menu and then the **Custom Object** menu item.

8. Enter the following field values:

    a. **Label**: `Example Object`

    b. **Plural Label**: `Example Objects`

    c. **Starts with vowel sound**: `Checked`

    d. **Object Name**: `Example_Object`

9. Click the **Save** button, which will open the detail page for the new custom object.

10. Click **Fields & Relationships**.

11. Click **New**.

12. In Step 1 of the new custom field wizard, select **Text** as the data type and then click **Next**.

13. In Step 2, enter the following field values, then click **Next**:

    a. **Field Label**: `Example Field`

    b. **Length**: `50`

    c. **Field Name**: `Example_Field`

14. In Step 3, just click **Next**.

15. In Step 4, click **Save**.

Now that we have some new metadata components, we can view the changes that are tracked by the CLI. Return to Visual Studio, open the integrated terminal, and execute the following CLI command:

```
$ sfdx force:source:status
```

This command's parameters are

- `--local|-l`: Lists all the changes that have been made in the local Salesforce DX project. [Optional]
- `--remote|-r`: Lists all the changes that have been made in the source-tracked org. [Optional]
- `--targetusername|-u`: The username or alias of the source-tracked org to track changes with. [Optional]
- `--apiversion, --concise, --json, --loglevel`: Please refer to the discussion on global parameters in the section "Command-Line Parameters and Arguments" in Chapter 4, "Salesforce CLI."

The command will output the changes that have been made in the local Salesforce DX project, which is none so far, and the changes that have been made in the source-tracked org.

Listing 8-5. Tracked changes in a source-tracked org

```
Source Status
STATE       FULL NAME                                        TYPE            PROJECT PATH
─────────   ─────────────────────────────────────────────    ─────────────   ──────────────────

 Remote Add Example_Object__c.Example_Field__c               CustomField
 Remote Add Example_Object__c                                CustomObject
 Remote Add Example_Object__c-Example Object Layout          Layout
 Remote Add Admin                                            Profile
```

We can see the new custom object that we created in the scratch org, plus its page layout, and the new custom field. In the process of creating the custom object, the Salesforce Platform has added the `Admin` profile. We don't really want to synchronize the profile with our local Salesforce DX project as there is no need to push or deploy the profile to any other org. In the section "Excluding Source Format Files from Syncing and

Converting" later in the chapter, we will see how to prevent metadata components from syncing, which gives users full control over what they are pulling from an org. For now, we will allow the syncing to happen.

Use the following command in the integrated terminal to pull the changed metadata components to synchronize the source-tracked org with the local Salesforce DX project:

```
$ sfdx force:source:pull
```

The parameters that can be used for this command are as follows:

- `--forceoverwrite|-f`: If the CLI detects conflicts between the metadata components in the local Salesforce DX project and the source-tracked org, it displays those conflicts. Passing this parameter suppresses the display of conflicts and forces the pulled metadata components to overwrite the local components. [Optional]
- `--targetusername|-u`: The username or alias of the source-tracked org to pull metadata components from. [Optional]
- `--wait|-w`: The number of minutes that the command will wait for completion. Control will be returned to the terminal application when the command completes or when the wait period expires, whichever is the sooner. [Optional] [Default: `33`]
- `--apiversion, --json, --loglevel`: Please refer to the discussion on global parameters in the section "Command-Line Parameters and Arguments" in Chapter 4, "Salesforce CLI."

Note To pull changed metadata components from a default source-tracked org using the Visual Studio Code Command Palette, execute the command **SFDX: Pull Source from Default Scratch Org**. To force the overwrite of local metadata components when there are conflicts, execute the command **SFDX: Pull Source from Default Scratch Org and Override Conflicts**.

When the command completes, it will output a list of the metadata components that have been pulled, the metadata type of each component, and the path to the directories in the local Salesforce DX project where the source format files have been stored.

Listing 8-6. Metadata components pulled from a source-tracked org

```
=== Retrieved Source
 STATE    FULL NAME                                    TYPE         PROJECT PATH
 ───────  ──────────────────────────────────────────  ───────────  ─────────────
 Created Example_Object__c.Example_Field__c           CustomField  force-app/main/↩
   default/objects/Example_Object__c/fields/Example_Field__c.field-meta.xml
 Created Example_Object__c                            CustomObject force-app/main/↩
   default/objects/Example_Object__c/Example_Object__c.object-meta.xml
 Created Example_Object__c-Example Object Layout Layout       force-app/main/↩
   default/layouts/Example_Object__c-Example Object Layout.layout-meta.xml
 Created Admin                                        Profile      force-app/main/↩
   default/profiles/Admin.profile-meta.xml
```

Note To improve readability, the preceding listing has been modified with wrapping added.

Opening the directories in the Visual Studio Explorer displays the source format files that have been created.

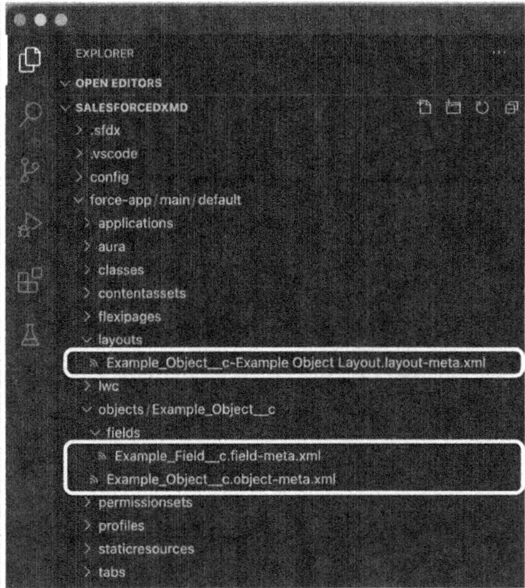

Figure 8-1. *Metadata components pulled from a scratch org*

We now have some new local metadata to work with. In the next section, we will make some local changes and push them to the source-tracked org.

Pushing Source Format Metadata to Source-Tracked Orgs

To synchronize changes made to metadata components stored using source format in a local Salesforce DX with a source-tracked org, we use the `force:source:push` command. Like the `force:source:pull` command, this will push new and changed metadata components to a source-tracked org, and it will delete from the source-tracked org any metadata components that have been deleted from a local Salesforce DX project.

To demonstrate pushing metadata components to a source-tracked org, we will first create some in the local Salesforce DX project. The most common local changes are development related, which will be covered in more detail in Chapter 12, "Development." For now, complete the following steps to create a simple trigger handler for the new `Example_Object__c` custom object that writes a welcome message to the `Example_Field__c` custom field that we created previously.

1. Launch Visual Studio Code if it's not already launched.

2. Open this chapter's `SalesforceDXMD` project.

3. Open the integrated terminal.
4. Execute the command:

```
sfdx force:apex:trigger:create \
-d ./force-app/main/default/triggers \
-n ExampleTrigger \
-s Example_Object__c
```

5. Open the newly created trigger handler file called `ExampleTrigger.trigger`, which can be found by expanding the `./force-app/main/default/triggers` directory in the Visual Studio Code Explorer.
6. Replace the source code with the code in the following listing.
7. Save the file.

Listing 8-7. Example trigger handler source code

```
trigger ExampleTrigger on Example_Object__c (before insert) {
    for (Example_Object__c exampleObject : Trigger.New) {
        exampleObject.Example_Field__c = 'Hello ' + UserInfo.
        getName() + '!';
    }
}
```

The `force:apex:trigger:create` command creates a new trigger handler in the Salesforce DX project's `triggers` directory. We won't dig into the command right now as we will be exploring it later in the book. The `ExampleTrigger` source code writes a welcome message to the user that is in context when the trigger handler runs.

If you now run the `force:source:status` command, it will show that there are some local changes.

Listing 8-8. Example trigger handler local metadata changes

```
Source Status
STATE      FULL NAME      TYPE        PROJECT PATH
─────────  ─────────────  ──────────  ──────────────────────────────────────
Local Add ExampleTrigger ApexTrigger force-app/main/default/↩
   triggers/ExampleTrigger.trigger
Local Add ExampleTrigger ApexTrigger force-app/main/default/↩
triggers/ExampleTrigger.trigger-meta.xml
```

To push these local changes to the default `MySO` scratch org, execute the following command in the Visual Studio Code integrated terminal:

```
$ sfdx force:source:push
```

The parameters that can be used for this command are as follows:

- `--forceoverwrite|-f`: If the CLI detects conflicts between the metadata components in the local Salesforce DX project and the source-tracked org, it displays those conflicts. Passing this parameter suppresses the display of conflicts and forces the pushed metadata components to overwrite the target org components. [Optional]
- `--ignorewarnings|-g`: If any warnings are generated during the push operation, using this parameter will ignore the warnings and complete the operation. [Optional]
- `--targetusername|-u`: The username or alias of the source-tracked org to push metadata components to. [Optional]
- `--wait|-w`: The number of minutes that the command will wait for completion. Control will be returned to the terminal application when the command completes or when the wait period expires, whichever is the sooner. [Optional] [Default: 33]
- `--apiversion, --json, --loglevel, --quiet`: Please refer to the discussion on global parameters in the section "Command-Line Parameters and Arguments" in Chapter 4, "Salesforce CLI."

Note To push changed metadata components to a default source-tracked org using the Visual Studio Code Command Palette, execute the command **SFDX: Push Source to Default Scratch Org**. To force the overwrite of source-tracked org metadata components when there are conflicts, execute the command **SFDX: Push Source to Default Scratch Org and Override Conflicts**.

On completion, the command will output the status of the push operation.

Listing 8-9. Metadata components pushed to a source-tracked org

```
*** Pushing with SOAP API v55.0 ***
Updating source tracking... done
=== Pushed Source
 STATE   FULL NAME      TYPE        PROJECT PATH
 ─────── ────────────── ─────────── ───────────────────────────────────────
 Created ExampleTrigger ApexTrigger force-app/main/default/↩
   triggers/ExampleTrigger.trigger
 Created ExampleTrigger ApexTrigger force-app/main/default/↩
   triggers/ExampleTrigger.trigger-meta.xml
```

Open the MySO scratch org using the `force:org:open` command and navigate to **Setup ➤ Custom Code ➤ Apex Triggers** where you can confirm that the Apex Trigger has been pushed to the scratch org.

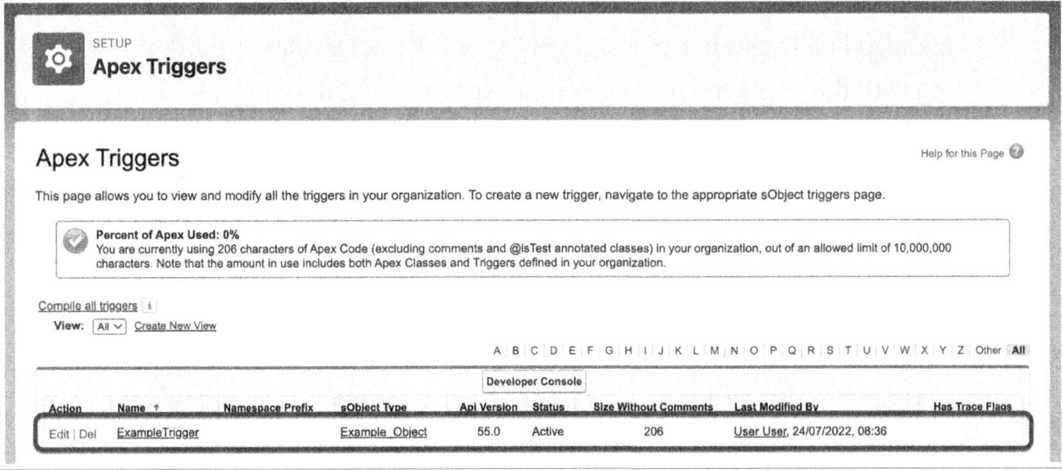

Figure 8-2. *Apex Trigger pushed to a source-tracked org*

We've covered how to synchronize source format metadata with source-tracked orgs; the next section will explore how to synchronize source format metadata with non-source-tracked orgs.

Synchronizing Source Format Metadata with Non-source-Tracked Orgs

So far, we have explored how to synchronize source format metadata components between a local Salesforce DX project and a source-tracked org. When developing applications or customizations for the Salesforce Platform, there are times when you will still need to synchronize with non-source-tracked orgs, such as Developer Edition orgs, Developer and Developer Pro sandboxes without source tracking enabled, Partial Copy sandboxes, Full sandboxes, and production orgs. For example:

- Internal development teams who are using source-tracked orgs for development and testing are still advised to perform User Acceptance Testing (UAT) using a Partial Copy sandbox and set up a staging environment using a Full sandbox, and they also need to deploy to production orgs of course.

- ISV development teams creating versions of first-generation managed packages in a packaging org, which is a Developer Edition org with the managed package's namespace configured, need to deploy their changes to that org.
- Internal development teams who are adopting Salesforce DX with a large, complex enterprise production environment may migrate to source-tracked orgs over time and will still need to synchronize with non-source-tracked orgs in the meantime.

This section covers synchronizing source format metadata with non-scratch orgs using the following `force:source` topic commands:

- **`force:source:retrieve`**: Retrieve metadata from a source-tracked or non-source-tracked org and store it in source format in a local Salesforce DX project.
- **`force:source:deploy`**: Deploy a local Salesforce DX project's source format metadata to a source-tracked or non-source-tracked org.
- **`force:source:deploy:cancel`**: Cancel an asynchronous deployment that was initiated with a `force:source:deploy` command.
- **`force:source:deploy:report`**: Report on the status of an asynchronous deployment that was initiated with a `force:source:deploy` command.

Note Unlike the `force:source:pull` and `force:source:push` commands, which only work with source format metadata files and source-tracked orgs, the preceding commands work with both source-tracked and non-source-tracked orgs. For example, if you want to run Apex tests in a scratch org, you can use the `force:source:deploy` command and specify the tests to run. Salesforce DX has the flexibility to work the way that you prefer to; however, we will focus on non-source-tracked orgs, although the commands work the same when working with source-tracked orgs.

First up, we shall see how to retrieve metadata from non-source-tracked orgs and store the metadata components in source format in a local Salesforce DX project.

Retrieving Source Format Metadata from Non-source-Tracked Orgs

In this section, we shall see how easy it is to retrieve metadata from a non-source-tracked org and store it locally in a Salesforce DX project in source format. While working with non-source-tracked orgs, you will then enjoy many of the benefits of working with source format metadata, such as more granular files to aid collaborative development and Salesforce DX commands for creating new metadata components.

Note We will be exploring new metadata component development using Salesforce DX in Chapter 12, "Development."

For this section, we will use a Developer Edition org as our non-source-tracked org, so head over to `https://developer.salesforce.com/signup` and sign up for a free one now. Follow the instructions and make a note of the username and password that you choose as they will be required to authorize the org with Salesforce DX next.

Once you have completed the sign-up process, authorize your new Developer Edition org with Salesforce DX by following these instructions:

1. If you have been following along with this chapter's examples so far, you will have existing metadata in your Salesforce DX project. If so, and to avoid any confusion, delete your existing `SalesforceDXMD` project or rename it.
2. Create a new `SalesforceDXMD` project; this time though, add the `--manifest|-x` parameter so that a `package.xml` file is added to the project. The command should be

   ```
   sfdx force:project:create -x \
   -n SalesforceDXMD
   ```
3. Launch Visual Studio Code if it's not already launched.
4. Open the `SalesforceDXMD` project.
5. Open the integrated terminal.

6. Use the `auth:web:login` command to authorize the new Developer Edition org, using the username and password that you made a note of when signing up. Set the alias to `MyDEOrg` and make it the org with the default username. Please refer to the section "Logging In to a Non-scratch Org" in Chapter 7, "Orgs," if you need a refresher on how to do this.

Run the `force:org:list` command to see that the Developer Edition org has been added to the list of authorized non-source-tracked orgs.

Listing 8-10. Authorized Developer Edition non-source-tracked org

```
=== Orgs

     ALIAS   USERNAME            ORG ID              CONNECTED STATUS
 ─── ─────   ────────────────    ──────────────────  ──────────────────
 (U) MyDEOrg ihdxde@example.com  00D4K000004iaUvUAI  Connected
 (D) MyDH    ihdxdh@example.com  00D4K0000015OzMUAU  Connected
```

If you have other orgs listed, there's no need to log out or delete them; as long as the Developer Edition org is the default org, the examples that follow will work just fine.

The next step is to create a metadata component in the non-source-tracked org so that we have something to retrieve. If you completed the example in the section "Pulling Source Format Metadata from Source-Tracked Orgs," you will notice that the steps to create a custom object with a custom field are the same; however, they are repeated here for convenience.

1. Launch Visual Studio Code if it's not already launched.
2. Open this chapter's `SalesforceDXMD` project.
3. Open the newly created org with the alias `MyDEOrg`.
4. Navigate to **Setup ➤ Objects and Fields ➤ Object Manager**.
5. Click the **Create** action menu and then the **Custom Object** menu item.
6. Enter the following field values:
   a. **Label**: `Example Object`
   b. **Plural Label**: `Example Objects`

c. **Starts with vowel sound**: `Checked`

d. **Object Name**: `Example_Object`

7. Click the **Save** button, which will open the detail page for the new custom object.

8. Click **Fields & Relationships**.

9. Click **New**.

10. In Step 1 of the new custom field wizard, select **Text** as the data type and then click **Next**.

11. In Step 2, enter the following field values, then click **Next**:

    a. **Field Label**: `Example Field`

    b. **Length**: `50`

    c. **Field Name**: `Example_Field`

12. In Step 3, just click **Next**.

13. In Step 4, click **Save**.

We will now create an unmanaged package that includes the new metadata components. Although this step isn't necessary when working with non-source-tracked orgs, later in this section there's an example of how to retrieve metadata components using packages, so it's worth setting one up now.

1. Navigate to **Setup ➤ Apps ➤ Packaging ➤ Package Manager**.

2. In the Packages section, click the **New** button.

3. In the Create a Package screen, enter the following field values, then click the **Save** button:

    a. **Package Name**: `Example Package`

4. The Example Package detail page should now be open. On the Components tab, click the **Add** button.

5. For the Component Type, select **Custom Object** from the picklist.

6. Enable the checkbox next to the `Example Object` custom object and click the **Add to Package** button.

The Example Package detail page will show that the custom object and its dependencies have been added to the unmanaged package.

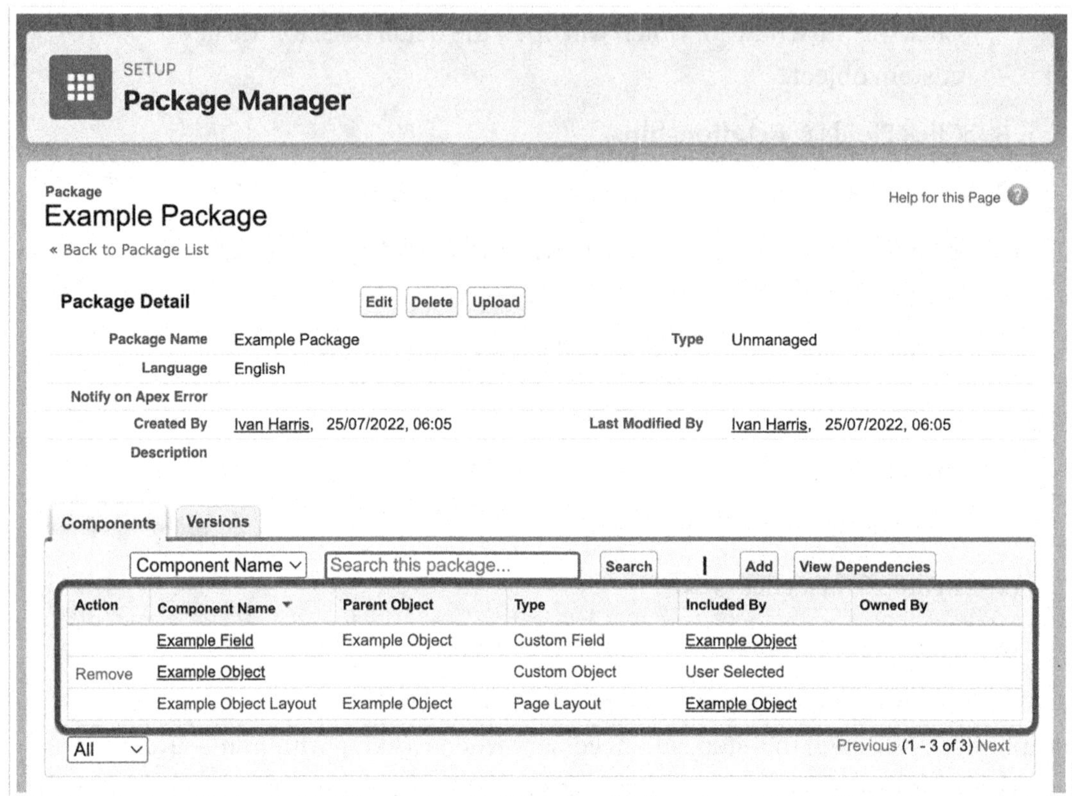

Figure 8-3. *An unmanaged package containing custom metadata components*

To complete the setup to support all the metadata retrieval examples, update the `package.xml` file that was added when creating the project. The file can be found in the `manifest` subdirectory below the project's root directory. Replace the contents with the following.

Listing 8-11. package.xml manifest to retrieve metadata components

```
<?xml version="1.0" encoding="UTF-8"?>
<Package xmlns="http://soap.sforce.com/2006/04/metadata">
    <types>
        <members>Example_Object__c.Example_Field__c</members>
        <name>CustomField</name>
    </types>
```

```
    <types>
        <members>Example_Object__c-Example Object Layout</members>
        <name>Layout</name>
    </types>
    <types>
        <members>Example_Object__c</members>
        <name>CustomObject</name>
    </types>
    <version>55.0</version>
</Package>
```

If you now execute the `force:source:status` command, unlike with source-tracked orgs, Salesforce DX is unable to track the changes that we just made and displays an error message instead.

Listing 8-12. Tracked changes are not supported with non-source-tracked orgs

```
ERROR running force:source:status:  This command can only be used on orgs
that have source tracking enabled, such as sandboxes and scratch orgs.
```

As changes are not tracked, we need to tell the Salesforce CLI what metadata components to retrieve, which can be done in several ways:

- A comma-separated list of metadata types and/or component names
- A comma-separated list of source file paths to retrieve
- A path to a `package.xml` manifest file that includes the metadata components to retrieve
- A comma-separated list of packages if the metadata components have been added to packages

This information is passed to the `force:source:retrieve` command as parameters. The complete list of parameters is described here.

```
$ sfdx force:source:retrieve
```

The parameters that can be used for this command are as follows:

- `--apiversion|-a`: Instructs the CLI to use a specific API version to retrieve metadata components. For example, if the API version specified in the `package.xml` file is older than the version supported by the CLI, setting this parameter will ensure that the CLI uses the `package.xml` API version. [Optional]
- `--forceoverwrite|-f`: If the CLI detects conflicts between the metadata components in the local Salesforce DX project and the source-tracked or non-source-tracked org, it displays those conflicts. Passing this parameter suppresses the display of conflicts and forces the retrieved metadata components to overwrite the local components. [Optional]
- `--metadata|-m`: A comma-separated list of metadata types and/or metadata components to retrieve. For example, `-m CustomObject` retrieves all metadata components of the `CustomObject` metadata type, and `-m CustomObject:Example_Object__c` retrieves the `Example_object__c` custom object. [Optional]
- `--packagenames|-n`: A comma-separated list of packages to retrieve. The packages contain metadata components and their dependencies. For example, `-n "Example Package"` retrieves the package with the name `Example Package`. [Optional]
- `--sourcepath|-p`: A comma-separated list of paths to directories or source files to retrieve. For example, to retrieve all custom objects, use `-p ./force-app/main/default/objects`, and to retrieve the `Example_Object__c` custom object, use `-p ./ force-app/main/default/objects/Example_Object__c/Example_Object__c.object-meta.xml`. [Optional]
- `--tracksource|-t`: Updates the tracking information that is used by the CLI to track differences between the metadata components in a source-tracked org and a local Salesforce DX project. Useful if the `force:source:retrieve` command is being used to retrieve a subset of metadata components from the source-tracked org rather

than using `force:source:pull`, which pulls all new and changed metadata components. Note, however, metadata components that have been deleted in the source-tracked org will not be deleted from the local Salesforce DX project. [Optional]

- `--targetusername`|`-u`: The username or alias of the source-tracked or non-source-tracked org to retrieve metadata components from. [Optional]
- `--wait`|`-w`: The number of minutes that the command will wait for completion. Control will be returned to the terminal application when the command completes or when the wait period expires, whichever is the sooner. [Optional] [Default: `33`]
- `--manifest`|`-x`: The path to a `package.xml` manifest file that lists the metadata components to retrieve, for example, `-x ./package.xml`. This parameter cannot be used in conjunction with the `--metadata`|`-m` or the `--sourcepath`|`-p` parameters. [Optional]
- `--json, --loglevel, --verbose`: Please refer to the discussion on global parameters in the section "Command-Line Parameters and Arguments" in Chapter 4, "Salesforce CLI."

Notes (1) The section "Excluding Source Format Files from Syncing and Converting" later in the chapter explains how to use the Metadata API Developer Guide to look up the correct metadata type name, source file path, and source file extensions for different metadata types.(2) If a parameter value's comma-separated list includes spaces, enclose the list in double quotes. On Windows, if the list contains commas, with or without spaces, enclose the list in double quotes. (3) To retrieve metadata components specified in a `package.xml` manifest from a default source-tracked or non-source-tracked org using the Visual Studio Code Command Palette, execute the command **SFDX: Retrieve Source in Manifest from Org**.

Earlier in this section, we set everything up that enables us to experiment with the various ways that we can instruct the force:source:retrieve command to retrieve metadata components. Executing any of the following commands will retrieve the Example_Object__c custom object, its dependent Example_Field__c custom field, and the Example_Object__c-Example Object Layout page layout:

```
$ sfdx force:source:retrieve \
    --metadata "
      CustomObject:Example_Object__c, \
      Layout:Example_Object__c-Example Object Layout"
```

```
$ sfdx force:source:retrieve \
    --sourcepath "
      ./force-app/main/default/objects/↩
        Example_Object__c/↩
        Example_Object__c.object-meta.xml, \
      ./force-app/main/default/objects/↩
        Example_Object__c/fields/↩
        Example_Field__c.field-meta.xml, \
      ./force-app/main/default/layouts/↩
        Example_Object__c-Example Object Layout.↩
        layout-meta.xml"
```

```
$ sfdx force:source:retrieve \
    --manifest ./manifest/package.xml
```

The first example illustrates how to pass a comma-separated list of metadata component names. The second uses a comma-separated list of source file paths. The final example passes a package.xml manifest file.

After running the force:source:retrieve command using the --metadata|-m parameter or the --manifest|-x parameter, the files created in the Salesforce DX project can be seen as in the following image. When using the --sourcepath|-p parameter, the metadata files must already exist in the Salesforce DX project, and the existing files are updated.

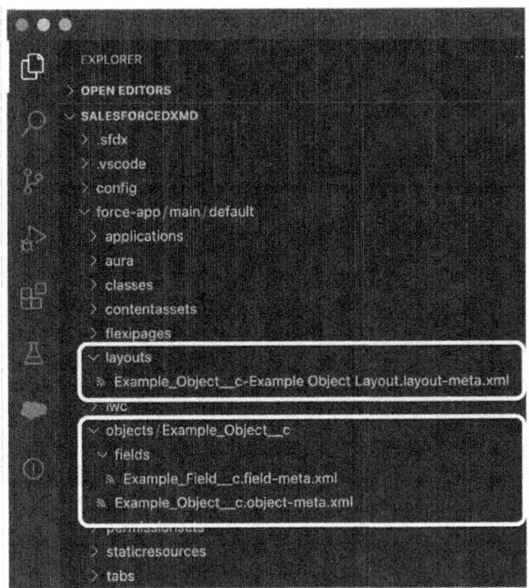

Figure 8-4. *Retrieved metadata source format files*

Whenever the `force:source:retrieve` command is run thereafter, the source format metadata files are updated, regardless of the `--metadata|-m`, `--sourcepath|-p`, or `--manifest|-x` parameter used. The command overwrites the files and does not attempt any merging, unlike the `force:source:pull` command, which only pulls new or changed metadata and deletes local metadata files when the corresponding metadata component is deleted in the source-tracked org.

The `--packagenames|-n` parameter behaves slightly differently as it will create a new directory in the local Salesforce DX project with the same name as the package. Run the following command in Visual Studio Code's integrated terminal:

```
$ sfdx force:source:retrieve \
    --packagenames "Example Package"
```

The VS Code Explorer shows that a new directory called `Example Package` has been created and the source format metadata files have been added.

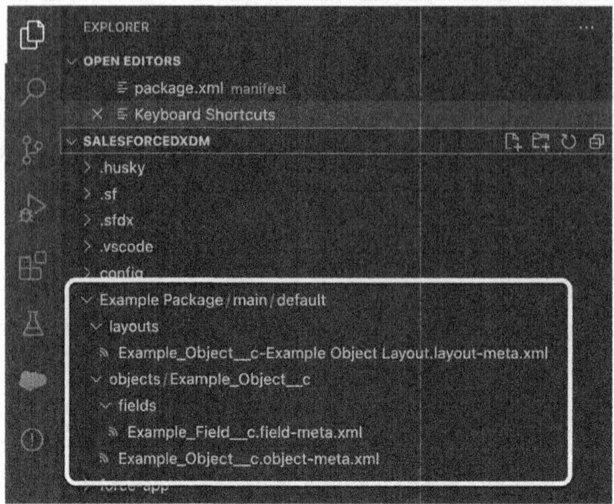

Figure 8-5. *Package directory and metadata source format files*

When we discuss deploying source format metadata to non-source-tracked orgs in the next section, you will discover that you cannot use a package name to deploy source format metadata components. The reason is that Salesforce DX supports deploying unpackaged metadata components, unlocked packages, and managed packages, but not unmanaged packages. Retrieving unmanaged packages is supported so that you can retrieve existing metadata for the first time. Imagine that you have some metadata components, which are a subset of a larger number of components, in a non-source-tracked org and you want to start using Salesforce DX and source format for their ongoing development. You could list the individual components to retrieve in a `package.xml` file, as metadata components using the `--metadata|-m` parameter or as source file paths using the `--sourcepath|-p` parameter. However, this could be a lengthy and complex process if there are a lot of components. Using an unmanaged package is a more convenient method for this purpose as many dependent metadata components are added automatically when adding components to the unmanaged package. The steps that you would follow are

1. Create a temporary unmanaged package in the non-source-tracked org.
2. Add all the unpackaged metadata components that need to be retrieved.

3. Retrieve the metadata components using the `--packagenames|-n` parameter.

4. Validate that all the required dependencies have been retrieved by pushing to a source-tracked org or deploying to a non-source-tracked org and performing some testing.

Thereafter, you can synchronize with orgs using unpackaged metadata, unlocked packages, or managed packages.

We have now covered how to retrieve metadata components from non-source-tracked orgs and store the metadata in a local Salesforce DX project in source format. The upcoming section will show how to deploy the metadata to non-source-tracked orgs.

Deploying Source Format Metadata to Non-source-Tracked Orgs

Metadata stored in a local Salesforce DX project in source format can be deployed to a source-tracked or non-source-tracked org using the `force:source:deploy` command; that said, it is primarily used to synchronize with non-source-tracked orgs for UAT testing, staging, and for deploying to production orgs. Unlike pushing source format metadata to source-tracked orgs using the `force:source:push` command, we need to tell the Salesforce CLI what source format metadata to deploy to a non-source-tracked org. This mirrors retrieving metadata from a non-source-tracked org and storing it in source format in the local Salesforce DX project using the `force:source:retrieve` command. We can tell the CLI what metadata components to deploy using one of the following methods:

- A comma-separated list of metadata types and/or component names
- A comma-separated list of source file paths to deploy
- A path to a `package.xml` manifest file that includes the metadata components to deploy

---

Note Unlike retrieving source format metadata from a non-source-tracked org, deploying using a package name is not supported. Please refer to the end of the previous section for the rationale.

As with the section "Pushing Source Format Metadata to Source-Tracked Orgs," we need to create some local source format metadata to deploy to the non-source-tracked org. We will follow the same steps to create an Apex class, with the steps repeated here for convenience.

1. Launch Visual Studio Code if it's not already launched.
2. Open this chapter's `SalesforceDXMD` project.
3. Open the integrated terminal.
4. Execute the command:

   ```
   sfdx force:apex:trigger:create \
     -d ./force-app/main/default/triggers \
     -n ExampleTrigger \
     -s Example_Object__c
   ```

5. Open the newly created trigger handler file called `ExampleTrigger.trigger`, which can be found by expanding the `force-app/main/default/triggers` directory in the Visual Studio Code Explorer.
6. Replace the source code with the trigger handler code in the following listing.
7. Save the file.

Listing 8-13. Example trigger handler source code

```
trigger ExampleTrigger on Example_Object__c (before insert) {
    for (Example_Object__c exampleObject : Trigger.New) {
        exampleObject.Example_Field__c = 'Hello ' + UserInfo.
        getName() + '!';
    }
}
```

As the `force:source:deploy` command can be used to deploy metadata components to a production org, we have the option to run Apex tests to achieve the 75% coverage requirement. Of course, these tests can also be run when deploying to other source-tracked and non-source-tracked orgs as well. To enable us to experiment with running Apex tests, let's create one for our `ExampleTrigger` trigger handler.

1. Assuming that the `SalesforceDXMD` project is still open in Visual Studio Code, execute the following command in the integrated terminal to create the Apex test class:

   ```
   sfdx force:apex:class:create \
     -d ./force-app/main/default/classes \
     -n TestExampleTrigger
   ```

2. Open the newly created Apex class file called `TestExampleTrigger.cls`, which can be found by expanding the `force-app/main/default/classes` directory in the Visual Studio Code Explorer.

3. Replace the source code with the trigger handler unit test code in the following listing.

4. Save the file.

Listing 8-14. Example trigger handler unit test source code

```
@isTest
private class TestExampleTrigger {
  @isTest static void TestExampleTriggerPositiveTest1() {

    // Create a test user.
    String username =
      'testUser' +
      DateTime.now().getTime() +
      '@example.com';
    String firstName = 'Inaya';
    String lastName = 'Hough';
    Profile p =
      [SELECT Id
```

```
      FROM Profile
      WHERE Name='Standard User'
      LIMIT 1];
    User testUser = new User (
      Alias = 'tstusr',
      Email = username,
      EmailEncodingKey = 'UTF-8',
      FirstName = firstName,
      LanguageLocaleKey = 'en_US',
      LastName = lastName,
      LocaleSidKey = 'en_GB',
      ProfileId = p.Id,
      TimeZoneSidKey = 'Europe/London',
      UserName = username);

    // Create an ExampleObject__c sObject.
    Example_Object__c newExampleObject = new Example_Object__c();

    // Insert the Example_Object__c record whilst running as the test user.
    System.runAs(testUser) {
      Test.startTest();
      insert newExampleObject;
      Test.stopTest();
    }

    // Query the inserted Example_Object__c record.
    Example_Object__c insertedExampleObject =
      [SELECT Example_Field__c
       FROM Example_Object__c
       WHERE Id = :newExampleObject.Id LIMIT 1];

    // Verify that the Example_Field__c was updated by the trigger handler.
    System.assertEquals(
      'Hello ' + firstName + ' ' + lastName + '!',
      insertedExampleObject.Example_Field__c);
  }
}
```

The preceding unit test performs the following tasks:

- Defines a test user using the Standard User profile. Note that this user and any other records created during a unit test are not persisted in the org as everything is rolled back at the end of the test.
- Creates an Example_Object__c record in memory.
- Runs the test as the test user, which simply inserts the Example_Object_c record. This will cause our trigger handler to run.
- Queries the inserted Example_Object__c record so that we can access the updated Example_Field__c value.
- Validates that the trigger handler has correctly updated the Example_Field__c field.

To deploy the trigger handler and unit test using a package.xml file, update the one created in the previous section as follows.

Listing 8-15. Updated package.xml manifest to deploy a trigger handler and unit test metadata components

```
<?xml version="1.0" encoding="UTF-8" standalone="yes"?>
<Package xmlns="http://soap.sforce.com/2006/04/metadata">
    <types>
        <members>TestExampleTrigger</members>
        <name>ApexClass</name>
    </types>
    <types>
        <members>ExampleTrigger</members>
        <name>ApexTrigger</name>
    </types>
    <types>
        <members>Example_Object__c.Example_Field__c</members>
        <name>CustomField</name>
    </types>
```

```
    <types>
        <members>Example_Object__c-Example Object Layout</members>
        <name>Layout</name>
    </types>
    <types>
        <members>Example_Object__c</members>
        <name>CustomObject</name>
    </types>
    <version>55.0</version>
</Package>
```

That completes the setup needed to illustrate the various methods for deploying source format metadata to a non-source-tracked org. To perform a deployment, use the following Salesforce CLI command:

```
$ sfdx force:source:deploy
```

The parameters that can be used for this command are as follows:

- `--checkonly|-c`: Validates a deployment without saving the metadata components in the target org. The Apex tests that run depend on the `--testlevel|-l` parameter value. When this parameter is used, an ID is returned that can be used with the `--validateddeployrequestid|-q` parameter to perform a Quick Deploy if the `--checkonly|-c` deployment was successful. [Optional] [Default: `false`]
- `--forceoverwrite|-f`: If the CLI detects conflicts between the metadata components in the local Salesforce DX project and the source-tracked or non-source-tracked org, it displays those conflicts. Passing this parameter suppresses the display of conflicts and forces the deployed metadata components to overwrite the target org components. [Optional]
- `--ignorewarnings|-g`: If a warning occurs during the deployment of any metadata component, the warning is ignored if this parameter is set to `true,` and the deployment will continue; otherwise, the warning is treated like an error, and whether the deployment continues or rolls back depends on the `--ignoreerrors|-o` parameter value. [Optional] [Default: `false`]

- `--testlevel|-l`: Specifies which Apex tests are executed during the deployment. [Optional]

  Allowed values are as follows:

  - `NoTestRun`: No Apex tests are executed during a deployment. [Default for (a) nonproduction orgs such as Developer Edition orgs and sandboxes and (b) for production orgs when the deployment does not include any Apex classes or triggers.]
  - `RunSpecifiedTests`: Execute the Apex tests listed in the `--runtests|-r` parameter. The tests must cover every Apex class and trigger that is being deployed, and each Apex class and trigger must achieve at least 75% coverage for the deployment to succeed. Note that this is different to `RunLocalTests` and `RunAllTestsInOrg` values where at least 75% coverage is required as an average across the org.
  - `RunLocalTests`: Execute all the Apex tests in the target org, including those in the deployment, except those in installed managed and unlocked packages. [Default for production orgs when a deployment includes Apex classes and/or triggers.]
  - `RunAllTestsInOrg`: Execute all the Apex tests in the target org, including those in the deployment and installed managed and unlocked packages.

- `--metadata|-m`: A comma-separated list of metadata types and/or metadata components to deploy. For example, `-m CustomObject` deploys all metadata components of the `CustomObject` metadata type, and `-m CustomObject:Example_Object__c` deploys the `Example_object__c` custom object. [Optional]
- `--ignoreerrors|-o`: Determines whether the deployment should continue if any errors occur or roll back. To continue with the deployment when errors occur, set to `true`. Set to `false` to roll back on error. This parameter must be set to `false` when deploying to a production org. [Optional] [Default: `false`]

- `--sourcepath|-p`: A comma-separated list of paths to directories or source files to deploy. For example, to deploy all custom objects, use `-p ./force-app/main/default/objects`, and to deploy the `Example_Object__c` custom object, use `-p ./ force-app/main/default/objects/Example_Object__c/Example_Object__c.object-meta.xml`. [Optional]
- `--validateddeployrequestid|-q`: Perform a quick deploy using the ID returned by a successful check-only deployment using the `--checkonly|-c` parameter. [Optional]
- `--runtests|-r`: If the `--testlevel|-l` parameter is set to `RunSpecifiedTests`, this parameter provides a comma-separated list of Apex test class names to execute during the deployment. The tests must achieve at least 75% coverage for each Apex class and trigger in the deployment. [Optional]
- `--tracksource|-t`: Updates the tracking information that is used by the CLI to track differences between the metadata components in a source-tracked org and a local Salesforce DX project. Useful if the `force:source:deploy` command is being used to deploy a subset of metadata components to the source-tracked org rather than using `force:source:push`, which pushes all new and changed metadata components. Note, however, unless the `--predestructivechanges` or `--postdestructivechanges` parameters are used to explicitly state the components to be deleted, metadata components that have been deleted in the local Salesforce DX project will not be deleted from the target org. [Optional]
- `--targetusername|-u`: The username or alias of the source-tracked or non-source-tracked org to deploy the metadata components to. [Optional]
- `--wait|-w`: The number of minutes that the command will wait for completion. Control will be returned to the terminal application when the command completes or when the wait period expires, whichever is the sooner. A value of `0` causes control to return

immediately and for the command to continue to execute asynchronously. Use the `force:source:deploy:report` command to check an asynchronous command status. [Optional] [Default: 33]

- `--manifest|-x`: The path to a `package.xml` manifest file that lists the metadata components to deploy, for example, `-x ./package.xml`. This parameter cannot be used in conjunction with the `--metadata|-m` or the `--sourcepath|-p` parameters. [Optional]
- `--coverageformatters`: A comma-separated list of formats for reporting code coverage results as an alternative to using the command output when the `--verbose` parameter is provided. By default, when the command completes, the CLI creates a directory in the local Salesforce DX project's root directory with the same name as the deployment ID that is returned by the `force:source:deploy` command. To specify a custom directory name, use the `--resultsdir` parameter. Within the directory, a `coverage` subdirectory is also created. The CLI then writes the code coverage results to the `coverage` directory in each of the formats provided to this parameter as arguments. [Optional]

  Allowed values are

  - `clover`
  - `cobertura`
  - `html-spa`
  - `html`
  - `json`
  - `json-summary`
  - `lcovonly`
  - `none`
  - `teamcity`
  - `text`
  - `text-summary`

- `--junit`: Provides an alternative to using the command output when the `--verbose` parameter is provided for reporting Apex test results. Like the `--coverageformatters` parameter, when the command completes the CLI creates a directory in the local Salesforce DX project's root directory with the same name as the deployment ID that is returned by the `force:source:deploy` command. Also, like the `--coverageformatters` parameter, this directory name can be overridden using the `--resultsdir` parameter. If both the `--coverageformatters` and the `--junit` parameters are used, they share the same directory. Within the directory, a `junit` subdirectory is also created. The CLI then writes Apex test results in JUnit format to the `junit` directory. [Optional]

- `--postdestructivechanges`: Uses a manifest file similar to a `package.xml` file to indicate which metadata components to delete in the target org after the deployment of the metadata components by the `force:source:deploy` command. [Optional]

- `--predestructivechanges`: Uses a manifest file similar to a `package.xml` file to indicate which metadata components to delete in the target org before the deployment of the metadata components by the `force:source:deploy` command. [Optional]

- `--purgeondelete`: By default, when the `--postdestructivechanges` or the `--predestructivechanges` parameter is used, deleted components in the target org are moved to the Recycle Bin. By using this parameter, the components are immediately eligible for deletion instead. [Optional]

- `--resultsdir`: By default, when the `--coverageformatters` and/or the `--junit` parameters are used, the CLI creates a directory in the local Salesforce DX project's root directory with the same name as the deployment ID that is returned by the `force:source:deploy` command. Use this parameter to provide a custom directory name. [Optional] [Default: The deployment ID that is returned by the `force:source:deploy` command.]

- `--soapdeploy`: By default, the CLI uses the REST API when executing the `force:source:deploy` command. Use this parameter to use the SOAP API rather than the REST API. [Optional]
- `--apiversion, --json, --loglevel, --verbose`: Please refer to the discussion on global parameters in the section "Command-Line Parameters and Arguments" in Chapter 4, "Salesforce CLI."

In the preceding parameter descriptions, we talk about default test execution behavior, which is worth summarizing.

Default Test Execution

If no `--testlevel|-l` parameter is specified, the default test execution behavior depends on whether the deployment is to a production or nonproduction org and whether the deployment includes any Apex classes or triggers. The following table summarizes the behaviors.

Table 8-2. *Default test execution behavior*

Deployment	Nonproduction Org	Production Org
Deployment includes Apex classes or triggers	No tests are run(equivalent to `NoTestRun`)	All Apex tests in the org, including those in the deployment, are run except those in installed managed and unlocked packages (equivalent to `RunLocalTests`)
Deployment does not include any Apex classes or triggers	No tests are run(equivalent to `NoTestRun`)	No tests are run(equivalent to `NoTestRun`)

Deploying metadata components can be executed synchronously, where the command waits until execution is completed before returning control back to the terminal application, or asynchronously, where control is returned immediately. We'll cover synchronous operation first in the next section.

Synchronous Deployment

To execute a deployment synchronously, the `--wait | -w` must have a value greater than zero. The parameter states the number of minutes that the `force:source:deploy` command will wait for completion before returning control to the terminal application, with a default of 33 minutes if the parameter is not provided.

These examples all synchronously deploy the metadata components that we created earlier to the non-source-tracked org with the default username, which should be `MyDEOrg` if you have been following along. The command also causes the `TestExampleTrigger` Apex test that is included in the deployment to be run.

```
$ sfdx force:source:deploy \
    --testlevel RunSpecifiedTests \
    --metadata " \
      ApexClass:TestExampleTrigger, \
      ApexTrigger:ExampleTrigger, \
      CustomObject:Example_Object__c, \
      Layout:↩
        Example_Object__c-Example Object Layout"\
    --runtests TestExampleTrigger
```

```
$ sfdx force:source:deploy \
    --testlevel RunSpecifiedTests \
    --sourcepath " \
      ./force-app/main/default/classes/↩
        TestExampleTrigger.cls-meta.xml, \
      ./force-app/main/default/triggers/↩
        ExampleTrigger.trigger-meta.xml, \
      ./force-app/main/default/objects/↩
        Example_Object__c/Example_Object__c.↩
        object-meta.xml, \
      ./force-app/main/default/objects/↩
        Example_Object__c/fields/Example_Field__c.↩
        field-meta.xml, \
      ./force-app/main/default/layouts/↩
```

```
        Example_Object__c-Example Object Layout.↩
        layout-meta.xml" \
    --runtests TestExampleTrigger

$ sfdx force:source:deploy \
    --testlevel RunSpecifiedTests \
    --runtests TestExampleTrigger \
    --manifest ./manifest/package.xml
```

The commands will complete, return control to the integrated terminal, and list the metadata components that have been successfully deployed.

Listing 8-16. Metadata components deployed to a non-source-tracked org

```
*** Deploying with SOAP API v55.0 ***
Deploy ID: 0Af4K00000KMTqLSAX
DEPLOY PROGRESS |
████████████████████████████████████████ | 6/6 Components

=== Deployed Source

FULL NAME                      TYPE        PROJECT PATH
─────────────────────────────  ──────────  ───────────────────

TestExampleTrigger             ApexClass   force-app/main/default/↩
  classes/TestExampleTrigger.cls

TestExampleTrigger             ApexClass   force-app/main/default/↩
  classes/TestExampleTrigger.cls-meta.xml

ExampleTrigger                 ApexTrigger force-app/main/default/↩
  triggers/ExampleTrigger.trigger

ExampleTrigger                 ApexTrigger force-app/main/default/↩
  triggers/ExampleTrigger.trigger-meta.xml
```

```
Example_Object__c.Example_Field__c      CustomField  force-app/main/default/↩
  objects/Example_Object__c/fields/Example_Field__c.field-meta.xml

Example_Object__c                       CustomObject force-app/main/default/↩
  objects/Example_Object__c/Example_Object__c.object-meta.xml

Example_Object__c-Example Object Layout Layout       force-app/main/default/↩
  layouts/Example_Object__c-Example Object Layout.layout-meta.xml

=== Test Results Summary

Passing: 1
Failing: 0
Total: 1
Time: 632
Deploy Succeeded.
```

To check the deployment status in the target org, use the `force:org:open` command to open the org and navigate to **Setup ➤ Environments ➤ Deploy ➤ Deployment Status**. This will list all failed and succeeded deployments.

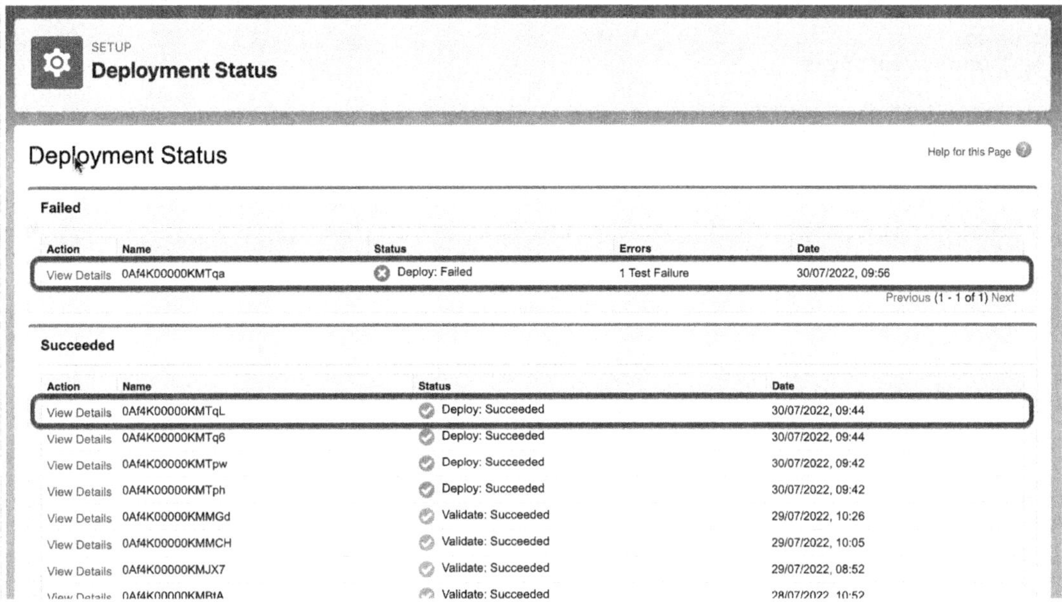

***Figure 8-6.** Failed and succeeded deployments*

Clicking the **View Details** link to the left of the deployment row will then display the deployment details.

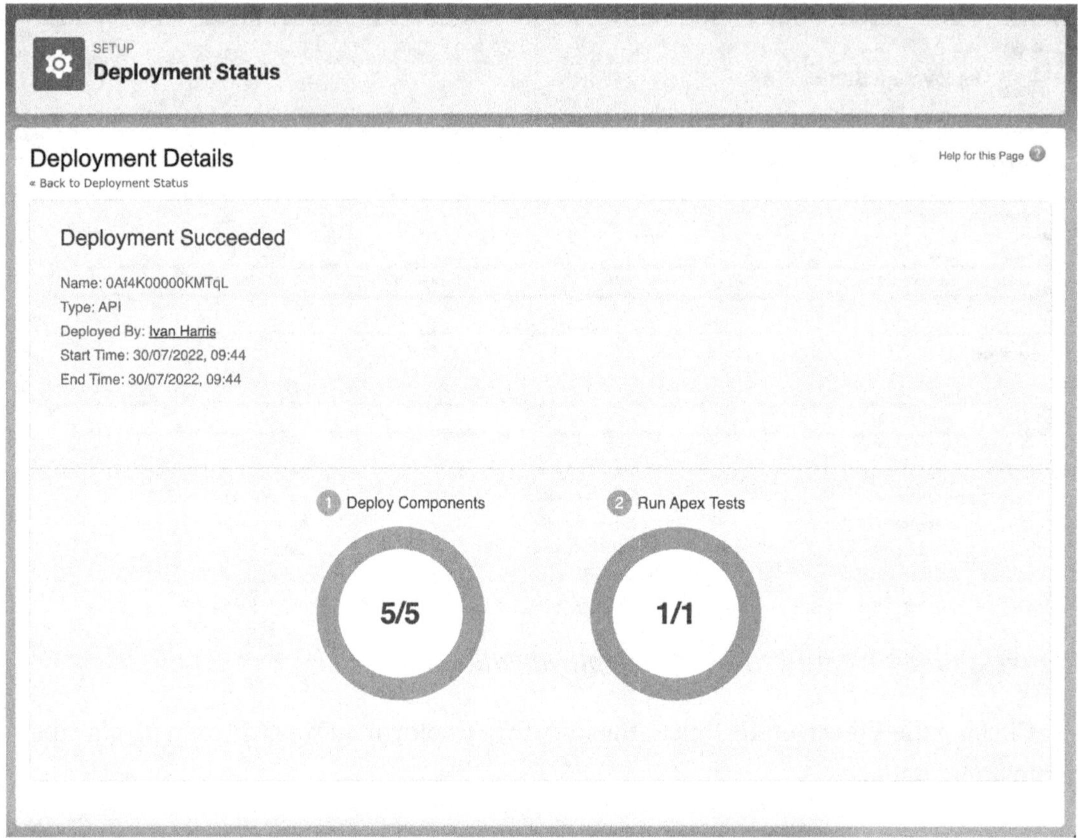

Figure 8-7. *Deployment details*

The details show that 5 out of 5 metadata components were successfully deployed and that 1 out of 1 Apex tests successfully executed.

We've explored synchronous deployments; in the next section, we will look at asynchronous deployments.

Asynchronous Deployment

Executing an asynchronous deployment returns control to the terminal application immediately after running the `force:source:deploy` command, allowing you to continue working while the command is in progress. To perform an asynchronous deployment, simply set the `--wait`|`-w` parameter to `0` (zero).

In the previous section, "Synchronous Deployment," we used three different commands to deploy some metadata stored in a local Salesforce DX project in source format to a non-source-tracked org. To see an asynchronous deployment in action, choose one of the commands and add the --wait|-w parameter. For example, in the following example we're using a manifest to perform the deployment:

```
$ sfdx force:source:deploy \
    --testlevel RunSpecifiedTests \
    --runtests TestExampleTrigger \
    --wait 0 \
    --manifest ./manifest/package.xml
```

The command will return immediately with a job ID that can be used to report on the status of the deployment or to cancel it. The output also lists the report and cancel commands that can be cut and pasted into the integrated terminal.

Listing 8-17. Output from an asynchronous deployment command

```
*** Deploying with SOAP API v55.0 ***
Deploy ID: 0Af4K00000KMTwYSAX
Deploy has been queued.

Run sfdx force:source:deploy:cancel -i 0Af4K00000KMTwYSAX -u
ihdxde@example.com to cancel the deploy.
Run sfdx force:source:deploy:report -i 0Af4K00000KMTwYSAX -u
ihdxde@example.com to get the latest status.
```

To report on the status of a deployment, use the following command and parameters:

```
$ sfdx force:source:deploy:report
```

The parameters that can be used for this command are as follows:

- --jobid|-i: The ID of the deployment to report on. The ID is returned when executing the force:source:deploy command. [Optional] [Default: The ID of the most recent deployment.]
- --targetusername|-u: The username or alias of the source-tracked or non-source-tracked org that is the target of the deployment to report on. [Optional]

- `--wait|-w`: The number of minutes that the command will wait for completion. Control will be returned to the terminal application when the command completes or when the wait period expires, whichever is the sooner. [Optional] [Default: 33]
- `--coverageformatters`: A comma-separated list of formats for reporting code coverage results as an alternative to using the command output when the `--verbose` parameter is provided. By default, when the command completes, the CLI creates a directory in the local Salesforce DX project's root directory with the same name as the deployment ID that is returned by the `force:source:deploy:report` command. To specify a custom directory name, use the `--resultsdir` parameter. Within the directory, a `coverage` subdirectory is also created. The CLI then writes the code coverage results to the `coverage` directory in each of the formats provided to this parameter as arguments. [Optional]

  Allowed values are

  - `clover`
  - `cobertura`
  - `html-spa`
  - `html`
  - `json`
  - `json-summary`
  - `lcovonly`
  - `none`
  - `teamcity`
  - `text`
  - `text-summary`
- `--junit`: Provides an alternative to using the command output when the `--verbose` parameter is provided for reporting Apex test results. Like the `--coverageformatters` parameter, when the command

completes the CLI creates a directory in the local Salesforce DX project's root directory with the same name as the deployment ID that is returned by the `force:source:deploy:report` command. Also, like the `--coverageformatters` parameter, this directory name can be overridden using the `--resultsdir` parameter. If both the `--coverageformatters` and the `--junit` parameters are used, they share the same directory. Within the directory, a `junit` subdirectory is also created. The CLI then writes Apex test results in JUnit format to the `junit` directory. [Optional]

- `--resultsdir`: By default, when the `--coverageformatters` and/or the `--junit` parameters are used, the CLI creates a directory in the local Salesforce DX project's root directory with the same name as the deployment ID that is returned by the `force:source:deploy:report` command. Use this parameter to provide a custom directory name. [Optional] [Default: The deployment ID that is returned by the `force:source:deploy:report` command.]
- `--apiversion, --json, --loglevel, --verbose`: Please refer to the discussion on global parameters in the section "Command-Line Parameters and Arguments" in Chapter 4, "Salesforce CLI."

Note Unlike the `force:source:deploy` command, you cannot pass a value of `0` for the `--wait` | `-w` parameter; the minimum value is `1` (minute). This means that it's not possible to use the `force:source:deploy:report` command to perform a quick check of the deployment status as you will always have to wait for at least a minute.

As an example, use the following command to wait for up to 33 minutes to report on the status of the deployment that we initiated asynchronously earlier:

```
$ sfdx force:source:deploy:report
```

When the command returns, the output will look like the following.

Listing 8-18. Status report for a completed asynchronous deployment

```
Deploy ID: 0Af4K00000KMTwYSAX
Status: Succeeded
Deployed: 5/5 Errors: 0
Tests Complete: 1/1 Errors: 0
```

When would you use the `--jobid|-i` parameter when one is not required when reporting on the most recent deployment? As the `force:source:deploy` command can be executed asynchronously by passing it a value of `0` for the `--wait|-w` parameter, you might want to kick off multiple asynchronous deployments, perhaps to different orgs, and each deployment will have its own job ID that you can then use to report on each deployment's status.

On some occasions, you might want to cancel a long-running asynchronous deployment, which can be done by using the following command:

```
$ sfdx force:source:deploy:cancel
```

The parameters that can be used for this command are as follows:

- `--jobid|-i`: The ID of the deployment to cancel. The ID is returned when executing the `force:source:deploy` command. [Optional] [Default: The ID of the most recent deployment.]
- `--targetusername|-u`: The username or alias of the source-tracked or non-source-tracked org that is the target of the deployment to be canceled. [Optional]
- `--wait|-w`: The number of minutes that the command will wait for completion. Control will be returned to the terminal application when the command completes or when the wait period expires, whichever is the sooner. The value must be greater than or equal to `1`. [Optional] [Default: `33`]
- `--apiversion, --json, --loglevel`: Please refer to the discussion on global parameters in the section "Command-Line Parameters and Arguments" in Chapter 4, "Salesforce CLI."

To cancel the asynchronous deployment that we initiated earlier and wait up to 33 minutes for the command to complete, you just need to execute the following:

```
$ sfdx force:source:deploy:cancel
```

When multiple asynchronous deployments are in progress, use the `--jobid|-i` parameter to specify which asynchronous job to cancel.

We've now explored how to use the `force:source` commands to work with source format metadata. We saw earlier, in the section "Pulling Source Format Metadata from Source-Tracked Orgs," that occasionally we encounter metadata that we do not want to synchronize between local Salesforce DX projects and target orgs. The next section will explain how to instruct the `force:source` commands to exclude metadata from synchronizing and converting.

Excluding Source Format Files from Syncing and Converting

As you develop customizations and applications using Salesforce DX, there will be times when you will want to prevent the synchronization of some source format files in your local Salesforce DX project with metadata components in an org and vice versa. Furthermore, if you are still working with legacy Metadata API format files, you might want to exclude source format files in your local Salesforce DX project when converting them from source format to Metadata API format.

When a Salesforce DX project is created, a file called `.forceignore` is added to the project's root directory. The file instructs the Salesforce CLI to ignore certain source format files and metadata components when executing synchronization and conversion commands. It has the following default contents.

Listing 8-19. Example .forceignore file contents

```
# List files or directories below to ignore them when running ↩
force:source:push, force:source:pull, and force:source:status
# More information: https://developer.salesforce.com/docs/atlas.en-↩
us.sfdx_dev.meta/sfdx_dev/sfdx_dev_exclude_source.htm
#

package.xml

# LWC configuration files
```

```
**/jsconfig.json
**/.eslintrc.json

# LWC Jest
**/__tests__/**
```

The Salesforce CLI skips over blank lines and comment lines, which begin with #. The remaining lines are patterns that match the source format files in your local Salesforce DX project and metadata components in an org that should be ignored. The syntax for ignoring source format files and metadata components are different. For example, if you create a new Apex class in your local Salesforce DX project and you want to prevent the source format files from being synchronized with an org, the `.forceignore` file entry would be as follows.

Listing 8-20. Excluding source format files from syncing and converting

```
force-app/main/default/classes/ExampleClass.cls
force-app/main/default/classes/ExampleClass.cls-meta.xml
```

However, if you create the Apex class in an org and you want to exclude the metadata component from being synchronized with your local Salesforce DX project, the file entry would be like the following.

Listing 8-21. Excluding a metadata component from syncing

```
ExampleClass.cls
```

If you want to prevent synchronization in both directions, you must include both preceding lines. The two syntaxes will be explained in more detail in a moment.

The Salesforce CLI commands that use the `.forceignore` file are as follows:

- **`force:source:convert`**: Converts source format files to Metadata API format files in your local Salesforce DX project.
- **`force:source:push`**: Synchronizes source format file changes in your local Salesforce DX project with the metadata components in a source-tracked org.
- **`force:source:pull`**: Synchronizes metadata component changes in a source-tracked org with the source format files in your local Salesforce DX project.

- **`force:source:deploy`**: Synchronizes source format files in your local Salesforce DX project with the metadata components in a source-tracked or a non-source-tracked org.
- **`force:source:retrieve`**: Synchronizes metadata components in a source-tracked or non-source-tracked org with the source format files in your local Salesforce DX project.
- **`force:source:status`**: Lists the differences between the source format files in your local Salesforce DX project and the metadata components in a source-tracked org.

The CLI commands `force:source:push`, `force:source:deploy`, `force:source:status`, and `force:source:convert` rely on the source format syntax, while the commands `force:source:pull`, `force:source:retrieve`, and `force:source:status` rely on the metadata component syntax.

We'll now dive deeper into the `.forceignore` entry syntax for ignoring source format files.

Ignoring Source Format Files

A `.forceignore` file entry that instructs the `force:source` commands to ignore source format files in a local Salesforce DX when syncing with an org, or when converting source format files to Metadata API format, uses a syntax that is very similar to the format of a `.gitignore` file, which is described in full here:

- `https://git-scm.com/docs/gitignore`

Note A `.gitignore` file is used to instruct the Git version control system to ignore certain untracked files.

Rather than explicitly listing each source format file to ignore, the `.forceignore` file uses pattern matching to ignore multiple files. The Salesforce documentation is a bit light when it comes to describing all of the available pattern formats, so please refer to the .gitignore documentation if you need to learn more, which includes the following examples:

- abc/**: Matches all files inside the directory abc.
- hello.*: Matches any file or directory that begins with hello.
- foo/: Matches a directory and all paths underneath it. It will not match files called foo.

Note that all directory and file paths are relative to the directory where the .forceignore is located.

Referring back to the .forceignore file that is added when a Salesforce DX project is created, we can now decipher the patterns as follows:

- package.xml: Exclude this file wherever it might be in the directory hierarchy.
- **/jsconfig.json and **/.eslintrc.json: Exclude these files wherever they might be in the directory hierarchy.
- **/__tests__/**: Match __tests__ in any directory, then exclude the directory and all the files in the directory.

Using the earlier example from Listing 8-20, the two source format files associated with the ExampleClass Apex class can now be excluded using a single line in the .forceignore file rather than two as follows.

Listing 8-22. Excluding multiple source format files from syncing and converting

```
force-app/main/default/classes/ExampleClass.*
```

To experiment with the .forceignore file syntax before performing any actual synchronizations or conversions, use the force:source:status CLI command to confirm that files have been successfully excluded as the command uses the .forceignore file.

We'll now see how to prevent metadata components in an org from synchronizing with source format files in a local Salesforce DX.

Ignoring Metadata Components

To prevent metadata components in a source-tracked or non-source-tracked org from synchronizing with your local Salesforce DX project, add an entry to the `.forceignore` file with the syntax `<api name>.<metadata type>`. For example, Listing 8-21 showed that the entry would be `ExampleClass.cls` for the Apex class that we created earlier, which had an `<api name>` of `ExampleClass`. The API name is easy enough, as it is provided when creating the Apex class using an org's Setup area or when using a CLI command. The `<metadata type>` is less intuitive, so let's look at how to determine what to use.

If you run the Salesforce CLI command `force:source:status` after creating the `ExampleClass` Apex class in a source-tracked org, you get the following output, which shows a metadata type of `ApexClass`. You might assume that this is what you should use for the `<metadata type>`, but hold that thought!

Listing 8-23. force:source:status output showing a new Apex class' metadata

```
Source Status
 STATE          FULL NAME          TYPE              PROJECT PATH
 ─────────────  ─────────────────  ────────────────  ────────────────
 Remote Add     ExampleClass       ApexClass
```

Rather confusingly, the `.forceignore` syntax doesn't need the metadata type, it actually needs the metadata type's file suffix. To find that, we need to look to the Metadata API Developer Guide, which can be found here:

- `https://developer.salesforce.com/docs/atlas.en-us.api_meta.meta/api_meta/meta_intro.htm`

If you look up the `ApexClass` metadata type in the Metadata API Developer Guide, either by using search or the navigation tree, you will find the following useful information.

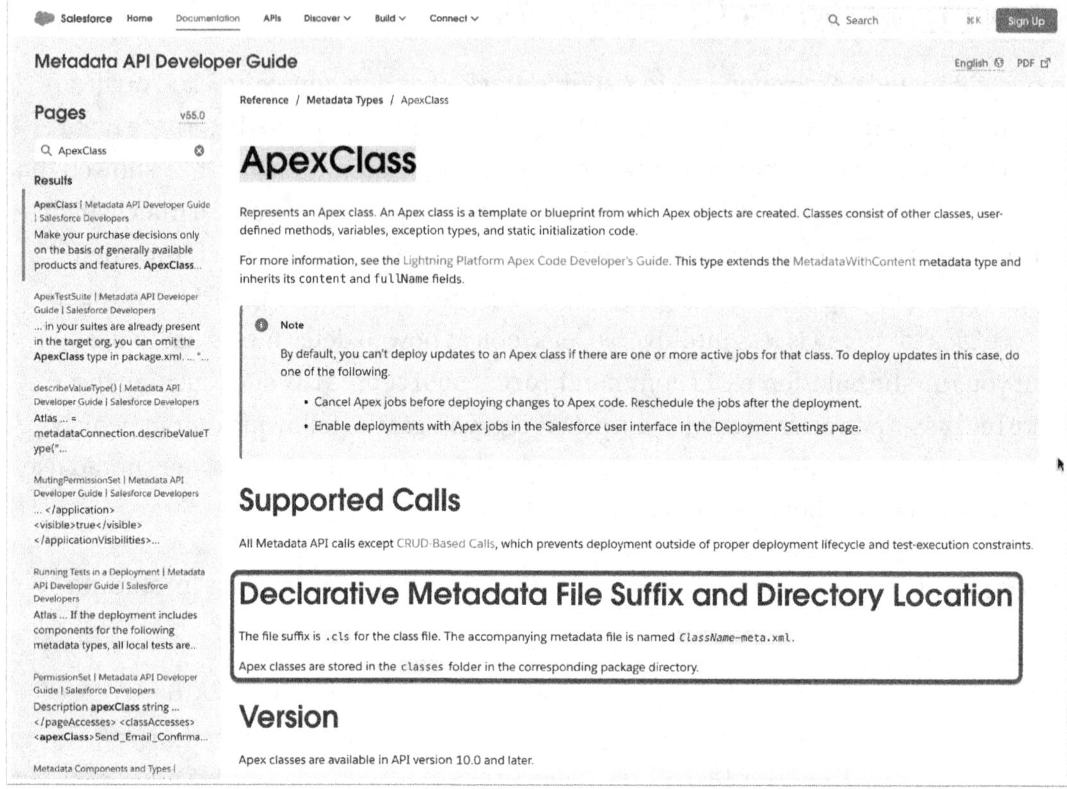

Figure 8-8. *Metadata type file suffix and directory location*

It shows that the file suffix for the `ApexClass` metadata type is `.cls` and that the directory location is the `classes` directory in your local Salesforce DX project's directory hierarchy. This tells us two things: (1) to use `.cls` as the `<metadata type>` in the `.forceignore` file to prevent metadata components of the `ApexClass` metadata type from synchronizing, and (2) after syncing, the source format file will be placed in the `./force-app/main/default/classes` project directory in a source file with a `.cls` extension and an accompanying metadata file with the `.cls-meta.xml` extension.

Note `./force-app` is the default package directory specified in the `sfdx-project.json` project configuration file, and `/main/default/classes` conforms with the standard Salesforce DX source format directory hierarchy.

As with source format file exclusions, explore the `.forceignore` file syntax for excluding metadata components from syncing by experimenting with the `force.source.status` command until you successfully exclude your metadata components before performing a synchronization. This will avoid inadvertently syncing metadata components that you would prefer not to.

So far, this chapter has focused on working with source format metadata as it's the recommended file format; however, there are good reasons for using Metadata API format files, which will be covered in the next section.

Synchronizing Metadata API Format Metadata with Source-Tracked and Non-source-Tracked Orgs

Although best practice is to store metadata components in your local Salesforce DX project in source format, to take advantage of the more granular file structure and tracked changes, there may be occasions when development teams will prefer to use the Metadata API format, such as the following:

- Although the team has adopted Salesforce DX, they have a large metadata estate and a trusted version control system, governance processes, and CI/CD pipelines that they are not ready to disturb yet.
- Related to the previous point, the team may be partway through a migration from Metadata API format to source format and need to continue working with Metadata API format for some customizations or applications.
- The team works with third parties, and the team is not ready to incur the direct and indirect cost of asking them to migrate yet.

In this section, we will explore the commands in the `force:mdapi` topic, which are used to synchronize metadata that is stored in Metadata API format with source-tracked and non-source-tracked orgs. When the Metadata API format is used, changes are not tracked when synchronizing whether the org is source-tracked or non-source-tracked orgs. Any metadata that is deployed or retrieved will overwrite the metadata in the org and the files in the local Salesforce DX project, respectively, which is the same behavior we experienced when using the `force:source:deploy` and `force:source:retrieve` commands. The commands that we will encounter in this section are as follows:

- **`force:mdapi:retrieve`**: Retrieve metadata from a source-tracked or non-source-tracked org and store it in Metadata API format in a local Salesforce DX project.
- **`force:mdapi:retrieve:report`**: Report on the status of a `force:mdapi:retrieve` command that is being executed asynchronously.
- **`force:mdapi:deploy`**: Deploy a local Salesforce DX project's Metadata API format metadata to a source-tracked or non-source-tracked org.
- **`force:mdapi:deploy:report`**: Report on the status of a `force:mdapi:deploy` command that is being executed asynchronously.
- **`force:mdapi:deploy:cancel`**: Cancel a `force:mdapi:deploy` command that is being executed asynchronously.

We'll start by retrieving metadata and storing it in Metadata API format in a local Salesforce DX project.

Retrieving Metadata API Format Metadata from Source-Tracked and Non-source-Tracked Orgs

We use the `force:mdapi:retrieve` command to retrieve metadata from source-tracked and non-source-tracked orgs and store it in Metadata API format files in a local Salesforce DX project. As the command does not support tracked changes, we need to tell the command what metadata to retrieve, and any retrieved metadata will overwrite the local Metadata API format files, that is, merging changes is not supported.

There are three methods that can be used to tell the Salesforce CLI which metadata components to retrieve:

- The path to a root directory of a source format metadata directory hierarchy that includes the metadata components in source format that are to be retrieved in Metadata API format.

- A path to a `package.xml` manifest file that includes the unpackaged metadata components to retrieve.
- A comma-separated list of managed or unmanaged packages that contain the packaged metadata components to retrieve.

Note When working directly with the Metadata API, it's possible to retrieve a mix of unpackaged and packaged metadata components in a single call. Although the `force:mdapi:retrieve` command uses the Metadata API, no mixed methods are allowed, so only one of the preceding methods can be used at a time.

We'll explore each of these methods in turn; however, we will first continue our practice of creating some metadata in an org to retrieve. We signed up for a Developer Edition org in the section "Retrieving Source Format Metadata from Non-source-Tracked Orgs" where we created some metadata components. We're going to create a different set of components in this section to illustrate retrieving multiple packages, so either delete the components from the existing org or sign up for a fresh one. The components that need deleting, in this order, if you wish to reuse your Developer Edition org are as follows:

- **Apex Trigger**: `ExampleTrigger`
- **Apex Class**: `TestExampleTrigger`
- **Custom Object**: `Example_Object__c`
- **Unmanaged Package**: `Example Package`

If you would prefer to start with a fresh Developer Edition org, log out of the existing Developer Edition org with the alias `MyDEOrg` using the `auth:logout` command. Then go to `https://developer.salesforce.com/signup` and sign up for another free Developer Edition org.

Note Although the `force:mdapi:retrieve` and `force:mdapi:deploy` commands can be used with source-tracked orgs, this section will illustrate how to retrieve and deploy unmanaged packages, which cannot be created in scratch orgs. We'll therefore be using a Developer Edition org, which is a non-source-tracked org.

If you have chosen to sign up for a fresh Developer Edition org, add the new org to the Salesforce CLI's list of authorized orgs by following these instructions:

1. If you have been following along with this chapter's examples so far, you will have existing metadata in your Salesforce DX project. If so, and to avoid any confusion, delete your `SalesforceDXMD` project or rename it.

2. Create a new `SalesforceDXMD` project and include a `package.xml` file by executing the command:

   ```
   sfdx force:project:create -x \
   -n SalesforceDXMD.
   ```

3. Launch Visual Studio Code if it's not already launched.

4. Open the `SalesforceDXMD` project.

5. Open the integrated terminal.

6. Use the `auth:web:login` command to authorize the new Developer Edition org, using the username and password that you made a note of when signing up. Set the alias to `MyDEOrg` and make it the org with the default username. Please refer to the section "Logging In to a Non-scratch Org" in Chapter 7, "Orgs," if you need a refresher on how to do this.

When retrieving metadata components in Metadata API format, a required parameter is the target directory where the Metadata API format files will be saved. Complete these steps to create the directory:

1. Launch Visual Studio Code if it's not already launched.

2. Open this chapter's `SalesforceDXMD` project.

3. In the Side Bar Explorer, create a directory called `mdapi` below the project's root directory.

The project structure should look like the following.

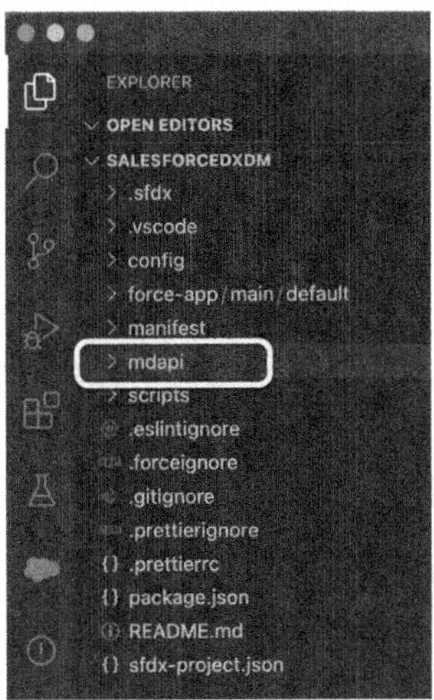

Figure 8-9. *Metadata API format target directory*

To create some metadata components that we can retrieve from the Developer Edition org, follow these steps:

1. Launch Visual Studio Code if it's not already launched.
2. Open this chapter's `SalesforceDXMD` project.
3. Open the newly created Developer Edition org with the alias `MyDEOrg`.
4. Navigate to **Setup ➤ Objects and Fields ➤ Object Manager**.
5. Click the **Create** action menu and then the **Custom Object** menu item.
6. Enter the following field values:
   a. **Label**: `Example Object 1`
   b. **Plural Label**: `Example Object 1s`
   c. **Starts with vowel sound**: `Checked`
   d. **Object Name**: `Example_Object_1`
7. Click the **Save** button, which will open the detail page for the new custom object.

8. Click **Fields & Relationships**.
9. Click **New**.
10. In Step 1 of the new custom field wizard, select **Text** as the data type and then click **Next**.
11. In Step 2, enter the following field values, then click **Next**:
    a. **Field Label**: `Example Field`
    b. **Length**: `50`
    c. **Field Name**: `Example_Field`
12. In Step 3, just click **Next**.
13. In Step 4, click **Save**.
14. Repeat steps 4–13, this time using the following field values for the custom object (the custom field name can be the same as in the previous steps):
    a. **Label**: `Example Object 2`
    b. **Plural Label**: `Example Object 2s`
    c. **Starts with vowel sound**: `Checked`
    d. **Object Name**: `Example_Object_2`

We will now create two unmanaged packages that include the new metadata components.

1. Navigate to **Setup ➤ Apps ➤ Packaging ➤ Package Manager**.
2. In the Packages section, click the **New** button.
3. In the Create a Package screen, enter the following field values, then click the **Save** button:
    a. **Package Name**: `Example Package 1`
4. The Example Package detail page should now be open. On the Components tab, click the **Add** button.
5. For the Component Type, select **Custom Object** from the picklist.

6. Enable the checkbox next to the `Example Object 1` custom object and click the **Add to Package** button.

7. Repeat steps 1-6 and create an unmanaged package called `Example Package 2` and add the `Example Object 2` custom object.

The final step that enables us to experience all the retrieval options is to update the `package.xml` file that was added when creating the project. The file can be found in the `manifest` subdirectory below the project's root directory. Replace the contents with the following.

Listing 8-24. package.xml manifest to retrieve metadata components

```
<?xml version="1.0" encoding="UTF-8"?>
<Package xmlns="http://soap.sforce.com/2006/04/metadata">
    <types>
        <members>Example_Object_1__c.Example_Field__c</members>
        <members>Example_Object_2__c.Example_Field__c</members>
        <name>CustomField</name>
    </types>
    <types>
        <members>Example_Object_1__c-Example Object 1 Layout</members>
        <members>Example_Object_2__c-Example Object 2 Layout</members>
        <name>Layout</name>
    </types>
    <types>
        <members>Example_Object_1__c</members>
        <members>Example_Object_2__c</members>
        <name>CustomObject</name>
    </types>
    <version>55.0</version>
</Package>
```

With our environment setup, let's look at the command that we will be using to retrieve metadata components in Metadata API format:

```
$ sfdx force:mdapi:retrieve
```

The parameters that can be used with this command are as follows:

- --apiversion|-a: Instructs the CLI to use a specific API version to retrieve metadata components. For example, if the API version specified in the package.xml file is older than the version supported by the CLI, setting this parameter will ensure that the CLI uses the package.xml API version. [Optional]
- --sourcedir|-d: When retrieving metadata components that are specified using the contents of a source format directory structure, this parameter is used to override the default package directory that's in the project configuration file (sfdx-project.json). [Optional]
- --unpackaged|-k: The path to a package.xml manifest file that lists the metadata components to retrieve, for example, -k ./package.xml. [Optional]
- --zipfilename|-n: By default, the CLI uses unpackaged.zip for the name of the zip file containing the retrieved metadata components. Override the default filename using this parameter, for example, -n mycomponents. [Optional]
- --packagenames|-p: A comma-separated list of packages to retrieve. The packages contain metadata components and their dependencies. For example, -p "Example Package 1" retrieves the package with the name Example Package 1. [Optional]
- --retrievetargetdir|-r: The path to a directory where the retrieved metadata components will be written. For example, -r ./mdapi. The metadata components are contained in a zip file called unpackaged.zip, unless overridden using the --zipfilename|-n parameter, regardless of which method is used to retrieve the metadata components. [Required]
- --singlepackage|-s: This parameter is used in conjunction with the --packagenames|-p parameter and is ignored if used with the other two methods for retrieving metadata components. The parameter indicates that the zip file containing the retrieved metadata components contains a single package and will adjust the

compressed directory structure accordingly. [Optional] [Default: If the parameter is omitted, the zip file directory structure is set up for multiple packages, even if it contains a single package.]

- `--targetusername | -u`: The username or alias of the source-tracked or non-source-tracked org to retrieve the metadata components from. [Optional]
- `--wait | -w`: The number of minutes that the command will wait for completion. Control will be returned to the terminal application when the command completes or when the wait period expires, whichever is the sooner. A value of `0` causes control to return immediately and for the command to continue to execute asynchronously. Use the `force:mdapi:retrieve:report` command to check an asynchronous command status. [Optional] [Default: `1440`]
- `--unzip | -z`: Automatically unzips the zip file containing the retrieved metadata components. [Optional]
- `--json, --loglevel, --verbose`: Please refer to the discussion on global parameters in the section "Command-Line Parameters and Arguments" in Chapter 4, "Salesforce CLI."

When we looked at deploying source format metadata earlier in the chapter, we saw that the `force:source:deploy` command can be executed synchronously or asynchronously. The same is true for the `force:mdapi:retrieve` and `force:mdapi:deploy` commands. We will first explore synchronous retrievals.

Synchronous Retrieval

To retrieve Metadata API format metadata components synchronously using the `force:mdapi:retrieve` command, either don't include the `--wait | -w` parameter or pass it a value greater than `0`. Passing `-1` causes the command to wait indefinitely. We'll soon see that passing a value of `0` causes the command to execute asynchronously.

The first of the three methods for retrieving metadata components and saving them locally in Metadata API format that we will look at is using a source format directory structure. This method makes use of the default package directory in the project configuration file (`sfdx-project.json`), which can be overridden by the `force:mdapi:retrieve` command's `--sourcedir|-d` parameter. The following listing highlights the default package directory, which in this case is `force-app`.

Listing 8-25. The project configuration file's default package directory

```
{
  "packageDirectories": [
    {
      "path": "force-app",
      "default": true
    }
  ],
  "name": "SalesforceDXMD",
  "namespace": "",
  "sfdcLoginUrl": "https://login.salesforce.com",
  "sourceApiVersion": "55.0"
}
```

Using a source format directory structure asks the CLI to retrieve the unpackaged components that are contained in the directory from a source-tracked or non-source-tracked org and save them in Metadata API format in another directory. You would then have source format and Metadata API format copies of the same metadata components. Question: Why would you want to do this? Answer: If a development team is still using Metadata API format as its primary format in a version control system, but developers want to use source format to take advantage of tracked changes, scratch orgs, and source format. After working in source format, the metadata components need to be converted back to Metadata API format before committing to a version control system. This command offers an alternative to the `force:source:convert` command that we will come across in the section "Converting Between Metadata API Format and Source Format" later in the chapter. Both commands enable you to convert source format metadata components to Metadata API format; whereas `force:source:convert` converts source format files in the local Salesforce DX project to Metadata API format and saves them in another Salesforce DX project directory, `force:mdapi:retrieve` uses the same source format metadata components in the Salesforce DX project to tell the command which components to retrieve from an org of your choice and save them in Metadata API format in another Salesforce DX project folder.

To use this command, we first need some metadata in source format. Follow these steps to create an Apex class in your `SalesforceDXMD` project:

1. Launch Visual Studio Code if it's not already launched.
2. Open this chapter's `SalesforceDXMD` project.
3. Right-click the project's `force-app/main/default/classes` directory.
4. Click the **SFDX: Create Apex Class** menu item.
5. Enter `ExampleClass` for the filename and hit **Enter**.
6. Hit **Enter** again to accept the default directory, which will create the file in the `force-app/main/default/classes` directory.
7. Right-click the `force-app/main/default/classes` directory again.
8. Click the **SFDX: Deploy Source to Org** menu item.

This will deploy the Apex class to the default org, which should be the `MyDEOrg` if you have been following along. We will now make a slight change to the Apex class to confirm that the class will be retrieved from the org rather than from the local source format directory structure. Perform these steps:

1. Open the default `MyDEOrg` using the `force:org:open` command.
2. Navigate to **Setup ➤ Custom Code ➤ Apex Classes**.
3. Click the **Edit** link next to the `ExampleClass` Apex class.
4. Add a comment to the class as highlighted in the following listing.
5. Click the **Save** button.

Listing 8-26. Updated Apex class

```
public with sharing class ExampleClass {
    public ExampleClass() {
        // My example class.
    }
}
```

To retrieve the metadata components contained in the source format directory, execute this command:

```
$ sfdx force:mdapi:retrieve \
    --retrievetargetdir ./mdapi
```

This is the most minimal form of the command. As we created the Apex class in the default package directory, we don't have to add the `--sourcedir|-d` to specify the source directory. The command will retrieve the Apex class from the default `MyDEOrg` org compressed in a zip file called `unpackaged.zip`, which will be written to the `./mdapi` directory along with a new `package.xml` file. To view the zip file contents:

1. Right-click the `unpackaged.zip` file in the VS Code Explorer.
2. Click the **Reveal in Finder** menu item (or the equivalent if you are not using macOS).
3. Double-click the zip file to uncompress it.

The Apex class in Metadata API format is present (1), and when it is opened, you can see that the comment we added in the org is present (2), which verifies that the component was retrieved from the org.

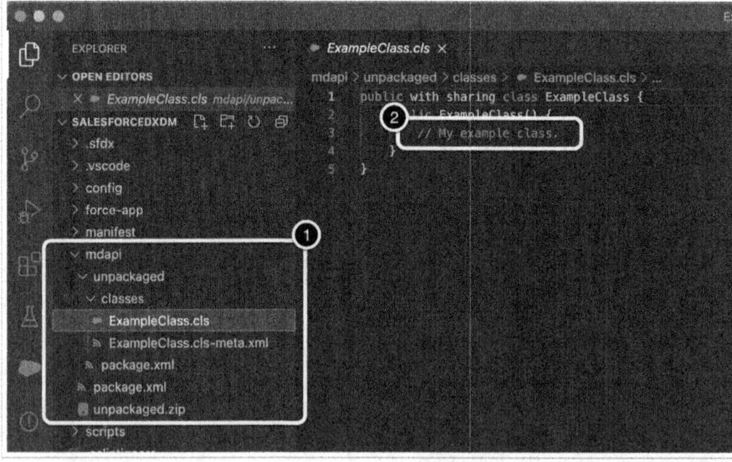

***Figure 8-10.** Metadata API format components retrieved using a source directory*

To see the --sourcedir|-d parameter used to override the default package directory, make a copy of the force-app package directory hierarchy and call it force-app-copy, then use the following command, which also uses a custom zip file name and automatically uncompresses the file for you:

```
$ sfdx force:mdapi:retrieve \
    --sourcedir ./force-app-copy \
    --zipfilename mycomponents \
    --retrievetargetdir ./mdapi \
    --unzip
```

The second of the three methods that can be used to retrieve metadata components in Metadata API format is to use a package.xml manifest specified using the --unpackaged|-k parameter to retrieve unpackaged metadata components. Delete the contents of the ./mdapi directory and execute the following command to retrieve metadata components using the manifest that we created earlier. The retrieved components are unpackaged; that is, they are not packaged by a managed or unmanaged package.

```
$ sfdx force:mdapi:retrieve \
    --unpackaged ./manifest/package.xml \
    --retrievetargetdir ./mdapi \
    --unzip
```

The command retrieves the Example_Object_1__c and Example_Object_2__c metadata components in a compressed zip file called unpackaged.zip, which is written to the ./mdapi directory and is automatically uncompressed thanks to the --unzip parameter.

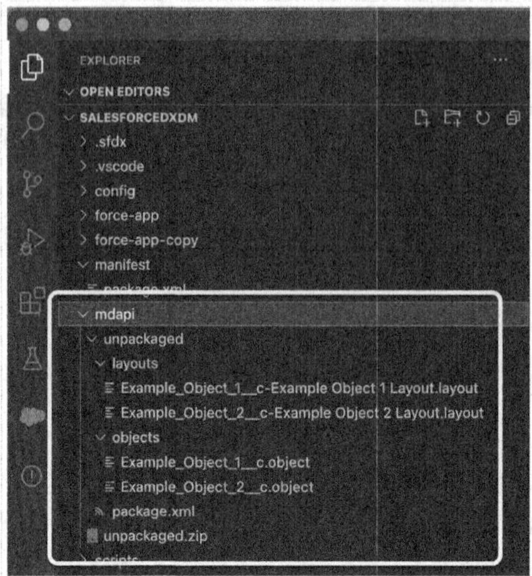

***Figure 8-11.** Metadata API format components retrieved using a manifest*

The third and final method for retrieving metadata components in Metadata API format is to retrieve components that are packaged in a managed package or an unmanaged package using the `--packagenames|-p` parameter. The parameter accepts a comma-separated list of package names. To retrieve the `Example Package 1` and `Example Package 2` unmanaged packages that we created earlier, delete the contents of the `./mdapi` directory and execute the following CLI command:

```
$ sfdx force:mdapi:retrieve \
    --packagenames \
      "Example Package 1","Example Package 2" \
    --retrievetargetdir ./mdapi \
    --unzip
```

Note Enclose package names that contain spaces in quotes.

The command retrieves the two packages with the packaged metadata components in a compressed zip file called `unpackaged.zip`, which is written to the `./mdapi` directory and automatically unzipped. Yes, by default the zip file is called `unpackaged.zip` even though the metadata components are packaged! You can override this filename using the `--zipfilename|-n` parameter if you wish.

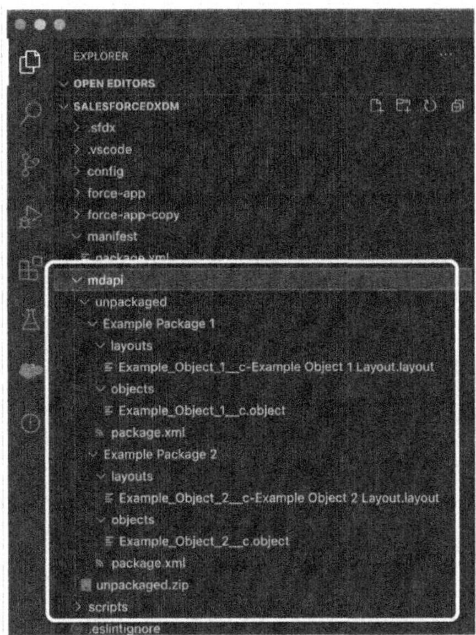

Figure 8-12. *Metadata API format components retrieved using packages*

A single package can, of course, be retrieved by only naming a single package, as in the following command:

```
$ sfdx force:mdapi:retrieve \
    --packagenames "Example Package 1" \
    --retrievetargetdir ./mdapi \
    --unzip
```

As expected, the `Example Package 1` files in Metadata API format are present.

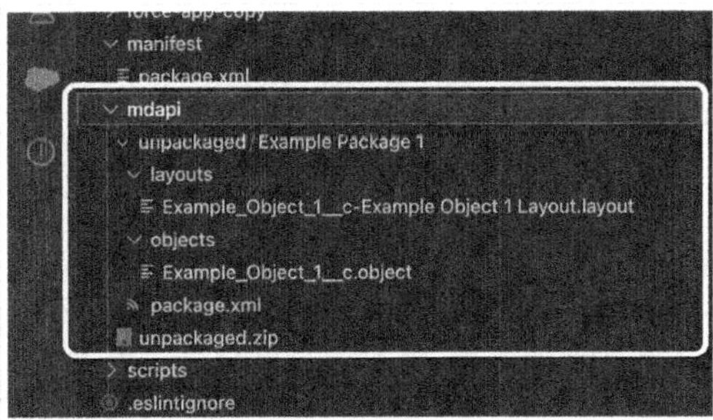

Figure 8-13. *Retrieved single package in Metadata API format*

We can see that, whether we are retrieving multiple packages or a single package, the command creates a directory within the `./mdapi` directory with the same name as the zip file. A subdirectory is then created for each retrieved package with the same name as the package.

When retrieving a single package, the `--singlepackage|-s` parameter can be used. This prevents the package subdirectory from being created, resulting in one less directory in the hierarchy. To illustrate this, execute the following command:

```
$ sfdx force:mdapi:retrieve \
    --packagenames "Example Package 1" \
    --retrievetargetdir ./mdapi \
    --singlepackage \
    --unzip
```

The uncompressed structure can be seen in the following screenshot.

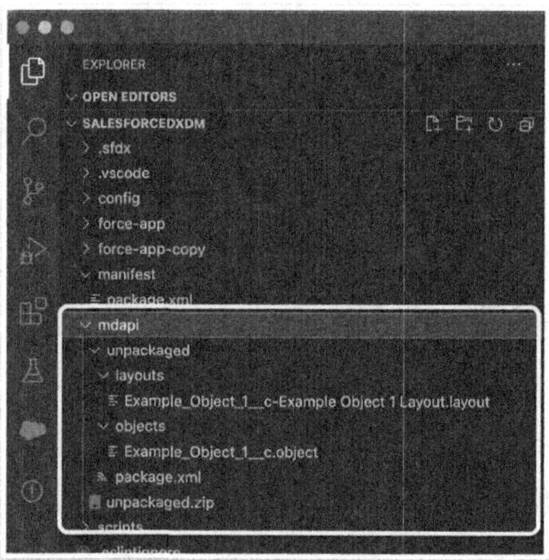

***Figure 8-14.** Retrieved single package in Metadata API format using the `--singlepackage|-s` parameter*

Note Attempting to use the `--singlepackage|-s` parameter when multiple package names are passed to the `--packagenames|-p` parameter results in an error.

Remember, the unpackaged directory name can be overridden using the --zipfilename|-n parameter if needed, for example, to be the same name as the package that is being retrieved.

That concludes synchronous retrieval of metadata components and saving the components locally in Metadata API format. Let's move on to asynchronous retrieval.

Asynchronous Retrieval

In the previous section, "Synchronous Retrieval," we experimented with three methods for retrieving metadata components that are then stored in Metadata API format in the local Salesforce DX project, namely:

- The path to a root directory of a source format metadata directory hierarchy, using the --sourcedir|-d parameter
- A path to a package.xml manifest file that includes the unpackaged metadata components to retrieve, using the --unpackaged|-k parameter
- A comma-separated list of managed or unmanaged packages that contain the packaged metadata components to retrieve, using the --packagenames|-p parameter

To illustrate how to retrieve metadata components asynchronously, we will focus on the package.xml manifest method. Once this method is understood, with the knowledge of how all the methods work synchronously, it's easy to deduce how the other methods work asynchronously.

If you find that metadata retrieval is taking a long time and you'd prefer not to wait for the job to finish, control can be returned to the terminal application immediately after executing the force:mdapi:retrieve command by setting the --wait|-w parameter to 0, as in the following command:

```
$ sfdx force:mdapi:retrieve \
    --unpackaged ./manifest/package.xml \
    --retrievetargetdir ./mdapi \
    --wait 0 \
    --unzip
```

The command output will indicate that the command is running asynchronously and how to check the asynchronous job status.

Listing 8-27. Asynchronous Metadata API format retrieve output

```
Retrieve ID: 09S4K000003Wx8fUAC
Retrieving metadata from ihdxde@example.com... queued
To check the status of this retrieve, run "sfdx force:mdapi:retrieve:
report --jobid 09S4K000003Wx8fUAC --retrievetargetdir /Users/ivanharris/
Documents/Book/Code/SalesforceDXMD/mdapi".
If the retrieve request has completed, the retrieved metadata zip file will
be written to the retrieve target dir.
```

As we are not retrieving a large number of metadata components, certainly less than the 10,000 files or 400 MB (39 MB compressed) limit, this job will complete by the time you execute the `force:mdapi:retrieve:report` command. Interestingly, if you inspect the `./mdapi` directory before running the `report` command, you will find that the `unpackaged.zip` file has not been saved there yet. This allows you to change the target directory if you wish, which we'll do here.

```
$ sfdx force:mdapi:retrieve:report \
    --jobid 09S4K000003Wx8fUAC \
    --retrievetargetdir ./mdapi2 \
    --unzip
```

If you now inspect the local Salesforce DX project's directory hierarchy, you will see that there is a new `./mdapi2` directory that includes the asynchronously retrieved metadata components, which have been automatically uncompressed as we used the `--unzip` parameter.

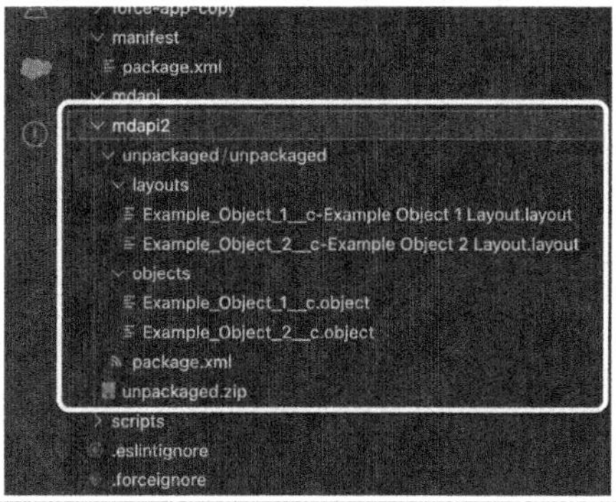

Figure 8-15. *Asynchronously retrieved metadata components*

Now that we understand how to retrieve Metadata API format components, we will now turn our attention to deploying Metadata API format components to source-tracked and non-source-tracked orgs.

Deploying Metadata API Format Metadata to Source-Tracked and Non-source-Tracked Orgs

To deploy metadata components to a source-tracked or non-source-tracked org, when the metadata is stored in Metadata API format in a local Salesforce DX project, we use the `force:mdapi:deploy` command. The command can be executed synchronously, where control is returned to the terminal application when it has completed or the period specified by the `--wait|-w` parameter expires, whichever is the sooner. It can also be executed asynchronously by passing `0` to the `--wait|-w` parameter, in which case control returns immediately to the terminal application and the `force:mdapi:deploy:report` command is used to check on the asynchronous command status.

There are two methods for deploying Metadata API format components:

- Passing the command a deployment directory that includes a `package.xml` manifest that states what components to deploy. The deployment directory can contain unpackaged components or packaged components, but not both. Components can be packaged in unmanaged or managed packages. This method uses the `--deploydir|-d` parameter.

- Providing a compressed zip archive of the preceding deployment directory. This method uses the `--zipfile|-f` parameter. When deploying packaged components, the `--singlepackage|-s` parameter can be used to specify that the zip archive contains a single package.

For this section, we will deploy metadata components that we retrieved using the `force:mdapi:retrieve` command that we encountered in the previous section. If you want to follow along with the examples, please complete the previous section first.

The format of the Metadata API format deployment command is as follows:

```
$ sfdx force:mdapi:deploy
```

The parameters that can be used for this command are as follows:

- `--checkonly|-c`: Validates a deployment without saving the metadata components in the target org. The Apex tests that run depend on the `--testlevel|-l` parameter value. When this parameter is used, an ID is returned that can be used with the `--validateddeployrequestid|-q` parameter to perform a Quick Deploy if the `--checkonly|-c` deployment was successful. [Optional] [Default: `false`]
- `--deploydir|-d`: The root of the directory hierarchy that contains uncompressed, unpackaged metadata components that have typically been retrieved using a `force:mdapi:retrieve` command with the `--source|-d` or `--unpackaged|-k` parameters. Use either `--deploydir|-d` or `--zipfile|-f`; an error is reported if both are used. [Optional]
- `--zipfile|-f`: A directory that contains a compressed zip file containing unpackaged metadata components that have typically been retrieved using a `force:mdapi:retrieve` command with the `--source|-d` or `--unpackaged|-k` parameters. Use either `--deploydir|-d` or `--zipfile|-f`; an error is reported if both are used. [Optional]
- `--ignorewarnings|-g`: If any warnings are generated during the deploy operation, using this parameter will ignore the warnings and complete the operation. [Optional]

- `--testlevel|-l`: Specifies which Apex tests are executed during the deployment. [Optional]

  Allowed values are as follows:

  - `NoTestRun`: No Apex tests are executed during a deployment. [Default for (a) nonproduction orgs such as Developer Edition orgs and sandboxes and (b) for production orgs when the deployment does not include any Apex classes or triggers.]
  - `RunSpecifiedTests`: Execute the Apex tests listed in the `--runtests|-r` parameter. The tests must cover every Apex class and trigger that is being deployed, and each Apex class and trigger must achieve at least 75% coverage for the deployment to succeed. Note that this is different to `RunLocalTests` and `RunAllTestsInOrg` values where at least 75% coverage is required as an average across the org.
  - `RunLocalTests`: Execute all the Apex tests in the target org, including those in the deployment, except those in installed managed and unlocked packages. [Default for production orgs when a deployment includes Apex classes and/or triggers.]
  - `RunAllTestsInOrg`: Execute all the Apex tests in the target org, including those in the deployment and installed managed and unlocked packages.
- `--ignoreerrors|-o`: Determines whether the deployment should continue or roll back if any errors occur. To continue with the deployment when errors occur, set to `true`. Set to `false` to roll back on error. This parameter must be set to `false` when deploying to a production org. [Optional] [Default: `false`]
- `--validateddeployrequestid|-q`: Perform a quick deploy using the ID returned by a successful check-only deployment using the `--checkonly|-c` parameter. [Optional]

- `--runtests|-r`: If the `--testlevel|-l` parameter is set to `RunSpecifiedTests`, this parameter provides a comma-separated list of Apex test class names to execute during the deployment. The tests must achieve at least 75% coverage for each Apex class and trigger in the deployment. [Optional]
- `--singlepackage|-s`: When deploying a compressed zip archive containing packaged metadata components, this parameter specifies that the archive contains a single package. It is often used in conjunction with the `--zipfile|-f` parameter, when the archive to deploy has previously been retrieved using the `force:mdapi:retrieve` command using both the `--packagenames|-p` and `--singlepackage|-s` parameters. Please refer to the "Synchronous Retrieval" section for more information about the handling of single vs. multiple packages. [Optional] [Default: If the parameter is omitted, it is assumed that the compressed zip archive passed to the `--zipfile|-f` parameter contains one or more package subdirectories, one for each package that the archive contains.]
- `--targetusername|-u`: The username or alias of the source-tracked or non-source-tracked org to deploy metadata components to. [Optional]
- `--wait|-w`: The number of minutes that the command will wait for completion. Control will be returned to the terminal application when the command completes or when the wait period expires, whichever is the sooner. A value of `0` causes control to return immediately and for the command to continue to execute asynchronously. A value of `-1` causes the command to wait indefinitely. Use the `force:mdapi:deploy:report` command to check an asynchronous command status. [Optional] [Default: `0`, the command will return immediately.]
- `--coverageformatters`: A comma-separated list of formats for reporting code coverage results as an alternative to using the command output when the `--verbose` parameter is provided. By default, when the command completes, the CLI creates a directory in the local Salesforce DX project's root directory with

the same name as the deployment ID that is returned by the `force:mdapi:deploy` command. To specify a custom directory name, use the `--resultsdir` parameter. Within the directory, a `coverage` subdirectory is also created. The CLI then writes the code coverage results to the `coverage` directory in each of the formats provided to this parameter as arguments. [Optional]

Allowed values are

- `clover`
- `cobertura`
- `html-spa`
- `html`
- `json`
- `json-summary`
- `lcovonly`
- `none`
- `teamcity`
- `text`
- `text-summary`

- `--junit`: Provides an alternative to using the command output when the `--verbose` parameter is provided for reporting Apex test results. Like the `--coverageformatters` parameter, when the command completes the CLI creates a directory in the local Salesforce DX project's root directory with the same name as the deployment ID that is returned by the `force:mdapi:deploy` command. Also, like the `--coverageformatters` parameter, this directory name can be overridden using the `--resultsdir` parameter. If both the `--coverageformatters` and the `--junit` parameters are used, they share the same directory. Within the directory, a `junit` subdirectory is also created. The CLI then writes Apex test results in JUnit format to the `junit` directory. [Optional]

- `--resultsdir`: By default, when the `--coverageformatters` and/or the `--junit` parameters are used, the CLI creates a directory in the local Salesforce DX project's root directory with the same name as the deployment ID that is returned by the `force:mdapi:deploy` command. Use this parameter to provide a custom directory name. [Optional] [Default: The deployment ID that is returned by the `force:mdapi:deploy` command.]
- `--soapdeploy`: By default, the CLI uses the REST API when executing the `force:mdapi:deploy` command. Use this parameter to use the SOAP API rather than the REST API. [Optional]
- `--apiversion, --concise, --json, --loglevel, --verbose`: Please refer to the discussion on global parameters in the section "Command-Line Parameters and Arguments" in Chapter 4, "Salesforce CLI."

Note We won't repeat here how to use the `--runtests|-r` and `--testlevel|-l` parameters to execute Apex tests on deployment; instead, please refer to the section "Deploying Source Format Metadata to Non-source-Tracked Orgs" earlier in the chapter as the parameters behave exactly the same for the `force:source:deploy` and `force:mdapi:deploy` commands.

We will look at synchronous deployment first, before moving on to asynchronous deployment.

Synchronous Deployment

If you are happy to wait for the command to complete when deploying Metadata API format metadata components to a source-tracked or non-source-tracked org, you can execute the `force:mdapi:deploy` command synchronously. Control will be returned to the terminal application when the command has completed or after the wait period passed to the `--wait|-w` parameter has expired, whichever is the sooner. The `--wait|-w` parameter can take the following values in units of minutes:

- `-1`: The command will wait indefinitely to complete.

- `0`: The command will return control to the terminal application immediately and continue executing asynchronously. This is the default.
- `1` or higher: The command will wait up to the defined number of minutes before returning control to the terminal application. If the command completes before the wait period expires, control will be returned to the terminal application.

Of the two methods for deploying Metadata API format metadata components listed at the start of this section, we will first deploy using a compressed zip archive. We'll see how to deploy unpackaged and packaged components using this method, as well as how to work with single packages.

To ensure that there are fresh unpackaged metadata components to deploy, open this chapter's `SalesforceDXMD` project and execute the following command using the integrated terminal to retrieve the unpackaged metadata components that were deployed in the previous section:

```
$ sfdx force:mdapi:retrieve \
    --unpackaged ./manifest/package.xml \
    --retrievetargetdir ./mdapi \
    --wait 30
```

This will retrieve the unpackaged metadata components from the default target org with the alias `MyDEOrg` and write a compressed zip archive called `unpackaged.zip` to the directory `./mdapi` in the local Salesforce DX project. Any existing file called `unpackaged.zip` will be overwritten.

To deploy the unpackaged metadata components in the compressed zip archive back to the same target org, execute the following CLI command:

```
$ sfdx force:mdapi:deploy \
    --zipfile ./mdapi/unpackaged.zip \
    --wait -1
```

The command will execute synchronously and wait indefinitely to complete due to the `-1` value passed to the `--wait|-w` parameter. In this case, we are deploying back to the target org that we've just retrieved from, but we could deploy to any other source-tracked or non-source-tracked org should we wish to. When it has completed, the command will output its success status.

Listing 8-28. Synchronous unpackaged Metadata API format deploy output

```
Deploy ID: 0Af3G00000QmOm6SAB
*** Deploying with SOAP ***
DEPLOY PROGRESS | ████████████████████████████████████████ | 6/6 Components
```

We can use the same command to deploy packaged metadata components; to illustrate this, retrieve the packaged metadata components that were deployed in the previous section, by executing this command:

```
$ sfdx force:mdapi:retrieve \
    --packagenames \
      "Example Package 1","Example Package 2" \
    --retrievetargetdir ./mdapi \
    --wait 30
```

To deploy these packaged components, execute the following deploy command again:

```
$ sfdx force:mdapi:deploy \
    --zipfile ./mdapi/unpackaged.zip \
    --wait -1
```

The command outputs the same success status as when we deployed unpackaged metadata.

Listing 8-29. Synchronous packaged Metadata API format deploy output

```
Deploy ID: 0Af4K00000KMkzRSAT
*** Deploying with SOAP ***
DEPLOY PROGRESS | ████████████████████████████████████████ | 6/6 Components
```

Although the commands used to deploy unpackaged and packaged metadata components are the same, we didn't need to tell the CLI that we are deploying packaged metadata components because the `package.xml` file that was created when we retrieved packaged metadata components includes the package name.

Listing 8-30. Package name in a package.xml file

```
<?xml version="1.0" encoding="UTF-8"?>
<Package xmlns="http://soap.sforce.com/2006/04/metadata">
    <fullName>Example Package 1</fullName>
    <types>
        <members>Example_Object_1__c.Example_Field__c</members>
        <name>CustomField</name>
    </types>
    <types>
        <members>Example_Object_1__c</members>
        <name>CustomObject</name>
    </types>
    <types>
        <members>Example_Object_1__c-Example Object 1 Layout</members>
        <name>Layout</name>
    </types>
    <version>55.0</version>
</Package>
```

The command is therefore able to determine that we are deploying packaged components.

An assumption that the CLI makes when deploying packaged components is that the compressed zip archive contains multiple packages. Referring to the previous section on retrieving Metadata API format metadata components, the directory structure in the compressed zip archive differs between retrieving multiple and single packages. To retrieve and then deploy a single package, execute the following commands:

```
$ sfdx force:mdapi:retrieve \
    --packagenames \
      "Example Package 1" \
    --retrievetargetdir ./mdapi \
    --singlepackage \
    --wait 30
```

```
$ sfdx force:mdapi:deploy \
    --zipfile ./mdapi/unpackaged.zip \
    --singlepackage \
    --wait -1
```

The command will output a success status similar to the output we saw when deploying multiple packages, except that it reports the deployment of three components, rather than six.

Note The `--singlepackage|-s` parameter must be used in both the retrieve and deploy commands for packaged components; any other combination results in an error.

The second method for deploying Metadata API format components uses a deployment directory. Internally, the Salesforce CLI compresses the directory into a zip archive before calling the Metadata API, so it removes a deployment step. Execute the following command again to retrieve the unpackaged metadata components:

```
$ sfdx force:mdapi:retrieve \
    --unpackaged ./manifest/package.xml \
    --retrievetargetdir ./mdapi \
    --wait 30 \
    --unzip
```

The compressed `unpackaged.zip` file and the uncompressed metadata components can be viewed in VS Code.

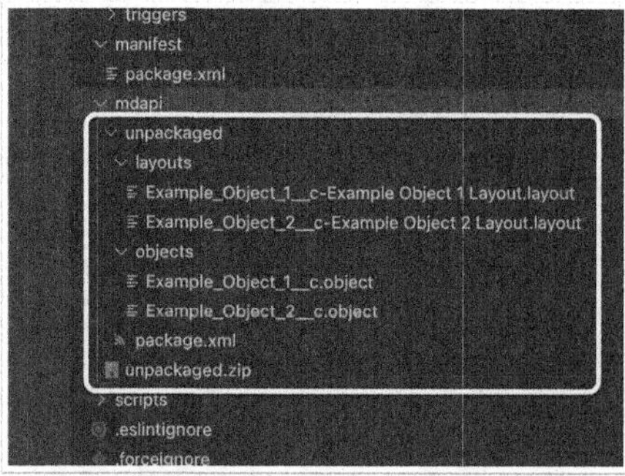

***Figure 8-16.** Retrieved unpackaged metadata components*

At this point in a development lifecycle, you would add additional metadata components to the directory structure and to the `package.xml` manifest. Then you would either compress the directory structure into a zip archive and deploy it, or you would deploy the directory. The following command is used to deploy the directory:

```
$ sfdx force:mdapi:deploy \
    --deploydir ./mdapi/unpackaged/unpackaged \
    --wait -1
```

The command will output the same success status as when deploying unpackaged metadata using a zip archive earlier.

For large deployments, you don't necessarily want to wait until the deployment completes before you can get on with some other work! That's a problem solved by asynchronous deployments.

Asynchronous Deployment

To execute an asynchronous deployment of Metadata API format metadata components, you must set the `--wait`|`-w` parameter to `0`. This will cause the `force:mdapi:deploy` command to return control to the terminal application so that you can continue working, while the command executes asynchronously. To check on the status of the asynchronous deployment, use the `force:mdapi:deploy:report` command, and to cancel an asynchronous execution, use the `force:mdapi:deploy:cancel` command.

To demonstrate an asynchronous deployment, we'll use the `package.xml` manifest method that we encountered in the previous synchronous deployment section; note, the process is the same when deploying using a deployment directory, so we won't show both methods. First, retrieve some Metadata API format metadata components using the following command:

```
$ sfdx force:mdapi:retrieve \
    --unpackaged ./manifest/package.xml \
    --retrievetargetdir ./mdapi \
    --wait 30
```

To perform an asynchronous deployment, set the `--wait`|`-w` parameter to `0`:

```
$ sfdx force:mdapi:deploy \
    --zipfile ./mdapi/unpackaged.zip \
    --wait 0
```

The command outputs a status message explaining that the command has not yet finished executing, along with the commands that can be used to cancel or to check the status of the asynchronous execution using the command's job ID.

Listing 8-31. Asynchronous Metadata API deployment started output

```
Deploy ID: 0Af4K00000KMoKmSAL
*** Deploying with SOAP ***
Deploy has been queued.

Run sfdx force:mdapi:deploy:cancel -i 0Af4K00000KMoKmSAL -u ihdxde@example.
com to cancel the deploy.
Run sfdx force:mdapi:deploy:report -i 0Af4K00000KMoKmSAL -u ihdxde@example.
com to get the latest status.
```

Executing the `force:mdapi:deploy:report` command will show the following status once the asynchronous command has completed executing.

Listing 8-32. Asynchronous Metadata API deployment completed output

```
Deploy ID: 0Af4K00000KMoKmSAL
Status: Succeeded
Deployed: 6/6 Errors: 0
Tests Complete: 0/0 Errors: 0
```

The command defaults to checking the status of the most recently executed asynchronous deployment. If you have kicked off multiple asynchronous deployments, you can check the status of a specific deployment by passing its ID to the `--jobid|-i` parameter. The full set of parameters are described here:

```
$ sfdx force:mdapi:deploy:report
```

The parameters that can be used for this command are as follows:

- `--jobid|-i`: The ID of the deployment to report on. The ID is returned when executing the `force:mdapi:deploy` command. [Optional] [Default: The ID of the most recent deployment.]
- `--targetusername|-u`: The username or alias of the source-tracked or non-source-tracked org that is the target of the deployment to report on. [Optional]

- `--wait|-w`: The number of minutes that the command will wait for completion. Control will be returned to the terminal application when the command completes or when the wait period expires, whichever is the sooner. A value of `0` causes control to return immediately and for the command to continue to execute asynchronously. A value of `-1` causes the command to wait indefinitely. [Optional] [Default: `0`, the command will return immediately.]
- `--coverageformatters`: A comma-separated list of formats for reporting code coverage results as an alternative to using the command output when the `--verbose` parameter is provided. By default, when the command completes, the CLI creates a directory in the local Salesforce DX project's root directory with the same name as the deployment ID that is returned by the `force:mdapi:deploy` command. To specify a custom directory name, use the `--resultsdir` parameter. Within the directory, a `coverage` subdirectory is also created. The CLI then writes the code coverage results to the `coverage` directory in each of the formats provided to this parameter as arguments. [Optional]

  Allowed values are

  - `clover`
  - `cobertura`
  - `html-spa`
  - `html`
  - `json`
  - `json-summary`
  - `lcovonly`
  - `none`
  - `teamcity`
  - `text`
  - `text-summary`

- `--junit`: Provides an alternative to using the command output when the `--verbose` parameter is provided for reporting Apex test results. Like the `--coverageformatters` parameter, when the command completes the CLI creates a directory in the local Salesforce DX project's root directory with the same name as the deployment ID that is returned by the `force:mdapi:deploy` command. Also, like the `--coverageformatters` parameter, this directory name can be overridden using the `--resultsdir` parameter. If both the `--coverageformatters` and the `--junit` parameters are used, they share the same directory. Within the directory, a `junit` subdirectory is also created. The CLI then writes Apex test results in JUnit format to the `junit` directory. [Optional]

- `--resultsdir`: By default, when the `--coverageformatters` and/or the `--junit` parameters are used, the CLI creates a directory in the local Salesforce DX project's root directory with the same name as the deployment ID that is returned by the `force:mdapi:deploy` command. Use this parameter to provide a custom directory name. [Optional] [Default: The deployment ID that is returned by the `force:mdapi:deploy` command.]

- `--apiversion, --json, --loglevel, --concise, --verbose`: Please refer to the discussion on global parameters in the section "Command-Line Parameters and Arguments" in Chapter 4, "Salesforce CLI."

There may be occasions when you will want to terminate a long-running asynchronous deployment, which can be done using the following command:

```
$ sfdx force:mdapi:deploy:cancel
```

The parameters that can be used for this command are as follows:

- `--jobid|-i`: The ID of the deployment to cancel. The ID is returned when executing the `force:mdapi:deploy` command. [Optional] [Default: The ID of the most recent deployment.]

- `--targetusername|-u`: The username or alias of the source-tracked or non-source-tracked org that is the target of the deployment to be canceled. [Optional]

- `--wait|-w`: The number of minutes that the command will wait for completion. Control will be returned to the terminal application when the command completes or when the wait period expires, whichever is the sooner. The value must be greater than or equal to `1`. [Optional] [Default: `33`]
- `--apiversion, --json, --loglevel`: Please refer to the discussion on global parameters in the section "Command-Line Parameters and Arguments" in Chapter 4, "Salesforce CLI."

As the `--jobid|-i` parameter defaults to the most recently executed asynchronous deployment, use the following command to cancel the asynchronous deployment that we initiated earlier. The command will wait up to the default 33 minutes to complete.

```
$ sfdx force:mdapi:deploy:cancel
```

To cancel an asynchronous deployment that is not the most recent one that was executed, pass the ID returned by the `force:mdapi:deploy` command as the value for the `--jobid|-i` parameter.

So far, this chapter has explained how to synchronize metadata components that are stored locally in source format or Metadata API format between a local Salesforce DX project and source-tracked and non-source-tracked orgs. We will now learn how to convert locally stored data between source format and Metadata API format.

Converting Between Metadata API Format and Source Format

Salesforce DX offers the choice of working with metadata components that are stored locally in source format, Metadata API format, or a mix of the two. Although the recommended storage method is source format, there may be times when you will need to convert between formats. This might be a one-off exercise, when converting existing applications and customizations from Metadata API format to source format. Alternatively, it may occur when different teams are using a mix of source and Metadata API formats, such as prior to a source code repository completing its migration from Metadata API to source format.

We will explore the following commands in this section:

- **force:source:convert**: Convert metadata components that are stored in source format to Metadata API format.
- **force:mdapi:convert**: Convert metadata components that are stored in Metadata API format to source format.

First, we will see how to convert from source format to Metadata API format, which will be followed by converting from Metadata API format to source format.

Converting from Source Format to Metadata API Format

To convert from source format to Metadata API format, the following command is used:

```
$ sfdx force:source:convert
```

The parameters that can be used for this command are as follows:

- `--outputdir|-d`: The directory where the converted files in Metadata API format will be written. [Optional] [Default: `metadataPackage_XXXXXXXXXXXXX`, where `XXXXXXXXXXXXX` is a unique 13-digit number created by the CLI each time the `force:source:convert` command is executed.]
- `--metadata|-m`: A comma-separated list of metadata components to convert from source format to Metadata API format. [Optional]
- `--packagename|-n`: The name of a managed or unmanaged package that will be used to package the converted metadata components. [Optional]
- `--sourcepath|-p`: A comma-separated list of directory and file paths. All source format files in a directory and its subdirectories will be converted to Metadata API format. Individual files can be specified using a file path. [Optional]
- `--rootdir|-r`: Overrides the default package directory in the `sfdx-project.json` project configuration file. [Optional]
- `--manifest|-x`: The path to a `package.xml` manifest containing the metadata components to convert. [Optional]

- `--json, --loglevel`: Please refer to the discussion on global parameters in the section "Command-Line Parameters and Arguments" in Chapter 4, "Salesforce CLI."

There are three different methods available for converting source format metadata components to Metadata API format:

- Using the default package directory, the `--rootdir|-r` parameter, or the `--sourcepath|-p` parameter to specify directories or files containing source format metadata components to convert.
- Providing a list of metadata components to convert using the `--metadata|-m` parameter.
- Using a `package.xml` manifest that contains the metadata types to convert. This uses the `--manifest|-x` parameter.

To convert some metadata components to Metadata API format, we need some in source format first. Let's assume that you haven't completed the steps in the previous sections, in which case we need to create some new metadata components.

1. If you have been following along with this chapter's examples so far, you will have existing metadata in your Salesforce DX project. If so, and to avoid any confusion, either delete the existing `SalesforceDXMD` project or rename it.
2. Create a new `SalesforceDXMD` project and include a `package.xml` manifest file using the following command:

   ```
   sfdx force:project:create -x \
   -n SalesforceDXMD.
   ```

3. Launch Visual Studio Code if it's not already launched.
4. Open the new `SalesforceDXMD` project.
5. Open the integrated terminal.
6. Create a new scratch org and make it the org with the default username.
7. Open the scratch org.
8. Navigate to **Setup ➤ Objects and Fields ➤ Object Manager**.

9. Click the **Create** action menu and then the **Custom Object** menu item.
10. Enter the following information in the New Custom Object page:
    a. **Label**: `Example Object`
    b. **Plural Label**: `Example Objects`
    c. **Starts with vowel sound**: `Checked`
    d. **Object Name**: `Example_Object`
11. Click the **Save** button, which will open the detail page for the new custom object.
12. Click **Fields & Relationships**.
13. Click **New**.
14. In Step 1 of the new custom field wizard, select **Text** as the data type and then click **Next**.
15. In Step 2, enter the following field values, then click **Next**:
    a. **Field Label**: `Example Field`
    b. **Length**: `50`
    c. **Field Name**: `Example_Field`
16. In Step 3, just click **Next**.
17. In Step 4, click **Save**.

Now that there are some metadata components in your scratch org, execute the following command in Visual Studio Code's integrated terminal to show the differences between the scratch org and your local Salesforce DX project:

```
$ sfdx force:source:status
```

The output shows the newly created custom object and custom field components, plus a system-generated profile that has been modified.

Listing 8-33. New scratch or metadata components

```
Source Status
 STATE      FULL NAME                               TYPE        PROJECT PATH
 ──────────  ──────────────────────────────────────  ─────────   ────────────
 Remote Add Example_Object__c.Example_Field__c      CustomField
 Remote Add Example_Object__c                       CustomObject
 Remote Add Example_Object__c-Example Object Layout Layout
 Remote Add Admin                                   Profile
```

We don't want to pull the profile changes as they are not part of the changes that we want to include in our application or customization. We learned in the section "Excluding Source Format Files from Syncing and Converting" earlier in the chapter that we can exclude these components from syncing and converting by updating the `.forceignore` file. Add the following to the `.forceignore` file to prevent the profile from being pulled from the scratch org.

Listing 8-34. Excluding profiles from being pulled from a scratch org

```
# Ignore profiles.
Admin.profile
```

To pull the new metadata components from the scratch org and save them in source format in your local Salesforce DX project, execute the following command:

```
$ sfdx force:source:pull
```

The new components are stored in source format in the local Salesforce DX project's default package directory, which is called `force-app` in the project configuration file that is created by default.

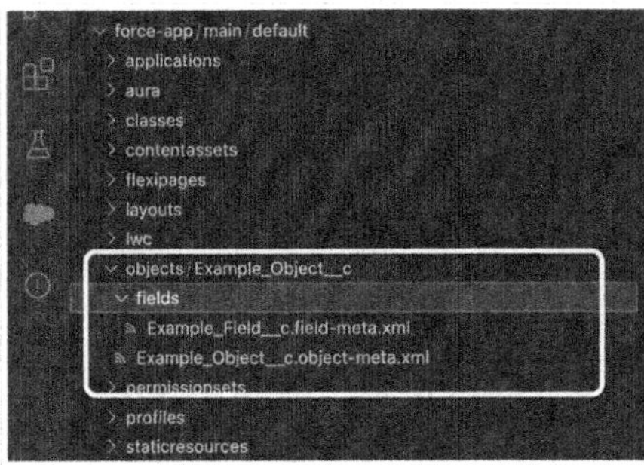

Figure 8-17. *Pulled metadata components stored in the default package directory*

We are now set up to illustrate the three methods for converting the source format metadata components to Metadata API format that we mentioned earlier, namely, (1) listing the directories and files to convert, (2) listing the metadata components, or (3) using a `package.xml` manifest.

The first method that we will explore is to use source format directory and file paths. There are three ways to specify the directories and files to convert:

- Use the default package directory in the `sfdx-project.json` project configuration file.
- Override the default package directory using the `--rootdir|-r` parameter.
- Use the `--sourcepath|-p` parameter to specify directories or files containing source format metadata components to convert.

The first way to use the `force:source:convert` command, where no parameters are needed, uses the default package directory in the `sfdx-project.json` project configuration file.

```
$ sfdx force:source:convert
```

The command creates a new, uniquely named directory in the Salesforce DX project in which it stores the Metadata API format files.

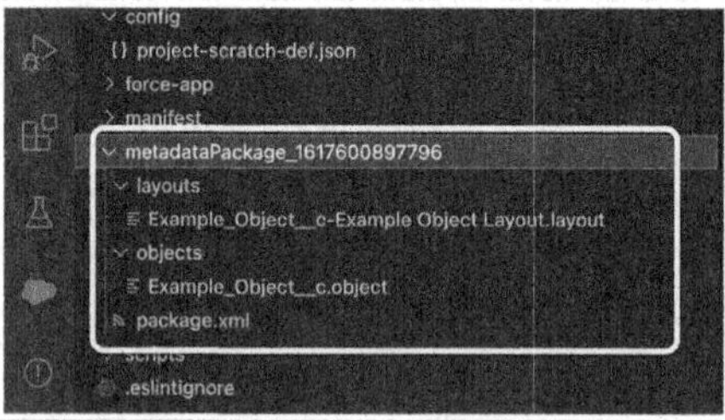

Figure 8-18. *Converted Metadata API components*

To store the converted files in a directory with a name of your choice, include the output directory name in the command using the `--outputdir|-d` parameter as follows:

```
$ sfdx force:source:convert \
    --outputdir ./mdapi/unpackaged
```

The command will create the directory if it doesn't already exist, and it will store the converted Metadata API format components there.

Note We are using an output directory called `./mdapi/unpackaged` to mirror the directory structure that is created when retrieving Metadata API format components. It also allows us to compress the `unpackaged` directory ready for deployment without proliferating files in the Salesforce DX project's root directory.

The second way to use source format directories and files to specify what to convert is to override the default package directory. To illustrate this, copy the `force-app` default package directory to a new directory hierarchy, such as `force-app-copy`, as in the following screenshot.

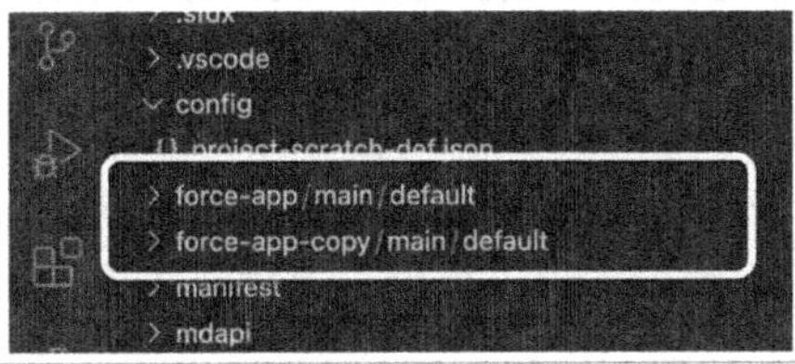

***Figure 8-19.** Duplicated package directory*

To let the Salesforce CLI know that this is a package directory, add it to the `sfdx-project.json` file as in the next listing.

Listing 8-35. A second package directory in the sfdx-project.json file

```
{
  "packageDirectories": [
    {
      "path": "force-app",
      "default": true
    },
    {
      "path": "force-app-copy"
    }
  ],
```

```
  "name": "SalesforceDXMD",
  "namespace": "",
  "sfdcLoginUrl": "https://login.salesforce.com",
  "sourceApiVersion": "55.0"
}
```

To use the nondefault package directory, pass its root directory to the `--rootdir|-r` parameter:

```
$ sfdx force:source:convert \
    --outputdir ./mdapi/unpackaged \
    --rootdir ./force-app-copy
```

The result should be the same as when converting using the default package directly; that is, a new `./mdapi` directory is created if it doesn't already exist, and the source format metadata component files in the new, nondefault package directory are converted to Metadata API format and stored there.

The third and final way to use source format directories and files to instruct the `force:source:convert` which components to convert is to use the `--sourcepath|-p` parameter. To achieve the same result as the previous two ways that we used for conversion, execute the following command:

```
$ sfdx force:source:convert \
  --outputdir ./mdapi/unpackaged \
  --sourcepath \
    "./force-app/main/default/layouts/↩
    Example_Object__c-Example Object Layout.↩
    layout-meta.xml",↩
    ./force-app/main/default/objects
```

It's a bit tricky to read due to the line wraps, but we're passing a file and a directory to the `--sourcepath|-p` parameter, separated by a comma. The file path is to the `Example Object Layout` component, and it is surrounded by double quotation marks due to the spaces in the path. The directory path is to the `object` directory, which will convert all objects in the directory and its subdirectories.

Having seen how to use three ways to perform the directories and files method for specifying which metadata components to convert from source format to Metadata API format, we'll move on to the second method, which is to list the metadata components to convert using the --metadata|-m parameter. To convert the same source format metadata components to Metadata API format that we converted using the directories and files method, use this command:

```
$ sfdx force:source:convert \
  --outputdir ./mdapi/unpackaged \
  --metadata \
    "Layout:Example_Object__c-Example Object↩
    Layout","CustomObject:Example_Object__c"
```

The format of each metadata component name that is passed to the --metadata|-m parameter is

```
<metadata type>:<metadata component>
```

The <metadata type> name can be found in the reference section of the Metadata API Developer Guide.

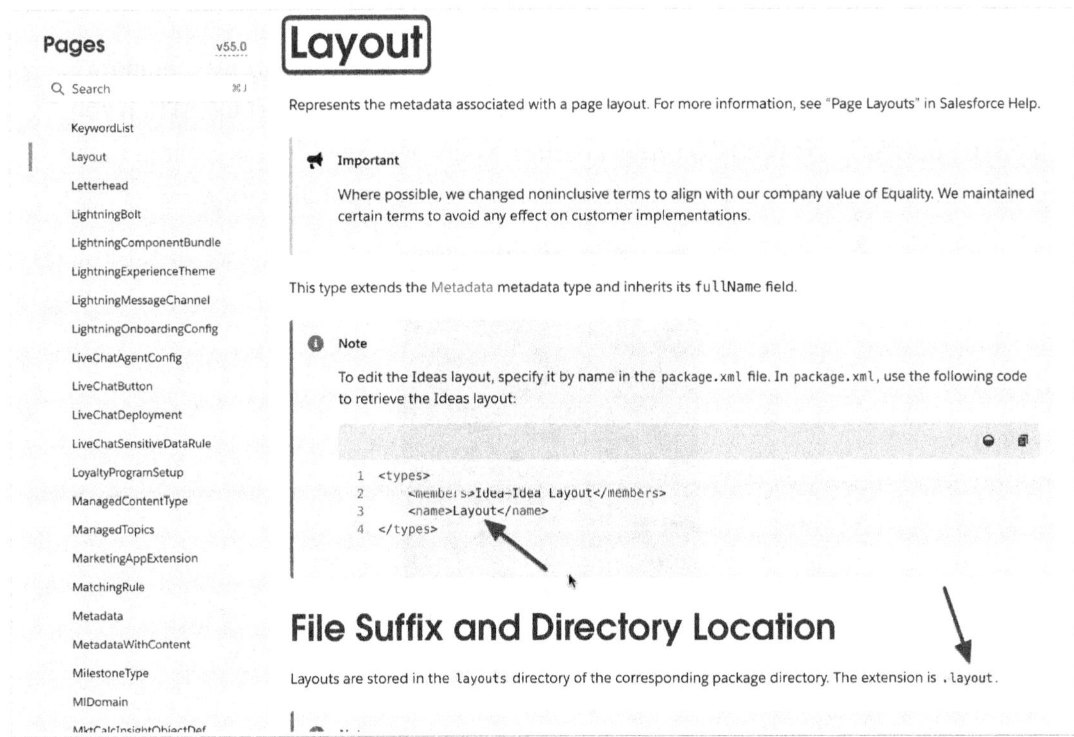

Figure 8-20. *Metadata type name*

Note The Metadata API Developer Guide can be found here: https://developer.salesforce.com/docs/atlas.en-us.api_meta.meta/api_meta/meta_intro.htm.

The <metadata component> name is the same as the metadata component's source format filename.

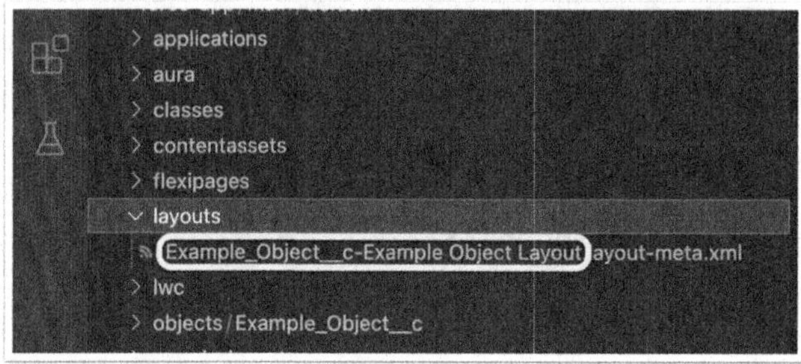

Figure 8-21. Metadata component name

The third and final method that can be used to convert source format metadata components to Metadata API format is to use a package.xml manifest file. When you created the new SalesforceDXMD project earlier, a package.xml file was created in the manifest directory, which is a subdirectory in the project's root directory.

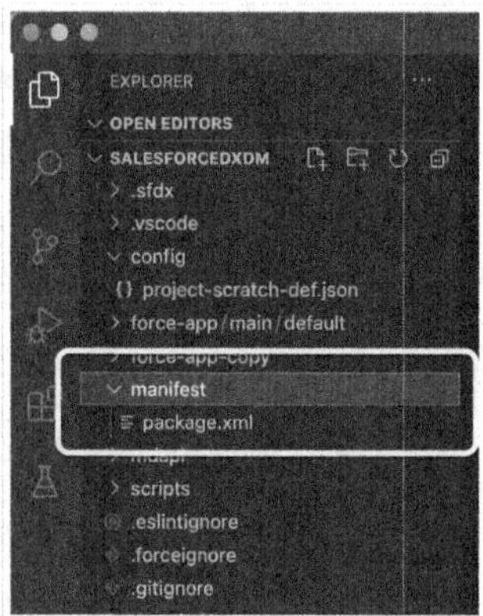

Figure 8-22. Default manifest file location

Replace the contents with the following.

Listing 8-36. Source format conversion manifest

```
<?xml version="1.0" encoding="UTF-8" standalone="yes"?>
<Package xmlns="http://soap.sforce.com/2006/04/metadata">
  <types>
    <name>Layout</name>
    <members>Example_Object__c-Example Object Layout</members>
  </types>
  <types>
    <name>CustomObject</name>
    <members>Example_Object__c</members>
  </types>
  <types>
    <name>CustomField</name>
    <members>Example_Object__c.Example_Field__c</members>
  </types>
    <version>55.0</version>
</Package>
```

Note The source format conversions that have been done so far created a `package.xml` file in the output directory that has these contents, which can be cut and pasted if you wish.

To perform a source format to Metadata API format conversion using this manifest file, execute the following command:

```
$ sfdx force:source:convert \
    --outputdir ./mdapi/unpackaged \
    --manifest ./manifest/package.xml
```

As before, the converted Metadata API files can be found in the `./mdapi` output directory.

To associate converted metadata components with a package name, use the `--packagename|-n` parameter with any of the preceding commands. For example, to convert the source format metadata in the default package directory and associate the converted Metadata API format components with a package called `Example Package`, the command would be:

```
$ sfdx force:source:convert \
    --outputdir ./mdapi/unpackaged \
    --packagename "Example Package"
```

Inspecting the `package.xml` manifest file that the command creates in the output directory confirms that the package name has been added, which can be seen in the following.

Listing 8-37. Source format converted with an associated package name

```
<?xml version="1.0" encoding="UTF-8"?>
<Package xmlns="http://soap.sforce.com/2006/04/metadata">
    <types>
        <members>Example_Object__c.Example_Field__c</members>
        <name>CustomField</name>
    </types>
    <types>
        <members>Example_Object__c</members>
        <name>CustomObject</name>
    </types>
    <types>
        <members>Example_Object__c-Example Object Layout</members>
        <name>Layout</name>
    </types>
    <version>55.0</version>
    <fullName>Example Package</fullName>
</Package>
```

To validate that a package is created that contains the converted metadata components, compress the `unpackaged` directory into a zip archive and deploy it to the Developer Edition org with the alias `MyDEOrg` that you created earlier in the chapter, although any org will work.

```
$ sfdx force:mdapi:deploy \
    --zipfile ./mdapi/unpackaged.zip \
    --targetusername MyDEOrg \
    --wait 30
```

Open the org and navigate to **Setup ➤ Apps ➤ Packaging ➤ Package Manager** and click **Example Package**. This displays the unmanaged package's contents, which include the converted components.

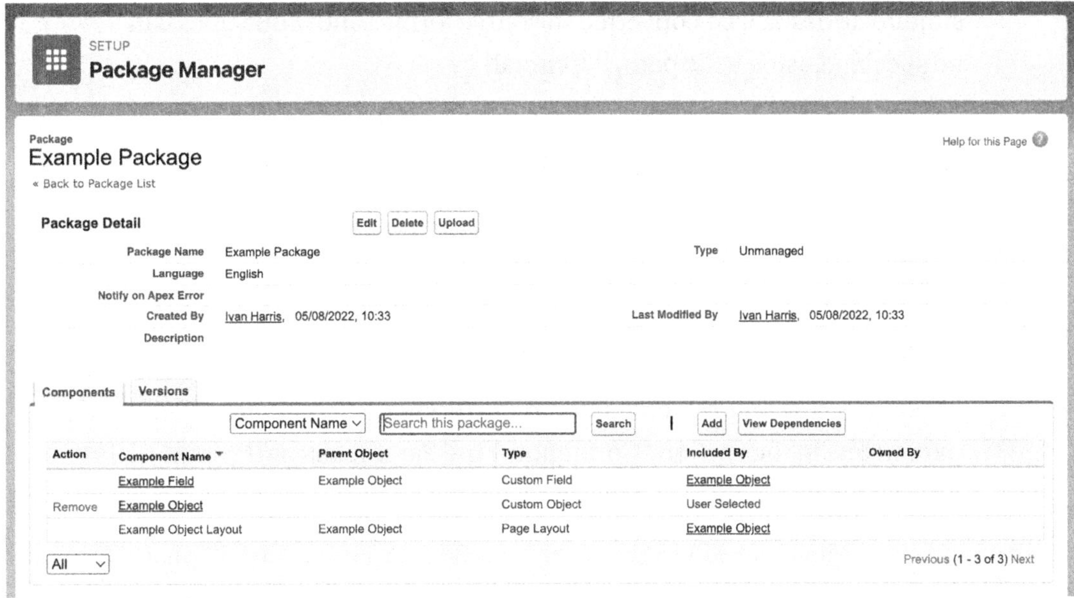

***Figure 8-23.** Packaged converted components*

Next up, we will see how to convert Metadata API format metadata components to source format.

Converting from Metadata API Format to Source Format

To convert metadata components from Metadata API format to source format, the following command is used:

```
$ sfdx force:mdapi:convert
```

This command's parameters are as follows:

- `--outputdir|-d`: The directory where the files that have been converted to source format will be written. [Optional]
- `--metadata|-m`: A comma-separated list of metadata components to convert from Metadata API format to source format. [Optional]
- `--metadatapath|-p`: A comma-separated list of directory and file paths. All Metadata API format files in a directory and its subdirectories will be converted to source format. Individual files can be specified using a file path. [Optional]
- `--rootdir|-r`: The root directory of the directory hierarchy that contains the Metadata API format files to convert to source format. All files in the directory and its subdirectories will be converted. [Required]
- `--manifest|-x`: The path to a `package.xml` manifest containing the metadata components to convert. [Optional]
- `--json, --loglevel`: Please refer to the discussion on global parameters in the section "Command-Line Parameters and Arguments" in Chapter 4, "Salesforce CLI."

To create some Metadata API format files to convert to source format, please use one of the methods in the previous section, "Converting from Source Format to Metadata API Format." This will store some Metadata API format files in the `./mdapi/unpackaged` directory, which should look like this in Visual Studio Code.

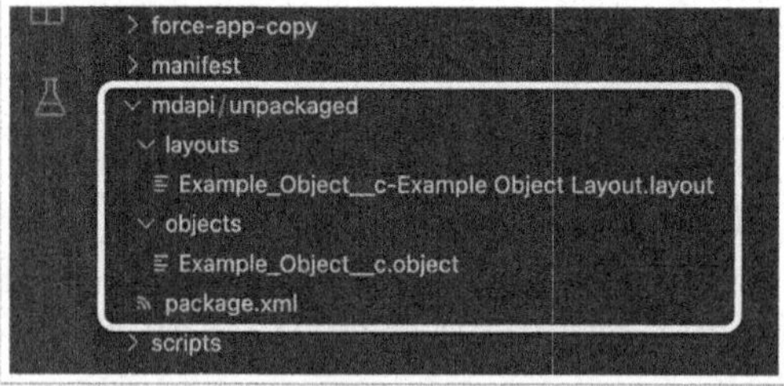

Figure 8-24. *Metadata API format files*

The most minimal form of the `force:mdapi:convert` command takes the single `--rootdir|-r` required parameter, which specifies the root of the directory hierarchy where the Metadata API format files are located.

```
$ sfdx force:mdapi:convert \
  --rootdir ./mdapi/unpackaged
```

All the files in the directory, plus all of its subdirectories, are converted to source format and stored in the default package directory that is specified by the `sfdx-project.json` project configuration file.

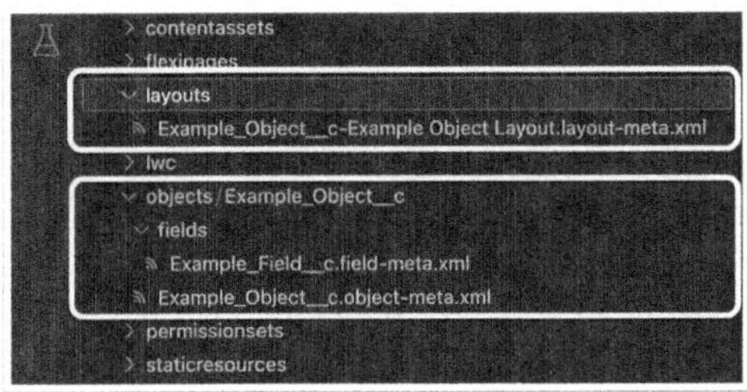

Figure 8-25. *Converted source format files*

To store the converted source format files in a directory that is not the default package directory, use the `--outputdir|-d` parameter as follows:

```
$ sfdx force:mdapi:convert \
  --outputdir ./src-format \
  --rootdir ./mdapi/unpackaged
```

This will create the `./src-format` directory if it does not already exist and will store the converted source format files there.

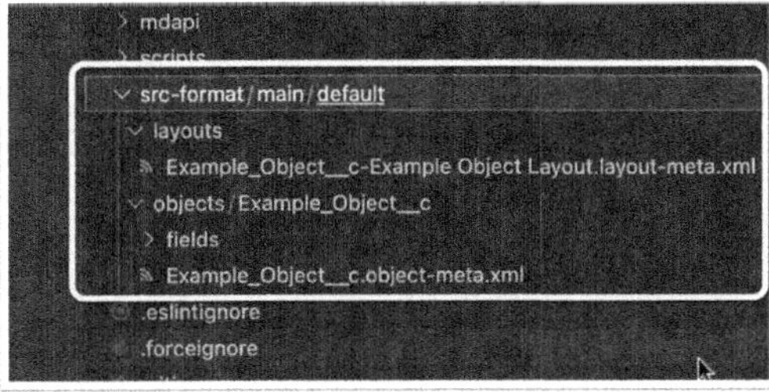

Figure 8-26. *Converted source format files in a new output directory*

So far, the `force:mdapi:convert` command has been used to convert all of the files in the directory hierarchy defined by the `--rootdir|-r` parameter. Using the `--metadata|-m`, `--metadatapath|-p`, and `--manifest|-x` parameters, it's possible to convert a subset of the files in the directory hierarchy. Each of the following three commands results in only the `Example_Object__c` page layout being converted, and not the `Example_Object__c` custom object and `Example_Field__c` custom field:

```
$ sfdx force:mdapi:convert \
  --outputdir ./src_format \
  --metadatapath \
    "./mdapi/unpackaged/layouts/↩
    Example_Object__c-Example Object ↩
    Layout.layout" \
  --rootdir ./mdapi/unpackaged

$ sfdx force:mdapi:convert \
  --outputdir ./src-format \
  --metadatapath ./mdapi/unpackaged/layouts \
  --rootdir ./mdapi/unpackaged

$ sfdx force:mdapi:convert \
  --outputdir ./src-format \
  --metadata \
    "Layout:Example_Object__c-↩
      Example Object Layout" \
  --rootdir ./mdapi/unpackaged

$ sfdx force:mdapi:convert \
  --outputdir ./src-format \
  --rootdir ./mdapi/unpackaged \
  --manifest ./manifest/package.xml
```

Note For the last example to work as expected, edit the ./manifest/package.xml file to remove the entries for the Example_Object__c custom object and Example_Field__c custom field. The resulting file should look like the following:

```
<?xml version="1.0" encoding="UTF-8" standalone="yes"?>
<Package xmlns="http://soap.sforce.com/2006/04/metadata">
  <types>
    <name>Layout</name>
    <members>Example_Object__c-Example Object Layout</members>
  </types>
    <version>55.0</version>
</Package>
```

The first example uses the `--metadatapath | -p` parameter to provide the path to a Metadata API format file to convert. The second uses the same parameter to provide the path to a directory containing Metadata API files to convert, in this case a single file, but it could be more. The third example uses the `--metadata | -m` parameter to specify the name of a Metadata API format component to convert. The final example uses the `--manifest | -x` to name a `package.xml` manifest file to use that lists the Metadata API format components to convert.

We've covered a lot of ground in this chapter, let's summarize what we've learned.

Chapter Summary

This extensive chapter focused on how to work with metadata components that are stored in either source format or Metadata API format in a local Salesforce DX project. We examined the difference between the two file formats and the benefits of working with the source format that Salesforce DX introduced. With these two metadata component file formats and two types of orgs (source-tracked and non-source-tracked), we illustrated how to synchronize metadata components in both formats with both org types, including when to use the appropriate synchronization method according to leading practices. Finally, we saw how to convert between the two file formats and explained when this might be required.

In this chapter, we touched upon storing metadata component files in a version control system as part of the application lifecycle model. The next chapter will explore how to use a version control system with Salesforce DX.

CHAPTER 9

Version Control

In Chapter 13, "Package Development," we will learn about the three application development models that Salesforce supports and where the metadata source of truth resides:

- **Change Set Development Model**: The production org is the source of truth. Salesforce DX does not support change sets.
- **Org Development Model**: A version control system is the source of truth. Salesforce DX supports this model.
- **Package Development Model**: A version control system is the source of truth. Salesforce DX supports this model.

We'll defer a more comprehensive description of the three models until Chapter 13; suffice to say, a version control system, or "VCS," being the source of truth is a fundamental aspect of Salesforce DX. There are several benefits to using a version control system when developing applications or customizations for Salesforce:

- **Branching and Merging**: Various branching and merging strategies can be utilized to support concurrent and collaborative development, testing, versioning, patching, etc.
- **Traceability**: Code lineage can be tracked, an audit trail of all changes exists, and code can be rolled back to previous versions if needed.
- **CI/CD**: Continuous integration and continuous delivery (or deployment) tools can be integrated with a version control system to automate the build, test, and deployment of applications or customizations.

I. Harris, *Beginning Salesforce DX*, https://doi.org/10.1007/978-1-4842-8114-7_9

- **Backup, Restore, and Archive**: Repository lifecycles can be managed like other digital assets as part of a company's business continuity and disaster recovery processes.
- **Agility**: Development teams can move at pace, release incremental changes, roll back if necessary, and quickly resolve issues thanks to the comprehensive audit trail.

There are plenty of version control systems to choose from and many excellent books available should you wish to explore the pros and cons of each. As this chapter is about how a version control system can be used with Salesforce DX, we'll choose just one to work with, which is Git.

Git, GitHub, and GitHub Desktop

In this book, we've standardized on using Microsoft's Visual Studio Code (VS Code) integrated development environment. Given that VS Code supports the Git version control system out of the box, and Git being the most used version control system by 3m+ organizations and 65m+ users, we will be using Git in this chapter. Having said that, Visual Studio Code does support other version control systems using extensions available on the VS Code Marketplace.

Note The Visual Studio Code documentation refers to a version control system as a source control manager, or "SCM."

To find an SCM extension, do the following:

- Launch Visual Studio Code.
- Click the Extensions icon in the Activities Bar, which is labeled (1) in the following screenshot. This will display the most popular extensions on the VS Code Marketplace.
- Enter `@category:"scm providers"` in the search box labeled (2) in the screenshot to filter extensions from SCM providers.

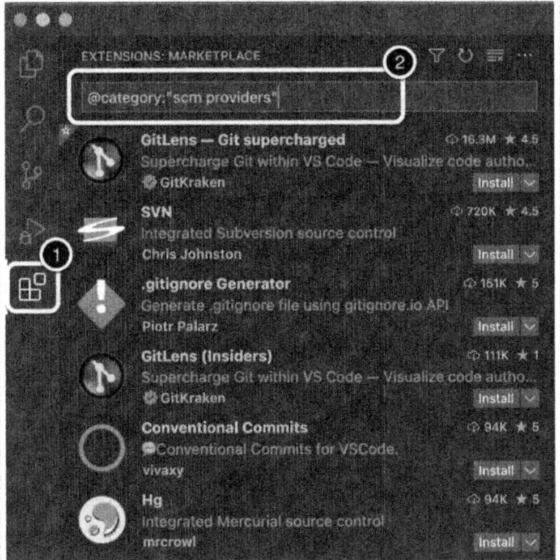

Figure 9-1. *Visual Studio Code extensions*

Some examples of popular version control system extensions include the following:

- **SVN**: Integrated Subversion source control
- **Hg**: Integrated Mercurial source control
- **Perforce for VS Code**: Perforce integration with VS Code's SCM features

---

Note An alternative method for browsing extensions is to visit the VS Code Marketplace at `https://marketplace.visualstudio.com/` and enter `SCM` in the search box.

There are two categories of version control system - centralized VCS and distributed VCS. A centralized VCS follows a client-server architecture, where a server stores a remote repository of code, including all the branches and change history. To modify any code stored in the remote repository, a developer downloads the code from the server, stores it on their computer, modifies it, and then commits it back to the remote repository. A distributed VCS on the other hand is more like a peer-to-peer architecture, where each developer clones a complete copy of the remote repository to a local repository on their computer. The developer can then work independently, and any changes are committed to their local repository first, which is then synchronized with the remote repository. Git is a free and open source distributed version control system (VCS).

Note that even with a distributed VCS, a repository needs to be hosted somewhere for multiple developers to collaborate with, which is where solutions like GitHub come in. GitHub is a repository hosting service built on top of Git that adds a graphical user interface and its own features, such as access control mechanisms, collaboration, pull requests, forking, and much more. In a team development environment, the hosted repository acts as the remote repository that developers can clone local repositories from. Visit `https://github.com/` to explore GitHub's features further, and there are alternatives to GitHub for hosting repositories, including the following, among others:

- **GitLab**: `https://gitlab.com/`
- **Bitbucket**: `https://bitbucket.com/`
- **SourceForge**: `https://sourceforge.net/`

Whereas GitHub provides a user-friendly graphical user interface for viewing and managing hosted repositories, when Git is installed on a developer's local computer, the out-of-the-box interface is via the command line. That said, there are several Git clients available to add a graphical user interface to the local repository experience, one being GitHub Desktop (`https://desktop.github.com/`), from the same stable as GitHub; others include

- **Sourcetree**: `www.sourcetreeapp.com/`
- **GitKraken**: `www.gitkraken.com/`
- **Git Tower**: `www.git-tower.com/`

Note In addition to Git clients that add a graphical user interface, other development tools that integrate with Git on a developer's computer are also Git clients, including Visual Studio Code. We won't be including GitHub Desktop in this chapter's examples; that said, it's a handy tool to have in your toolbelt and well worth exploring further as it will help you navigate complex branches with many changes (we will only use two branches and four new files in the examples).

In summary, the version control system solutions that we will be using in this chapter are as follows:

- **Git**: A distributed version control system. Each developer that is collaborating on a project using a remote Git repository hosted by GitHub will install Git on their local development computer. Developers clone the hosted remote repository as a local repository, commit any changes to their local repository, and then synchronize those changes with the hosted remote repository.
- **GitHub**: A Git repository hosting service that will be used to host the remote repository that developers will collaborate on and clone as a local repository.

The relationship between solution components is illustrated in the following diagram.

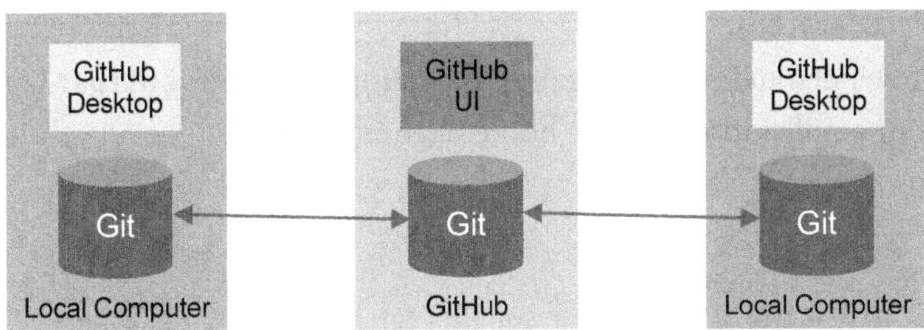

***Figure 9-2.** Git solutions*

In the forthcoming sections, we will create a GitHub account and install Git on our development computer. We'll start by creating a GitHub account.

Creating a GitHub Account

When multiple developers are collaborating in a business environment, such as when developing Salesforce applications and customizations, a GitHub account is needed in order to host the remote repository; additionally, each developer needs their own GitHub account. Administrators of the GitHub account that hosts the remote repository can then add collaborators using the developers' GitHub accounts and control each developer's access to the repository.

If we were exploring team collaboration using GitHub in depth, we'd probably create a GitHub account to host the remote repository and at least two developer GitHub user accounts to illustrate collaboration workflows; however, that's beyond the scope of this book as we're introducing how to use a version control system with Salesforce DX, so we will create a single GitHub account to host a remote repository and use the same account for the developer's account.

Note To learn more about GitHub accounts and collaboration teams, look up "Teams" and "Organizations" in the GitHub documentation, which can be found here: `https://docs.github.com/`. An Organization account supports the creation of teams that are assigned access to repositories with more fine-grained permissions than are available with a personal user account. In a business environment, the GitHub account that hosts the remote repository will most likely be an Organization or Enterprise account.

Creating a free personal GitHub account is as simple as visiting `https://github.com/` and entering your email address on the home page as follows.

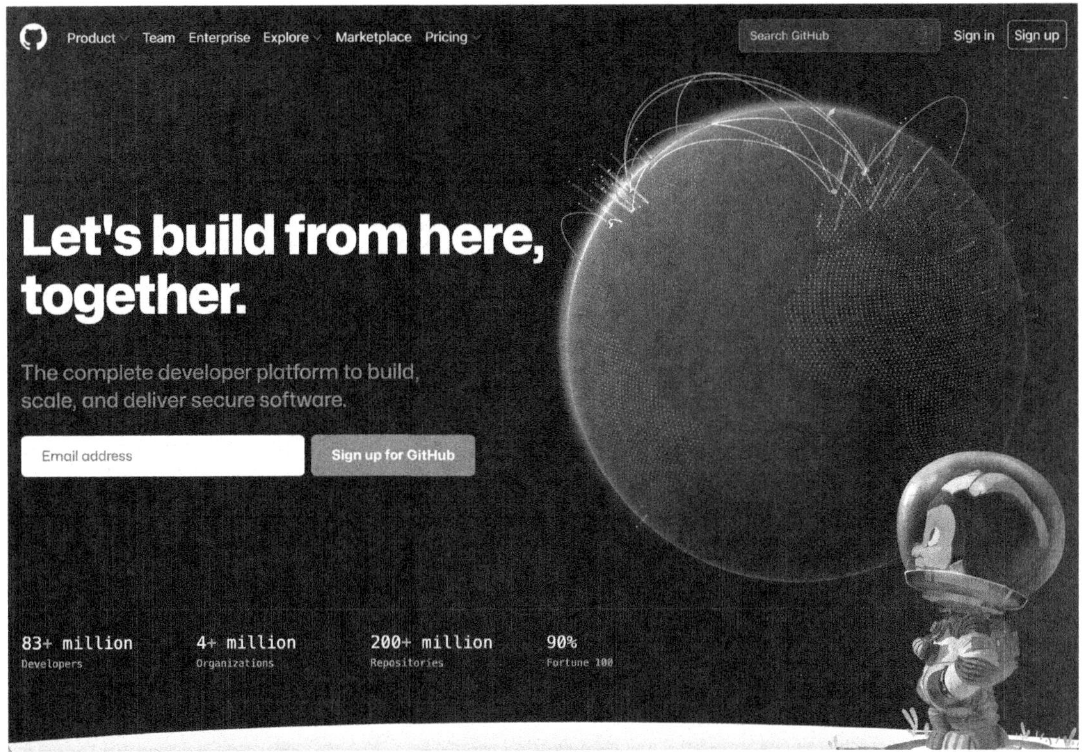

Figure 9-3. *GitHub home page*

With the free edition of GitHub, you receive the following benefits:

- Unlimited public and private repositories
- Unlimited collaborators
- 500MB of Packages storage

Once the sign-up process is complete, your dashboard will be displayed.

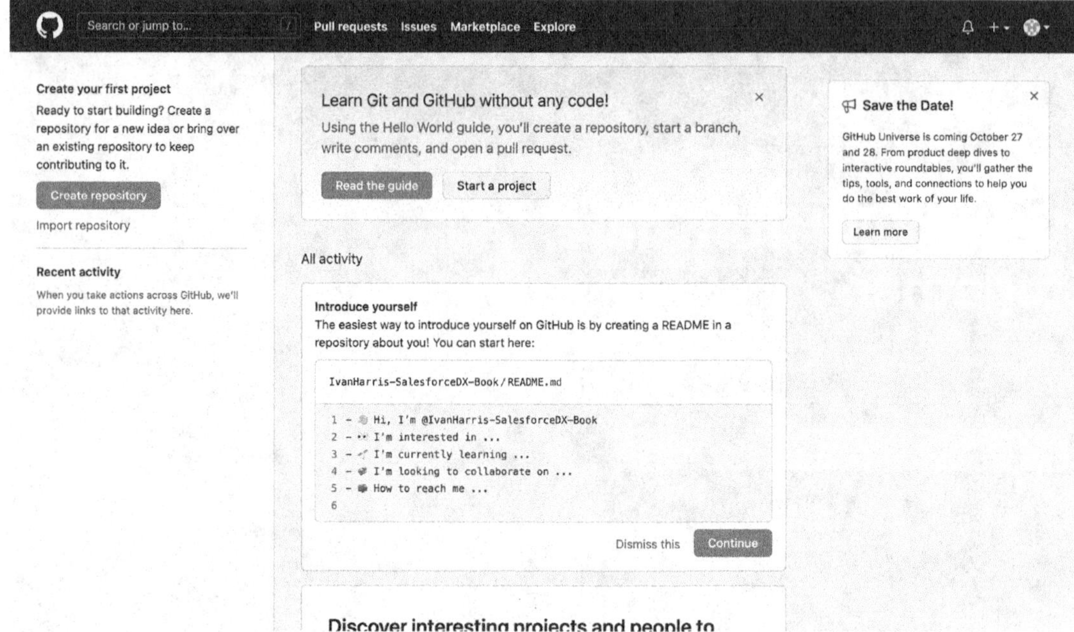

Figure 9-4. *GitHub dashboard*

The next job is to install Git on our development computer.

Installing Git

Git is a free and open source distributed version control system (VCS) that we will be using to illustrate how to use a VCS when developing applications or customizations with Salesforce DX. To install Git, visit the following website page and follow the instructions for your operating system:

- `https://git-scm.com/book/en/v2/Getting-Started-Installing-Git`

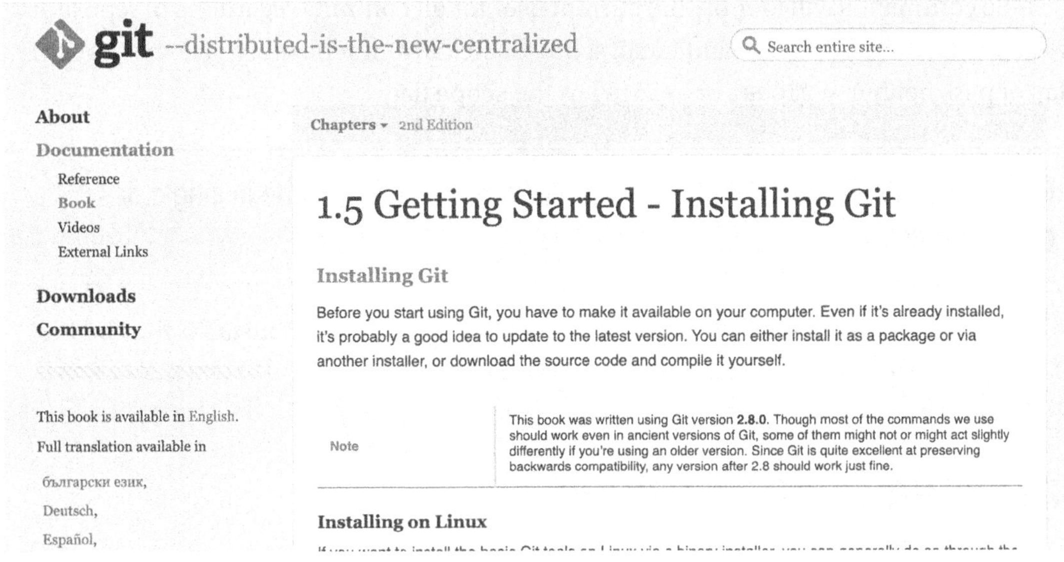

Figure 9-5. *Git installation page*

To confirm that Git is installed, run the following command in a terminal application:

```
$ git --version
```

The output should look like this.

Listing 9-1. Git version information

```
git version 2.37.1
```

To make it easier to identify who has made commits in a collaborative development environment, it's good practice to set up each author's Git identity.

Setting Up Your Git Identity

If this is the first time that you have used Git on your development computer, you should set up your Git identity, which will be used to identify your commits. Set your author's name and author email address using the following commands:

```
$ git config --global user.name <your-name>
$ git config --global user.email <your-email>
```

The commands will identify the current user for all commits regardless of repository. To define the author's name and email scope to the current repository, use the `--local` flag or pass neither `--global` or `--local` as the scope flag.

Note If `your-name` contains spaces, enclose the whole name in single or double quotes.

Although not an essential component, the final Git solution to install is the GitHub Desktop, which makes it easier to examine local repositories.

Installing GitHub Desktop

GitHub Desktop is a Git client that is installed on the same computer as Git that provides a graphical user interface alternative to using the Git command line. To install the GitHub Desktop, visit the following web page and follow the instructions for your operating system:

- `https://desktop.github.com/`

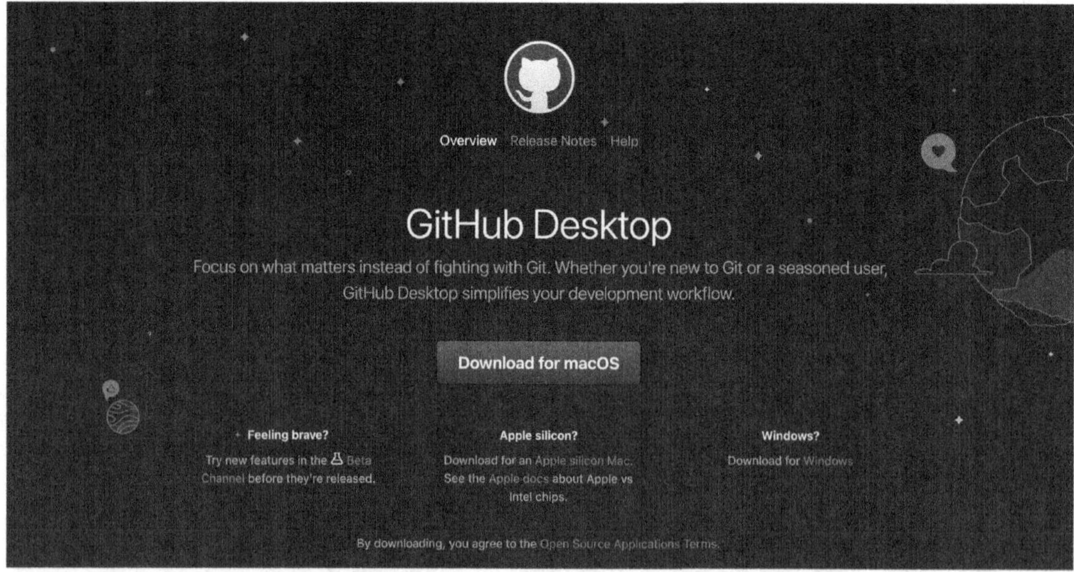

***Figure 9-6.** GitHub Desktop installation page*

When opening the application for the first time, the Welcome screen prompts you to sign in to GitHub.com. Click the **Sign in to GitHub.com** button.

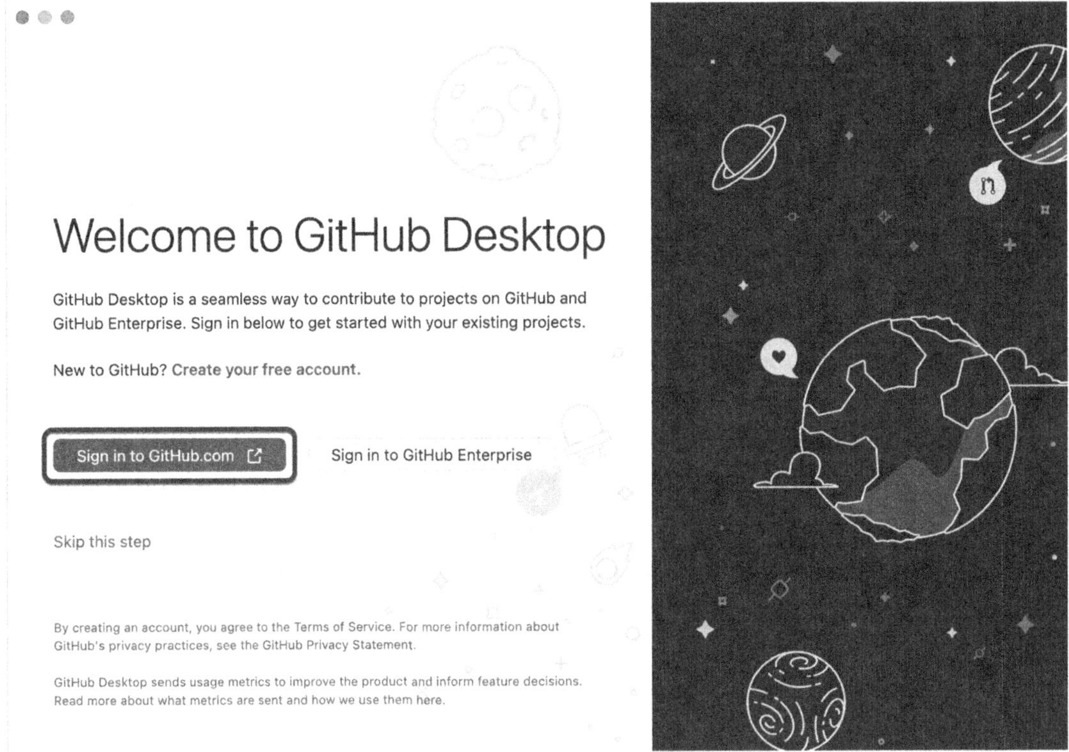

Figure 9-7. *GitHub Desktop welcome screen*

If you are currently logged out of GitHub.com, the sign-in page is presented. Sign in using the credentials that you used when creating your free personal GitHub account earlier. If you are in a business environment, where the GitHub account hosting the remote repository and your personal GitHub account are different, the credentials that you enter here are for your personal GitHub account.

Note If this is not the first time that you have opened GitHub Desktop on your development computer, navigate to **GitHub Desktop ➤ Preferences ➤ Accounts** via the application's menu bar to sign in and out of your personal GitHub account. It's here that you can also log in to your company's GitHub Enterprise account to access the hosted remote repositories that you can collaborate on.

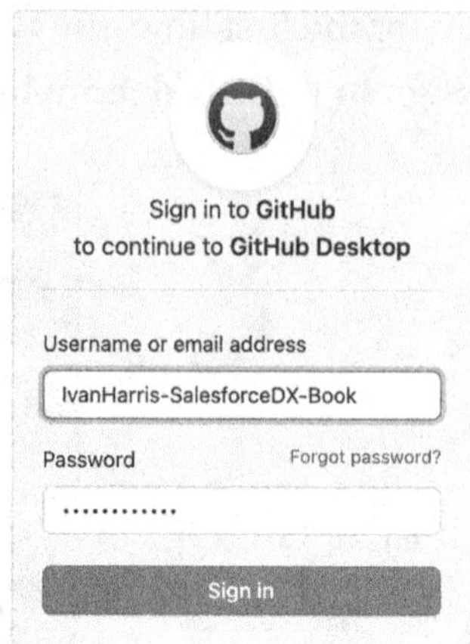

Figure 9-8. *GitHub.com sign-in page*

The next page to appear is the OAuth authorization screen to provide GitHub Desktop access to your personal GitHub account. Click the **Authorize desktop** button.

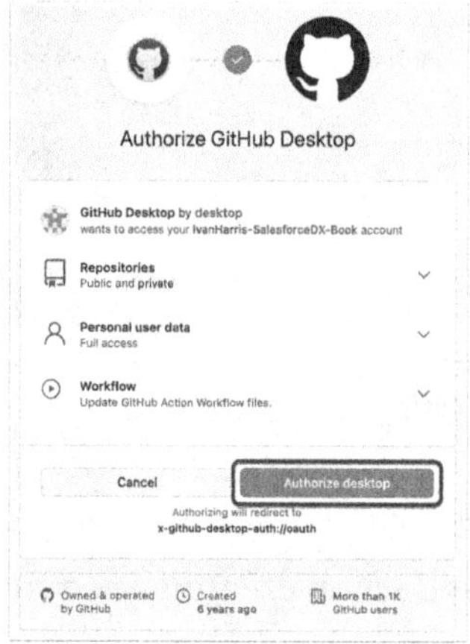

Figure 9-9. *GitHub OAuth authorization page*

The final screen presented by the GitHub Desktop application is the Configure Git screen; accept the defaults by clicking the **Finish** button.

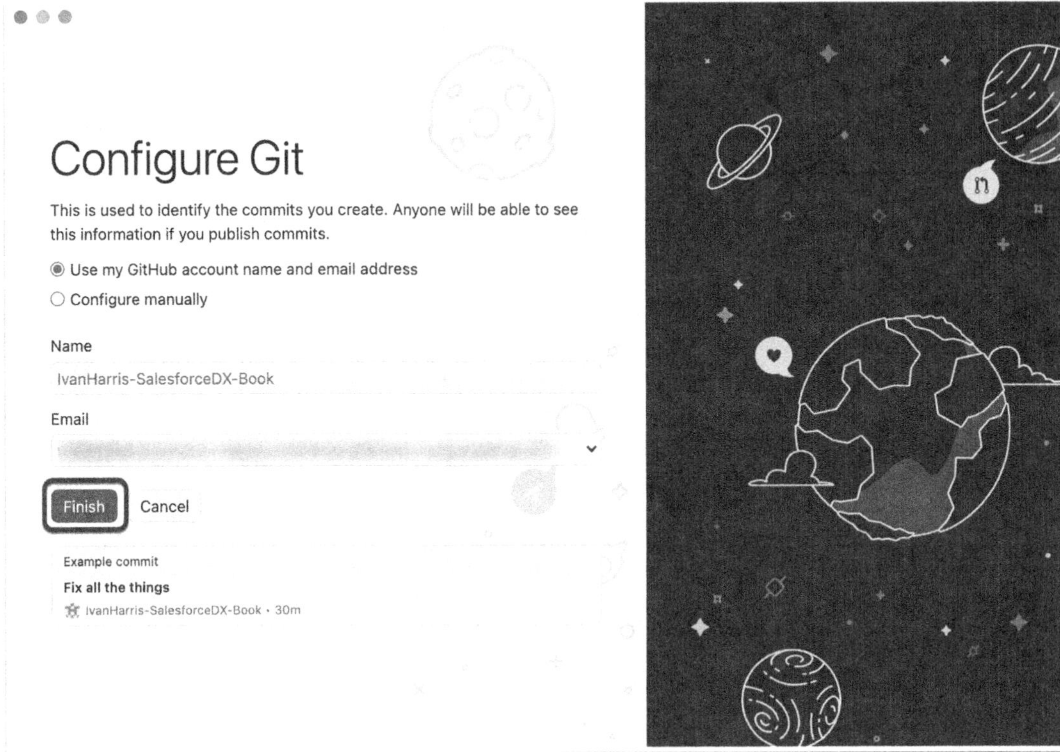

Figure 9-10. *GitHub Desktop Configure Git screen*

Note As mentioned earlier in the chapter, we won't be including GitHub Desktop in this chapter's examples. It is a handy tool however that's worth exploring further for when you start collaborating on complex branches and many changes.

All the solutions are now in place to collaboratively develop Salesforce applications or customizations with a version control system as the source of truth. The upcoming sections will illustrate how to start collaborating on a new Salesforce DX project that has yet to be added to a hosted remote GitHub repository vs. one that already exists.

Working with a New Salesforce DX Project

In this section, we will create a new Salesforce DX project and add it to a remote Git repository that is hosted by GitHub for other development team members to access.

Creating a Remote GitHub Repository

To collaborate on a Salesforce DX project, we must first create a hosted remote Git repository using GitHub. Open the GitHub account that you signed up for earlier and click the **New repository** option as illustrated in the following screenshot.

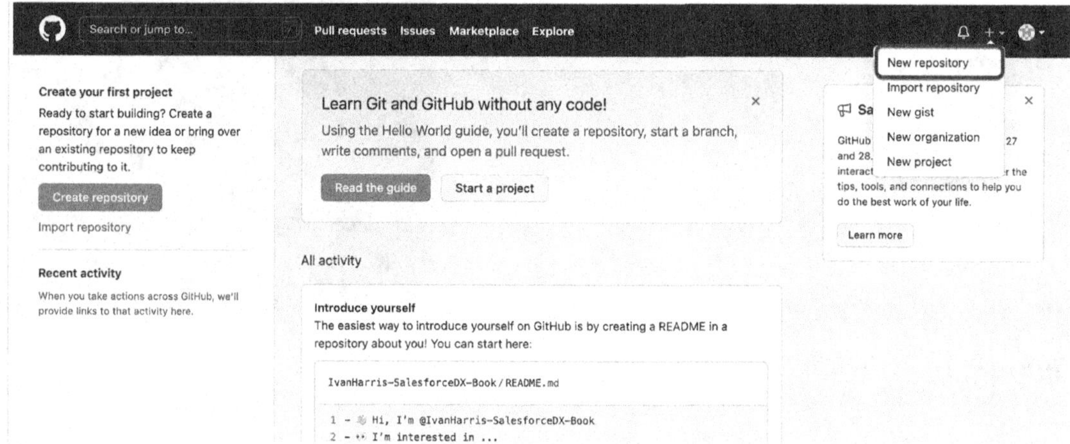

***Figure 9-11.** Create a new repository option*

In the Create a new repository screen, enter the following:

1. **Repository name**: `SalesforceDXVCS`.
2. **Private**: Select as we will not be sharing our project publicly.
3. **Add a README file**: Deselect.
4. **Add .gitignore**: Select **None**.
5. **Choose a license**: Select **None**.
6. Click the **Create repository** button.

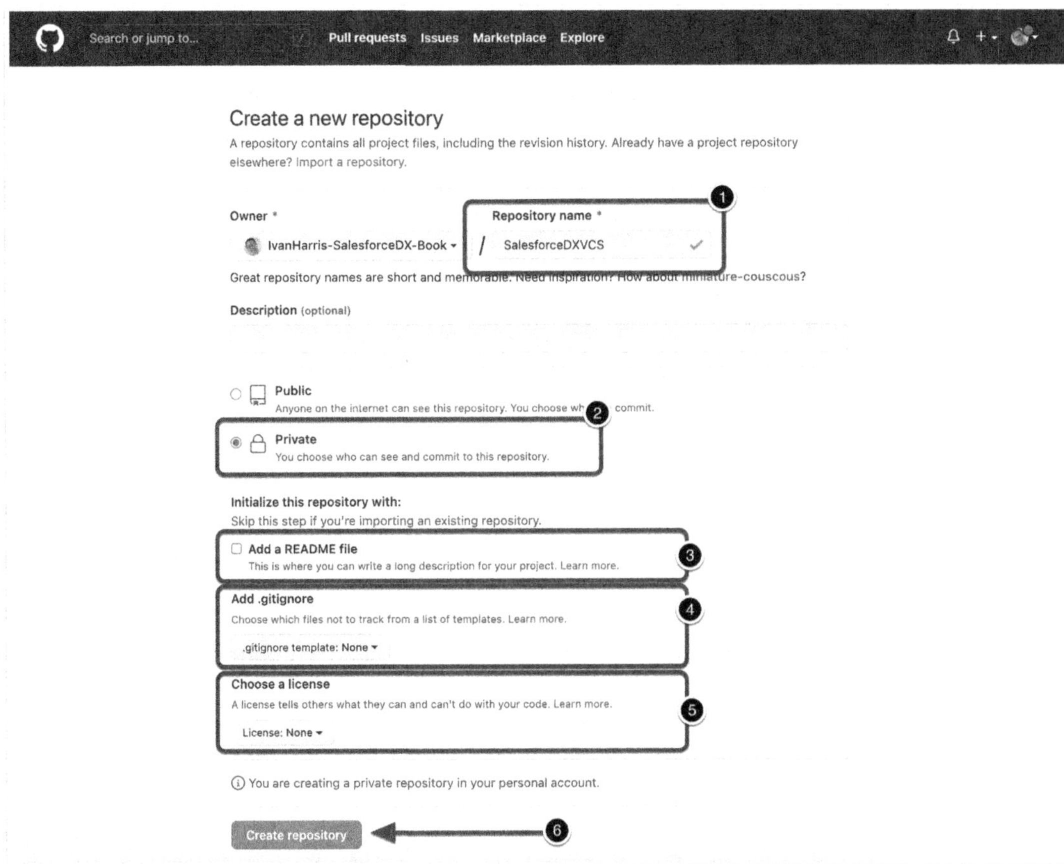

***Figure 9-12.** Create a new repository screen*

Note Options 3 and 4 were deselected to create a bare repository as the `README.md` and `.gitignore` files will be created in the Salesforce DX project and then added to the repository.

We will now create a new Salesforce DX project, which will be added to the GitHub repository later.

This Chapter's Project

Please follow the instructions in Chapter 6, "Projects," to create a new Salesforce DX project, name the project `SalesforceDXVCS`, and use the default standard template. Also, make sure that you have a default Dev Hub org authorized with an alias of `MyDH`, which is described in Chapter 5, "Dev Hub," as we will be using scratch orgs. Finally, use the instructions in Chapter 7, "Orgs," to create a scratch org with the alias `MySO` and assign it as having the default username. Running the `force:org:list` command will list the new org.

Listing 9-2. Chapter org list

```
=== Orgs

     ALIAS   USERNAME              ORG ID                 CONNECTED STATUS
 ─── ─────── ───────────────────── ────────────────────── ──────────────────
 (D) MyDH    ihdxdh@example.com    00D4K0000015OzMUAU     Connected
     ALIAS   USERNAME                          ORG ID                 EXPIRATION DATE
 ─── ─────── ───────────────────────────────── ────────────────────── ───────────────
 (U) MySO    test-5im0swpr5lrt@example.com     00D3G0000001OHwUAM     2022-09-06
```

It's OK if you have other orgs listed, if you have a new default scratch org, we're good to go.

To share new and updated metadata components from your Salesforce DX project with other developers, a local Git repository is needed, which we can synchronize with the hosted remote repository.

Creating a Local Repository

If you have been following this chapter so far, you will have created a new remote `SalesforceDXVCS` Git repository hosted by GitHub and a new Salesforce DX project on your local development computer. The two are unconnected at this point, so it is not possible to synchronize any changes between them. A local repository is needed to track the changes made to the Salesforce DX project, and the local repository can then be synchronized with the hosted remote repository.

To create a local repository and ask Git to track any changes to the Salesforce DX project, perform the following steps:

1. Launch Visual Studio Code.
2. Open this project's Salesforce DX project, called `SalesforceDXVCS`.
3. Open the integrated terminal.
4. Enter the command `git init` using the integrated terminal's command line.

The command should output the following on completion.

Listing 9-3. git init command output

```
Initialized empty Git repository in ↩
  /Users/ivanharris/Documents/Book/Code/SalesforceDXVCS/.git/
```

The output explains that an empty Git repository has been created in the root directory of the Salesforce DX project. Git will now track all file changes in the root directory and its subdirectories.

We don't need to add every file in our Salesforce DX project to version control, so the `.gitignore` file will determine what files to exclude.

The .gitignore File

In Chapter 8, "Metadata," we learned that a `.forceignore` file instructs the Salesforce CLI to ignore certain source format files and metadata components when performing synchronization and conversion commands. The `.forceignore` file format is based on the `.gitignore` file format, which performs a similar function, namely, to instruct Git to ignore certain files and exclude them when tracking changes. When we created the GitHub remote repository, we chose not to add a `.gitignore` file as one is added when creating the Salesforce DX project. It can be found in the project's root directory and contains the following contents.

Listing 9-4. Default .gitignore file contents

```
# This file is used for Git repositories to specify intentionally untracked
files that Git should ignore.
# If you are not using git, you can delete this file. For more information
see: https://git-scm.com/docs/gitignore
# For useful gitignore templates see: https://github.com/github/gitignore

# Salesforce cache
.sf/
.sfdx/
.localdevserver/
deploy-options.json

# LWC VSCode autocomplete
**/lwc/jsconfig.json

# LWC Jest coverage reports
coverage/

# Logs
logs
*.log
npm-debug.log*
yarn-debug.log*
yarn-error.log*

# Dependency directories
node_modules/

# Eslint cache
.eslintcache

# MacOS system files
.DS_Store
```

```
# Windows system files
Thumbs.db
ehthumbs.db
[Dd]esktop.ini
$RECYCLE.BIN/

# Local environment variables
.env
```

Having created the local repository, we can now commit all the new Salesforce DX files to it before we synchronize the local repository with the hosted remote repository.

Performing the Initial Add and Commit

At this point, we have created a new Salesforce DX project and initialized a new local Git repository. To perform an initial commit, first add all the files that we want Git to track, a process known as staging, by executing the following command in VS Code's integrated terminal:

```
$ git add .
```

Now execute the following command to see the staged files that Git is tracking:

```
$ git status
```

The command should generate the following output.

Listing 9-5. Files staged in a local Git repository

```
On branch master

No commits yet

Changes to be committed:
  (use "git rm --cached <file>..." to unstage)
        new file:   .eslintignore
        new file:   .forceignore
        new file:   .gitignore
        new file:   .husky/pre-commit
        new file:   .prettierignore
```

```
        new file:   .prettierrc
        new file:   .vscode/extensions.json
        new file:   .vscode/launch.json
        new file:   .vscode/settings.json
        new file:   README.md
        new file:   config/project-scratch-def.json
        new file:   force-app/main/default/aura/.eslintrc.json
        new file:   force-app/main/default/lwc/.eslintrc.json
        new file:   jest.config.js
        new file:   package.json
        new file:   scripts/apex/hello.apex
        new file:   scripts/soql/account.soql
        new file:   sfdx-project.json
```

To create a snapshot of all the Salesforce DX project's changes, as captured in the staged files, the next step is to commit them to the local repository, which is performed using the following command in VS Code's integrated terminal:

```
$ git commit --message "Initial commit"
```

The output should look like the following.

Listing 9-6. Files committed to a local Git repository

```
[master (root-commit) 2a4b1da] Initial commit
 18 files changed, 255 insertions(+)
 create mode 100644 .eslintignore
 create mode 100755 .forceignore
 create mode 100644 .gitignore
 create mode 100755 .husky/pre-commit
 create mode 100755 .prettierignore
 create mode 100755 .prettierrc
 create mode 100644 .vscode/extensions.json
 create mode 100644 .vscode/launch.json
 create mode 100644 .vscode/settings.json
 create mode 100644 README.md
 create mode 100644 config/project-scratch-def.json
 create mode 100644 force-app/main/default/aura/.eslintrc.json
```

```
create mode 100644 force-app/main/default/lwc/.eslintrc.json
create mode 100644 jest.config.js
create mode 100644 package.json
create mode 100644 scripts/apex/hello.apex
create mode 100644 scripts/soql/account.soql
create mode 100644 sfdx-project.json
```

The next step is not required, although it is highly recommended.

Changing the Branch Name

When initializing a local Git repository using the `git init` command, the default branch is named `master`. As we reflect on the historical use of certain terms, `master` (especially in the context of `master-slave`) is quite rightly being replaced with more appropriate alternatives. Good practice is to rename the `master` branch to `main` (or another name of your choice) by executing the following command in VS Code's integrated terminal:

```
$ git branch -m master main
```

Alternatively, to avoid having to perform this step for every new local repository, execute the following command to change the default branch name:

```
$ git config --global init.defaultBranch main
```

So far, we have created a Salesforce DX project and tracked its changes in a local Git repository. We also created a hosted remote repository in GitHub. We will now link the local repository and hosted remote repository so that we can synchronize the changes.

Linking a Local and Hosted Remote Repository

Linking, or connecting, a local repository to a hosted remote repository provides an alias for the remote repository that can be used as an alternative to the remote repository's lengthy URL. The connection is made using this command in Visual Studio Code's integrated terminal:

```
$ git remote add origin \
    https://github.com/<uname>/SalesforceDXVCS.git
```

where uname is replaced by the GitHub username that we used when creating the GitHub account earlier, in this case IvanHarris-SalesforceDX-Book, and origin is the new alias. Running git remote --verbose will display the remote connections, as shown here.

Listing 9-7. Git remote connections

```
origin  https://github.com/IvanHarris-SalesforceDX-Book/SalesforceDXVCS.
git (fetch)
origin  https://github.com/IvanHarris-SalesforceDX-Book/SalesforceDXVCS.
git (push)
```

With a connection established between the local repository and the hosted remote repository, we can synchronize the tracked changes next.

Synchronizing Tracked Changes

To synchronize the changes being tracked by the local repository with the hosted remote repository, we push the changes using this command in VS Code's integrated terminal:

```
$ git push --set-upstream origin main
```

If this is the first time that you have used a Git command to interact with the newly linked hosted remote repository, you may be notified that authorization to access GitHub is required. This is the first dialog that is displayed; click the **Allow** button.

Figure 9-13. *Authorization to access GitHub is required*

This will open the following page in a browser; click the **Continue** button.

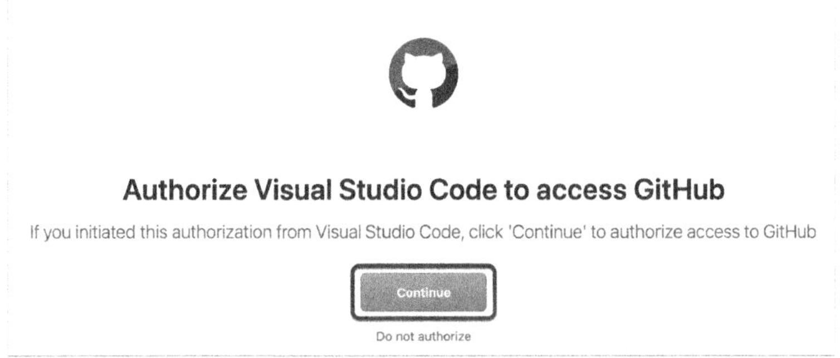

Figure 9-14. *Start VS Code authorization to access GitHub*

OAuth is used to authorize Visual Studio Code access to the GitHub hosted remote repository. Click the **Authorize github** button in the next page that appears.

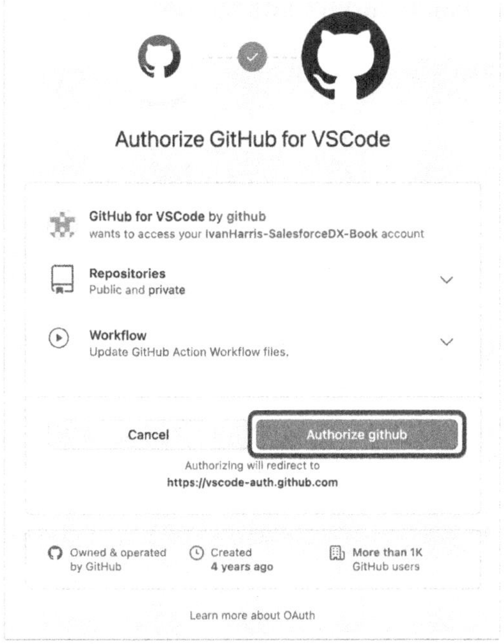

Figure 9-15. *Approve VS Code access to GitHub using OAuth*

Enter your GitHub password that you made a note of when signing up for an account in the Confirm Access dialog box, then click the **Confirm password** button.

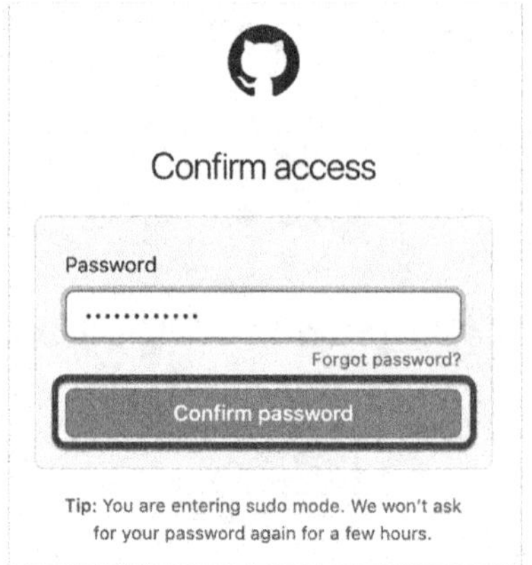

Figure 9-16. *Confirm VS Code access to GitHub*

The final OAuth stage is a redirect back to Visual Studio Code to complete the authorization flow. The first of two dialogs that will appear requests permission to open VS Code. Click the **Open Visual Studio Code** button.

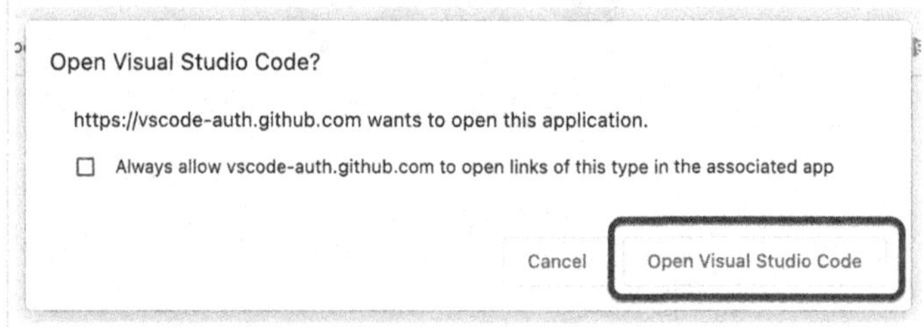

Figure 9-17. *Redirect from GitHub to VS Code*

The second dialog requests permission for a VS Code extension to open the GitHub authentication URI. Click the **Open** button.

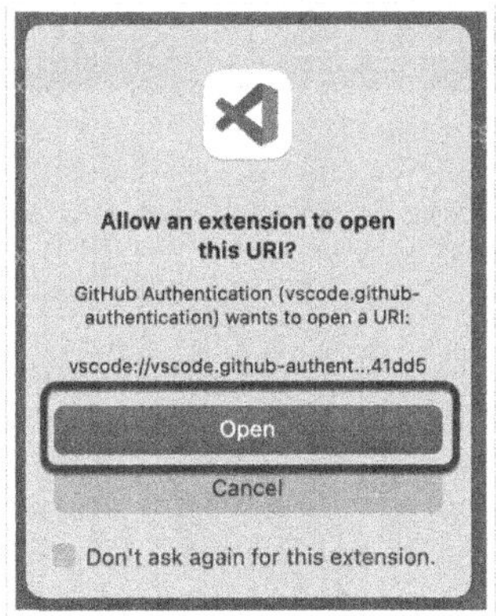

Figure 9-18. *Approve an extension to open the URI*

With access to GitHub authorized, the `git push --set-upstream origin main` command continues to run and pushes all the tracked changes from the local repository's `main` branch to a new branch on the remote repository of the same name. As we created a bare repository, this will create the default branch in the remote repository using the name `main`. The command will output a completion statement such as this.

Listing 9-8. Git push output status

```
Enumerating objects: 31, done.
Counting objects: 100% (31/31), done.
Delta compression using up to 8 threads
Compressing objects: 100% (24/24), done.
Writing objects: 100% (31/31), 5.04 KiB | 2.52 MiB/s, done.
Total 31 (delta 0), reused 0 (delta 0), pack-reused 0
To https://github.com/IvanHarris-SalesforceDX-Book/SalesforceDXVCS.git
 * [new branch]      main -> main
branch 'main' set up to track 'origin/main'.
```

To view the synchronized files in GitHub, log in and navigate to the `SalesforceDXVCS` repository, which will show that the files are now present. Other developers can now pull the contents of this repository to add their own changes.

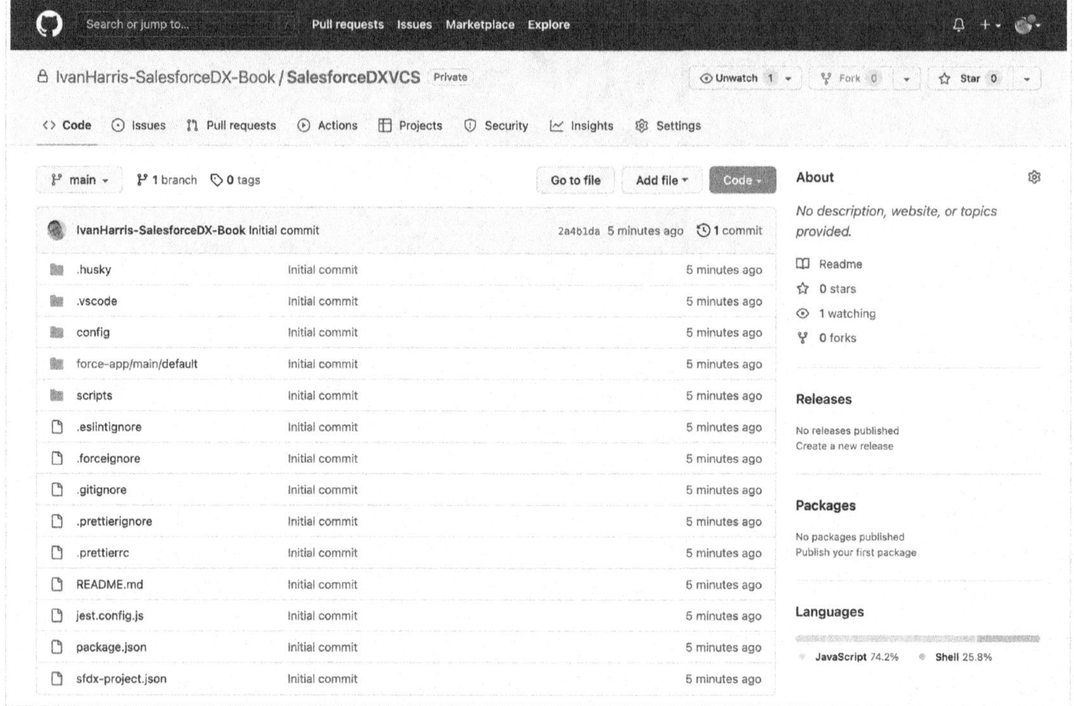

Figure 9-19. *Synchronized remote repository*

In this section, we started with a new Salesforce DX project and added it to a hosted remote repository in GitHub, which makes it available to other developers to collaborate on. The hosted remote repository has the same name as the Salesforce DX project and mirrors its branch structure.

What if you have an existing set of applications and customizations that have been added to a production org using change sets, and you wish to transition from the production org being the source of truth to a version control system being the source of truth? To do this, follow the instructions in the section "Converting from Metadata API Format to Source Format" in Chapter 8, "Metadata," to synchronize the production org with a Salesforce DX project, and then follow the preceding instructions to add the Salesforce DX project to a GitHub hosted remote repository. Developers can then collaboratively evolve the applications and customizations using the GitHub repository as the source of truth.

Although it's useful to understand how to add an existing Salesforce DX project to a version control system, we often start collaborating on a Salesforce DX project that is already under source control, which we will cover next; that said, feel free to skip to the "Example Git Workflow" section if you want to move straight to working with the Salesforce DX project that we created in this section.

Working with an Existing Salesforce DX Project

Often, we start collaborating on an existing Salesforce DX project that is in a version control system rather than adding a new one. The `git clone` command creates a local working copy of a hosted remote repository and links the local repository with the hosted remote repository. To illustrate the process, we will clone Salesforce's Dreamhouse app repository.

Note The Dreamhouse app can be found, along with many more sample Salesforce projects, on the Code Samples and SDKs site, which can be found here: `https://developer.salesforce.com/code-samples-and-sdks`.

To clone the Dreamhouse remote repository, perform the following steps:

1. Open a terminal application.
2. Navigate to a directory where you would like to create the Dreamhouse Salesforce DX directory.
3. Execute the command:

   ```
   git clone ↩
     https://github.com/↩
     dreamhouseapp/dreamhouse-lwc
   ```

4. Launch Visual Studio Code and open the `dreamhouse-lwc` directory that the `git clone` command created.

The `git clone` command has created a Salesforce DX project and a local Git repository linked to the hosted remote repository. You're now ready to follow the Git workflow that will be explained in the next section to make changes to the Salesforce DX project and share those changes with your colleagues.

Example Git Workflow

Once a Salesforce DX project has been created, a local Git repository has been set up to track changes to the project, and the local repository has been linked to a hosted remote repository, we're ready to start collaborating on the project. The steps to be followed when adding new features, or changing existing features, typically follow this workflow:

1. Create and switch to a local feature branch.
2. Add, delete, and change Salesforce metadata components.
3. Test the changes in a scratch org or a source tracking-enabled sandbox.
4. Stage the changes in the local repository.
5. Repeat steps 2, 3, and 4 until the feature is complete.
6. Commit the changes to the local repository.
7. Push the local repository's feature branch to the hosted remote repository.
8. Generate a pull request for team members to review the new feature changes.
9. Merge the feature branch in the hosted remote repository to the hosted remote repository's default branch.
10. Optionally, delete the feature branches in the local and hosted remote repositories, unless they will be reused.

Note The preceding list is an example of a Centralized Workflow. To discover more about alternative workflow types, simply search for "Git workflows" to find a wide range of scholarly articles.

We'll follow these steps to make a change to the new `SalesforceDXVCS` Salesforce DX project created in the "Working with a New Salesforce DX Project" section earlier in the chapter.

Creating a Local Feature Branch

Creating a local feature branch allows developers to work on a project's files without disrupting the default `main` branch. A local feature branch can be deleted, for example, if you were just experimenting with an idea, without fear of making inadvertent changes to the default branch. Alternatively, the feature branch changes can be committed to the local repository's default `main` branch, which can then be pushed to the hosted remote repository and merged with its `main` branch. The changes then become part of the project's code base and will be available to all the other developers who are collaborating on the project.

Before we start, make sure that you have launched Visual Studio Code and that the `SalesforceDXVCS` project that we created earlier is open.

In Visual Studio Code Status Bar, you can easily see which branch you are on; in our case, it should be `main`, as shown in this screenshot.

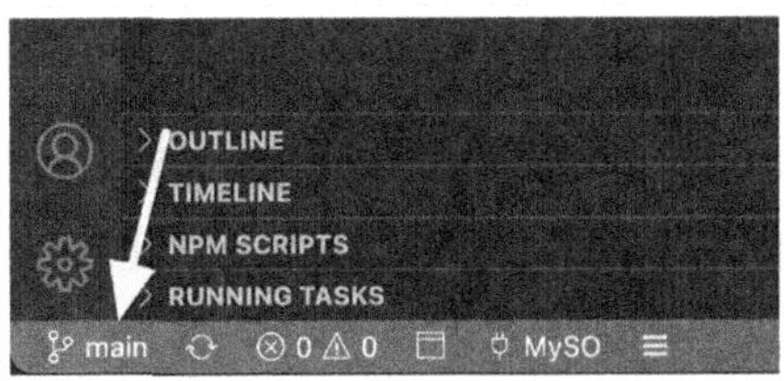

Figure 9-20. *Git main branch in VCS*

To create a new feature branch, and switch to it straightaway, execute the following Git command in VS Code's integrated terminal:

```
$ git checkout -b feature-x
```

Visual Studio Code will now show that we have switched to the `feature-x` branch.

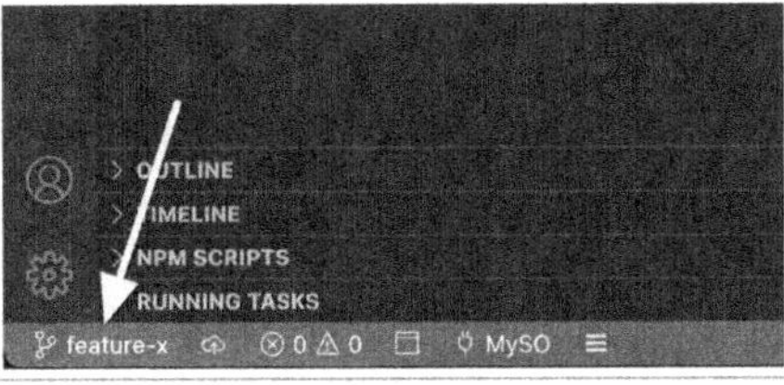

Figure 9-21. *Git feature-x branch in VCS*

Note Git commands are available in the Visual Studio Code Command Palette and if you click the branch indicator in the Visual Studio Code Status Bar, which is shown in the previous figure. Furthermore, by clicking the Source Control icon ( ) in VS Code's Activity Bar (on the left-hand side of the user interface), you can interact with Git to view changed files, perform differences, execute Git commands such as commits, and much more. It's left as an exercise for the reader to explore further and boost their collaborative productivity!

To view local branches, execute the `git branch` command, which will display the branches and indicate the branch that you are on with an asterisk.

Listing 9-9. Listing of local Git branches

```
* feature-x
  main
```

With a local feature branch created, we can make some project modifications with confidence that we are not going to change anything in the `main` branch. We'll make some changes now.

Creating a Lightning Web Component

To illustrate the Git workflow, we will make a modification to the project by adding a simple Lightning web component. Assuming that the `SalesforceDXVCS` project is still open in Visual Studio Code, create the Lightning web component's scaffolding by performing the following steps:

1. In VS Code's Explorer in the Side Bar, expand the nodes **force-app/main/default** and right-click the **lwc** node.

2. In the context menu, click the menu item called **SFDX: Create Lightning Web Component**.

3. In the Enter desired filename box that appears at the top of VS Code's user interface, type `helloWorld` and hit **Enter**.

4. Hit Enter again to select the default directory for the files to be created in, which will be **force-app/main/default/lwc/helloWorld**.

The VS Code Explorer will show the newly created files.

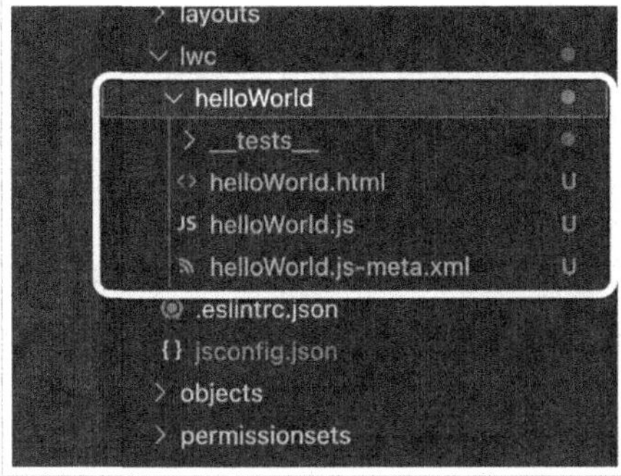

Figure 9-22. *New LWC files in Visual Studio Code*

If you now execute the `git status` command, it will show that changed files exist, but they have not yet been added to the Git staging area using the `git add` command, nor have they been saved to the project timeline using the `git commit` command. They are therefore untracked by Git.

Listing 9-10. Unstaged, changed files

```
On branch feature-x
Untracked files:
  (use "git add <file>..." to include in what will be committed)
        force-app/main/default/lwc/helloWorld/

nothing added to commit but untracked files present (use "git add"
to track)
```

The Lightning web component's scaffolding doesn't do anything that we can observe in the Salesforce user interface. We'll make some changes to the files to correct that. First, change the contents of the `helloWorld.html` file to the following.

Listing 9-11. helloWorld.html

```
<template>
    <lightning-card title="Hello World" icon-name="utility:world">
        <div class="slds-m-around_medium">
            <p>Hello there!</p>
        </div>
    </lightning-card>
</template>
```

So that we can add the Lightning web component to a Home Page using Lightning App Builder, update the `helloWorld.js-meta.xml` file to the following.

Listing 9-12. helloWorld.js-meta.xml

```
<?xml version="1.0" encoding="UTF-8"?>
<LightningComponentBundle xmlns="http://soap.sforce.com/2006/04/metadata">
    <apiVersion>55.0</apiVersion>
    <isExposed>true</isExposed>
    <targets>
        <target>lightning__HomePage</target>
    </targets>
</LightningComponentBundle>
```

Now let's test the component in a scratch org.

Testing the Component in a Scratch Org

To test our new Lightning web component in a scratch org, start by pushing the new files to the org by executing the `sfdx force:source:push` command, which will push the files to the default scratch org with the alias `MySO` if you have been following along with this chapter.

Open the default scratch org using the `sfdx force:org:open` command. When the org is open in a browser, click the App Launcher (⁝⁝⁝) icon and then click the **Sales** app. Next, click the cog (⚙) icon and then click **Edit Page**. This will open the Lightning App Builder for the Sales app's Home Page.

In the list of components will be our new `helloWorld` custom component (1).

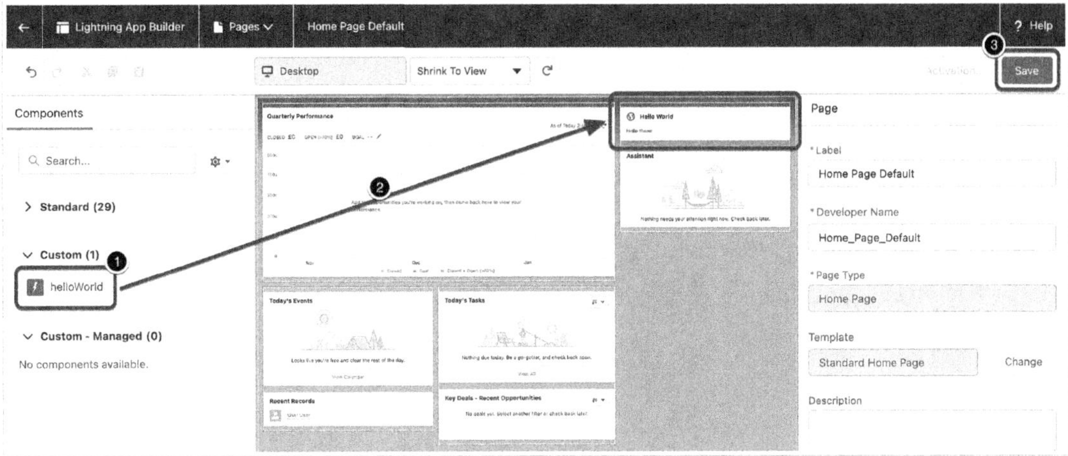

Figure 9-23. *Lightning App Builder*

Drag the `helloWorld` custom component onto the Page Canvas (2) and then click the **Save** button (3). In the Page Saved confirmation dialog, click the **Activate** button.

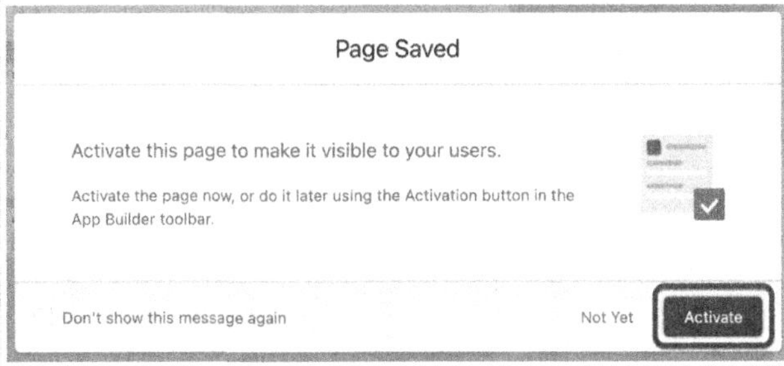

Figure 9-24. *Page Saved confirmation dialog*

This will open the Activation: Home Page Default dialog; click the **Assign as Org Default** button.

***Figure 9-25.** Activation: Home Page Default dialog*

Click the **Save** button in the Set as Org Default: Home Page Default dialog that appears.

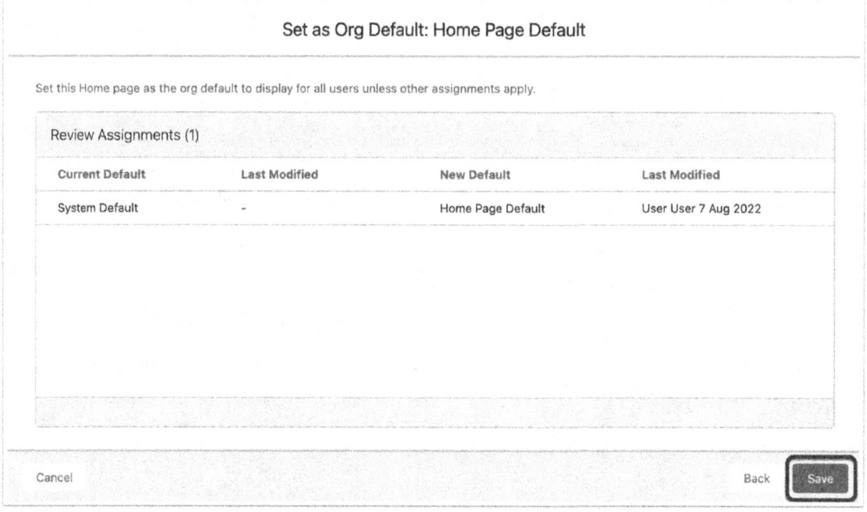

***Figure 9-26.** Set as Org Default: Home Page Default dialog*

Exit the Lightning App Builder by clicking the arrow button (←).

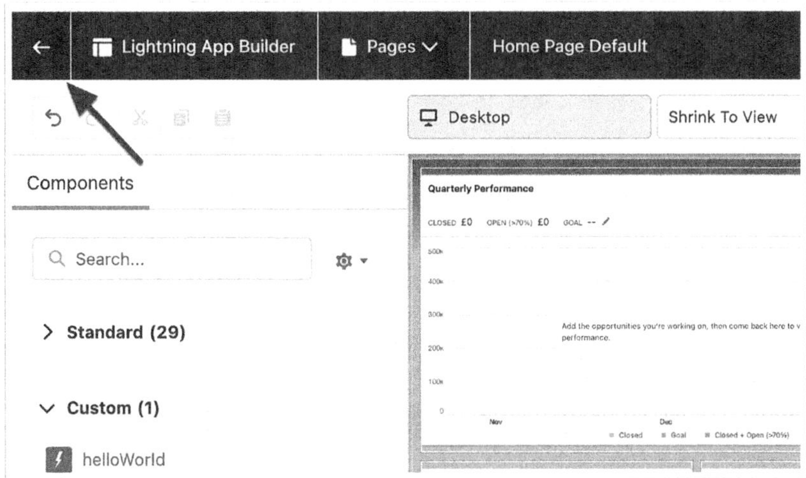

***Figure 9-27.** Exiting Lightning App Builder*

This returns us the Sales app's Home Page where we can confirm that our Lightning web component is present.

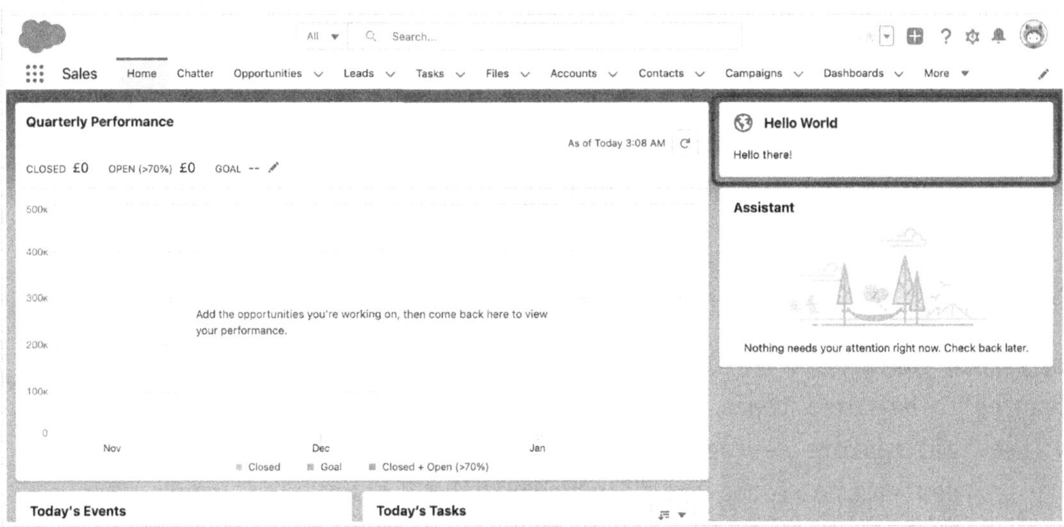

***Figure 9-28.** The Sales app with a new Lightning web component*

Note Let's imagine for the purposes of this exercise that we only wish to place the Lightning web component under source control. We will therefore not be adding the Sales app Home Page changes that we made using Lightning App Builder.

Granted, our Lightning web component isn't particularly exciting! Having said that, we've tested that the component displays correctly in the Lightning Experience user interface, and we now have some changed files to add to the Git staging area for Git to track.

Adding the Component to the Git Staging Area

Git's staging area is a collection of changes that are to be included in the next commit. If you are developing a new feature, for example, you might work on one aspect of the feature until you are happy with the results and add the changes to the staging area before moving on to the next aspect of the feature. When your feature development is complete, you'll commit your changes, which will be covered in the next section.

To add the new Lightning web component files to Git's staging area, execute the following command in the Visual Studio Code's integrated terminal:

```
$ git add .
```

Running the `git status` command again will show that we have staged files ready to commit.

Listing 9-13. Staged Lightning web component files

```
On branch feature-x
Changes to be committed:
  (use "git restore --staged <file>..." to unstage)
        new file:   force-app/main/default/lwc/helloWorld/__tests__/
        helloWorld.test.js
        new file:   force-app/main/default/lwc/helloWorld/helloWorld.html
        new file:   force-app/main/default/lwc/helloWorld/helloWorld.js
        new file:   force-app/main/default/lwc/helloWorld/helloWorld.
        js-meta.xml
```

As mentioned earlier, we would most likely move on to develop another aspect of our feature; however, in this instance, we are going to move straight to committing the changes.

Committing the Component Changes

When a complete set of changed files have been added to Git's staging area using the `git add` command, those changes can be committed to the project's history as a snapshot of changes using the following Git command:

```
$ git commit -m "Added new Hello World LWC."
```

Git confirms that a snapshot has been created that includes changes to the files that make up our Lightning web component.

Listing 9-14. Committed Lightning web component files

```
[feature-x f95a925] Added new Hello World LWC.
 4 files changed, 43 insertions(+)
 create mode 100644 force-app/main/default/lwc/helloWorld/__tests__/
 helloWorld.test.js
 create mode 100644 force-app/main/default/lwc/helloWorld/helloWorld.html
 create mode 100644 force-app/main/default/lwc/helloWorld/helloWorld.js
 create mode 100644 force-app/main/default/lwc/helloWorld/helloWorld.
 js-meta.xml
```

Executing the `git status` command one more time shows that there are no untracked files and no files in the staging area to commit.

Listing 9-15. No more untracked or uncommitted files

```
On branch feature-x
nothing to commit, working tree clean
```

Our local repository has an updated project with the Lightning web component committed changes in a feature branch. The next step in the workflow is to push those changes to the hosted remote repository.

Pushing Changes from the Local to the Remote Repository

Up to this point, the Lightning web component is committed to our local repository's feature branch, meaning that our local repository has the complete project history up until the point where we created and switched to the new `feature-x` branch plus the Lightning web component changes. To make these changes visible to the other developers on our team, they need to be synchronized with the hosted remote repository that our local repository is linked to. This is a three-step process:

1. Push the local feature branch's changes to the hosted remote repository. If the feature branch that has been created in the local repository doesn't exist in the hosted remote repository, a new one of the same name will be created.

2. Create a GitHub pull request to let other developers know that you have pushed changes to the hosted remote repository. This allows the changes to be reviewed before the changes are merged with the hosted remote repository's `main` branch.

3. Merge the changes with the hosted remote repository's default `main` branch.

To perform the first step and push the locally committed changes to the hosted remote repository, execute the following command:

```
$ git push origin feature-x
```

The command output shows that a new branch has been created in the hosted remote repository.

Listing 9-16. Pushing changes to a hosted remote repository

```
Enumerating objects: 17, done.
Counting objects: 100% (17/17), done.
Delta compression using up to 8 threads
Compressing objects: 100% (9/9), done.
Writing objects: 100% (12/12), 1.46 KiB | 1.46 MiB/s, done.
Total 12 (delta 1), reused 0 (delta 0), pack-reused 0
remote: Resolving deltas: 100% (1/1), completed with 1 local object.
```

```
remote:
remote: Create a pull request for 'feature-x' on GitHub by visiting:
remote:      https://github.com/IvanHarris-SalesforceDX-Book/
SalesforceDXVCS/pull/new/feature-x
remote:
To https://github.com/IvanHarris-SalesforceDX-Book/SalesforceDXVCS.git
 * [new branch]      feature-x -> feature-x
```

Viewing the <> **Code** tab on the hosted remote repository in GitHub shows the following:

1. The `feature-x` branch was recently pushed.
2. Two branches now exist in the hosted remote repository.
3. A `feature-x` branch has been created in the hosted remote repository.
4. A pull request can now be created for the changes that have been pushed to the new `feature-x` branch in the hosted remote repository.

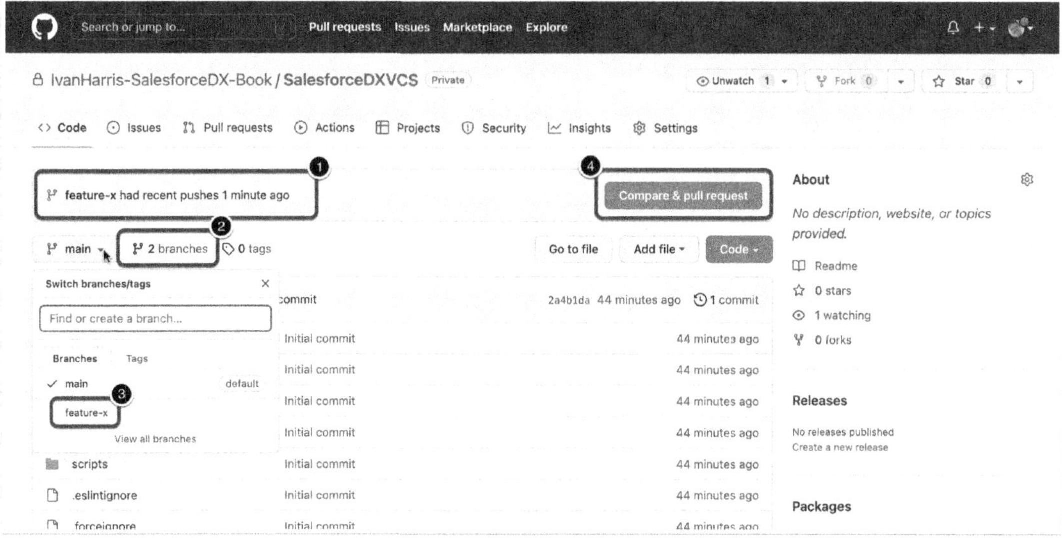

***Figure 9-29.** The hosted remote repository with pushed changes*

Click the **Compare & pull request** button to start the pull request creation process that will be covered in the next section.

Creating a Pull Request

When the **Compare & pull request** button that is shown in the previous screenshot is clicked, the Open a pull request page is displayed.

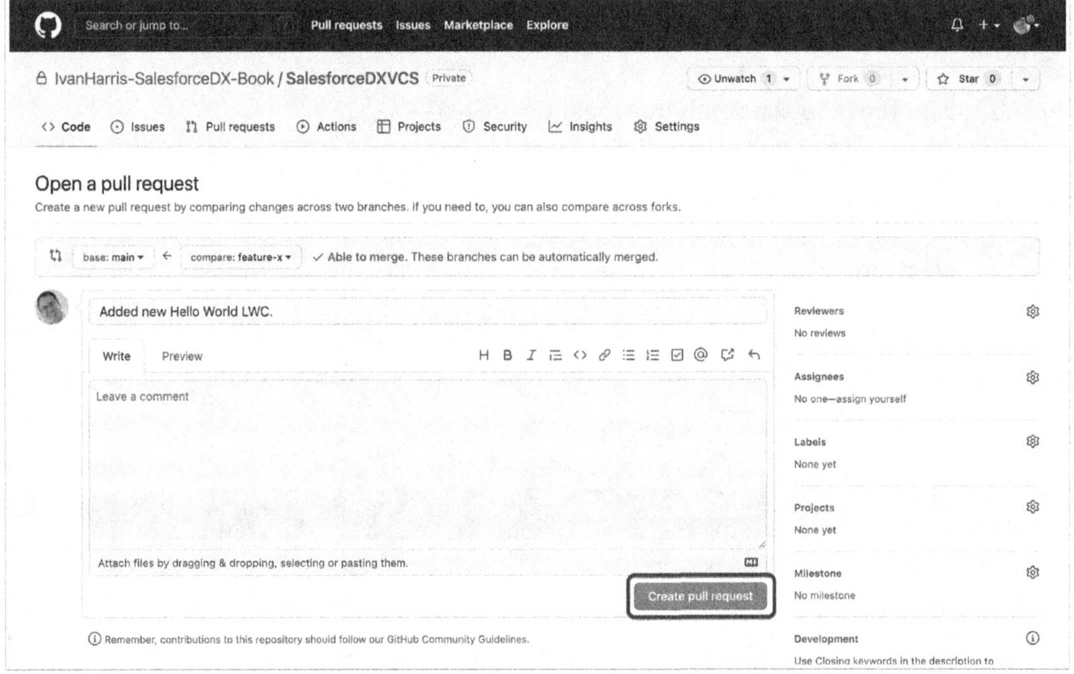

Figure 9-30. *Open a pull request page*

Click the **Create pull request** button to do just that, after which the pull request page is displayed.

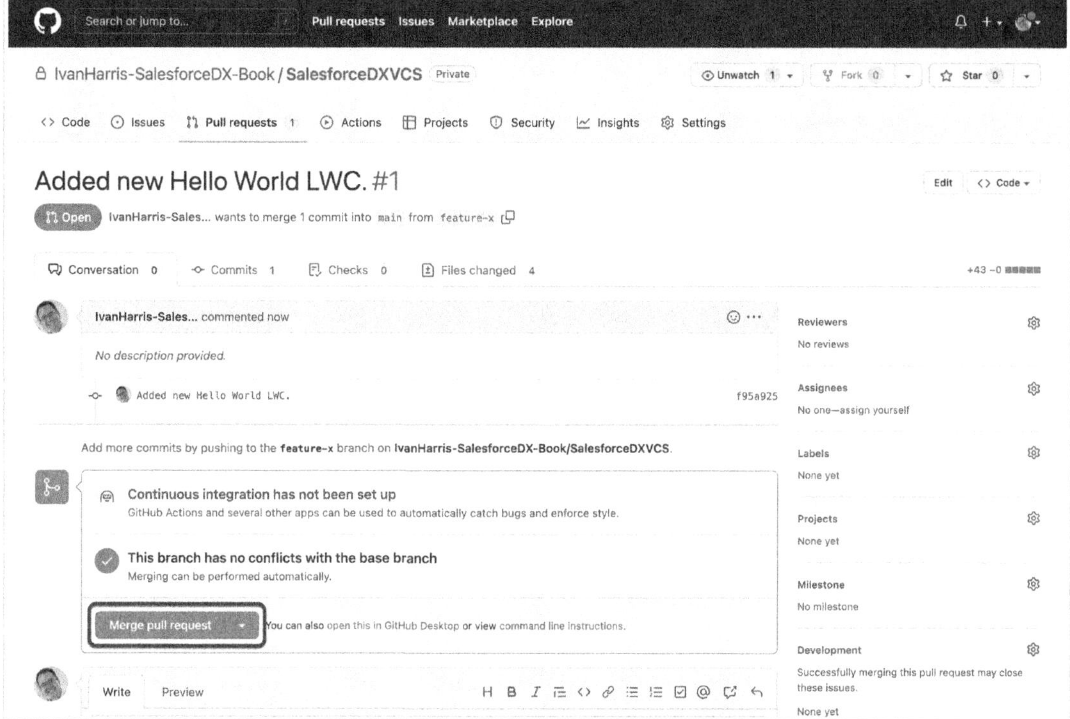

Figure 9-31. *Pull request page*

Team members can now collaboratively review the proposed changes that are part of the pull request. When any suggested modifications are made, and there is consensus that the changes are ready to be merged into the default `main` branch, click the **Merge pull request** button.

Merging Changes

Clicking the **Merge pull request** button in the previous screenshot changes the button to **Confirm merge**; go ahead and click the button.

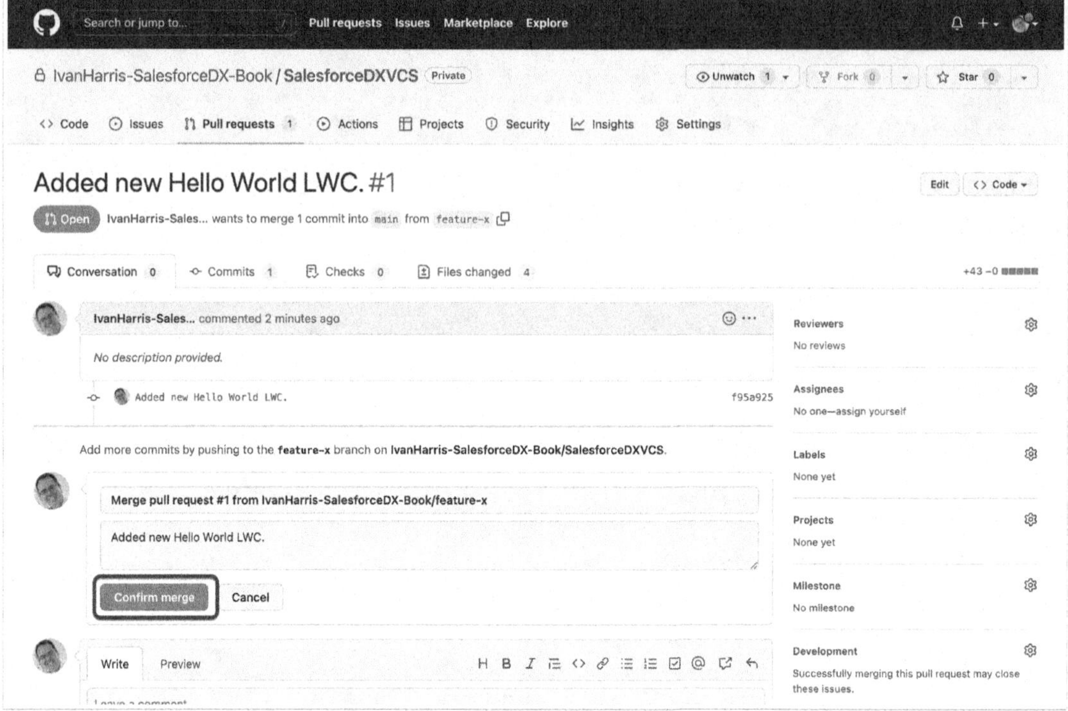

Figure 9-32. *Confirm merge request*

The merge is shown as successfully completed (1), and you now have the option to optionally delete the `feature-x` branch should you wish (2), although it's not uncommon to reuse the branches for further changes.

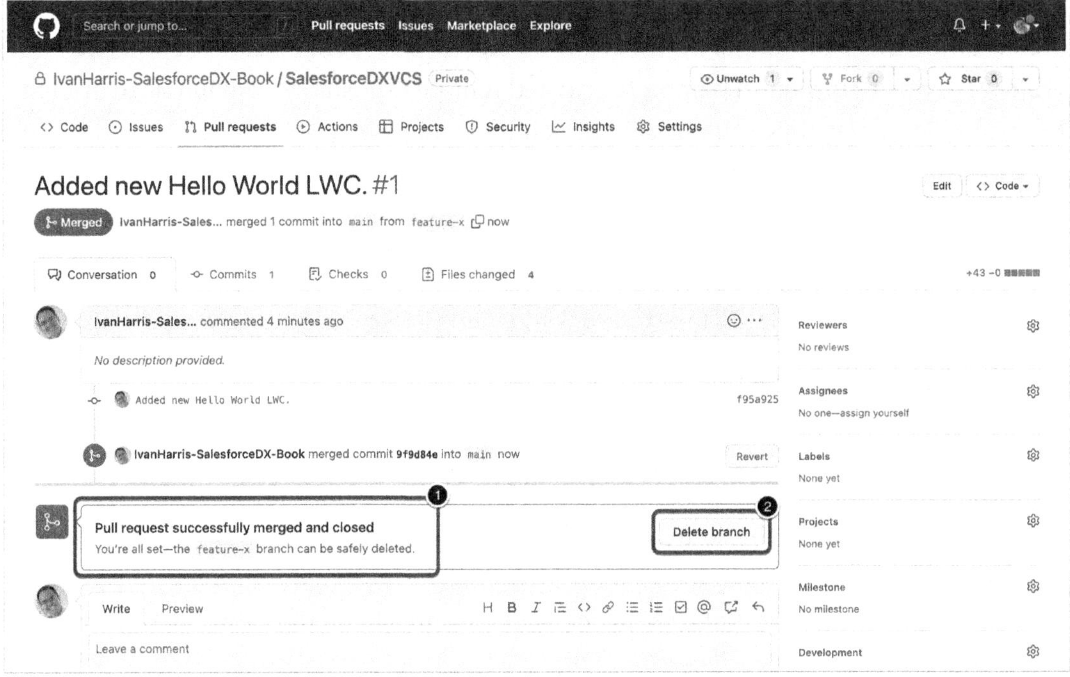

Figure 9-33. *Successful merge*

If you click the <> **Code** tab (1), select the **Main** branch (2), and navigate to **force-app/main/default/lwc/helloWorld** directory (3), you can see the Lightning web component files that have been merged (4).

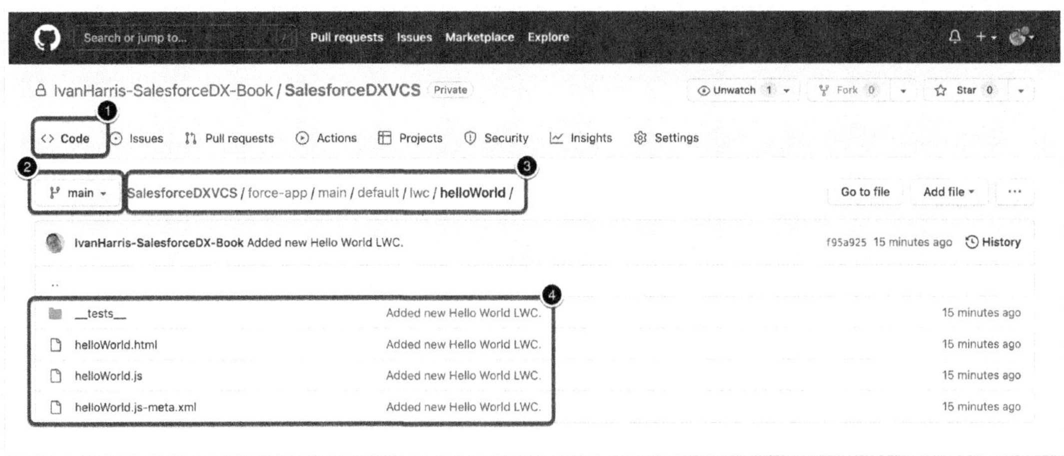

Figure 9-34. *Merged Lightning web component files*

The Lightning web component changes are now part of the project's code base. The next time that a developer on the team executes a `git pull` command or a `git fetch/git merge` command pair on the hosted remote repository's default `main` branch, they will synchronize these changes with their local repository.

We have just executed an end-to-end version control system workflow using Salesforce DX, Git, and GitHub. We'll now summarize what we have explored in this chapter.

Chapter Summary

In this chapter, we learned how to install and set up the various Git solutions needed to collaboratively develop applications or customizations using Salesforce DX where a version control system is the source of truth. We walked through how to start working on a new Salesforce DX project or an existing one. Finally, we stepped through a typical Git workflow to make changes that were synchronized with a hosted remote Git repository for other developers to have access to.

In the next chapter, we will show how to add test users to a scratch org so that an application or customization can be tested using a user account with specific permissions.

CHAPTER 10

Test Users

When a scratch org is created, a user called `User User` is automatically added that has the System Administrator profile assigned to it. Here's the user, which can be viewed by opening a scratch org and navigating to **Setup ➤ Users ➤ Users**.

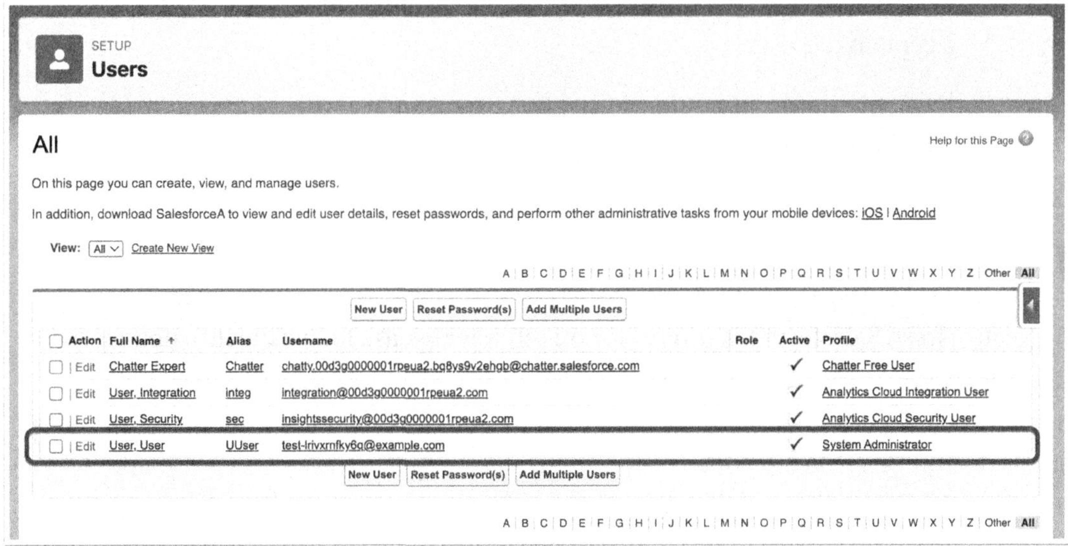

Figure 10-1. *A new scratch org's User User*

If your application or customization is only used by system administrators, you can perform testing with this user. Having said that, you will normally want to perform testing with different end users in mind, such as service agents and account executives; therefore, it makes much more sense to test with a user that has the same permissions as the end users in your production org. You can create additional users in a scratch org, assign them a profile such as Standard User, and then assign feature license and permission sets to mimic your production org end users.

Before we see how to create these additional users, let's summarize the commands that will be covered in this chapter.

I. Harris, *Beginning Salesforce DX*, https://doi.org/10.1007/978-1-4842-8114-7_10

This Chapter's Commands

The commands that we will explore in this chapter for creating users, assigning permission sets, and generating passwords belong to the `force:user` topic:

- **`force:user:create`**: Creates a new user in a scratch org
- **`force:user:display`**: Displays information about a scratch org user
- **`force:user:list`**: Lists scratch org users
- **`force:user:permset:assign`**: Assigns permission sets to scratch org users
- **`force:user:password:generate`**: Generates a random password for a scratch org user

We'll delve into the commands shortly; first, as usual, we will create a new Salesforce DX project for the chapter.

This Chapter's Project

To create a fresh Salesforce DX project for this chapter, please follow the instructions in Chapter 6, "Projects," and name the project `SalesforceDXTestUsers` using the default standard template. As we will be working with scratch orgs, please also make sure that you have a default Dev Hub org authorized with an alias of `MyDH` as described in Chapter 5, "Dev Hub." Finally, create a scratch org with the alias `MySO` and assign it as having the default username. Please refer to Chapter 7, "Orgs," for scratch org creation instructions. If you now run the `force:org:list` command, you should get an output similar to the following.

Listing 10-1. Chapter org list

```
=== Orgs

     ALIAS  USERNAME                      ORG ID              CONNECTED STATUS
───  ─────  ────────────────────────────  ──────────────────  ────────────────
(D)  MyDH   ihdxdh@example.com            00D4K0000015OzMUAU  Connected

     ALIAS  USERNAME                      ORG ID              EXPIRATION DATE
───  ─────  ────────────────────────────  ──────────────────  ────────────────
(U)  MySO   test-lrivxrnfky6q@example.com 00D3G0000001RPEUA2  2022-09-06
```

If you have additional orgs, that's OK as long as you have a new default scratch org.

With everything set up, we can move on and look at creating scratch org users, assigning permission sets, and generating passwords. First up, we'll see how to go about creating a new scratch org user.

Creating Scratch Org Users

To create, view, and list scratch org users, we will use the following commands from the **force:user** topic in this section:

- **force:user:create**: Creates a new user in a scratch org
- **force:user:display**: Displays information about a scratch org user
- **force:user:list**: Lists scratch org users

To create a user in a scratch org, execute the following CLI command. If you have been following this chapter so far, no other options are required because you have set up a default Dev Hub, with the alias MyDH, and you have created a default scratch org, with the alias MySO.

```
$ sfdx force:user:create \
    --setalias MyUser
```

The complete set of parameters that can be used for this command are as follows:

- --setalias|-a: Provides an alias for the user to be created that can be used to reference the user rather than using its username. [Optional]
- --definitionfile|-f: The path to a user definition file that can be used to customize a user. [Optional]
- --setuniqueusername|-s: Ensures that a unique username is created by appending the org ID to the username that's specified in the user definition file. [Optional]
- --targetusername|-u: The username or alias of the scratch org where the user should be created. [Optional]

- `--targetdevhubusername|-v`: The username or alias of the Dev Hub org that was used to create the scratch org where the user should be created. [Optional]
- `--apiversion, --json, --loglevel`: Please refer to the discussion on global parameters in the section "Command-Line Parameters and Arguments" in Chapter 4, "Salesforce CLI."

The command output states that a user has been successfully created.

Listing 10-2. Successful user creation

```
Successfully created user "1659935975571_test-mesmas4s0rtd@example.com"
with ID 0050C000005zJ64QAE for org 00D0C0000001j51UAA.
You can see more details about this user by running "sfdx
force:user:display -u 1659935975571_test-mesmas4s0rtd@example.com".
```

The preceding command will create a user with the Standard User profile assigned to it and the alias `MyUser`. To view the new user and all the other users in your scratch org, execute the following command:

```
$ sfdx force:user:list
```

This command's parameters are as follows:

- `--targetusername|-u`: The username or alias of the scratch org containing the users to list. [Optional]
- `--targetdevhubusername|-v`: The username or alias of the Dev Hub org that was used to create the scratch org containing the users to list. [Optional]
- `--apiversion, --json, --loglevel`: Please refer to the discussion on global parameters in the section "Command-Line Parameters and Arguments" in Chapter 4, "Salesforce CLI."

The command's output should look like the following.

Listing 10-3. List of scratch org users

```
=== Users in org 00D0C0000001j51UAA

Default Alias  Username                                    Profile Name
─────── ────── ─────────────────────────────────────────── ────────────────────
(A)     MySO   test-mesmas4s0rtd@example.com               System Administrator
        MyUser 1659935975571_test-mesmas4s0rtd@example.com Standard User
```

Note The preceding output has had the User Id column removed to aid readability.

The username of the new user, with the alias `MyUser`, is formed by adding a timestamp, in this case `1659935975571_`, to the beginning of the default user's username to ensure that it is unique. The advantage of creating an alias is clear, as using the full username would be rather cumbersome!

Note By setting the `Username` field in the user definition file, you can create a user with a username of your choice. To ensure that a unique username is generated, use the `--setuniqueusername | -s` parameter, which causes the CLI to append the org Id to the definition file's `Username` to make it unique.

To define additional user characteristics, a user definition file can be created and added to your Salesforce DX project. The file allows you to assign values to any field on the User record that will be created and to set the following Salesforce DX–specific parameters:

- `permsets`: Assign permission sets to the user.
- `generatePassword`: Generate a random password for the user.
- `profileName`: Assign a profile to the user.

Note The complete list of fields on the User standard object can be found in the SOAP API Developer Guide, which can be found here: `https://developer.salesforce.com/docs/atlas.en-us.api.meta/api/sforce_api_objects_user.htm`.

The user definition file can be stored anywhere that the Salesforce CLI can access. I prefer to store the file within the Salesforce DX project's `config` directory as it simplifies version control and keeps all the scratch org-related configuration files together. In Visual Studio Code, create a new file in the `config` folder, which can be found in the root folder of the Salesforce DX project. Give the file a descriptive name and make sure that the file extension is `json`. I call mine `project-user-def.json` to be consistent with the scratch org definition file that is in the same directory. Copy the following JSON into the file and save it.

Listing 10-4. Example user definition file

```
{
    "CompanyName": "Acme",
    "Department": "R&D",
    "Division": "Renewable Energy",
    "profileName": "Chatter Free User"
}
```

The user definition file sets three fields on the new User record, namely, `CompanyName`, `Department`, and `Division`. It also sets the `profileName` parameter to assign the `Chatter Free User` profile to the created user.

Run the following CLI command to create a user using the new user definition file:

```
$ sfdx force:user:create \
    --setalias MyUser2 \
    --definitionfile ./config/project-user-def.json
```

Running the `force:user:list` command again shows the newly created user.

Listing 10-5. List of scratch org users with the second user added

```
=== Users in org 00D0C0000001j51UAA

 Default Alias    Username                                     Profile Name
 ─────── ──────── ──────────────────────────────────────────── ──────────────
 (A)     MySO     test-mesmas4s0rtd@example.com                System Administrator
         MyUser   1659935975571_test-mesmas4s0rtd@example.com Standard User
         MyUser2  1659937828150_test-mesmas4s0rtd@example.com Chatter Free User
```

Note Scratch orgs include a limited number of Salesforce user licenses. If all the licenses have been used, the creation of a user will fail. The simplest solution to follow these exercises is to delete the scratch org and create a fresh one if this occurs.

Open your scratch org using the `force:org:open` command, and navigate to **Setup ➤ Users ➤ Users** where you can see the two new users that we just created.

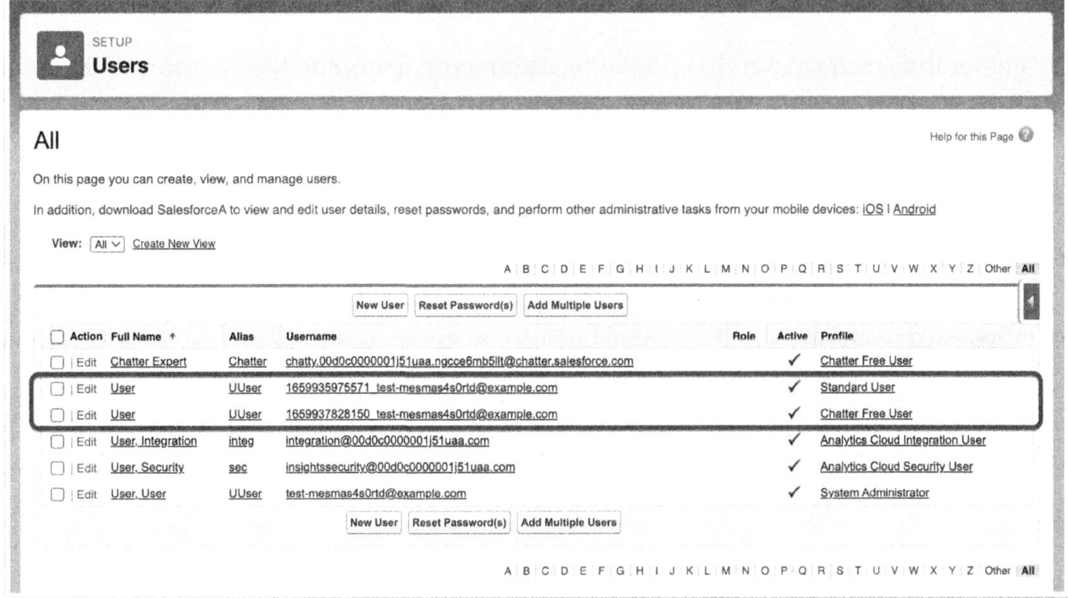

Figure 10-2. *Two new scratch org users viewed in Setup*

The most recently created user is the second one that has the `Chatter Free User` profile assigned to it. Click its **Username** to open the User record, which will look like the following, where the `Company/Department/Division` (1) and `Profile` (2) are set to the values in the user definition file.

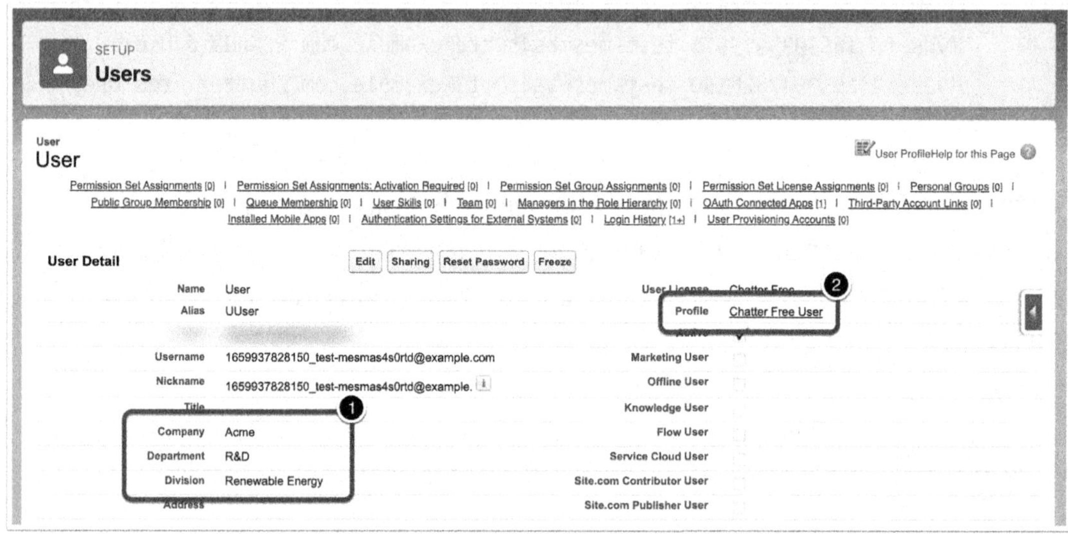

***Figure 10-3.** User record with user definition file settings*

Rather than using a user definition file, user record fields and the Salesforce DX parameters can be set on the `force:user:create` command line. For example, to create a third user with the same settings as the previous user, you would execute the following CLI command:

```
$ sfdx force:user:create \
    --setalias MyUser3 \
    CompanyName=Acme \
    Department="R&D" \
    Division="Renewable Energy" \
    profileName="Chatter Free User"
```

Note Quotes must be used to enclose parameter values that have spaces or ampersands.

Running the `force:user:list` command one more time shows the third user that we have created.

Listing 10-6. List of scratch org users with the third user added

```
=== Users in org 00D0C0000001j51UAA

 Default Alias   Username                                       Profile Name
 ─────── ─────   ────────────────────────────────────────────   ────────────────────
 (A)     MySO    test-mesmas4s0rtd@example.com                  System Administrator
         MyUser  1659935975571_test-mesmas4s0rtd@example.com    Standard User
         MyUser2 1659937828150_test-mesmas4s0rtd@example.com    Chatter Free User
         MyUser3 1659943083345_test-mesmas4s0rtd@example.com    Chatter Free User
```

To view detailed information about a user, the following command is used:

```
$ sfdx force:user:display
```

The parameters that can be used with this command are as follows:

- `--targetusername|-u`: The username or alias of the user to display detailed information about. [Optional]
- `--targetdevhubusername|-v`: The username or alias of the Dev Hub org that was used to create the scratch org containing the user to display detailed information about. [Optional]
- `--apiversion, --json, --loglevel`: Please refer to the discussion on global parameters in the section "Command-Line Parameters and Arguments" in Chapter 4, "Salesforce CLI."

The command's output should look like the following.

Listing 10-7. Detailed user information

```
Sharing this information is equivalent to logging someone in under the
current credential, resulting in unintended access and escalation of
privilege.
For additional information, please review the authorization section of the
https://developer.salesforce.com/docs/atlas.en-us.sfdx_dev.meta/sfdx_dev/
sfdx_dev_auth_web_flow.htm

=== User Description
```

```
key           label
────────────  ──────────────────────────────────────────────────────
Username      test-mesmas4s0rtd@example.com
Profile Name  System Administrator
Id            0050C000005zATAQA2
Org Id        00D0C0000001j51UAA
Access Token  00D0C0000001j5...
Instance Url  https://fun-inspiration-9305-dev-ed.my.salesforce.com
Login Url     https://CS110.salesforce.com
Alias         MySO
```

While it is possible to assign one or more permission sets to a user using the `permsets` parameter in the user definition file, you can also use the `force:user:permset:assign` CLI command to assign a permission set after a user has been created. We'll dig into permission set assignment next.

Assigning Permission Sets to Users

Permission sets include settings and permissions that provide user's access to platform capabilities, objects, and fields. We encountered user definition files in the previous section, which can be used for assigning permission sets to users like this.

Listing 10-8. Adding permission sets to a user definition file

```
{
    "CompanyName": "Acme",
    "Department": "R&D",
    "Division": "Renewable Energy",
    "permsets": ["Permset1", "Permset2"],
    "profileName": "Standard User"
}
```

For some use cases, you might need to assign permission sets after a user has been created; for example, you may want to run some tests using the same user with different permission sets. Let's create a couple of permission sets to assign to a user by following these steps:

1. Launch VS Code and open this project's `SalesforceDXTestUsers` Salesforce DX project if it's not already open.
2. Open the Terminal window.
3. Open your scratch org by running the CLI command `force:org:open`.
4. Navigate to **Setup ➤ Users ➤ Permission Sets**.
5. Click the **New** button.
6. Enter the following field values:
    a. **Label**: ExamplePermSet1
    b. **API Name**: ExamplePermSet1
7. Click the **Save** button.
8. Repeat steps 4–7, this time entering the following field values for the permission set:
    a. **Label**: ExamplePermSet2
    b. **API Name**: ExamplePermSet2

Of course, these permission sets don't provide a user with any settings or permissions as we haven't modified it, although it will suffice for illustrating permission set assignment. To assign the permission sets to a user with the necessary permissions to assign permission sets, use the following CLI command:

```
$ sfdx force:user:permset:assign \
    --permsetname ExamplePermSet1,ExamplePermSet2
```

Here are this command's available parameters:

- `--permsetname|-n`: A comma-separated list of permission sets to assign to one or more users. [Required]
- `--onbehalfof|-o`: A comma-separated list of usernames or aliases to assign one or more permission sets to. Use this parameter to assign permission sets to users without the necessary permissions to assign permission sets. [Optional]
- `--targetusername|-u`: A comma-separated list of usernames or aliases to assign one or more permission sets to. Use this parameter to assign permission sets to users with the necessary permissions to assign permission sets. [Optional]
- `--apiversion, --json, --loglevel`: Please refer to the discussion on global parameters in the section "Command-Line Parameters and Arguments" in Chapter 4, "Salesforce CLI."

The command assigns the permission set to the default target username, which is the user with the alias `MySO` in our case.

Listing 10-9. Permission sets assigned to a user

```
=== Permsets Assigned
 Username                       Permission Set Assignment
 ─────────────────────────────  ───────────────────────────────────
 test-mesmas4s0rtd@example.com ExamplePermSet1
 test-mesmas4s0rtd@example.com ExamplePermSet2
```

Note Although we have not done so here, the permission sets can be pulled using the `force:source:pull` command and deployed to a scratch org using the `force:source:push` command before creating users and then assigning the permission sets to those users, all using the Salesforce CLI.

To assign the permission set to a user without the necessary permissions to assign permission sets, the following CLI command is used:

```
$ sfdx force:user:permset:assign \
    --permsetname ExamplePermSet1,ExamplePermSet2 \
    --onbehalfof MyUser
```

What does "users with the necessary permissions to assign permission sets" mean, and why are there two different parameters to list the usernames or aliases of users to assign permission sets to? To assign permission sets, a user must have the following permissions:

- Assign Permission Sets
- View Setup and Configuration

The profiles that are assigned to the four scratch org users are as follows:

- **MySO**: `System Administrator`
- **MyUser**: `Standard User`
- **MyUser2**: `Chatter Free User`
- **MyUser3:** `Chatter Free User`

Of the three profiles, only the `System Administrator` profile has the necessary permissions to assign permission sets, and users with these permissions can either assign permission sets to themselves, or they can assign permission sets to users who do not have the necessary permissions. Therefore, follow these rules:

- To assign permission sets to users with the necessary permissions to assign permission sets, pass their usernames or aliases to the `--targetusername|-u` parameter. In our examples, we have a default target username with the alias `MySO`, which has the `System Administrator` profile, so we don't need to use the `--targetusername|-u` parameter.
- To assign permission sets to users without the necessary permissions to assign permission sets, pass the username or alias of a user with the necessary permissions to the `--targetusername|-u` parameter and the users without the necessary permissions to

the --onbehalfof|-o parameter. Again, in our examples, we have a default target username with the alias MySO, which has the System Administrator profile, so we don't need to use the --targetusername|-u parameter.

That's a lot of convoluted words! Here are some examples to illustrate the principles:

```
$ sfdx force:user:permset:assign \
    --permsetname ExamplePermSet1,ExamplePermSet2 \
    --targetusername MySO

$ sfdx force:user:permset:assign \
    --permsetname ExamplePermSet1,ExamplePermSet2 \
    --targetusername MySO \
    --onbehalfof MyUser

$ sfdx force:user:permset:assign \
    --permsetname ExamplePermSet1,ExamplePermSet2 \
    --targetusername MySO \
    --onbehalfof MyUser2,MyUser3
```

Note The --targetusername|-u parameter in the preceding examples could be omitted as MySO is the default target username.

The first example assigns permission sets to the MySO user, which is assigned the System Administrator profile and therefore has the necessary permissions to assign permission sets to itself or other users. The last two examples assign permission sets to users without the necessary permissions to assign permission sets, where the MySO user is used to assign the permission sets on behalf of those users.

Passing the incorrect types of users to the --targetusername|-u and --onbehalf|-o parameters will result in one of the following two errors.

Listing 10-10. Permission set assignment error 1

```
=== Failures

 Username  Error Message
 ────────  ─────────────────────────────────────────────────────────────
 MySO      entity type cannot be inserted: Permission Set Assignment
 MySO      entity type cannot be inserted: Permission Set Assignment
```

Listing 10-11. Permission set assignment error 2

```
ERROR running force:user:permset:assign:  No authorization information
found for MyUser1.
```

To see an example of the successful permission set assignments, open the scratch org and navigate to **Setup ➤ Users ➤ Permission Sets** and click the **ExamplePermSet1**, then click the **Manage Assignments** button.

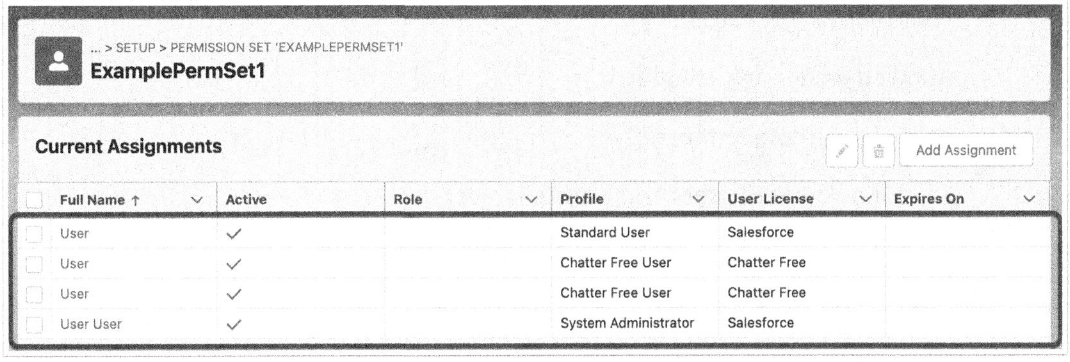

Figure 10-4. *A permission set assigned to users*

We've looked at creating scratch org users and assigning them permission sets. The last aspect of managing test users in scratch orgs that we will explore is how to generate passwords for the users.

Generating User Passwords

When a user is created in a scratch org, which can either be the initial System Administrator that is added when the scratch org is created or when additional users are created using the `force:user:create` command, the user does not have a password. A password is not normally required as OAuth is used to access the scratch org when using the Salesforce CLI. However, there may be situations where you need a login password, for example, to test login Flows or password policies. Adding a password can be performed using a password reset, which is done via the scratch org's Setup area, using the Salesforce API, or by using the `force:user:password:generate` command as follows:

```
$ sfdx force:user:password:generate \
    --onbehalfof MyUser3
```

The parameters that are available for this command are as follows:

- `--complexity|-c: Defines the password complexity. [Optional] [Default: 5]`

  Allowed values are as follows:

  - `0`: Lowercase letters only
  - `1`: Lowercase letters and numbers only
  - `2`: Lowercase letters and symbols only
  - `3`: Lowercase and uppercase letters and numbers only
  - `4`: Lowercase and uppercase letters and symbols only
  - `5`: Lowercase and uppercase letters and numbers and symbols only
- `--length|-l: The length of password to generate, which can be between 8 and 1000 characters. [Optional] [Default: 13]`
- `--onbehalfof|-o`: A comma-separated list of usernames or aliases of users to generate passwords for. Use this parameter to generate passwords for users without the necessary permissions to generate passwords. [Optional]

- `--targetusername|-u`: A comma-separated list of usernames or aliases of users to generate passwords for. Use this parameter to generate passwords for users with the necessary permissions to generate passwords. [Optional]
- `--targetdevhubusername|-v`: The username or alias of the Dev Hub org that manages the scratch org containing the users for whom passwords should be generated. [Optional]
- `--apiversion, --json, --loglevel`: Please refer to the discussion on global parameters in the section "Command-Line Parameters and Arguments" in Chapter 4, "Salesforce CLI."

In order to perform a password reset, a user must have the following permission:

- Reset User Passwords and Unlock Users

As with assigning permission sets, which was discussed in the previous section, the only user with the necessary permissions to reset passwords is the `MySO` user that has the `System Administrator` profile assigned to it. Again, as with assigning permission sets, this dictates how to use the `--targetusername|-u` and `--onbehalfof|-o` parameters. Please refer to the previous section to understand the rationale.

Executing the preceding command will generate the following output.

Listing 10-12. Generating a user password output

```
Successfully set the password "(u8jqfgRokbyo" for user 1659943083345_test-
mesmas4sOrtd@example.com.
You can see the password again by running "sfdx force:user:display -u
1659943083345_test-mesmas4sOrtd@example.com".
```

As the output suggests, to view a user's password and their details, execute the `force:use:display` command, which will generate the following output with the password highlighted.

Listing 10-13. Detailed user information, including their password

```
=== User Description

 key          label
 ──────────── ────────────────────────────────────────────────────────────
 Username     1659943083345_test-mesmas4s0rtd@example.com
 Profile Name Chatter Free User
 Id           0050C000005zJ93QAE
 Org Id       00D0C0000001j51UAA
 Access Token 00D0C0000001j5...
 Instance Url https://fun-inspiration-9305-dev-ed.my.salesforce.com
 Login Url    https://fun-inspiration-9305-dev-ed.my.salesforce.com
 Alias        MyUser3
 Password     (u8jqfgRokbyo
```

To mirror the examples for assigning permission sets, here are some examples for generating passwords for the users that we have created in this chapter:

```
$ sfdx force:user:password:generate \
    --targetusername MySO
```

```
$ sfdx force:user:password:generate \
    --targetusername MySO \
    --onbehalfof MyUser
```

```
$ sfdx force:user:password:generate \
    --targetusername MySO \
    --onbehalfof MyUser2,MyUser3
```

Note The `--targetusername` | `-u` parameter in the preceding examples could be omitted as `MySO` is the default target username.

The first example generates a password for the `MySO` user as the user specified using the `--targetusername|-u` parameter has the necessary permissions to reset passwords. In the last two examples, the same user is used to generate passwords on behalf of the `MyUser`, `MyUser2`, and `MyUser3` users, as they do not have the permissions necessary to reset passwords.

That rounds out managing scratch org users, so let's wrap up the chapter.

Chapter Summary

In this chapter, we introduced how to create additional scratch org users, how to assign permission sets, and how to generate passwords for them when required. These users are normally created for testing purposes and are therefore often created alongside test data, which we'll explore in the next chapter.

CHAPTER 11

Test Data

The Salesforce Developers Blog "Month of Testing: Why We Test"[1] reveals that the IBM System Science Institute discovered that it costs nearly seven times as much to fix a bug in production compared to during the testing phase of the application lifecycle. So, the more bugs we catch during predeployment testing, the better! Apex unit tests provide their own test data to achieve the 75% coverage required before Apex classes can be deployed to production. To perform end-to-end testing of your application or customization, you will need some additional test data. That same test data needs to be added to each scratch org and sandbox used during the application lifecycle to achieve consistent levels of test coverage and results. Sample data can be added to a scratch org using the `hasSampleData` parameter in the scratch org definition file; however, if you don't want to depend on data that you have no control over, or if you want to use the same data in scratch orgs and sandboxes, or if you want to add test data for custom objects and custom fields, sample data isn't the answer. Instead, you can create your own custom test data and use the Salesforce CLI commands in the `force:data` topic to manage the data in scratch orgs and sandboxes. We will explore these commands in this chapter.

This Chapter's Commands

This chapter introduces the following Salesforce CLI commands from the `force:data` topic, grouped by subtopic, which are used to manage test data in scratch orgs and sandboxes:

- Subtopic: **`force:data:soql`**
  - **`force:data:soql:query`**: Execute SOQL queries.

[1] `https://developer.salesforce.com/blogs/2018/05/why-we-test.html`

I. Harris, *Beginning Salesforce DX*, https://doi.org/10.1007/978-1-4842-8114-7_11

- Subtopic: **force:data:record**
    - **force:data:record:create**: Create a record.
    - **force:data:record:get**: Read a record.
    - **force:data:record:update**: Update a record.
    - **force:data:record:delete**: Delete a record.
- Subtopic: **force:data:bulk**
    - **force:data:bulk:upsert**: Bulk upsert data.
    - **force:data:bulk:status**: Check bulk status.
    - **force:data:bulk:delete**: Bulk delete data.
- Subtopic: **force:data:tree**
    - **force:data:tree:export**: Export sObject trees.
    - **force:data:tree:import**: Import sObject trees.

Note The `force:data` commands also work with production orgs; however, as we are focusing on test data, we will only refer to scratch orgs and sandboxes as targets for the commands.

Before introducing the first of the `force:data` commands, we need to create a new Salesforce DX project for this chapter.

This Chapter's Project

Follow the instructions in Chapter 6, "Projects," to create a fresh Salesforce DX project for this chapter called `SalesforceDXTestData`, using the default `standard` template. Set the contents of the scratch org definition file in the newly created project to the following.

Listing 11-1. Scratch org definition file for this chapter's Salesforce DX project

```
{
  "orgName": "Using Test Data",
  "edition": "Developer",
  "hasSampleData": true,
  "features": ["EnableSetPasswordInApi"],
  "settings": {
    "lightningExperienceSettings": {
      "enableS1DesktopEnabled": true
    },
    "mobileSettings": {
      "enableS1EncryptedStoragePref2": false
    }
  }
}
```

Although we won't be using the sample data for testing purposes, it has been added so that we can demonstrate the `force:data:soql` commands, which is the subject of the next section.

As we will be working with scratch orgs in this chapter, please ensure that you have a default Dev Hub authorized with an alias of `MyDH` as described in Chapter 5, "Dev Hub."

Executing SOQL Queries

When developing applications or customizations for Salesforce, you will frequently find yourself needing to query for records in a scratch org or sandbox. Until now, we would typically turn to the Developer Console, Workbench, or another third-party tool in order to run a query. Today, the Salesforce CLI includes the `force:data:soql` subtopic commands, which enable you to execute SOQL queries directly from the Visual Studio Code integrated terminal command line without switching environments. The `force:data:soql` subtopic consists of the following single command:

- **`force:data:soql:query`**: Execute SOQL queries.

To see it in action, first open the `SalesforceDXTestData` Salesforce DX project that we are using for this chapter in Visual Studio Code. Next, create a new scratch org with the alias `MySO` and set it as the default username. Finally, open the integrated terminal and execute the following Salesforce CLI command to perform a SOQL query:

```
$ sfdx force:data:soql:query \
    --query "SELECT Name, Rating FROM Account"
```

This command's parameters are as follows:

- `--soqlqueryfile|-f`: The path to a file containing the SOQL query to execute. One of the parameters `--query|-q` or `--soqlqueryfile|-f` must be provided, but not both. [Optional]
- `--query|-q`: The SOQL query to execute. One of the parameters `--query|-q` or `--soqlqueryfile|-f` must be provided, but not both. [Optional]
- `--resultformat|-r`: This parameter modifies the format of the command output. Note that the `--json` parameter overrides this parameter. [Optional] [Default: `human`]
- Allowed values are as follows:
    - `human`: Output in a human-readable format
    - `csv`: Output as comma-separated field values
    - `json`: Output in JavaScript Object Notation format
- `--usetoolingapi|-t`: Instructs the command to use the Tooling API for fine-grained access to metadata, which supports interactive applications. [Optional]
- `--targetusername|-u`: The username or alias of the org to be queried. [Optional]
- `--apiversion, --json, --loglevel, --perflog`: Please refer to the discussion on global parameters in the section "Command-Line Parameters and Arguments" in Chapter 4, "Salesforce CLI."

Note To run a SOQL query from the Visual Studio Code Command Palette, execute the command **SFDX: Execute SOQL Query...**. Alternatively, write the SOQL query in any file, select the text and run the Command Palette command **SFDX: Execute SOQL Query with Currently Selected Text**.

The query will return all Accounts and their ratings, which will look like this as we have included sample data in the scratch org.

Listing 11-2. Output from a SOQL query of Account records

```
NAME                                              RATING
────────────────────────────────────────────────  ────────
Sample Account for Entitlements                   null
Edge Communications                               Hot
Burlington Textiles Corp of America Warm
Pyramid Construction Inc.                         null
Dickenson plc                                     null
Grand Hotels & Resorts Ltd                        Warm
United Oil & Gas Corp.                            Hot
Express Logistics and Transport                   Cold
University of Arizona                             Warm
United Oil & Gas, UK                              null
United Oil & Gas, Singapore                       null
GenePoint                                         Cold
sForce                                            null
Total number of records retrieved: 13.
Querying Data... done
```

By default, the `force:data:soql:query` command uses the Lightning Platform REST API. The `--usetoolingapi|-t` parameter instructs the command to use the Tooling API instead. The following is an example Tooling API query for the DebugLevel sObject, which is an sObject that is not supported by the Lightning Platform REST API:

```
$ sfdx force:data:soql:query \
    --query "SELECT Id, DeveloperName, System \
            FROM DebugLevel" \
    --usetoolingapi
```

And this is the resulting output.

Listing 11-3. Output from a SOQL query of DebugLevel records using the Tooling API

```
 ID                          DEVELOPERNAME           SYSTEM
 ─────────────────────────── ─────────────────────── ─────────
 7dl3G0000004fmJQAQ          SFDC_DevConsole         DEBUG
Total number of records retrieved: 1.
Querying Data... done
```

Note For further information about the Tooling API, please refer to the Salesforce documentation here: `https://developer.salesforce.com/docs/atlas.en-us.api_tooling.meta/api_tooling/intro_api_tooling.htm`.

That concludes our review of the `force:data:soql` subtopic commands. We'll now turn our attention to the `force:data:record` subtopic commands for manipulating individual records in a scratch org or sandbox.

Record CRUD Commands

Suppose that you need to quickly manipulate an individual record without having to create a CSV file (which is needed for the `force:data:bulk` subtopic commands) or an sObject tree file (which is needed for the `force:data:tree` subtopic commands). The `force:data:record` subtopic commands can be used to create, read, update, and delete (CRUD) individual records in scratch orgs and sandboxes. The commands in this subtopic are as follows:

- **`force:data:record:create`**: Create a new record.
- **`force:data:record:get`**: Read a record.
- **`force:data:record:update`**: Update a record.
- **`force:data:record:delete`**: Delete a record.

In this section, we will create, read, update, and delete a single Case record using the Lightning Platform REST API and a single DebugLevel record using the Tooling API. Let's start with creating the records.

Creating Records

To create a Case record using the `force:data:record:create` command, open the `SalesforceDXTestData` Salesforce DX project that we are using for this chapter in Visual Studio Code, then run the following Salesforce CLI command from the integrated terminal:

```
$ sfdx force:data:record:create \
    --sobjecttype Case \
    --values \
      "Subject='Generator fuel gauge is inaccurate'"
```

The parameters that can be used with this command are as follows:

- `--sobjecttype|-s`: The type of standard or custom object to create a record for. [Required]
- `--usetoolingapi|-t`: Instructs the command to use the Tooling API. [Optional]
- `--targetusername|-u`: The username or alias of the org where the record will be created. [Optional]
- `--values|-v`: Space-separated field-value pairs that specify the fields to set values for on creation. [Required]
- `--apiversion, --json, --loglevel, --perflog`: Please refer to the discussion on global parameters in the section "Command-Line Parameters and Arguments" in Chapter 4, "Salesforce CLI."

The command will return the Id of the record that has been created. Make a note of this as you will be using it for the other commands in this subtopic. If you forget to make a note of the Id, don't worry, just remember that you can run the following `force:data:soql` command to query for Case record Ids:

```
$ sfdx force:data:soql:query \
    --query "SELECT Id, Subject \
             FROM Case \
             WHERE IsClosed=false"
```

This will return the Id and Subject for all open cases, including the Case record that you just created, which is the final one in this listing.

Listing 11-4. The Case created with the force:data:record:create command

```
 ID                 SUBJECT
 ────────────────── ──────────────────────────────────────────────────────
 5003G000000gNVlQAM Seeking guidance on electrical wiring installation
 for GC5060
 5003G000000gNVzQAM Maintenance guidelines for generator unclear
 5003G000000gNW7QAM Design issue with mechanical rotor
 5003G000007ugPcQAI Generator fuel gauge is inaccurate
Total number of records retrieved: 4.
Querying Data... done
```

As an example of how to use the Tooling API, this command creates a new DebugLevel sObject record, which cannot be done using the REST API.

```
$ sfdx force:data:record:create \
    --sobjecttype DebugLevel \
    --usetoolingapi \
    --values \
      "ApexCode=DEBUG \
       DeveloperName=ExampleDebugLevel \
       MasterLabel=ExampleDebugLevel \
       System=ERROR \
       Visualforce=DEBUG"
```

If you tried to create this record without using the Tooling API, you would get the following error.

Listing 11-5. Error when trying to create a Tooling API sObject using the REST API

```
ERROR running force:data:record:create:  The requested resource does
not exist
Creating record for DebugLevel... done
```

Having created new records, we can now move on to reading them.

Reading Records

To read the newly created Case record, execute the following CLI command after replacing <Case record Id> with the Id of the Case record that you created in the previous section:

```
$ sfdx force:data:record:get \
    --sobjectid <Case record Id> \
    --sobjecttype Case
```

This command's parameters are as follows:

- --sobjectid|-i: The Id of the record to read. [Optional: You must provide this parameter or the --where|-w parameter.]
- --sobjecttype|-s: The type of standard or custom object to read a record for. [Required]
- --usetoolingapi|-t: Instructs the command to use the Tooling API. [Optional]
- --targetusername|-u: The username or alias of the org containing the record to be read. [Optional]
- --where|-w: Provides space-separated <fieldName>=<value> pairs to read a record. The combination of <fieldName>=<value> pairs must uniquely identify a record; otherwise, you will get an error. [Optional: You must provide this parameter or the --sobjectid|-i parameter.]
- --apiversion, --json, --loglevel, --perflog: Please refer to the discussion on global parameters in the section "Command-Line Parameters and Arguments" in Chapter 4, "Salesforce CLI."

The command will return all the sObject's fields and their values, as in the following listing.

Listing 11-6. The Case record read using the force:data:record:get command

```
attributes:
  type: Case
  url: /services/data/v55.0/sobjects/Case/5003G000007ugPcQAI
Id: 5003G000007ugPcQAI
IsDeleted: false
MasterRecordId: null
CaseNumber: 00001026
ContactId: null
AccountId: null
AssetId: null
ParentId: null
SuppliedName: null
SuppliedEmail: null
SuppliedPhone: null
SuppliedCompany: null
Type: null
Status: New
Reason: null
Origin: null
Subject: Generator fuel gauge is inaccurate
Priority: Medium
Description: null
IsClosed: false
ClosedDate: null
IsEscalated: false
OwnerId: 0053G000002uT3YQAU
CreatedDate: 2022-08-09T06:38:20.000+0000
CreatedById: 0053G000002uT3YQAU
LastModifiedDate: 2022-08-09T06:38:20.000+0000
LastModifiedById: 0053G000002uT3YQAU
SystemModstamp: 2022-08-09T06:38:20.000+0000
ContactPhone: null
ContactMobile: null
ContactEmail: null
```

```
ContactFax: null
Comments: null
LastViewedDate: 2022-08-09T06:38:20.000+0000
LastReferencedDate: 2022-08-09T06:38:20.000+0000
EngineeringReqNumber__c: null
SLAViolation__c: null
Product__c: null
PotentialLiability__c: null
Getting Record... done
```

To read the same record using the `--where|-w` parameter, rather than the `--sobjectid|-i` parameter, execute the following command after replacing `<Case record Id>` with the actual record Id:

```
$ sfdx force:data:record:get \
    --sobjecttype Case \
    --where "Id=<Case record Id>"
```

The `--where|-w` parameter must resolve to a single record; otherwise, you will get the following error.

Listing 11-7. Error when the force:data:record:get command retrieves multiple records

```
Getting Record... failed
ERROR running force:data:record:get:  IsClosed=false is not a unique
qualifier for Case; 4 records were retrieved.
Retrieve only one record.
```

However, you can pass multiple `<fieldName>=<value>` pairs to the parameter to be more specific and retrieve a single record.

Using the `--usetoolingapi|-t` parameter, you can read the DebugLevel record that you created in the previous section by executing the following command after replacing `<DebugLevel record Id>` with the actual Id. Execute the Tooling API SOQL query example in the "Executing SOQL Queries" section earlier if you didn't make a note of the Id.

```
$ sfdx force:data:record:get \
    --sobjectid <DebugLevel record Id> \
    --sobjecttype DebugLevel \
    --usetoolingapi
```

The resulting command output should resemble this.

Listing 11-8. The DebugLevel record read using the force:data:record:get command and the Tooling API

```
attributes:
  type: DebugLevel
  url: /services/data/v55.0/tooling/sobjects/DebugLevel/7dl3G0000004frsQAA
Id: 7dl3G0000004frsQAA
IsDeleted: false
DeveloperName: ExampleDebugLevel
Language: en_US
MasterLabel: ExampleDebugLevel
CreatedDate: 2022-08-09T06:43:14.000+0000
CreatedById: 0053G000002uT3YQAU
LastModifiedDate: 2022-08-09T06:43:14.000+0000
LastModifiedById: 0053G000002uT3YQAU
SystemModstamp: 2022-08-09T06:43:14.000+0000
Workflow: INFO
Validation: INFO
Callout: INFO
ApexCode: DEBUG
ApexProfiling: INFO
Visualforce: DEBUG
System: ERROR
Database: INFO
Wave: INFO
Nba: INFO
Getting Record... done
```

So far, you've created and read individual records. Sometimes, you will need to modify the data to cover different use cases and test paths, which we will do next.

Updating Records

To update the Case record, execute the following command, replacing `<Case record Id>` with the Id of the Case that you created earlier:

```
$ sfdx force:data:record:update \
    --sobjectid <Case record Id> \
    --sobjecttype Case \
    --values \
      "Subject='Fuel gauge cable missing' \
       SuppliedName='Joe Bloggs'"
```

The parameters that can be used for this command are as follows:

- `--sobjectid|-i`: The Id of the record to update. [Optional: You must provide this parameter or the `--where|-w` parameter.]
- `--sobjecttype|-s`: The type of standard or custom object to update a record for. [Required]
- `--usetoolingapi|-t`: Instructs the command to use the Tooling API. [Optional]
- `--targetusername|-u`: The username or alias of the org containing the record to be updated. [Optional]
- `--values|-v`: Space-separated field-value pairs that specify which fields to update. [Required]
- `--where|-w`: Provides space-separated `<fieldName>=<value>` pairs to update a record. The combination of `<fieldName>=<value>` pairs must uniquely identify a record; otherwise, you will get an error. [Optional: You must provide this parameter or the `--sobjectid|-i` parameter.]
- `--apiversion, --json, --loglevel, --perflog`: Please refer to the discussion on global parameters in the section "Command-Line Parameters and Arguments" in Chapter 4, "Salesforce CLI."

By re-running the `force:data:record:get` command, you will observe that the `Subject` and `SuppliedName` fields will have been updated.

Listing 11-9. The Case record updated using the force:data:record:update command

```
attributes:
  type: Case
  url: /services/data/v55.0/sobjects/Case/5003G000007ugPcQAI
Id: 5003G000007ugPcQAI
IsDeleted: false
MasterRecordId: null
CaseNumber: 00001026
ContactId: null
AccountId: null
AssetId: null
ParentId: null
SuppliedName: Joe Bloggs
SuppliedEmail: null
SuppliedPhone: null
SuppliedCompany: null
Type: null
Status: New
Reason: null
Origin: null
Subject: Fuel gauge cable missing
Priority: Medium
Description: null
IsClosed: false
ClosedDate: null
IsEscalated: false
OwnerId: 0053G000002uT3YQAU
CreatedDate: 2022-08-09T06:38:20.000+0000
CreatedById: 0053G000002uT3YQAU
LastModifiedDate: 2022-08-09T07:14:18.000+0000
LastModifiedById: 0053G000002uT3YQAU
```

```
SystemModstamp: 2022-08-09T07:14:18.000+0000
ContactPhone: null
ContactMobile: null
ContactEmail: null
ContactFax: null
Comments: null
LastViewedDate: 2022-08-09T07:18:04.000+0000
LastReferencedDate: 2022-08-09T07:18:04.000+0000
EngineeringReqNumber__c: null
SLAViolation__c: null
Product__c: null
PotentialLiability__c: null
Getting Record... done
```

As the usage of these parameters is exactly the same as for the `force:data:record:get` command, rather than provide more examples, have a go yourself. Try updating the Case record using the `--where|-w` parameter rather than the `--sobjectid|-i` parameter. Then have a go at using the Tooling API to update and then read the DebugLevel record that you created earlier.

To complete the CRUD cycle, we'll now delete the records that you created, read, and updated.

Deleting Records

Using the `force:data:record:delete` command, you can delete the Case and DebugLevel records that you have created. Start by deleting the Case record by running the following command once you have replaced `<Case record Id>` with the actual Case record Id:

```
$ sfdx force:data:record:delete \
    --sobjectid <Case record Id> \
    --sobjecttype Case
```

The parameters used for this command are as follows:

- `--sobjectid|-i`: The Id of the record to delete. [Optional: You must provide this parameter or the `--where|-w` parameter.]

- `--sobjecttype|-s`: The type of standard or custom object to delete a record for. [Required]
- `--usetoolingapi|-t`: Instructs the command to use the Tooling API. [Optional]
- `--targetusername|-u`: The username or alias of the org containing the record to be deleted. [Optional]
- `--where|-w`: Provides space-separated `<fieldName>=<value>` pairs to delete a record. The combination of `<fieldName>=<value>` pairs must uniquely identify a record; otherwise, you will get an error. [Optional: You must provide this parameter or the `--sobjectid|-i` parameter.]
- `--apiversion, --json, --loglevel, --perflog`: Please refer to the discussion on global parameters in the section "Command-Line Parameters and Arguments" in Chapter 4, "Salesforce CLI."

If all is well, the command will confirm that the record has been successfully deleted.

By now, you should have enough knowledge to delete the DebugLevel sObject using the Tooling API, which will be left for you as an exercise.

You have now executed each of the `force:data:record` subtopic commands to manage the create, read, update, and delete (CRUD) lifecycle of a single Case record using the Lightning Platform REST API and a single DebugLevel record using the Tooling API. In the next chapter, we will use the `force:data:bulk` subtopic commands to import and delete large volumes of records using CSV files.

Bulk Data Commands

The `force:data:bulk` subtopic commands use a CSV file to import large volumes of test data into a scratch org or sandbox or to delete large volumes of test data from a scratch org or sandbox. The following commands in this subtopic take advantage of the Bulk API under the hood to interact with orgs:

- **`force:data:bulk:upsert`**: Bulk upsert data from a CSV file.
- **`force:data:bulk:status`**: Check the status of a `force:data:bulk:upsert` or `force:data:bulk:delete` command.
- **`force:data:bulk:delete`**: Bulk delete data using a CSV file.

Note To learn more about the Bulk API, please refer to the Bulk API Developer Guide, which can be found here: `https://developer.salesforce.com/docs/atlas.en-us.226.0.api_asynch.meta/api_asynch/asynch_api_intro.htm`.

Those familiar with the Bulk API will notice that there are no separate `force:data:bulk` commands for the Bulk API's insert and update commands; instead, the single command `force:data:bulk:upsert` is used for performing inserts, updates, and upserts. We'll explore this upserting command first.

Bulk Upserting

The `force:data:bulk:upsert` command upserts large volumes of data contained in a CSV file to a scratch org or sandbox. Each row of data in the CSV file corresponds to a standard or custom object record in the org that needs to be updated or inserted. When upserting, if a record already exists in the org that matches a row in the CSV file, the record in the org is updated with the row's data; otherwise, a new record is created. But how does the upsert command know if a record already exists in the org? What fields in the org record and the CSV file row are compared to determine if there's a match? The answer is an External ID field.

An External ID is a custom field on a standard or custom object that prevents duplicate records from being created when using the Bulk API's upsert command. A typical use case for the Bulk API is to regularly import large volumes of data into a Salesforce production org that has been exported from a third-party system, such as an ERP system. The third-party, or "external," system will have its own unique Id for each record that it exports, which will be used as the External ID column in the export's CSV file. When the first upsert into Salesforce occurs, none of the records in Salesforce will have an External ID set yet, so all the records in the CSV file will be inserted. When the next upsert into Salesforce occurs, for each row in the CSV file, the Bulk API checks if the External ID exists in Salesforce; if it does, the record with the matching External ID is updated; otherwise, a new record is inserted, including its External ID field. And so, the process can repeat without duplicate records!

Note If you're only inserting data once and not updating it later, you do not need a custom External ID field, just set the `force:data:bulk:upsert` command's `--externalid` parameter to `id` and omit the External ID column from the CSV file; however, this will create duplicate records if you upsert more than once. If you do upsert more than once for the Account, Person Account, Contact, or Lead standard objects, be aware of any duplicate rules that might be enabled that could cause the upsert to fail.

As our data does not originate from an external system, we will create a synthetic External ID. This will enable us to insert fresh data into a scratch org or sandbox and then modify it later if needed. To get ready for upserting some data, perform the following steps to add an External ID custom field to the Contact and Case standard objects:

1. Open the `SalesforceDXTestData` Salesforce DX project that we are using for this chapter in VS Code.
2. Open the scratch org with the `MySO` alias.
3. In the scratch org, navigate to **Setup ➤ Objects and Fields ➤ Object Manager**.
4. In the Object Manager list view, scroll down and click the **Contact** object.
5. In the left-hand navigation bar, click the **Fields & Relationships** link.
6. Click the **New** button.
7. In Step 1 of the New Custom Field wizard, select the **Number** data type.
8. Click the **Next** button.
9. In Step 2 of the New Custom Field wizard, enter the following field values:
   a. **Field Label**: External ID
   b. **Length**: 18

   c. **Decimal Places**: 0

   d. **Field Name**: External_ID

   e. **External ID**: Checked

10. Click the **Next** button.

11. In Step 3 of the New Custom Field wizard, click the **Next** button.

12. In Step 4 of the New Custom Field wizard, click the **Save** button.

13. Repeat steps 3–12 for the Case object.

The Contact and Case objects now have a custom External ID field, so we are ready to upsert some data.

Note Although the field name is `External_ID`, when referencing the field in a CSV file, you need to append `__c`, for example, `External_ID__c`.

Add a directory called `data` to your Salesforce DX project's root directory.

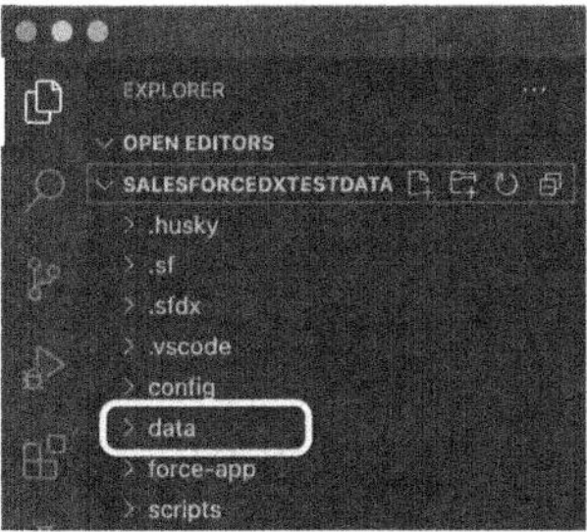

***Figure 11-1.** Salesforce DX project with a data directory added*

Now create a file called `contacts.csv` with the following contents and save it in the `data` directory.

Listing 11-10. Contacts CSV file

```
External_ID__c,FirstName,LastName,Email
1,Devon,Salter,devon.salter@example.com
2,Lily,Brewer,lily.brewer@example.com
```

The file contains data that will be used to insert new, or update existing, Contact records in our scratch org. The first row specifies the fields that we want to set on Contact records, and the remaining two rows supply the field values for two records. The External ID field is in the first column with unique values for each row, in this case simply an incrementing row number.

As these records do not yet exist in the scratch org, two new Contact records will be created, one for Devon Salter and the other for Lily Brewer. To bulk upsert these records, open the integrated terminal and execute the following command:

```
$ sfdx force:data:bulk:upsert \
    --csvfile ./data/contacts.csv \
    --externalid External_ID__c \
    --sobjecttype Contact
```

The parameters that can be used with this command are as follows:

- `--csvfile|-f`: The path to the CSV file containing the data to upsert. [Required]
- `--externalid|-i`: The field that contains the External ID. [Required]
- `--serial|-r`: Runs all batches in a job in serial rather than parallel mode. [Optional]
- `--sobjecttype|-s`: The type of standard or custom object that will be upserted. [Required]
- `--targetusername|-u`: The username or alias of the org to upsert data to. [Optional]
- `--wait|-w`: How long to wait, in minutes, for the command to complete. If the parameter is not provided, the command returns immediately. Otherwise, the command will wait up to the specified number of minutes and will return earlier if the command completes. [Optional]
- `--apiversion, --json, --loglevel`: Please refer to the discussion on global parameters in the section "Command-Line Parameters and Arguments" in Chapter 4, "Salesforce CLI."

The `force:data:bulk:upsert` command output provides the Ids of the job and the batches that have been created. In this example, only one batch was created as the CSV file only contains two records.

Listing 11-11. The force:data:bulk:upsert command output

```
Check batch #1's status with the command:
sfdx force:data:bulk:status -i 7503G000001IKveQAG -b 7513G000001ac9CQAQ
Bulk Upsert... done
```

If the CSV file contains more than 10,000 records, the Bulk API will create a batch per 10,000 records, in which case the `force:data:bulk:upsert` command output will provide the Ids for each batch; here's an example:

Listing 11-12. The force:data:bulk:upsert command output for multiple batches

```
Check batch #5's status with the command:
sfdx force:data:bulk:status -i 7503G000001ILScQAO -b 7513G000001acaXQAQ
Check batch #4's status with the command:
sfdx force:data:bulk:status -i 7503G000001ILScQAO -b 7513G000001acacQAA
Check batch #3's status with the command:
sfdx force:data:bulk:status -i 7503G000001ILScQAO -b 7513G000001acahQAA
Check batch #1's status with the command:
sfdx force:data:bulk:status -i 7503G000001ILScQAO -b 7513G000001acamQAA
Check batch #2's status with the command:
sfdx force:data:bulk:status -i 7503G000001ILScQAO -b 7513G000001acarQAA
Bulk Upsert... done
```

To check the upsert status of a batch, execute one of the status commands in the previous listings. The same command with the long name version of its parameters is

```
$ sfdx force:data:bulk:status \
    --batchid 7513G000001ac9CQAQ \
    --jobid 7503G000001IKveQAG
```

Here are the command's available parameters:

- `--batchid|-d`: The Id of one of the batches in a job whose status is to be viewed. [Optional]

- `--jobid|-i`: The Id of the job whose status is to be viewed, or the Id of a job containing the batch specified by the `--batchid|-d` whose status is to be viewed. [Required]
- `--targetusername|-u`: The username or alias of the org that is executing the bulk job or batch whose status is to be viewed. [Optional]
- `--apiversion, --json, --loglevel`: Please refer to the discussion on global parameters in the section "Command-Line Parameters and Arguments" in Chapter 4, "Salesforce CLI."

The output of the `force:data:bulk:status` command when both the job Id and the batch Id are provided shows the status of an individual batch, which here shows that two records were processed and that there were no failures.

Listing 11-13. The force:data:bulk:status command output for a batch

```
=== Batch Status

jobId:                     7503G000001IKveQAG
state:                     Completed
createdDate:               2022-08-09T08:07:45.000Z
systemModstamp:            2022-08-09T08:07:46.000Z
numberRecordsProcessed:    2
numberRecordsFailed:       0
totalProcessingTime:       770
apiActiveProcessingTime:   593
apexProcessingTime:        0
Getting Status... done
```

When only the job Id is provided, the `force:data:bulk:status` command outputs the status of the overall job, which includes one or more batches. In this listing, five batches were successfully completed, with a total of 43,991 records.

Listing 11-14. The force:data:bulk:status command output for a job

```
=== Job Status

id:                        7503G000001ILScQAO
operation:                 upsert
object:                    Contact
createdById:               0053G000002uT3YQAU
createdDate:               2022-08-09T11:15:38.000Z
systemModstamp:            2022-08-09T11:15:41.000Z
state:                     Closed
externalIdFieldName:       External_ID__c
concurrencyMode:           Parallel
contentType:               CSV
numberBatchesQueued:       0
numberBatchesInProgress:   0
numberBatchesCompleted:    5
numberBatchesFailed:       0
numberBatchesTotal:        5
numberRecordsProcessed:    43991
numberRetries:             0
apiVersion:                55.0
numberRecordsFailed:       250
totalProcessingTime:       577970
apiActiveProcessingTime:   555468
apexProcessingTime:        0
```

To illustrate a failed insert, here is the `force:data:bulk:status` command output when the CSV file includes a field called `Bad_Field__c` that isn't a standard or custom field on the Contact object.

Listing 11-15. force:data:bulk:status command showing a failed insert

```
=== Batch Status

jobId:                     7503G000001ILVfQAO
state:                     Failed
stateMessage:              InvalidBatch : Field name not found : Bad_Field__c
```

```
createdDate:              2022-08-09T11:43:28.000Z
systemModstamp:           2022-08-09T11:43:28.000Z
numberRecordsProcessed:   0
numberRecordsFailed:      0
totalProcessingTime:      0
apiActiveProcessingTime:  0
apexProcessingTime:       0
Getting Status... done
```

To confirm that the contacts have been upserted into the scratch org, open the scratch org and navigate to **App Launcher ➤ Service**; then click the **Contacts** tab, which should list the new Contacts as follows.

***Figure 11-2.** Contacts upserted using the force:data:bulk:upsert command*

Note I created a custom list view with a filter to only show the Contacts that have an External ID that is not equal to null. This ensures that the sample data that we included in the scratch org is not listed.

Now create a file called `cases.csv` that contains the following rows and add it to the same data directory where the `contacts.csv` file is saved.

Listing 11-16. Cases CSV file

```
External_ID__c,Subject,Priority,Contact.External_ID__c
1,"Faulty fuel gauge",High,1
2,"Excessive noise",Medium,2
3,"Smokey exhaust",Low,2
```

Each Case has an External ID, and note the use of dotted notation to relate a Case to a Contact using the Contact's External ID. In this example, the Case with the External ID of 3 will be related to the Contact with an External ID of 2.

Notes 1. Any indexed, unique field on the parent record can be used to establish a relationship; for example, a Contact record can be the parent of another Contact record, in which case the relationship field column header in the CSV file could use `ReportsTo.Email`, as email addresses are unique. However, as we are adding an External ID field to our sObjects anyway, we may as well use this field.

2. If you use a custom master-detail or lookup field, rather than a standard field, to relate a child record to a parent record, use the `__r` notation. For example, for a lookup field called Parent__c, reference the parent's External ID field using `Parent__r.External_ID__c` in the child record's CSV file header row.

To perform the bulk insert of the Case records, execute the following Salesforce CLI command:

```
$ sfdx force:data:bulk:upsert \
    --csvfile ./data/cases.csv \
    --externalid External_ID__c \
    --sobjecttype Case
```

View the newly upserted Cases by opening the scratch org and navigating to **App Launcher ➤ Service**; then click the **Cases** tab.

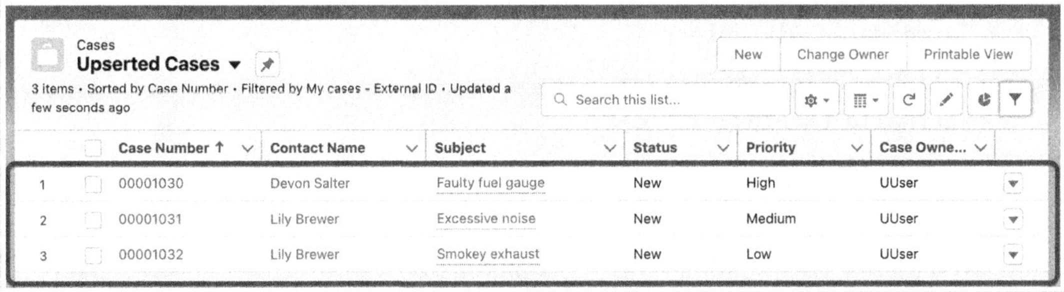

Figure 11-3. *Cases upserted using the force:data:bulk:upsert command*

Note As with the Contacts list view, I created a custom list view with a filter to show the Cases that have an External ID that is not equal to null. This ensures that only the imported data and not the sample data is listed.

You can see from the Contact Name column that the Cases have been correctly related to the Contacts that we inserted earlier.

So far, we have used the `force:data:bulk:upsert` command to insert new records. To demonstrate how the command can update existing records while inserting new records, update the `cases.csv` file to include the following contents.

Listing 11-17. Updated Cases CSV file

```
External_ID__c,Subject,Priority,Contact.External_ID__c
1,"Faulty fuel gauge",High,1
2,"Excessive noise",Medium,2
3,"Smokey exhaust",High,2
4,"Unreliable cold start",Medium,1
```

There are two changes to the file:

1. The row with the External ID of `3` has changed its `Priority` from `Low` to `High`.
2. A new row with the External ID of `4` has been added.

Re-run the `force:data:bulk:upsert` command to upsert the `cases.csv` file, but this time add the `--wait|-w` parameter:

```
$ sfdx force:data:bulk:upsert \
    --csvfile ./data/cases.csv \
    --externalid External_ID__c \
    --sobjecttype Case \
    --wait 5
```

As we saw earlier, without the `--wait|-w` parameter, the `force:data:bulk:upsert` command returns immediately and will output the `force:data:bulk:status` command that can be used to check the status of the command's job or batches. When the `--wait|-w` parameter is included, the command will wait for up to the specified number of minutes for the job and batches to complete. As soon as they have completed, the `force:data:bulk:upsert` command returns and outputs the job and batch results, as shown in the following.

Listing 11-18. Completed force:data:bulk:upsert command after waiting

```
Will poll the batch statuses every 5 seconds
To fetch the status on your own, press CTRL+C and use the command:
sfdx force:data:bulk:status -i 7503G000001ILXlQAO -b [<batchId>]
Batch #1 queued (Batch ID: 7513G000001acd7QAA).

=== Batch #1

=== Batch Status

id:                        7513G000001acd7QAA
jobId:                     7503G000001ILXlQAO
state:                     Completed
createdDate:               2022-08-09T12:30:55.000Z
systemModstamp:            2022-08-09T12:30:56.000Z
numberRecordsProcessed:    4
numberRecordsFailed:       0
totalProcessingTime:       288
apiActiveProcessingTime:   174
apexProcessingTime:        0

=== Job Status

id:                        7503G000001ILXlQAO
operation:                 upsert
object:                    Case
createdById:               0053G000002uT3YQAU
createdDate:               2022-08-09T12:30:55.000Z
systemModstamp:            2022-08-09T12:30:56.000Z
state:                     Closed
externalIdFieldName:       External_ID__c
concurrencyMode:           Parallel
contentType:               CSV
numberBatchesQueued:       0
```

```
numberBatchesInProgress: 0
numberBatchesCompleted:  1
numberBatchesFailed:     0
numberBatchesTotal:      1
numberRecordsProcessed:  4
numberRetries:           0
apiVersion:              55.0
numberRecordsFailed:     0
totalProcessingTime:     288
apiActiveProcessingTime: 174
apexProcessingTime:      0
Bulk Upsert... done
```

To see the upserted data, refresh the Cases list view in the scratch org, which will show the updated record (1) and the new one (2), as illustrated in the following.

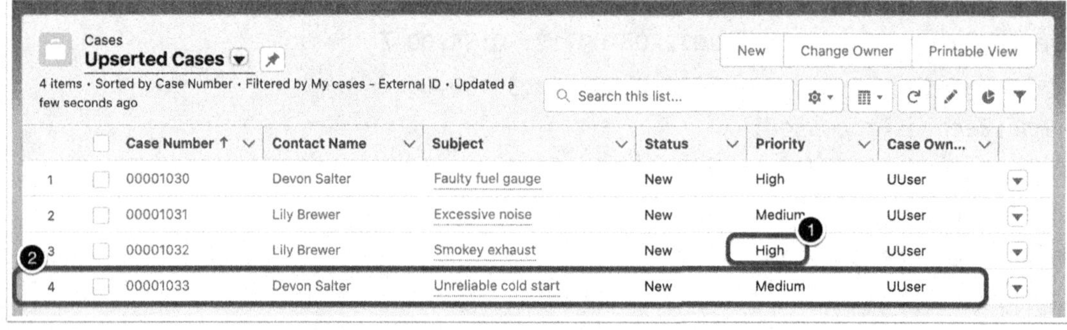

***Figure 11-4.** Cases updated and inserted using the force:data:bulk:upsert command*

Having upserted a large volume of test data, there may be occasions where you will want to delete the data from a scratch org or sandbox. Let's look at that next.

Bulk Deleting

The `force:data:bulk:delete` command is used to delete large volumes of data from a scratch org or sandbox. The command requires a CSV file with a single `Id` column and a row containing the Salesforce record Id for each record to be deleted. To get the

Salesforce record Id, the records need to be queried using a command such as the following, which returns all records where the External ID has been set. Because the External ID has been set, the query only returns imported data:

```
$ sfdx force:data:soql:query \
    --query \
      "SELECT Contact.Name, Id, Contact.Id \
       FROM Case \
       WHERE External_ID__c != null"
```

This will return the following.

Listing 11-19. Record Ids of inserted Contacts and Cases

```
CONTACT.NAME CONTACT.ID         ID
──────────── ────────────────── ──────────────────────────
Devon Salter 0033G0000099BHHQA2 5003G000007uga2QAA
Lily Brewer  0033G0000099BHIQA2 5003G000007uga3QAA
Lily Brewer  0033G0000099BHIQA2 5003G000007uga4QAA
Devon Salter 0033G0000099BHHQA2 5003G000007ugaCQAQ
```

Let's assume that you want to delete the Contact called `Devon Salter` and his related Cases. To do this, start by creating a file called `delete_cases.csv` and save the file in the `data` directory. Add to the file the Ids of the two Cases that are related to the `Devon Salter` Contact as follows.

Listing 11-20. Delete Cases CSV file

```
Id
5003G000007uga2QAA
5003G000007ugaCQAQ
```

Then create a file called `delete_contacts.csv` in the `data` directory and add the Id of the Contact called `Devon Salter`, like this.

Listing 11-21. Delete Contacts CSV file

```
Id
0033G0000099BHHQA2
```

Now execute the following two commands to delete the Cases and Contacts, respectively:

```
$ sfdx force:data:bulk:delete \
    --csvfile ./data/delete_cases.csv \
    --sobjecttype Case

$ sfdx force:data:bulk:delete \
    --csvfile ./data/delete_contacts.csv \
    --sobjecttype Contact
```

The parameters that can be used with this command are as follows:

- `--csvfile|-f`: The path to the CSV file containing the Ids of the records to delete. [Required]
- `--sobjecttype|-s`: The type of standard or custom object for the records to be deleted. [Required]
- `--targetusername|-u`: The username or alias of the org where the records to be deleted are stored. [Optional]
- `--wait|-w`: How long to wait, in minutes, for the command to complete. If the parameter is not provided, the command returns immediately. Otherwise, the command will wait up to the specified number of minutes and will return earlier if the command completes. [Optional]
- `--apiversion, --json, --loglevel`: Please refer to the discussion on global parameters in the section "Command-Line Parameters and Arguments" in Chapter 4, "Salesforce CLI."

Like the `force:data:bulk:upsert` command, this command returns immediately and displays the `force:data:bulk:status` command that you can execute to check the status of the job or batches.

Listing 11-22. The force:data:bulk:delete command output

```
Check batch #1's status with the command:
sfdx force:data:bulk:status -i 7503G000001ILZhQAO -b 7513G000001ace0QAA
Bulk Delete... done
```

When the batch has completed, the `force:data:bulk:status` command returns the following.

Listing 11-23. The force:data:bulk:status command output on completion

```
=== Batch Status

jobId:                     7503G000001ILZhQAO
state:                     Completed
createdDate:               2022-08-09T12:47:25.000Z
systemModstamp:            2022-08-09T12:47:26.000Z
numberRecordsProcessed:    2
numberRecordsFailed:       0
totalProcessingTime:       519
apiActiveProcessingTime:   355
apexProcessingTime:        0
Getting Status... done
```

Open the scratch org and navigate to the Contacts and Cases list views in the Service app, and you will observe that the Cases and the Contact have been successfully deleted.

You've learned that the `force:data:bulk` subtopic commands are useful when there are large volumes of records to upsert or delete. Example use cases that need large data volumes are when building Einstein models or testing analytics, reports, and dashboards. In most other scenarios, we can take advantage of the `force:data:tree` subtopic commands, which operate on more modest data volumes and are easier to work with; we'll explore these commands next.

SObject Tree Commands

The `force:data:record` subtopic commands are ideal for manipulating individual records, and the `force:data:bulk` subtopic commands are great for upserting and deleting large volumes of data. But what if you only want to export and import a few hundred records? What if you don't want to modify your standard and custom objects to add External ID custom fields just to support the upserting of test data? This is where the `force:data:tree` subcategory of commands is useful. The commands in this subtopic are as follows:

- **`force:data:tree:export`**: Export an sObject tree.
- **`force:data:tree:import`**: Import an sObject tree.

The commands use the Salesforce REST API's `tree` endpoint to export and import hierarchies of parent-child records that have a common root standard or custom object type and can be up to five levels deep.

Note To learn more about the REST API `tree` endpoint, please refer to the REST API Developer Guide, which can be found here: `https://developer.salesforce.com/docs/atlas.en-us.api_rest.meta/api_rest/resources_composite_sobject_tree.htm`.

The REST API Developer Guide states that a request can contain the following:

- Up to a total of 200 records across all trees
- Up to five records of different types
- SObject trees up to five levels deep

Note The `export` command can actually export up to 2000 records, while the `import` command is limited to 200 records. Therefore, to import 2000 records, the export needs to be split up and imported separately.

The `force:data:tree:export` and `force:data:tree:import` commands can operate in two modes: with and without a plan definition file. Without a plan definition file, all exported objects are written to a single JSON file, and the hierarchical relationships are maintained using nested JSON objects. When a plan definition file is used, separate JSON files are created for each sObject type that is exported, and the hierarchical relationships are maintained using references between the files. We will delve into the mode that doesn't use a plan definition file first, as this most closely resembles how the underlying REST API `tree` endpoint is used. We will then look at the plan definition file mode, where the Salesforce CLI team has added some extra logic to simplify test data maintenance.

Note If you are new to JSON, you can learn more about the format here: `www.json.org/json-en.html`.

Before experimenting with the commands, we need to set up some test data.

Creating Hierarchical Test Data

To try the `force:data:tree` subtopic commands, we first need to create some test data, which will be a four-level deep hierarchy of custom objects in a scratch org. This data can then be exported and imported into another scratch org or sandbox. To create the hierarchy of test data, first create the four custom objects that will be part of the hierarchy by following these steps:

1. Open the `SalesforceDXTestData` Salesforce DX project that we are using for this chapter in VS Code.
2. Open the scratch org with the `MySO` alias.
3. In the scratch org, navigate to **Setup ➤ Objects and Fields ➤ Object Manager**.
4. Click the **Create** menu button and then the **Custom Object** menu item.
5. Create the first custom object with the following field values:
    a. **Label**: `Level 1`
    b. **Plural Label**: `Level 1s`
    c. **Object Name**: `Level_1`
    d. **Record Name**: `Level 1 Name`
    e. **Data Type**: `Text`

Repeat steps 3–5 for levels 2–4 by changing the `1` in the field values to the level number; for example, the level 4 label would be `Level 4`.

To confirm that the custom objects have all been created, navigate back to **Setup ➤ Objects and Fields ➤ Object Manager**, and enter `Level` in the Quick Find field, which should show the four custom objects like the following.

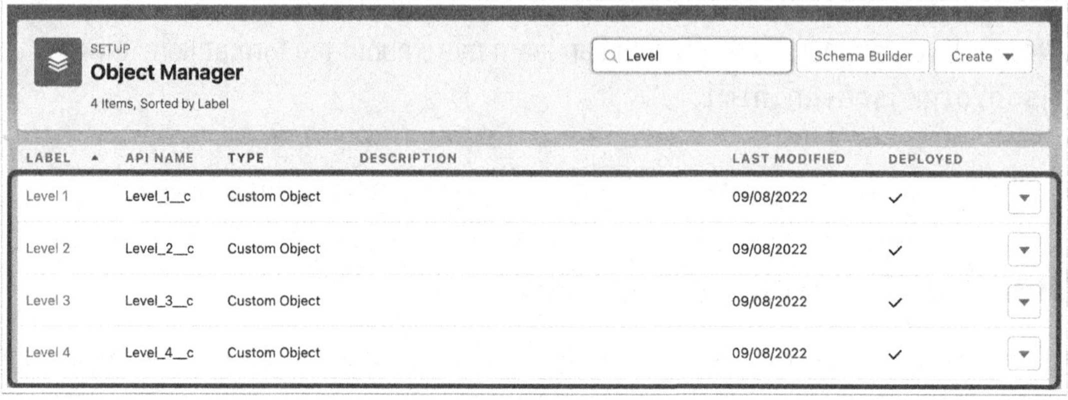

SETUP
Object Manager
4 Items, Sorted by Label

Level | Schema Builder | Create

LABEL	API NAME	TYPE	DESCRIPTION	LAST MODIFIED	DEPLOYED
Level 1	Level_1__c	Custom Object		09/08/2022	✓
Level 2	Level_2__c	Custom Object		09/08/2022	✓
Level 3	Level_3__c	Custom Object		09/08/2022	✓
Level 4	Level_4__c	Custom Object		09/08/2022	✓

Figure 11-5. *Four new custom objects for the four-level test data hierarchy*

To access the custom object hierarchy in the Salesforce user interface, for example, to add or view test data records, we need to add a custom object tab by performing the following steps:

1. Navigate to **Setup ➤ User Interface ➤ Tabs** in the scratch org.
2. Click the **New** button in the Custom Object Tabs section.
3. In Step 1 of the New Custom Object Tab wizard, enter the following field values, then click the **Next** button:
   a. **Object**: Select **Level 1**.
   b. **Tab Style**: Select the **Hexagon** tab style.
4. In Step 2 of the New Custom Object Tab wizard, accept the defaults by clicking the **Next** button.
5. In Step 3 of the New Custom Object Tab wizard, accept the defaults by clicking the **Save** button.

Open an app such as Sales from the App Launcher (⁝⁝⁝) to see the tab, as illustrated in the next figure (you might have to click **More** to see the **Level 1s** tab).

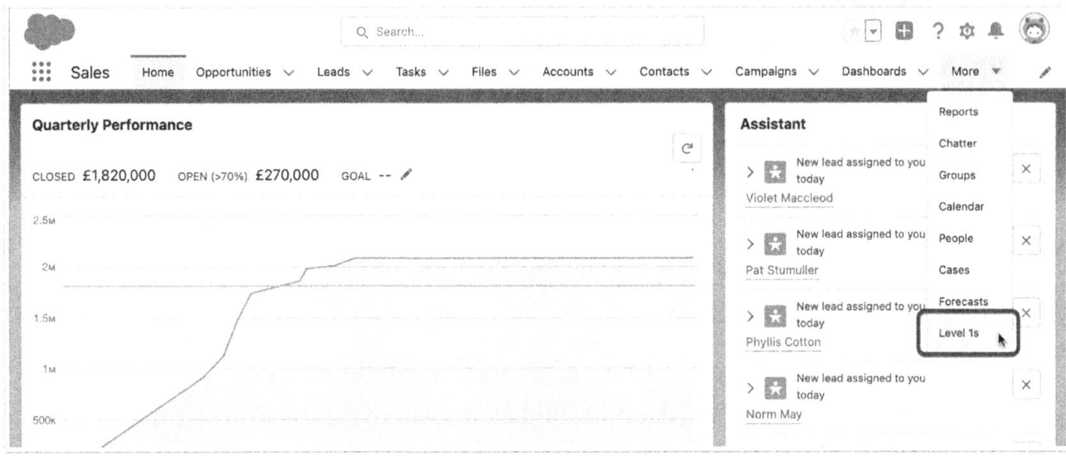

***Figure 11-6.** The new custom object tab in the Sales app*

Complete the following steps to add a master-detail field to custom objects Level_2__c, Level_3__c, and Level_4__c with a relationship to the level above, which will create the hierarchy:

1. In the scratch org, navigate to **Setup ➤ Objects and Fields ➤ Object Manager**.
2. Enter `Level` in the Quick Find field and click the object with the label **Level 2**.
3. Click the **Fields & Relationships** item in the left-hand navigation pane.
4. Click the **New** button to create a new custom field.
5. In Step 1 of the New Custom Field wizard, select the **Master-Detail Relationship** data type, then click the **Next** button.
6. In Step 2 of the New Custom Field wizard, select **Level 1** for the **Related To** field, then click the **Next** button.
7. In Step 3 of the New Custom Field wizard, leave the following default field values, then click the **Next** button:
    a. **Field Label:** `Level 1`
    b. **Field Name**: `Level_1`

    c. **Child Relationship Name**: `Level 2s`

8. In Step 4 of the New Custom Field wizard, accept the defaults by clicking the **Next** button.

9. In Step 5 of the New Custom Field wizard, accept the defaults by clicking the **Next** button.

10. In Step 6 of the New Custom Field wizard, accept the defaults by clicking the **Save** button.

The preceding steps create a parent-child relationship between the Level_1__c (parent) object and the Level_2__c (child) object. Repeat the steps to create a Level_2__c (parent) and Level_3__c (child) relationship and a Level_3__c (parent) and Level_4__c (child) relationship.

Having created the four-level hierarchy of custom objects, it's now time to create some test data records. To do this, you can either use the **Level 1s** tab in the Salesforce user interface, or you can use the `force:data:record:create` Salesforce CLI command. As this book is about Salesforce DX, let's use the CLI command!

Note To refresh your memory of the `force:data:record` subtopic commands, please refer to the section earlier in this chapter.

Starting at the top of the hierarchy, create a Level_1__c object record by executing the following CLI command in VS Code's integrated terminal:

```
$ sfdx force:data:record:create \
    --sobjecttype Level_1__c \
    --values "Name='This is the first level'"
```

The command's success status output will include the record Id of the newly created record, as shown in the following.

Listing 11-24. Newly created record Id

```
Successfully created record: a003G000006TQXUQA4.
Creating record for Level_1__c... done
```

When creating the Level_2__c child record, this is the value that should be assigned to the Level_1__c field to relate the Level_2__c child record to the Level_1__c parent record. Run the following command to create the Level_2__c record:

```
$ sfdx force:data:record:create \
    --sobjecttype Level_2__c \
    --values \
      "Name='This is the second level' \
       Level_1__c= a003G000006TQXUQA4"
```

Again, make a note of the newly created record Id and plug this into a `force:data:record:create` command to create a Level_3__c record and repeat the process to create a Level_4__c record. Confirm that the records have been created by viewing the Level_1__c record in the list view of the **Level 1s** tab that you created earlier and by drilling down to the other levels via each record's related list.

We're almost ready to start using the `force:data:tree:export` command to export our first sObject tree; however, the command requires a SOQL statement, so let's revisit the `force:data:soql:query` command for a moment.

Export Command SOQL Queries

The `force:data:tree:export` command requires a SOQL query to tell it what records to export. Sometimes, it can take a few iterations to get a SOQL query right; fortunately, you can experiment with a query using the `force:data:soql:query` command that we introduced earlier in the chapter. For example, to query for the Level_1__c records and their child Level_2__c records created in the previous section, use the following query:

```
$ sfdx force:data:soql:query \
    --query \
      "SELECT Name, \
        (SELECT Name \
         FROM Level_2s__r \
         ORDER BY Id) \
       FROM Level_1__c \
       ORDER BY Id"
```

The output from the command should resemble the following.

Listing 11-25. Level_1__c with Level_2__c hierarchy

```
NAME                      LEVEL_2S__R.NAME
───────────────────────── ─────────────────────────────
This is the first level This is the second level
Total number of records retrieved: 1.
Querying Data... done
```

Note The SOQL documentation specifically states that *"The order of results is not guaranteed unless you use an ORDER BY clause in a query."* By using the `ORDER BY Id` clause, we can ensure that the returned records are always in the same order, which is beneficial when stitching multiple export files together, as we shall see later. Refer here for the source of this quote: `https://developer.salesforce.com/docs/atlas.en-us.soql_sosl.meta/soql_sosl/sforce_api_calls_soql_select.htm`.

With a four-level hierarchy of test data set up, and a validated SOQL query, we can start to explore the `force:data:tree:export` command, firstly without a plan definition file, followed by with a plan definition file.

Exporting Without a Plan Definition File

The `force:data:tree:export` command takes an optional `--plan|-p` parameter, which determines whether the command uses a plan definition file or not. When the parameter is omitted, the command doesn't use a plan definition file. Without this file, all exported objects are written to a single JSON file and the relationship hierarchy is preserved using nested JSON objects, as we will see in a moment. The `force:data:tree` subtopic commands use the Lightning Platform REST API's `tree` endpoint for exporting and importing sObject trees. If you have previously used this endpoint, you will note that this file format of nested JSON objects is the same as the format used by the API.

To export the Level_1__c and Level_2__c test data records created earlier in the chapter, execute the following Salesforce CLI command, which assumes that the `data` directory you created earlier is present in your Salesforce DX project's root directory:

```
$ sfdx force:data:tree:export \
    --outputdir ./data \
    --query \
      "SELECT Name, \
        (SELECT Name \
         FROM Level_2s__r \
         ORDER BY Id) \
       FROM Level_1__c \
       ORDER BY Id" \
    --prefix noplan
```

This command's parameters are as follows:

- `--outputdir|-d`: The path to the directory where the exported data files will be written. [Optional]
- `--plan|-p`: Specifies whether a plan definition file is used. [Optional]
- `--query|-q`: The SOQL query used to indicate which records should be exported. [Required]
- `--targetusername|-u`: The username or alias of the org that the records should be exported from. [Optional]
- `--prefix|-x`: A prefix added to each file created by the export. This is useful when performing multiple exports on the same objects. [Optional]
- `--apiversion, --json, --loglevel`: Please refer to the discussion on global parameters in the section "Command-Line Parameters and Arguments" in Chapter 4, "Salesforce CLI."

A new file called `noplan-Level_1__c-Level_2__c.json` is created in the `data` directory. The filename consists of the `noplan` prefix followed by the names of the queried objects.

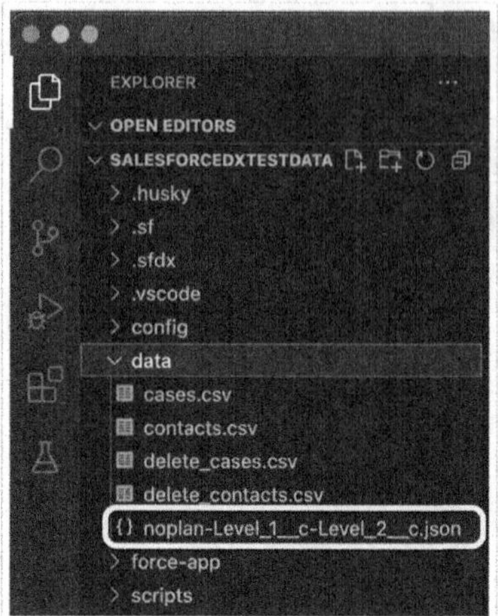

Figure 11-7. *Exported Level_1__c and Level_2__c file*

Open the file and you will see, as the filename extension indicates, that the contents are in JSON format and the record hierarchy is maintained by using nested JSON objects, which can be seen in the following listing.

Listing 11-26. Level_1__c with Level_2__c JSON export

```
{
    "records": [
        {
            "attributes": {
                "type": "Level_1__c",
                "referenceId": "Level_1__cRef1"
            },
            "Name": "This is the first level",
            "Level_2s__r": {
                "records": [
                    {
                        "attributes": {
                            "type": "Level_2__c",
                            "referenceId": "Level_2__cRef1"
                        },
                        "Name": "This is the second level"
                    }
```

```
                ]
            }
        }
    ]
}
```

So far so good, but this contains only two levels of the four-level hierarchy. How do we query for all four levels? After all, SOQL can only query two levels by design. The answer is to perform multiple queries and then "stitch" the files together. This might sound like a lot of work, but it's not uncommon to create and export test data a few times until you get it right and then to import it multiple times thereafter, so the up-front effort is recouped many times over. To capture the whole hierarchy, execute the following additional exports:

```
$ sfdx force:data:tree:export \
   --outputdir ./data \
   --query \
     "SELECT Name, \
       (SELECT Name \
        FROM Level_3s__r \
        ORDER BY Id) \
      FROM Level_2__c \
      ORDER BY Id" \
   --prefix noplan

$ sfdx force:data:tree:export \
   --outputdir ./data \
   --query \
     "SELECT Name, \
       (SELECT Name \
        FROM Level_4s__r \
        ORDER BY Id) \
      FROM Level_3__c \
      ORDER BY Id" \
   --prefix noplan
```

This will create two more files in the data directory containing the Level_2__c and Level_3__c exported records and the Level_3__c and Level_4__c exported records.

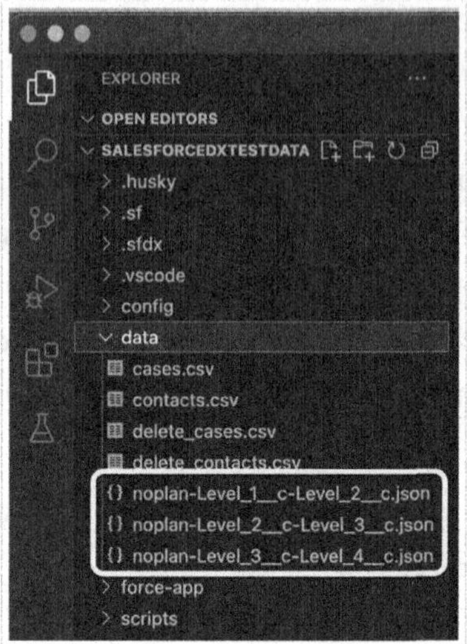

Figure 11-8. *Files containing four levels of export*

Because of the simplicity of the custom objects, it's not surprising that the three files containing the exported records look similar, and stitching them together will be fairly straightforward. Here, I've listed the Level_1__c with Level_2__c export file followed by the Level_2__c with Level_3__c file.

Listing 11-27. Level_1__c with Level_2__c JSON export

```
{
    "records": [
        {
            "attributes": {
                "type": "Level_1__c",
                "referenceId": "Level_1__cRef1"
            },
            "Name": "This is the first level",
            "Level_2s__r": {
                "records": [
                    {
                        "attributes": {
```

```
                        "type": "Level_2__c",
                        "referenceId": "Level_2__cRef1"
                    },
                    "Name": "This is the second level"
                }
            ]
        }
    }
  ]
}
```

Listing 11-28. Level_2__c with Level_3__c JSON export

```
{
    "records": [
        {
            "attributes": {
                "type": "Level_2__c",
                "referenceId": "Level_2__cRef1"
            },
            "Name": "This is the second level",
            "Level_3s__r": {
                "records": [
                    {
                        "attributes": {
                            "type": "Level_3__c",
                            "referenceId": "Level_3__cRef1"
                        },
                        "Name": "This is the third level"
                    }
                ]
            }
        }
    ]
}
```

Highlighted in the first listing are all the Level_2__c records that are related to the Level_1__c record, in this example just a single record. In the second listing, the Level_2__c record is highlighted again, this time with the Level_3__c records that are related to it. Because we used the `ORDER BY Id` clause in the SOQL query, if there were multiple Level_1__c, Level_2__c, and Level_3__c records, they would be in the same order in each export file; therefore, to stich the two files together, replace the highlighted rows in the first file with the highlighted rows from the second file. Finally, repeat the process for the Level_3__c with Level_4__c export file.

In the following listing, the stitching is complete, and it's saved in a file called `noplan-four_levels.json`. The nested records, represented by nested JSON objects, are highlighted in the listing.

Listing 11-29. Four-level stitched JSON export

```
{
    "records": [
        {
            "attributes": {
                "type": "Level_1__c",
                "referenceId": "Level_1__cRef1"
            },
            "Name": "This is the first level",
            "Level_2s__r": {
                "records": [
                    {
                        "attributes": {
                            "type": "Level_2__c",
                            "referenceId": "Level_2__cRef1"
                        },
                        "Name": "This is the second level",
                        "Level_3s__r": {
                            "records": [
                                {
                                    "attributes": {
                                        "type": "Level_3__c",
                                        "referenceId": "Level_3__cRef1"
                                    },
```

```
                                    "Name": "This is the third level",
                                    "Level_4s__r": {
                                        "records": [
                                            {
                                                "attributes": {
                                                    "type": "Level_4__c",
                                                    "referenceId":
                                                    "Level_4__cRef1"
                                                },
                                                "Name": "This is the
                                                fourth level"
                                            }
                                        ]
                                    }
                                }
                            ]
                        }
                    }
                ]
            }
        }
    ]
}
```

We now have a single file containing the test data records that can be imported into other scratch orgs using the `force:data:tree:import` command, which will be explained next.

Importing Without a Plan Definition File

The `force:data:tree:import` command imports up to 200 records contained in export files created by the `force:data:tree:export` command. To import the records contained in the `noplan-four_levels.json` file that we created in the previous section, create a fresh scratch org with the alias `MySO2`, and add the custom objects, custom object tab, and custom fields that you added to the scratch org with the alias `MySO`, which was used for the data export earlier.

Note Wasn't that a pain, recreating the same metadata components in the second scratch org? If you've jumped to this section, please refer to Chapter 8, "Metadata," where we look at migrating metadata components between orgs.

Now run the following command to import the data:

```
$ sfdx force:data:tree:import \
    --sobjecttreefiles \
        ./data/noplan-four_levels.json \
    --targetusername MySO2
```

The parameters that can be passed to this command are as follows:

- `-- sobjecttreefiles|-f`: A comma-separated list of files containing records to import. [Optional: Either this parameter or the `--plan|-p` parameter must be used.]
- `--plan|-p`: Path to the plan definition file to be used. [Optional: Either this parameter or the `-- sobjecttreefiles|-f` parameter must be present.]
- `--targetusername|-u`: The username or alias of the org that the data should be imported to. [Optional]
- `--confighelp`: Displays the schema of the plan definition file. [Optional: The `--plan|-p` parameter must be present, and the `--json` parameter is the only other parameter that can be present.]
- `--apiversion, --json, --loglevel`: Please refer to the discussion on global parameters in the section "Command-Line Parameters and Arguments" in Chapter 4, "Salesforce CLI."

This will create the four records in the new scratch org and output the Ids of the created records, as follows.

Listing 11-30. Import of the four-level stitched JSON export file

```
=== Import Results

Reference ID        Type          ID
──────────────────  ────────────  ───────────────────────
Level_1__cRef1      Level_1__c    a002z000001tCKLAA2
Level_2__cRef1      Level_2__c    a012z000002OBzbAAG
Level_3__cRef1      Level_3__c    a022z000002c4haAAA
Level_4__cRef1      Level_4__c    a032z000001tkgjAAA
```

The import can be confirmed by opening the scratch org that has the alias `MySO2`, launching any app from the App Launcher, clicking the **Level 1s** tab, viewing the Level_1__c custom object record, and drilling down the dependency tree using the related records.

So far, we've covered exporting and importing data without using a plan definition file. We will now move on to exporting and then importing with a plan definition file.

Exporting with a Plan Definition File

Using the Salesforce CLI `force:data:tree:export` and `force:data:tree:import` commands to export and import data without using a plan definition file is a convenient command-line wrapper around the Lightning Platform REST API's `tree` endpoint. The challenge is that a single JSON file contains test data for all the sObjects in a hierarchy, which can become difficult to maintain if you have a complex multilevel sObject hierarchy. Furthermore, if multiple developers are concurrently working on different sObjects in the hierarchy and they need to update the test data, those changes will need to be merged, adding to the complexity.

In their drive to increase the granularity of source files, which simplifies version control and speeds up source synchronization between Salesforce DX projects and scratch orgs, the Salesforce CLI team has added the plan definition file feature to the `force:data:tree` subtopic commands. When using a plan definition file, multiple files are generated during an export, rather than the single file that is generated without a plan definition file. Each sObject type is exported to its own file with hierarchical relationships maintained using references between the files. Finally, the plan definition file lists the sObject files that have been exported, and it instructs the CLI how to resolve the references between the files.

To use a plan definition file, simply add the `--plan|-p` parameter to the `force:data:tree:export` command. For example, to export the four-level hierarchy of test data records that we set up in the earlier section called "Exporting Without a Plan Definition File," execute the following three commands:

```
$ sfdx force:data:tree:export \
    --outputdir ./data \
    --plan \
    --query \
      "SELECT Name, \
        (SELECT Name \
         FROM Level_2s__r \
         ORDER BY Id) \
       FROM Level_1__c \
       ORDER BY Id" \
    --prefix plan12

$ sfdx force:data:tree:export \
    --outputdir ./data \
    --plan \
    --query \
      "SELECT Name, \
        (SELECT Name \
         FROM Level_3s__r \
       ORDER BY Id) \
       FROM Level_2__c \
       ORDER BY Id" \
    --prefix plan23

$ sfdx force:data:tree:export \
    --outputdir ./data \
    --plan \
    --query \
      "SELECT Name, \
        (SELECT Name \
         FROM Level_4s__r \
         ORDER BY Id) \
```

```
    FROM Level_3__c \
    ORDER BY Id" \
--prefix plan34
```

Each of the three commands will export the following files:

- Plan definition file, the format of which is <prefix>-<parent sObject>-<child sObject>-plan.json
- Parent sObject record file, the format of which is <prefix>-<parent SObject>s.json
- Child sObject record file, the format of which is <prefix>-<parent SObject>s.json

The resulting nine files can be seen in the following screenshot.

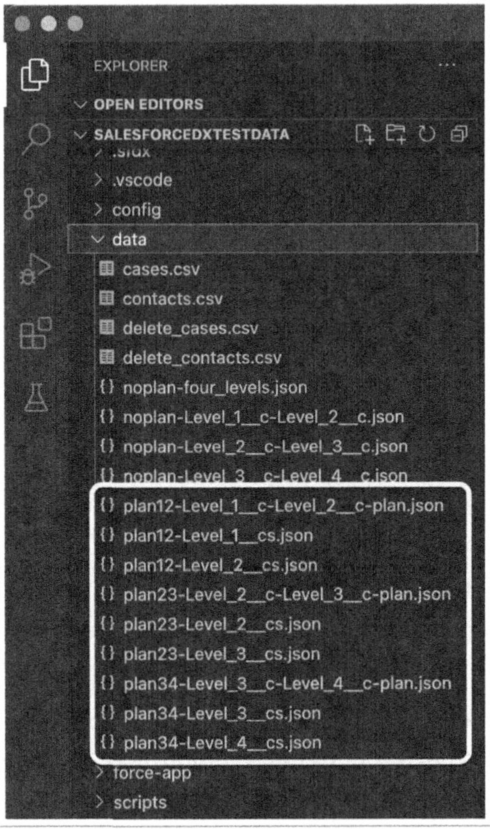

Figure 11-9. *Plan definition file and record file exports*

> **Note** The reason that we've used a different prefix for each of the three commands is to avoid the record files from being overwritten; for example, the first command creates a child sObject file called `plan12-Level_2__cs.json`, and the second command creates a parent sObject file called `plan23-Level_2__cs.json`. If I had used the same prefix for both commands, the second record file will have overwritten the first, and we would have lost the relationship between the `Level_1__c` parent and the `Level_2__c` child records.

Open the file containing the Level_1__c custom object records, which should resemble the following.

Listing 11-31. Exported Level_1__c record file

```
{
    "records": [
        {
            "attributes": {
                "type": "Level_1__c",
                "referenceId": "Level_1__cRef1"
            },
            "Name": "This is the first level"
        }
    ]
}
```

The file contains an array called `records` that contains a single JSON object representing the single Level_1__c record that we created earlier. If we had created further records, they would be included in this array. Within the record object, there is an `attributes` object, which contains information that is used by the `force:data:tree:import` command when deserializing the JSON file. The `type` attribute specifies the sObject type that the records should be created for, and the `referenceId` is a unique reference Id for each record in the file, which will be used to resolve any relationships between this parent record and any child records, as you shall see in a moment. After the attributes object come the field values that are returned by the SOQL query in the `force:data:tree:export` command; in this instance, just the `Name` field.

Opening the Level_2__c record file will reveal the following.

Listing 11-32. Exported Level_2__c record file

```
{
    "records": [
        {
            "attributes": {
                "type": "Level_2__c",
                "referenceId": "Level_2__cRef1"
            },
            "Name": "This is the second level",
            "Level_1__c": "@Level_1__cRef1"
        }
    ]
}
```

The format of this file is the same as the Level_1__c record file, except for the addition of the `Level_1__c` master-detail relationship field that establishes this record as a child of a Level_1__c record. Although we did not explicitly query this field, because we executed a SOQL subquery the Salesforce CLI ensured that this field was also queried to resolve the relationship hierarchy. You will notice that the `Level_1__c` field value is not a standard sObject record Id; rather, `@Level_1__cRef1` is the reference Id of the Level_1__c record that is the parent of this record. Actual record Ids cannot be used because when the `force:data:tree:import` command imports the data into a different scratch org or sandbox, new record Ids will be generated.

The plan definition file informs the `force:data:tree:import` command of the record files to use and whether or not to resolve any parent-child references between the files. The plan definition file looks like this.

Listing 11-33. Exported Level_1__c and Level_2__c plan definition file

```
[
    {
        "sobject": "Level_1__c",
        "saveRefs": true,
        "resolveRefs": false,
```

```
        "files": [
            "plan12-Level_1__cs.json"
        ]
    },
    {
        "sobject": "Level_2__c",
        "saveRefs": false,
        "resolveRefs": true,
        "files": [
            "plan12-Level_2__cs.json"
        ]
    }
]
```

The file contains a JSON array consisting of each sObject type that has been exported. The `sobject` field specifies the sObject type, and the `files` array lists the files that contain the exported records; note, there can be more than one record file. The `saveRefs` and `resolveRefs` values are used to instruct the CLI how to resolve parent-child relationships between records. When the `saveRefs` value is `true`, the Salesforce CLI keeps track of the `referenceId` value for each record in a record file along with the associated sObject record Id when the records are inserted. When the `resolveRefs` value is `true`, the CLI resolves the parent relationship in a child record by replacing the `@<referenceId>` reference in the child record file with the parent sObject's record Id, which is being tracked by the CLI thanks to the `saveRefs` value being set to `true` on the parent sObject. In our example, when the Level_1__c record is created, the CLI keeps track of the sObject record Id for the corresponding `Level_1__cRef1` reference Id. Before the Level_2__c record is inserted, the CLI replaces the `@Level_1__cRef1` reference with the parent's sObject record Id so that the `Level_1__c` master-detail relationship field is populated with the parent sObject Id when it is inserted. All without the need for an External ID!

As with exporting without a plan definition file, the SOQL query can only query two levels deep, so we now need to stitch together the exported plan definition files and record files so that the `force:data:tree:import` command can import all of the levels in the hierarchy in one go.

Stitching together the plan definition files is very straightforward as the files consist of a JSON array of sObjects, so there's no deeply nested JSON objects to negotiate. Create a new plan definition file, which we shall call `plan-Level_1_to_4-plan.json`, that includes the Level_1__c, Level_2__c, Level_3__c, and Level_4__c JSON objects from the exported plan definition files as follows.

Listing 11-34. Level_1__c to Level_4__c plan definition files

```
[
    {
        "sobject": "Level_1__c",
        "saveRefs": true,
        "resolveRefs": false,
        "files": [
            "plan-Level_1__cs.json"
        ]
    },
    {
        "sobject": "Level_2__c",
        "saveRefs": true,
        "resolveRefs": true,
        "files": [
            "plan-Level_2__cs.json"
        ]
    },
    {
        "sobject": "Level_3__c",
        "saveRefs": true,
        "resolveRefs": true,
        "files": [
            "plan-Level_3__cs.json"
        ]
    },
    {
        "sobject": "Level_4__c",
        "saveRefs": false,
```

```
        "resolveRefs": true,
        "files": [
            "plan-Level_4__cs.json"
        ]
    }
]
```

Note the following about the new plan definition file:

- `saveRefs` has been set to `true` for levels 1 through 3 as these levels all have child records.
- `resolveRefs` has been set to `true` for levels 2 through 4 as these levels all have parent records.
- The record file names have been changed to use the `plan` prefix that we are using for this plan definition file.

Recall that we have nine exported files, three plan definition files, and six record files. The six record files are as follows:

- The Level_1__c and Level_2__c exported record files
    - `plan12-Level_1__cs.json`: Top of tree parent
    - `plan12-Level_2__cs.json`: Child of Level_1__c
- The Level_2__c and Level_3__c exported record files
    - `plan23-Level_2__cs.json`: Intermediate parent
    - `plan23-Level_3__cs.json`: Child of Level_2__c
- The Level_3__c and Level_4__c exported record files
    - `plan34-Level_3__cs.json`: Intermediate parent
    - `plan34-Level_4__cs.json`: Child of Level_3__c

The record files of interest when stitching the files together are the top of tree parent and the three record files that have a child to parent relationship. If we were only exporting and importing two levels of related records, we could use the exported plan definition file, the top of tree parent record file, and the child of Level_1__c record file as is. However, because we are stitching together four levels, we performed two extra exports so that we can establish the syntax for the child of Level_2__c and child of

Level_3__c record files, that is, levels 3 and 4, respectively. The intermediate parents are there just to get the subquery outputs for the Level_3__c and Level_4__c records, so they can be discarded.

Simply rename the four record files of interest to use the same `plan` prefix as the stitched plan definition file. You should now have the following record files:

- `plan-Level_1__cs.json`
- `plan-Level_2__cs.json`
- `plan-Level_3__cs.json`
- `plan-Level_4__cs.json`

Note As long as no new records were inserted, or existing records deleted, between the three export commands, the child record to parent record references in the record files will be consistent across the three sets of exported files because we used the `ORDER BY Id` clause in the SOQL queries.

That stitching was easier, wasn't it? Thank you, Salesforce CLI team! And remember, if you are only working on the Level_3__c custom object and you want to update your test data, you only have to modify the `plan-Level_3__cs.json` file. Let's see how to import this data into another scratch org.

Importing with a Plan Definition File

To perform an import of the stitched together four-level data using a plan definition file, start by creating a fresh scratch org with the alias `MySO3`. Add the custom objects, custom object tab, and custom fields that you added to the `MySO` scratch org that was used for the data export.

Note Alternatively, reuse the scratch org that you used in the section "Importing Without a Plan Definition File." To do this, open the scratch org with the alias `MySO2`, open the **Sales** app, navigate to the **Level 1s** tab, and delete the Level 1 record. This will delete the Level 2, 3, and 4 records as well, due to the master-detail relationships.

Now run the following command to import the data:

```
$ sfdx force:data:tree:import \
    --plan ./data/plan-Level_1_to_4-plan.json \
    --targetusername MySO3
```

The command should output the following results, which shows the records that were inserted and the sObject record Ids that replaced the reference Ids to resolve the parent-child relationships.

Listing 11-35. Import of the four-level stitched JSON plan definition file

```
=== Import Results

 Reference ID           Type            ID
 ─────────────────────  ──────────────  ─────────────────────────
 Level_1__cRef1         Level_1__c      a003G000000qgbNQAQ
 Level_2__cRef1         Level_2__c      a013G000000Ex6pQAC
 Level_3__cRef1         Level_3__c      a023G000000fvKKQAY
 Level_4__cRef1         Level_4__c      a033G000000ETC8QAO
```

As you can see, the `force:data:tree` subcategory of commands greatly simplifies the management of test data and should be preferred over the `force:data:bulk` subcategory of commands, except when very large volumes of data are involved of course.

Let's wrap up the chapter.

Chapter Summary

Effective testing relies on sufficient, good quality data to cover your application or customization's use cases. In this chapter, you learned about the various methods that Salesforce DX provides for managing test data in scratch orgs and sandboxes to support your testing efforts. Salesforce CLI commands provide data management for standard objects, standard fields, custom objects, and custom fields. They support data queries, CRUD operations on individual records, bulk export and import of large data volumes, and finally a convenient way for exporting and importing hierarchical sObject trees of data.

In the next chapter, we will look at how to use Salesforce DX for developing metadata components such as Apex classes and Lightning web components.

CHAPTER 12

Development

The Setup area in a Salesforce org is predominantly used for no-code and low-code metadata component development. An example of no-code development is the point-and-click creation of a custom object or a custom field. Working with validation rules and formula fields are examples of low-code development. Changes made using an org's Setup area are synchronized from the org to a Salesforce DX project using Salesforce CLI commands in the `force:source` or `force:mdapi` topics. For pro-code development, such as writing Apex classes or Lightning web components, developers often turn to development environments such as Visual Studio Code with the Salesforce Extensions for Visual Studio Code and the Salesforce CLI to develop the metadata components on a local computer. The commands in the CLI's `force:source` or `force:mdapi` topics are then used to synchronize a Salesforce DX project that contains the changes to a Salesforce org.

To improve developer productivity, the Salesforce CLI includes commands to create boilerplate code for several metadata components that can then be further developed using the pro-code approach. In this chapter, we will encounter the commands that kick-start the development of the following components:

- Apex classes
- Custom metadata types
- Experience Cloud sites
- Lightning web components
- Static resources
- Visualforce pages and components

I. Harris, *Beginning Salesforce DX*, https://doi.org/10.1007/978-1-4842-8114-7_12

Note When exploring the Salesforce CLI commands, you may notice the `force:analytics` topic, which has a command to create boilerplate code for CRM Analytics templates. You might be wondering why it's not included in this chapter. The recommended method for pro-code CRM Analytics development using Salesforce DX is to install the `@salesforce/analytics` plug-in for the Salesforce CLI, which adds many more commands in addition to the template create command. The range of plug-ins that are available won't be covered in this book; otherwise, it would extend to over 1000+ pages! If you're interested in CRM Analytics development using Salesforce DX, simply search for "`Salesforce Analytics CLI Plugin`" to learn more.

Before we dive into this chapter's CLI commands, let's summarize the commands that will be covered and set up the Salesforce DX project for the chapter.

This Chapter's Commands

Commands in the following Salesforce CLI topics will be covered in this chapter:

- **`force:apex`**: Create Apex classes and triggers, retrieve Apex logs, and run unit tests.
- **`force:cmdt`**: Create custom metadata types, add fields, and create records for the custom metadata type.
- **`force:community`**: Create an Experience Cloud site from a template and publish it.
- **`force:lightning`**: Create and test Aura and Lightning web components.
- **`force:staticresource`**: Create static resources.
- **`force:visualforce`**: Create Visualforce pages and components.

First things first, let's create our Salesforce DX project for this chapter.

This Chapter's Project

As usual, please follow the instructions in Chapter 6, "Projects," to create a project called SalesforceDXDev using the default standard template. As we will be using scratch orgs, please ensure that you have a default Dev Hub org authorized with an alias of MyDH, which is described in Chapter 5, "Dev Hub." Also, create a scratch org with the alias MySO by following the instructions in Chapter 7, "Orgs," and make it the org with the default username. If you now execute the force:org:list command, the output should resemble the following listing.

Listing 12-1. Chapter org list

```
=== Orgs
     ALIAS USERNAME             ORG ID             CONNECTED STATUS
 ─── ───── ──────────────────── ────────────────── ────────────────
 (D) MyDH  ihdxdh@example.com   00D4K0000015OzMUAU Connected
     ALIAS USERNAME                       ORG ID             EXPIRATION DATE
 ─── ───── ────────────────────────────── ────────────────── ──────────
 (U) MySO  test-rncsfeckoidh@example.com 00D3G0000001YF5UAM 2022-08-17
```

It's not a problem if you have other orgs in your list, so long as you have a fresh scratch org with the alias MySO and it has the default username.

The first Salesforce CLI topic that we will explore is force:apex, which includes command for working with Apex classes and triggers.

Working with Apex Classes

The Salesforce CLI force:apex topic includes the following commands that we will explore in this section:

- **force:apex:execute**: Executes anonymous Apex that is entered on the command line or using a file
- **force:apex:class:create**: Creates the metadata and boilerplate code for an Apex class

- **force:apex:trigger:create**: Creates the metadata and boilerplate code for an Apex trigger
- **force:apex:log:list**: Lists the debug logs in an org
- **force:apex:log:get**: Retrieves one or more debug logs from an org and optionally saves them as files
- **force:apex:log:tail**: Starts debugging in an org and displays the debug log files in the terminal application
- **force:apex:test:run**: Executes Apex unit tests in an org
- **force:apex:test:report**: Displays the results from a test run executed using the `force:apex:test:run` command

The first command from the list that we will look at is the `force:apex:execute` command, which executes anonymous Apex.

Executing Anonymous Apex

On occasion, it is useful to be able to execute anonymous Apex from the Salesforce CLI command line as you would using the Execute Anonymous Window in the Developer Console. To see an example of this, first follow these steps:

1. Launch Visual Studio Code if it's not already launched.
2. Open this chapter's `SalesforceDXDev` project.
3. Open the integrated terminal.

Then execute the following CLI command in the integrated terminal:

```
$ sfdx force:apex:execute
```

All of the `force:apex:execute` command parameters are optional. Those that can be used are as follows:

- `--apexcodefile|-f`: Path to a file containing anonymous Apex, which can be used instead of entering the code interactively. [Optional]
- `--targetusername|-u`: The username or alias of the org to execute the anonymous Apex in. [Optional]

- `--apiversion`, `--json`, `--loglevel`: Please refer to the discussion on global parameters in the section "Command-Line Parameters and Arguments" in Chapter 4, "Salesforce CLI."

Note To execute anonymous Apex using the Visual Studio Code Command Palette, display some Apex code in an editor window. Then execute one of the following two commands:

SFDX: Execute Anonymous Apex with Currently Selected Text

SFDX: Execute Anonymous Apex with Editor Contents

The first command requires Apex code to be selected in the editor window first. An example Apex code file is included in a new Salesforce DX project: `./scripts/apex/hello.apex`.

The `force:apex:execute` command will output the following as a prompt to start entering anonymous Apex.

Listing 12-2. Salesforce CLI anonymous Apex prompt

```
Start typing Apex code. Press the Enter key after each line, then press
CTRL+D when finished.
```

Type the following Apex statement, then press the **Enter** key. At this point, you could add another Apex statement; however, our Apex code consists of one line, so press the key combination **CTRL+D** to return to the integrated terminal prompt.

```
System.debug(
  'Org Name: ' +
  UserInfo.getOrganizationName());
```

The Salesforce CLI will execute the anonymous Apex in the org with the default username, which in our case is `MySO`. The output will resemble the following listing, where the result of the `System.debug` method is the line that includes "`USER_DEBUG|[1]|DEBUG|Org Name: ivanharris company`".

Listing 12-3. Execute anonymous Apex output

```
Compiled successfully.
Executed successfully.

55.0 APEX_CODE,DEBUG;APEX_PROFILING,INFO
Execute Anonymous: System.debug(
Execute Anonymous:   'Org Name: ' +
Execute Anonymous:   UserInfo.getOrganizationName());
Execute Anonymous:
07:22:03.20 (20489300)|USER_INFO|[EXTERNAL]|0053G000002ukoz|test-
rncsfeckoidh@example.com|(GMT+01:00) British Summer Time (Europe/
London)|GMT+01:00
07:22:03.20 (20544209)|EXECUTION_STARTED
07:22:03.20 (20562421)|CODE_UNIT_STARTED|[EXTERNAL]|execute_anonymous_apex
07:22:03.20 (21721822)|USER_DEBUG|[1]|DEBUG|Org Name: ivanharris company
07:22:03.21 (21800304)|CUMULATIVE_LIMIT_USAGE
07:22:03.21 (21800304)|LIMIT_USAGE_FOR_NS|(default)|
  Number of SOQL queries: 0 out of 100
  Number of query rows: 0 out of 50000
  Number of SOSL queries: 0 out of 20
  Number of DML statements: 0 out of 150
  Number of Publish Immediate DML: 0 out of 150
  Number of DML rows: 0 out of 10000
  Maximum CPU time: 0 out of 10000
  Maximum heap size: 0 out of 6000000
  Number of callouts: 0 out of 100
  Number of Email Invocations: 0 out of 10
  Number of future calls: 0 out of 50
  Number of queueable jobs added to the queue: 0 out of 50
  Number of Mobile Apex push calls: 0 out of 10

07:22:03.21 (21800304)|CUMULATIVE_LIMIT_USAGE_END

07:22:03.20 (21870434)|CODE_UNIT_FINISHED|execute_anonymous_apex
07:22:03.20 (21882012)|EXECUTION_FINISHED
```

Anonymous Apex allows you to execute Apex code without persisting the code in the org. To persist Apex code, you need to create Apex classes or triggers and add them to an org. We'll cover creating Apex classes next.

Creating Apex Classes

To create an Apex class, we can use the `force:apex:class:create` CLI command. The command creates the metadata and boilerplate code for an Apex class in a Salesforce DX project. Commands in the `force:source` or `force:mdapi` CLI topics can then be used to add the metadata to an org.

To use the command, launch Visual Studio Code, open the `SalesforceDXDev` project, and execute the following CLI command in the integrated terminal:

```
$ sfdx force:apex:class:create \
    --outputdir ./force-app/main/default/classes \
    --classname ExampleDefaultApexClass
```

The full list of parameters that can be used with this command is as follows:

- `--outputdir|-d`: Path to the directory where the Apex class files will be created. [Optional] [Default: Current working directory (`.`)]
- `--classname|-n`: The name of the Apex class to be created. [Required]
- `--template|-t`: Templates for the types of Apex classes that can be created. [Optional] [Default: `DefaultApexClass`]

  Allowed values are as follows:

  - `ApexException`: Create a custom exception Apex class that extends the built-in `Exception` class.
  - `ApexUnitTest`: Create an Apex unit test class that includes a single test method.
  - `DefaultApexClass`: Create an Apex class that includes a constructor. [Default]

    - `InboundEmailService`: Create an Inbound Email Service Apex class that implements the `Messaging.InboundEmailHandler` interface.

- `--apiversion, --json, --loglevel`: Please refer to the discussion on global parameters in the section "Command-Line Parameters and Arguments" in Chapter 4, "Salesforce CLI."

Note To create an Apex class using the Visual Studio Code Command Palette, execute the command **SFDX: Create Apex Class**. To create an Apex class using Visual Studio Code context menus, right-click the `classes` directory and click the menu item **SFDX: Create Apex Class**. Even though you don't have the option to select a template, this is a quick way to create new default Apex classes.

The command creates the required source format metadata files in the `classes` directory as directed by the `--outputdir|-d` parameter. The files can be seen in this screenshot.

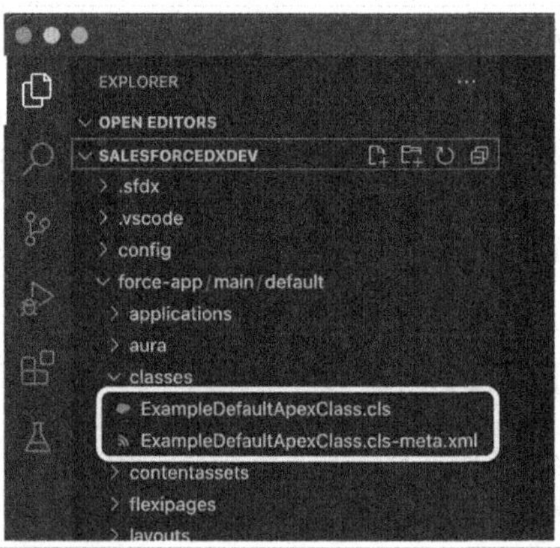

Figure 12-1. *New default Apex class files*

The following listings show the boilerplate code that is created for each of the template types that can be passed to the `--template|-t` parameter.

Listing 12-4. Apex exception class boilerplate code

```
public class ExampleApexException extends Exception {

}
```

Listing 12-5. Apex unit test class boilerplate code

```
/**
 * This class contains unit tests for validating the behavior of
Apex classes
 * and triggers.
 *
 * Unit tests are class methods that verify whether a particular piece
 * of code is working properly. Unit test methods take no arguments,
 * commit no data to the database, and are flagged with the testMethod
 * keyword in the method definition.
 *
 * All test methods in an org are executed whenever Apex code is deployed
 * to a production org to confirm correctness, ensure code
 * coverage, and prevent regressions. All Apex classes are
 * required to have at least 75% code coverage in order to be deployed
 * to a production org. In addition, all triggers must have some code
   coverage.
 *
 * The @isTest class annotation indicates this class only contains test
 * methods. Classes defined with the @isTest annotation do not
   count against
 * the org size limit for all Apex scripts.
 *
 * See the Apex Language Reference for more information about Testing and
   Code Coverage.
 */
@isTest
private class ExampleApexUnitTest {
```

```
    @isTest
    static void myUnitTest() {
        // TO DO: implement unit test
    }
}
```

Listing 12-6. Default Apex class boilerplate code

```
public with sharing class ExampleDefaultApexClass {
    public ExampleDefaultApexClass() {

    }
}
```

Listing 12-7. Inbound Email Service Apex class boilerplate code

```
/**
 * Email services are automated processes that use Apex classes
 * to process the contents, headers, and attachments of inbound
 * email.
 */
global class ExampleInboundEmailService implements Messaging.
InboundEmailHandler {

    global Messaging.InboundEmailResult handleInboundEmail(Messaging.
InboundEmail email, Messaging.InboundEnvelope envelope) {
        Messaging.InboundEmailResult result = new Messaging.
InboundEmailresult();

        return result;
    }
}
```

We'll now discover how to create the metadata and boilerplate code for Apex triggers.

Creating Apex Triggers

Similar to using the `force:apex:class:create` CLI command to create Apex classes, we can use the `force:apex:trigger:create` command to create the metadata and boilerplate code for an Apex trigger. To create an Apex trigger, launch Visual Studio Code if it's not already, open the `SalesforceDXDev` project, and use the integrated terminal to execute the following CLI command:

```
$ sfdx force:apex:trigger:create \
    --outputdir ./force-app/main/default/triggers \
    --triggername ExampleDefaultApexTrigger \
    --sobject Contact
```

The `force:apex:trigger:create` command supports the following parameters:

- `--outputdir`|`-d`: Path to the directory where the Apex trigger files will be created. [Optional] [Default: Current working directory (`.`)]
- `--triggerevents`|`-e`: A comma-separated list of events that will invoke the trigger. Due to the spaces in the event names, surround each event or the entire list with single or double quotes. [Optional] [Default: `before insert`]
- Allowed values are
    - `before insert` [Default]
    - `before update`
    - `before delete`
    - `after insert`
    - `after update`
    - `after delete`
    - `after undelete`
- `--triggername`|`-n`: The name of the Apex trigger to be created. [Required]

- `--sobject|-s`: The standard or custom object that the Apex trigger will be created for. [Optional] [Default: `SOBJECT`]
- `--template|-t`: Templates for the types of Apex triggers that can be created. Note that currently the only allowed value is `ApexTrigger`. [Optional] [Default: `ApexTrigger`]
- `--apiversion, --json, --loglevel`: Please refer to the discussion on global parameters in the section "Command-Line Parameters and Arguments" in Chapter 4, "Salesforce CLI."

Note To create an Apex trigger using the Visual Studio Code Command Palette, execute the command **SFDX: Create Apex Trigger**. To create an Apex trigger using Visual Studio Code context menus, right-click the `triggers` directory and click the menu item **SFDX: Create Apex Trigger**.

The trigger's source format metadata files are created in the directory specified by the `--outputdir|-d` parameter, which is the `triggers` directory in this instance.

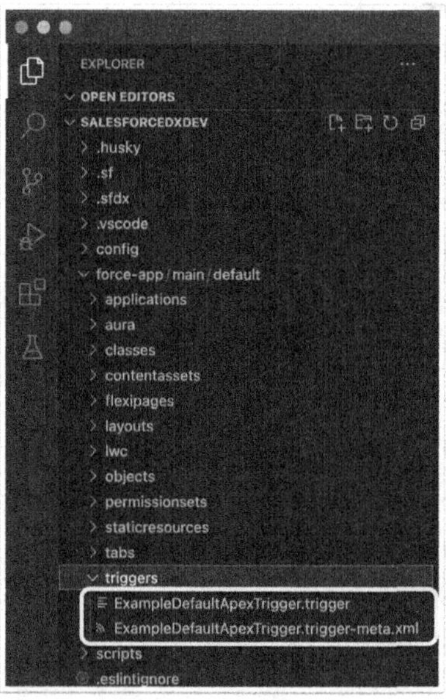

Figure 12-2. *New default Apex trigger files*

This is the boilerplate code that is created.

Listing 12-8. Apex trigger boilerplate code

```
trigger ExampleDefaultApexTrigger on Contact (before insert) {

}
```

Debugging is a fundamental activity when developing software applications, which is also true of Salesforce application and customization development. In the next section, we will see how we can access debug logs using Salesforce CLI commands.

Accessing Debug Logs

Debug logs contain a wealth of useful information that is collected when an Apex transaction or unit test is executed. Information includes, but is not limited to, database operations, Apex exceptions, resource usage, and information written to a log using methods from the `System` class, such as `System.debug`. Although debuggers are undoubtedly valuable tools, it's sometimes useful to export a log file to search for patterns and trends, such as the accumulating resource usage during a transaction.

Note The Salesforce Extensions for Visual Studio Code includes three Apex code debuggers. (1) The Apex Replay Debugger requires no additional licenses. (2) The Apex Interactive Debugger requires Apex Debugger Sessions – Performance Edition and Unlimited Edition orgs come with a single Apex Debugger Session, and additional Apex Debugger Sessions can be purchased for those org editions and for Enterprise Edition orgs. (3) The ISV Customer Debugger comes with the Apex Interactive Debugger and allows ISVs to collaborate with customers to debug managed packages in customer sandboxes. We won't be covering these debuggers in this book; please refer to the Salesforce Extensions for Visual Studio Code documentation if you wish to explore further.

In this section, we will be looking at the following commands in the `force:apex:log` subtopic, which provide access to debug logs in a target org:

- **`force:apex:log:list`**: Lists the debug logs in an org.
- **`force:apex:log:get`**: Retrieves one or more debug logs from an org and optionally saves them as files.
- **`force:apex:log:tail`**: Starts debugging in an org and displays the debug log files in the terminal application.

Note This section assumes that the reader has a working knowledge of debug logs, trace flags, and debug levels. To learn more, search for "Debugging Apex" in the Salesforce developer website, which can be found here: `https://developer.salesforce.com/`.

To trigger the generation of debug logs, trace flags must first be set; having said that, the Salesforce CLI doesn't currently include commands to set trace flags. Some options that can be considered for setting trace flags are as follows:

- **Developer Console**: Opening the target org's Developer Console will create a trace flag and a debug level automatically. Use the **Debug ➤ Change Log Levels...** dialog to manage trace flags and debug levels.
- **Setup**: Use Setup in the target org to set trace flags and debug levels in the **Environments ➤ Logs ➤ Debug Logs** area.
- **Scripting**: Write a script to call the `force:data:record:create` command and add trace flag and debug level records to the target org.
- **Command Palette**: Use the Visual Studio Code Command Palette to run the **SFDX: Turn On Apex Debug Log for Replay Debugger** and **SFDX: Turn Off Apex Debug Log for Replay Debugger** commands to set and unset trace flags, which effectively turns debugging on and off. These commands are available because the Salesforce Extensions for Visual Studio Code includes the free-to-use Apex Replay Debugger.

The scripting option is the preferred method when repeatable operations are needed, such as when turning debugging on and off in a CI/CD pipeline. If the generation of debug logs needs to be turned on and off during an interactive debugging session, the Developer Console, Setup, or Command Palette options can be used. We'll be using the Command Palette option to remove the need to open an org and switch to a different environment.

The `force:apex:log:list` command, which lists a target org's debug logs, is the first command that we will explore. To create a debug log to list, execute each of the following steps to turn on debugging, execute some anonymous Apex that writes to the debug log, and then turn off debugging:

1. Launch Visual Studio Code if it's not already launched.
2. Open this chapter's `SalesforceDXDev` project.
3. Using VS Code's Command Palette, ensure that a trace flag and debug level are active in the target org by executing the command **SFDX: Turn On Apex Debug Log for Replay Debugger**.
4. In the integrated terminal, run the command `sfdx force:apex:execute` to enter anonymous Apex that will be executed in the target org with the default username.
5. Enter the following Apex statement followed by hitting **Enter**, then **CTRL+D**:

   ```
   System.debug(
   'Org Name: ' +
   UserInfo.getOrganizationName());
   ```

6. Using VS Code's Command Palette, turn off debugging by executing the command **SFDX: Turn Off Apex Debug Log for Replay Debugger**.

Note The **SFDX: Turn On Apex Debug Log for Replay Debugger** command looks for an existing trace flag with a log type of `DEVELOPER_LOG` where the traced entity is the target org's user with the default username, which is `MySO` in our case. If an existing trace flag is found, it is reused; otherwise, a new trace flag and debug level are created.

To list the debug log that has just been created, execute the following command in the integrated terminal:

```
$ sfdx force:apex:log:list
```

The parameters that can be used with the command are as follows:

- `--targetusername|-u`: The username or alias of the org to extract the debug logs from. [Optional]
- `--apiversion, --json, --loglevel`: Please refer to the discussion on global parameters in the section "Command-Line Parameters and Arguments" in Chapter 4, "Salesforce CLI."

Using the preceding command without any parameters lists the debug logs in the target org with the default username. The command output is shown in the following listing.

Listing 12-9. Debug log list

```
APPLICATION  DURATION (MS)  ID                  LOCATION   SIZE (B)  LOG USER
───────────  ─────────────  ──────────────────  ─────────  ────────  ─────────────
Unknown      56             07L3G000002r9ERUAY  SystemLog  2643      User User

OPERATION  REQUEST  START TIME                STATUS
─────────  ───────  ────────────────────────  ───────
Api        Api      2022-08-10T07:11:16+0000  Success
```

Of course, the command may return additional debug logs that might already exist in the target org. To retrieve the debug log, execute the following command in the integrated terminal:

```
$ sfdx force:apex:log:get
```

Here are the parameters that can be used with the `force:apex:log:get` command:

- `--outputdir|-d`: Path to the directory where the debug logs will be saved as files. If the parameter is omitted, the debug logs are displayed in the terminal application and not saved as files. [Optional]

- `--logid|-i`: The ID of a specific debug log to retrieve. List the debug logs in a target org, including their IDs, using the `force:apex:log:list` command. [Optional]
- `--number|-n`: The number of most recent debug logs to retrieve. [Optional] [Default: `1`]
- `--targetusername|-u`: The username or alias of the org to extract the debug logs from. [Optional]
- `--apiversion, --json, --loglevel`: Please refer to the discussion on global parameters in the section "Command-Line Parameters and Arguments" in Chapter 4, "Salesforce CLI."

Note To retrieve a debug log using the Visual Studio Code Command Palette, execute the command **SFDX: Get Apex Debug Logs** and select one of the logs that is listed. The log is saved in the Salesforce DX project's `./.sfdx/tools/debug/logs` directory.

As we are using the command without any parameters, it retrieves the most recent debug log and displays it in the terminal application where the command was executed, which in this instance is the integrated terminal. The information written to the debug log using anonymous Apex is the line that includes "`USER_DEBUG|[1]|DEBUG|Org Name: ivanharris company`".

Listing 12-10. Retrieved debug log

```
55.0 APEX_CODE,FINEST;APEX_PROFILING,INFO;CALLOUT,INFO;DB,INFO;NBA,INFO;SYS
TEM,DEBUG;VALIDATION,INFO;VISUALFORCE,FINER;WAVE,INFO;WORKFLOW,INFO
Execute Anonymous: System.debug(
Execute Anonymous:    'Org Name: ' +
Execute Anonymous:    UserInfo.getOrganizationName());
Execute Anonymous:
08:11:16.22 (22111582)|USER_INFO|[EXTERNAL]|0053G000002ukoz|test-
rncsfeckoidh@example.com|(GMT+01:00) British Summer Time (Europe/
London)|GMT+01:00
08:11:16.22 (22145485)|EXECUTION_STARTED
08:11:16.22 (22150393)|CODE_UNIT_STARTED|[EXTERNAL]|execute_anonymous_apex
```

```
08:11:16.22 (22510515)|HEAP_ALLOCATE|[79]|Bytes:3
08:11:16.22 (22545369)|HEAP_ALLOCATE|[84]|Bytes:152
08:11:16.22 (22562506)|HEAP_ALLOCATE|[399]|Bytes:408
08:11:16.22 (22581001)|HEAP_ALLOCATE|[412]|Bytes:408
08:11:16.22 (22596171)|HEAP_ALLOCATE|[520]|Bytes:48
08:11:16.22 (22623860)|HEAP_ALLOCATE|[139]|Bytes:6
08:11:16.22 (22664557)|HEAP_ALLOCATE|[EXTERNAL]|Bytes:5
08:11:16.22 (22812342)|STATEMENT_EXECUTE|[1]
08:11:16.22 (22815082)|STATEMENT_EXECUTE|[1]
08:11:16.22 (22818295)|HEAP_ALLOCATE|[2]|Bytes:10
08:11:16.22 (22899866)|HEAP_ALLOCATE|[52]|Bytes:5
08:11:16.22 (22923922)|HEAP_ALLOCATE|[58]|Bytes:5
08:11:16.22 (22933223)|HEAP_ALLOCATE|[66]|Bytes:7
08:11:16.22 (22954286)|SYSTEM_MODE_ENTER|false
08:11:16.22 (22984005)|HEAP_ALLOCATE|[3]|Bytes:5
08:11:16.22 (23057892)|HEAP_ALLOCATE|[3]|Bytes:101
08:11:16.22 (23069600)|SYSTEM_METHOD_ENTRY|[1]|UserInfo.UserInfo()
08:11:16.22 (23075257)|STATEMENT_EXECUTE|[1]
08:11:16.22 (23082359)|SYSTEM_METHOD_EXIT|[1]|UserInfo
08:11:16.22 (23098830)|METHOD_ENTRY|[3]||System.UserInfo.
getOrganizationName()
08:11:16.22 (24152721)|METHOD_EXIT|[3]||System.UserInfo.
getOrganizationName()
08:11:16.22 (24172499)|SYSTEM_MODE_EXIT|false
08:11:16.22 (24198751)|HEAP_ALLOCATE|[2]|Bytes:28
08:11:16.22 (24256544)|USER_DEBUG|[1]|DEBUG|Org Name: ivanharris company
08:11:16.24 (24370666)|CUMULATIVE_LIMIT_USAGE
08:11:16.24 (24370666)|LIMIT_USAGE_FOR_NS|(default)|
  Number of SOQL queries: 0 out of 100
  Number of query rows: 0 out of 50000
  Number of SOSL queries: 0 out of 20
  Number of DML statements: 0 out of 150
  Number of Publish Immediate DML: 0 out of 150
  Number of DML rows: 0 out of 10000
  Maximum CPU time: 0 out of 10000
```

```
  Maximum heap size: 0 out of 6000000
  Number of callouts: 0 out of 100
  Number of Email Invocations: 0 out of 10
  Number of future calls: 0 out of 50
  Number of queueable jobs added to the queue: 0 out of 50
  Number of Mobile Apex push calls: 0 out of 10

08:11:16.24 (24370666)|CUMULATIVE_LIMIT_USAGE_END

08:11:16.22 (24450467)|CODE_UNIT_FINISHED|execute_anonymous_apex
08:11:16.22 (24467268)|EXECUTION_FINISHED
```

To retrieve a debug log using the Salesforce CLI and write it to a file in a directory called debug-logs, you would use this command:

```
$ sfdx force:apex:log:get \
    --outputdir ./debug-logs
```

In this figure, the debug log file can be seen in the Visual Studio Code Explorer view, and the file is shown open in an editor window.

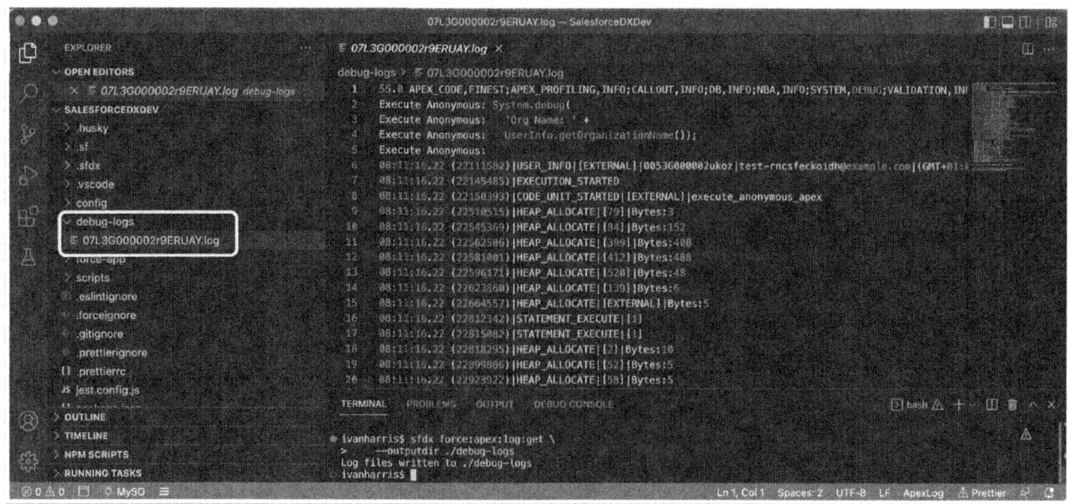

***Figure 12-3.** Debug log saved as a file*

The final command in the `force:apex:log` subtopic is the `force:apex:log:tail` command, which streams debug log entries to the terminal application where the command is executed for 30 minutes. The terminal application that we use is VS Code's integrated terminal. Before executing the command, make sure that debugging is enabled by executing the **SFDX: Turn On Apex Debug Log for Replay Debugger** command using VS Code's Command Palette.

Note The `force:apex:log:tail` command will reuse a debug level with the name `SFDC_DevConsole`, or a debug level that's related to a trace flag with a log type of `DEVELOPER_LOG`, regardless of the debug level's name; so, if you know that such a debug level exists, there is no need to run the **SFDX: Turn On Apex Debug Log for Replay Debugger** command.

To start streaming a debug log, enter the following command in the integrated terminal:

```
$ sfdx force:apex:log:tail
```

We're executing the command without any parameters; here are the ones that are available:

- `--color|-c`: Applies color coding to selected entries in the streamed debug log. [Optional]
- `--debuglevel|-d`: Trace flag records have a related debug level record, which includes logging levels, such as `Error` or `Info`, for different categories, such as `Apex Code` or `Database`. This parameter allows a trace flag record to be related to a different debug level record. [Optional]
- `--skiptraceflag|-s`: If a trace flag and debug level have already been set up for the command to use, this parameter will prevent the command from setting one up. [Optional]
- `--targetusername|-u`: The username or alias of the org to stream the debug logs from. [Optional]

- `--apiversion, --json, --loglevel`: Please refer to the discussion on global parameters in the section "Command-Line Parameters and Arguments" in Chapter 4, "Salesforce CLI."

After executing the `force:apex:log:tail` command, the integrated terminal is no longer interactive while it awaits debug log entries to be created. We'll generate some by performing a few actions in the scratch org. Open the default org by clicking the **Open Org** icon in Visual Studio Code's Status Bar.

Figure 12-4. *Open the default org*

In the scratch org, do the following, which will generate some debug log entries:

- Click the App Launcher icon (⁝⁝⁝).
- Click the **Sales** app (click **View All** first if the **Sales** app is not in the list).
- Click the **Leads** tab.
- Click the **New** action.
- Fill in the required fields in the New Lead dialog.
- Click the **Save** button.

Returning to Visual Studio Code, you will see that some debug log entries have been created and that the entries have been streamed to the integrated terminal.

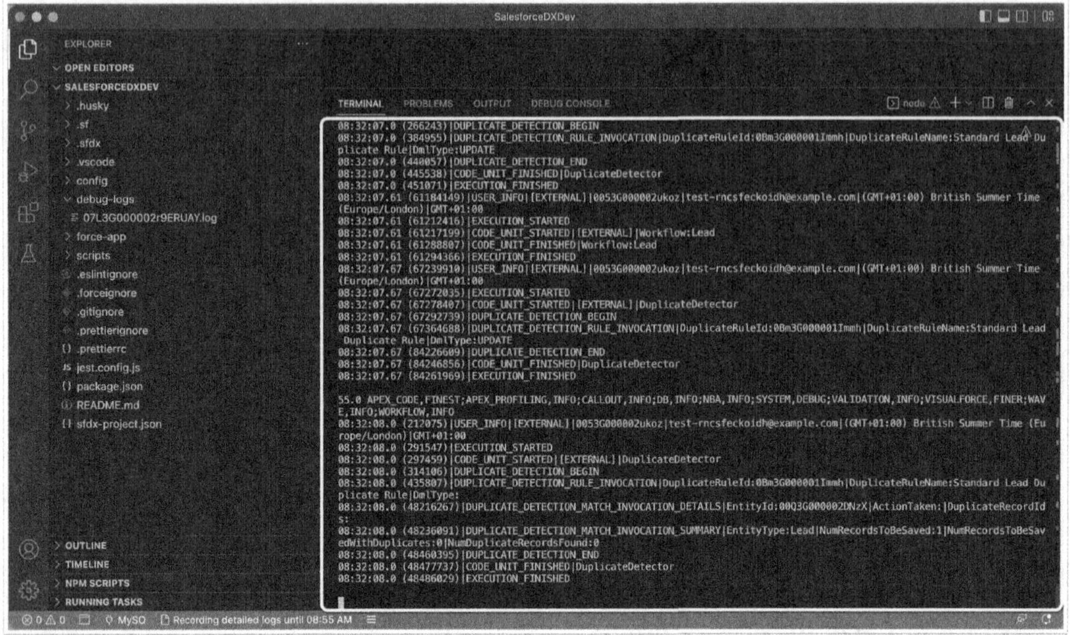

***Figure 12-5.** Streamed debug log entries*

Here's the same streamed debug log with the `--color|-c` parameter applied, which shows some entries in green.

Figure 12-6. *Streamed debug log entries using the* `--color|-c` *parameter*

The `--debuglevel|-d` parameter can be used to override the debug level that the `force:apex:log:tail` command sets up. Suppose that you only want the debug logs to contain entries for the ApexCode category. To do so, create a new debug level record called `ApexCode_Finest` by executing the following Salesforce CLI command in VS Code's integrated terminal:

```
$ sfdx force:data:record:create \
    --sobjecttype DebugLevel \
    --usetoolingapi \
    --values \
      "DeveloperName=ApexCode_Finest \
       MasterLabel='ApexCode Finest' \
       Language=en_US \
       ApexCode=FINEST \
       ApexProfiling=NONE \
       Callout=NONE \
       Database=NONE \
       Nba=NONE \
```

```
    System=NONE \
    Validation=NONE \
    Visualforce=NONE \
    Wave=NONE \
    Workflow=NONE"
```

Before using the new debug level, let's see the default debug level that the `force:apex:log:tail` command uses before we override it using the `--debuglevel|-d` parameter. Run the Visual Studio Code Command Palette command **SFDX: Turn On Apex Debug Log for Replay Debugger**. Open the `MySO` scratch org and navigate to **Setup ➤ Environments ➤ Logs ➤ Debug Logs**, where you can see the debug level that has been set up.

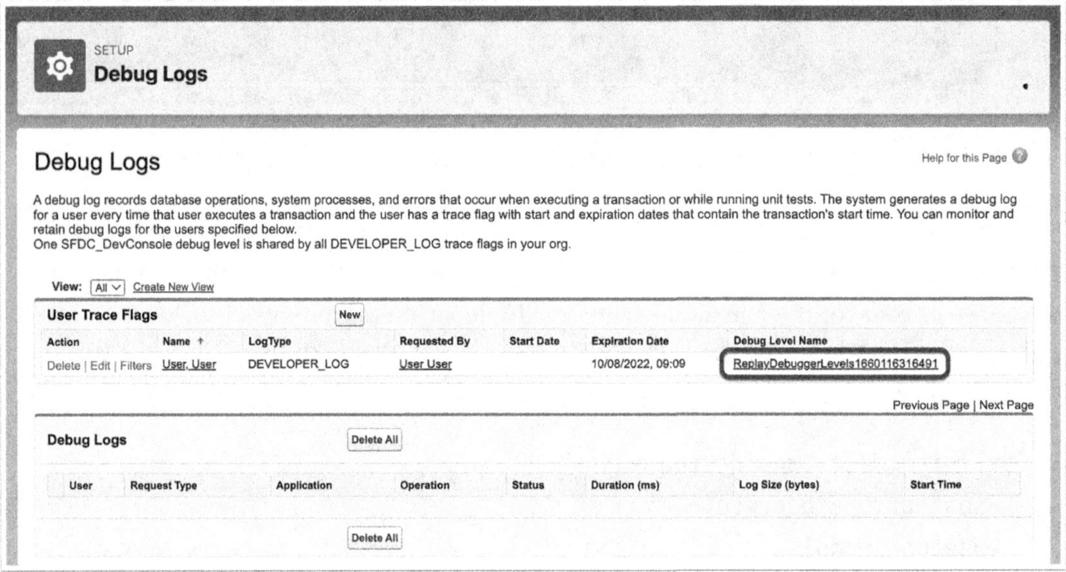

Figure 12-7. *The debug level set up by the **SFDX: Turn On Apex Debug Log for Replay Debugger** command*

In VS Code's integrated terminal, execute the following command to start streaming debug log entries using the `ApexCode_Finest` debug level that we created earlier:

```
$ sfdx force:apex:log:tail \
    --debuglevel ApexCode_Finest
```

Refreshing the Debug Logs screen in the scratch org will show that the new debug level is being used.

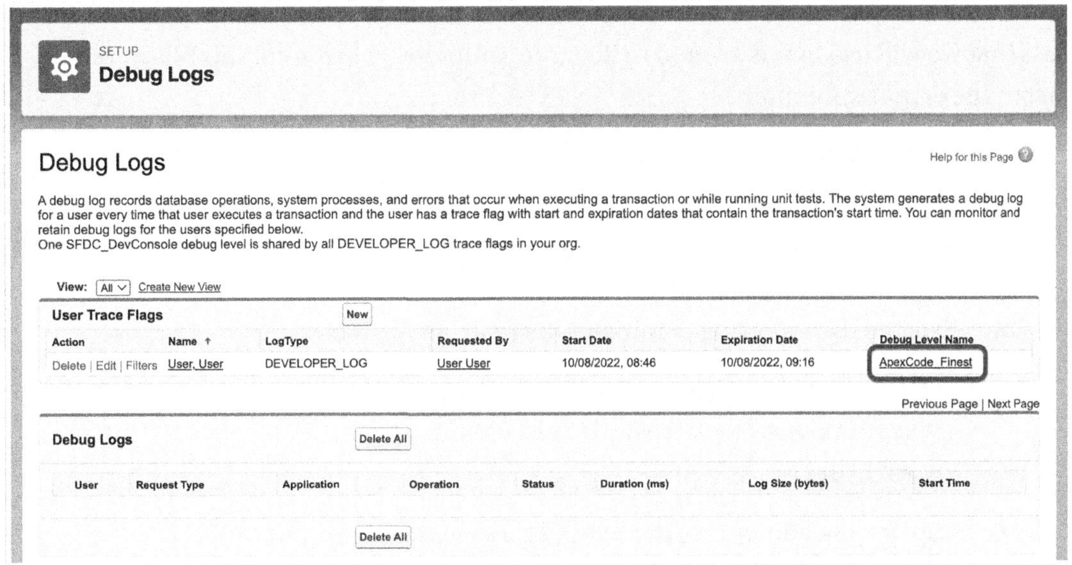

Figure 12-8. *Overridden debug level*

This will cut down the amount of streamed logging information while allowing you to focus on the Apex code detail.

The final subtopic in this section about Apex development details how to run Apex tests.

Running Apex Tests

In Chapter 8, "Metadata," we looked at how to run Apex tests when deploying metadata to orgs using the `force:source:deploy` and `force:mdapi:deploy` commands, usually to sandboxes without source tracking enabled and production orgs. Chapter 11, "Test Data," took a deep dive into how to create test data to be used in end-to-end testing, such as systems integration testing (SIT) or user acceptance testing (UAT). The end-to-end testing and deployment activities occur toward the end of the application development lifecycle; that said, we also need to continuously test earlier in the lifecycle to catch bugs before they become increasingly expensive to fix. We've seen how to create boilerplate code and metadata for Apex classes and triggers using the Salesforce CLI. As we flesh out our code and push the changes to an org, we need to perform unit testing. Although we can run unit tests using an org's Setup area or by using the Developer Console, the Salesforce CLI provides commands to execute unit tests, allowing us to develop, push, and test iteratively from the command line.

The following steps will create an Apex class and a corresponding Apex test class that we will use in this section to illustrate unit testing using commands in the `force:apex:test` subtopic:

1. Launch Visual Studio Code if it's not already launched.

2. Open this chapter's `SalesforceDXDev` project.

3. Open the integrated terminal.

4. Execute the following command to create an Apex class:

   ```
   sfdx force:apex:class:create \
   -d ./force-app/main/default/classes \
   -n MathsUtils
   ```

5. Replace the contents of the `MathsUtils` class with the code from Listing 12-11.

6. Execute the following command to create an Apex test class:

   ```
   sfdx force:apex:class:create \
   -d ./force-app/main/default/classes \
   -n TestMathsUtils
   ```

7. Replace the contents of the `TestMathsUtils` class with the code from Listing 12-12.

8. Push the changes to the `MySO` scratch org by executing the following command:

   ```
   sfdx force:source:push.
   ```

Listing 12-11. `MathsUtils` class

```
public inherited sharing class MathsUtils {
    public static Integer Add(Integer value1, Integer value2) {
        return value1 + value2;
    }
}
```

Listing 12-12. `TestMathsUtils` class

```
@isTest
private class TestMathsUtils {
    @isTest static void TestMathsUtilsPositiveTest1() {
        Integer value1 = 4;
        Integer value2 = 6;
        Integer addResult;
        Test.startTest();
        addResult = MathsUtils.Add(value1, value2);
        Test.stopTest();
        System.assertEquals(value1 + value2, addResult);
    }
}
```

To run all the tests in the target org's namespace, which is the single `TestMathsUtils.TestMathsUtilsPositiveTest1` test method in this example, use the following CLI command:

```
$ sfdx force:apex:test:run --synchronous
```

The parameters that can be used with this command are as follows:

- `--codecoverage|-c`: Includes code coverage information in the returned test results. Using this parameter causes the `force:apex:test:run` command to run synchronously. The `--resultformat|-r` parameter must also be provided when using this parameter. [Optional]
- `--outputdir|-d`: Specifies the directory where test result files will be written. [Optional]
- `--testlevel|-l`: Specifies which Apex tests are executed. [Optional]

Allowed values are as follows:

- `RunSpecifiedTests`: Execute the Apex tests listed in the `--classnames|-n`, `--suitenames|-s`, or `--tests|-t` parameters.
- `RunLocalTests`: Execute all the Apex tests in the target org's namespace, which includes tests in installed, non-namespaced unlocked packages. It excludes those tests in installed managed packages and unlocked packages that have a namespace.
- `RunAllTestsInOrg`: Execute all the Apex tests in the target org, including those in installed managed packages and unlocked packages that have a namespace.

- `--classnames|-n`: A comma-separated list of Apex test classes to run, such as `TestMathsUtils` in our example. This parameter cannot be used if the `--suitenames|-s` or `--tests|-t` parameters are being used. [Optional]
- `--resultformat|-r`: The format of the test run results that are streamed to the terminal application and also to the result files when the `--outputdir|-d` parameter is used. [Optional]

  Allowed values are as follows:

  - `human`: Human-readable formatted test results
  - `tap`: Test Anything Protocol (TAP) formatted test results
  - `junit`: JUnit XML formatted test results
  - `json`: JSON formatted test results

- `--suitenames|-s`: A comma-separated list of Apex test suites to run. Test suites are collections of test classes that can be executed as a group. There are currently no Salesforce CLI commands for creating test suites and adding test classes; however, the Visual Studio Code Command Palette has the following commands to work with test suites: **SFDX: Create Apex Test Suite**, **SFDX: Add Tests to Apex Test Suite**, and **SFDX: Run Apex Test Suite**. This parameter cannot be used if the `--classnames|-n` or `--tests|-t` parameters are being used. [Optional]

- `--tests | -t`: A comma-separated list of Apex test classes and/or Apex test methods to run, such as `TestMathsUtils` and/or `TestMathsUtils.TestMathsUtilsPositiveTest1` in our example. This parameter cannot be used if the `--classnames | -n` or `--suitenames | -s` parameters are being used. [Optional]
- `--targetusername | -u`: The username or alias of the org containing the Apex tests to run. [Optional]
- `--detailedcoverage | -v`: Displays more detailed coverage information per test. [Optional]
- `--wait | -w`: The number of minutes that the command will wait for completion. Control will be returned to the terminal application when the command completes or when the wait period expires, whichever is the sooner. The minimum value is 2 minutes. [Optional]
- `--synchronous | -y`: Causes the command to wait indefinitely for the command to complete, after which the test results will be displayed, and control will be returned to the terminal application. [Optional]
- `--apiversion, --json, --loglevel, --verbose`: Please refer to the discussion on global parameters in the section "Command-Line Parameters and Arguments" in Chapter 4, "Salesforce CLI."

Note To execute Apex tests using the Visual Studio Code Command Palette, use the command **SFDX: Run Apex Tests** or **SFDX: Run Apex Test Suite**. To execute Apex tests from the Visual Studio Code Editor, open the test class file in the Editor and click **Run All Tests** above the class definition to execute all the test methods in the class or click **Run Test** above a test method's definition to execute a single test method. To execute Apex tests using the Visual Studio Code Testing view, click the Testing icon ( ) in the Side Bar and click the Run All Tests or Run Test icons ( ) to run all the test methods in a test class or one, respectively.

As we have used the `--synchronous | -y` parameter when executing the `force:apex:test:run` command, it will execute synchronously. When the command completes, control is returned to the terminal application, the integrated terminal in this case, and the test results are displayed.

Listing 12-13. Synchronous Apex test results

```
=== Test Summary
NAME                 VALUE
───────────────────  ──────────────────────────────
Outcome              Passed
Tests Ran            1
Pass Rate            100%
Fail Rate            0%
Skip Rate            0%
Test Run Id          7073G000000PPOB
Test Execution Time  9 ms
Org Id               00D3G0000001YF5UAM
Username             test-rncsfeckoidh@example.com

=== Test Results
TEST NAME                                    OUTCOME  MESSAGE    RUNTIME (MS)
───────────────────────────────────────────  ───────  ─────────  ────────────
TestMathsUtils.TestMathsUtilsPositiveTest1   Pass                9
```

In the next example, more parameters are used. It executes synchronously, runs the test methods in the test class `TestMathsUtils`, writes the test results to files in the `./test-results` directory, includes code coverage information, and streams the test results in human-readable format to the integrated terminal.

```
$ sfdx force:apex:test:run \
    --codecoverage \
    --outputdir ./test-results \
    --classnames TestMathsUtils \
    --resultformat human \
    --synchronous
```

The following listing shows the command output with the included code coverage information.

Listing 12-14. Synchronous Apex test results with code coverage included

```
Test result files written to ./test-results
=== Test Summary
NAME                 VALUE
───────────────────  ──────────────────────────────
Outcome              Passed
Tests Ran            1
Pass Rate            100%
Fail Rate            0%
Skip Rate            0%
Test Run Id
Test Execution Time  85 ms
Org Id               00D3G0000001YF5UAM
Username             test-rncsfeckoidh@example.com
Org Wide Coverage    100%

=== Test Results
TEST NAME                                 OUTCOME  MESSAGE  RUNTIME (MS)
────────────────────────────────────────  ───────  ───────  ────────────
TestMathsUtils.TestMathsUtilsPositiveTest1  Pass            33

=== Apex Code Coverage by Class
CLASSES     PERCENT  UNCOVERED LINES
──────────  ───────  ───────────────
MathsUtils  100%
```

The following figure shows the files that are created, which also contain the test results and code coverage.

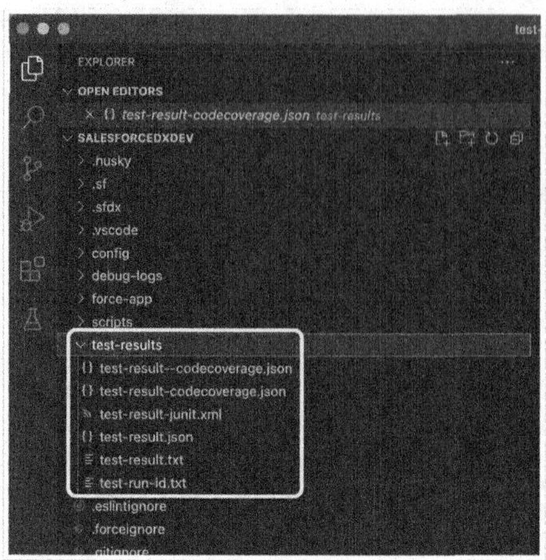

Figure 12-9. *Synchronous test result and code coverage files*

To execute the command asynchronously, omit both the `--wait|-w` and the `--synchronous|y` parameters. Here's an example:

```
$ sfdx force:apex:test:run \
    --outputdir ./test-results \
    --classnames TestMathsUtils
```

The command returns immediately and creates a file in the output directory that contains the test run ID.

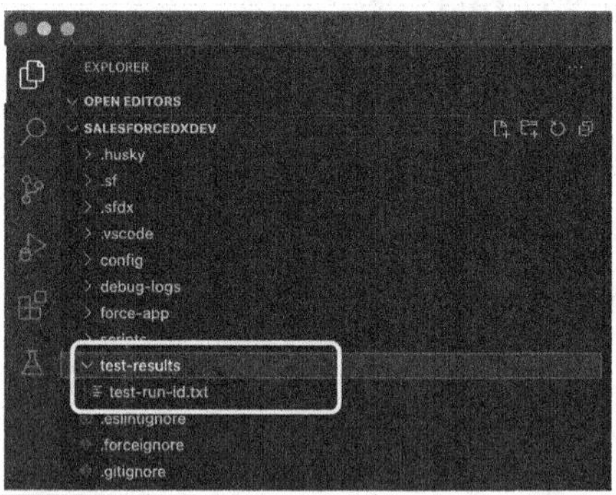

Figure 12-10. *Asynchronous test run ID file*

The command output in the integrated terminal displays the following.

Listing 12-15. Asynchronous Apex test output

```
Run "sfdx force:apex:test:report -i 7073G000000PPVU -u test-rncsfeckoidh@
example.com" to retrieve test results
```

The preceding output shows the command to use to retrieve the test results and display them in the integrated terminal. To achieve similar results as the previous synchronous command, we can add additional `force:apex:test:report` parameters:

```
$ sfdx force:apex:test:report \
    --codecoverage \
    --outputdir ./test-results \
    --testrunid 7073G000000PPVU \
    --resultformat human
```

Here are the parameters for the `force:apex:test:report` command:

- `--codecoverage|-c`: Includes code coverage information in the returned test results. The `--resultformat|-r` parameter must also be provided when using this parameter. [Optional]
- `--outputdir|-d`: Specifies the directory where test result files will be written. [Optional]
- `--testrunid|-i`: The ID of the test run to report the test results for. The ID is output by the `force:apex:test:run` command when it is initiated asynchronously. [Required]
- `--resultformat|-r`: The format of the test run results that are streamed to the terminal application and also to the result files when the `--outputdir|-d` parameter is used. Note that the `--json` parameter overrides this parameter. [Optional]

  Allowed values are as follows:

  - `human`: Human-readable formatted test results
  - `tap`: Test Anything Protocol (TAP) formatted test results
  - `junit`: JUnit XML formatted test results
  - `json`: JSON formatted test results

- `--targetusername|-u`: The username or alias of the org where the test run is being executed. [Optional]
- `--wait|-w`: The number of minutes that the command will wait for completion. Control will be returned to the terminal application when the command completes or when the wait period expires, whichever is the sooner. The minimum value is 2 minutes. [Optional]
- `--apiversion, --json, --loglevel, --verbose`: Please refer to the discussion on global parameters in the section "Command-Line Parameters and Arguments" in Chapter 4, "Salesforce CLI."

The asynchronous output in the integrated terminal is like the synchronous command output.

Listing 12-16. Asynchronous Apex test results with code coverage included Test result files written to ./test-results

```
=== Test Summary
NAME                 VALUE
───────────────────  ─────────────────────────────
Outcome              Passed
Tests Ran            1
Pass Rate            100%
Fail Rate            0%
Skip Rate            0%
Test Run Id          7073G000000PPVU
Test Execution Time  11 ms
Org Id               00D3G0000001YF5UAM
Username             test-rncsfeckoidh@example.com
Org Wide Coverage    100%

=== Apex Code Coverage for Test Run 7073G000000PPVU
TEST NAME                                  CLASS BEING TESTED OUTCOME PERCENT MESSAGE
─────────────────────────────────────────  ────────────────── ─────── ─────── ───────
TestMathsUtils.TestMathsUtilsPositiveTest1 MathsUtils         Pass    100%

RUNTIME (MS)
───────────
11
```

```
=== Apex Code Coverage by Class
CLASSES     PERCENT    UNCOVERED LINES
──────────  ─────────  ───────────────
MathsUtils  100%
```

The created test results and code coverage files are also similar to the synchronous command files, with the exception that the test run ID is included in the test result filenames.

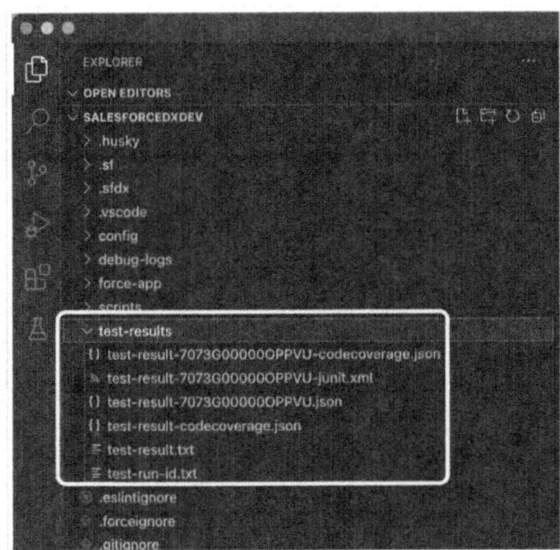

Figure 12-11. *Asynchronous test result and code coverage files*

The `force:apex:test:report` command concludes our journey through the commands in the `force:apex` topic. The next section will cover the commands used when working with custom metadata types.

Working with Custom Metadata Types

Custom metadata types are used to deploy application metadata to production orgs using change sets, unlocked packages, or managed packages. Application metadata is a way to store parameters for an application or customization. Unlike custom objects and custom settings, which can also be deployed, the structure of the custom metadata type objects and the records created for the objects are both considered metadata. To illustrate the point, consider the following:

- **Custom Objects and Custom Settings**: Custom objects and custom settings are examples of metadata. Records created for the objects or settings are data, not metadata. For example, if a custom object has a custom field called `MaxBonusPercent__c` and a record is created for the object where the value `10` is provided for the field, `MaxBonusPercent__c` is metadata and `10` is data. When deploying custom objects and custom settings, only the metadata is deployed. Any data, in the form of records, must be provided by other means, such as manually adding the records, using Data Loader or postinstall scripts.

- **Custom Metadata Types**: Using the preceding example, records containing field values, such as `10` for the `MaxBonusPercent__c` field, are also metadata. When deploying custom metadata types, the records containing field values can also be deployed. Extending this example, if a payroll application is being developed, custom metadata types specifying the maximum bonus that employees are eligible for in different countries can be defined and deployed along with the payroll application in a package.

To create custom metadata types in a local Salesforce DX project, these commands in the `force:cmdt` topic are used:

- **`force:cmdt:create`**: Creates a new custom metadata type in the local Salesforce DX project. No fields or records are created when using this command.

- **`force:cmdt:field:create`**: Creates a custom metadata type field.

- **`force:cmdt:record:create`**: Creates a single record for a custom metadata type.

- **`force:cmdt:record:insert`**: Creates multiple records for a custom metadata type from a CSV file.

The three-step process that we will follow to create a new custom metadata type, its fields, and its records is as follows:

1. Create the custom metadata type using the **force:cmdt:create** command.
2. Create the custom metadata type's fields using the **force:cmdt:field:create** command.
3. Create the custom metadata type's records using the **force:cmdt:record:create** command to create records individually or the **force:cmdt:record:insert** command to create multiple records from a CSV file.

We'll create a custom metadata type first.

Creating a Custom Metadata Type

To create a custom metadata type, execute the following Salesforce CLI command from the SalesforceDXDev project's root directory in Visual Studio Code's integrated terminal:

```
$ sfdx force:cmdt:create \
    --outputdir ./force-app/main/default/objects \
    --label 'Example CMDT' \
    --typename Example_CMDT \
    --plurallabel 'Example CMDTs'
```

The command's complete list of parameters is as follows:

- --outputdir|-d: The directory where the source format metadata files for the created custom metadata type will be stored. An absolute or relative path can be used; having said that, using the ./force-app/main/default/objects directory will ensure that the new custom metadata type will be located in the same directory as custom metadata types that are pulled from an org (assuming that force-app is the default path/packaging directory). Furthermore, the objects directory is the default when using the force:cmdt:record:create and force:cmdt:record:insert commands, which will be introduced shortly. [Optional] [Default: The current working directory (.)]

- `--label|-l`: The label for the custom metadata type that will be displayed in the Setup area of an org after the custom metadata type has been pushed or deployed to an org. If this parameter is not specified, the label will be the same as the value passed to the `--typename|-n` parameter. [Optional]
- `--typename|-n`: The API name of the custom metadata type, which must be unique in an org. [Required]
- `--plurallabel|-p`: The plural form of the value passed to the `--label|-l` parameter. If this parameter is not specified, the plural label will be the same as the value used by the `--label|-l` parameter. [Optional]
- `--visibility|-v`: The custom metadata type's visibility when it is deployed using a managed package. [Optional] [Default: `Public`]

  Allowed values are as follows:

  - `PackageProtected`: The custom metadata type is only accessible from within the same package that contains the custom metadata type. If multiple packages share the same namespace, other packages within the namespace cannot access the custom metadata type.
  - `Protected`: The custom metadata type is accessible from packages that share the same namespace as the package that contains the custom metadata type.
  - `Public`: The custom metadata type is accessible from within and from outside the managed package and namespace that contains the custom metadata type, including from the subscriber org.
- `--json, --loglevel`: Please refer to the discussion on global parameters in the section "Command-Line Parameters and Arguments" in Chapter 4, "Salesforce CLI."

The next step is to add a field to the custom metadata type.

Adding Custom Metadata Type Fields

To create a custom field for the new custom metadata type, use the following command in VS Code's integrated terminal from the `SalesforceDXDev` project's root directory:

```
$ sfdx force:cmdt:field:create \
    --outputdir ./force-app/main/default/objects/Example_CMDT__mdt \
    --fieldtype Number \
    --label 'Example Field' \
    --fieldname Example_Field \
    --decimalplaces 2
```

The parameters that can be used with the command are as follows:

- `--outputdir|-d`: The directory where the source format metadata file for the created custom metadata type field will be stored. An absolute or relative path can be used. To associate the field with a custom metadata type, pass the custom metadata type's directory, as in the preceding example. The command will create a `fields` subdirectory when the first field is created, which will be used to store all the field files. [Optional] [Default: The current working directory (`.`)]
- `--fieldtype|-f`: The type of field to create. [Required]

  Allowed values are

  - `Checkbox`
  - `Date`
  - `DateTime`
  - `Email`
  - `Number`
  - `Percent`
  - `Phone`
  - `Picklist`
  - `Text`
  - `TextArea`

    - `LongTextArea`
    - `Url`
- `--label|-l`: The label for the custom metadata type field that will be displayed in the Setup area of an org after the custom metadata type field has been pushed or deployed to an org. If this parameter is not specified, the label will be the same as the value passed to the `--fieldname|-n` parameter. [Optional]
- `--fieldname|-n`: The API name of the custom metadata type field. [Required]
- `--picklistvalues|-p`: A comma-separated list of picklist values. If any of the values contain spaces, enclose the value, or the whole list, in single or double quotes. [Required if the `--fieldtype|-f` parameter is set to `Picklist`]
- `--decimalplaces|-s`: The number of decimal places to use for fields that are of type `Number` or `Percent`. The value must be greater than or equal to `0` to create the metadata file for the field in the local Salesforce DX project. Note, however, that the field will fail to push or deploy to an org if the value is greater than 8, as the precision (the number of digits before the decimal places) must be greater than the scale (the number of decimal places). [Optional]
- `--json, --loglevel`: Please refer to the discussion on global parameters in the section "Command-Line Parameters and Arguments" in Chapter 4, "Salesforce CLI."

The third step is to create a custom metadata type record.

Creating Custom Metadata Type Records

Adding a single record to the custom metadata type can be accomplished with the following command, which assumes that you still have the `SalesforceDXDev` project open in Visual Studio Code and that the integrated terminal's working directory is the project's root directory:

```
$ sfdx force:cmdt:record:create \
    Example_Field__c=167.23 \
    --label 'Example Record 1' \
    --recordname Example_Record_1 \
    --typename Example_CMDT__mdt
```

The `force:cmdt:record:create` command can accept the following parameters:

- `--outputdir|-d`: The directory where the source format metadata file for the created custom metadata type record will be stored. An absolute or relative path can be used. [Optional] [Default: ./`force-app/main/default/customMetadata`]
- `--inputdir|-i`: The directory containing the source format metadata files of the custom metadata type that the record will be created for. An absolute or relative path can be used. The command appends the custom metadata type name specified by the `--typename|-t` parameter to the directory specified by this parameter to create the full path to the files. [Optional] [Default: ./`force-app/main/default/objects`]
- `--label|-l`: The label for the custom metadata type record that will be displayed in the Setup area of an org after the custom metadata type and its records have been pushed or deployed to an org. If this parameter is not specified, the label will be the same as the value passed to the `--recordname|-n` parameter. [Optional]
- `--recordname|-n`: The API name of the custom metadata type record. [Required]
- `--protected|-p`: Determines if the custom metadata type record is protected when deployed in a managed package. [Optional] [Default: `false`]

  Allowed values are as follows:

  - `false`: The custom metadata type record is accessible from within and from outside the managed package and namespace that contains the custom metadata type record, including from the subscriber org.

    - `true`: The custom metadata type record is accessible from all packages that share the same namespace as the package that contains the custom metadata type record.

- `--typename|-t`: The API name of the custom metadata type that the custom metadata type record will be created for. [Required]

- `--json, --loglevel`: Please refer to the discussion on global parameters in the section "Command-line Parameters and Arguments" in Chapter 4, "Salesforce CLI."

To create multiple custom metadata type records using the `force:cmdt:record:insert` command, create a CSV file with the record field values included. Here is an example for the custom metadata type that we have just created.

Listing 12-17. Custom metadata type records

```
Name,Example_Field__c
Example_Record_2,386.01
Example_Record_3,629.29
Example_Record_4,870.91
```

The file can be stored anywhere that is accessible by `force:cmdt:record:insert` command using an absolute or relative path. For this exercise, it is saved in the Salesforce DX project's `./config` directory as a file called `exampleCMDTRecords.csv`.

The file contains a header row with the field names and a row per record that includes the field values. The first column contains the record's Name, and the second column holds the value for the custom `Example_Field__c` field.

Note A current command limitation is that the CSV file cannot contain columns for both the record's Name, such as "Example_Record_1," and Label, such as "Example Record 1." By default, the Label is assigned the same value as the Name. A workaround is to replace `Name` in the first row of the CSV file with `Label` and in each row enter the value that you would like to use for the record's Label. Use `--namecolumn Label` as a parameter to instruct the command that the `Label` column should be used to create the record's Name. The command will autogenerate the record Name and use it for the filename in the `./force-app/`

main/default/customMetadata directory. Next, if the autogenerated filename is not what you need, rename it to the Name that you would like to use for the record when it is pushed or deployed to an org.

Now execute the following command to create the records in the ./force-app/main/default/customMetadata directory:

```
$ sfdx force:cmdt:record:insert \
    --filepath ./config/exampleCMDTRecords.csv \
    --typename Example_CMDT__mdt
```

See the following for the parameters that can be used with this command:

- --outputdir|-d: The directory where the source format metadata files for the created custom metadata type records will be stored. An absolute or relative path can be used. [Optional] [Default: force-app/main/default/customMetadata]
- --filepath|-f: The path to a CSV file containing field values to be used when creating the custom metadata type records. An absolute or relative path can be used. [Required]
- --inputdir|-i: The directory containing the source format metadata files of the custom metadata type that the records will be created for. An absolute or relative path can be used. The custom metadata type name specified by the --typename|-t parameter is appended to the directory specified by this parameter. [Optional] [Default: force-app/main/default/objects]
- --namecolumn|-n: The column in the CSV file specified by the --filepath|-f parameter that contains the API name to be used for the created custom metadata type record. [Optional] [Default: Name]
- --typename|-t: The API name of the custom metadata type that the custom metadata type records will be created for. [Required]
- --json, --loglevel: Please refer to the discussion on global parameters in the section "Command-Line Parameters and Arguments" in Chapter 4, "Salesforce CLI."

After executing the preceding commands, namely, `force:cmdt:create`, `force:cmdt:field:create`, `force:cmdt:record:create`, and `force:cmdt:record:insert`, the new source format metadata files in your Salesforce DX project should look like in the following figure, which includes (1) the CSV file containing field values for the additional three records that were inserted, (2) the custom metadata type record files that were created, and (3) the custom metadata type object and field files.

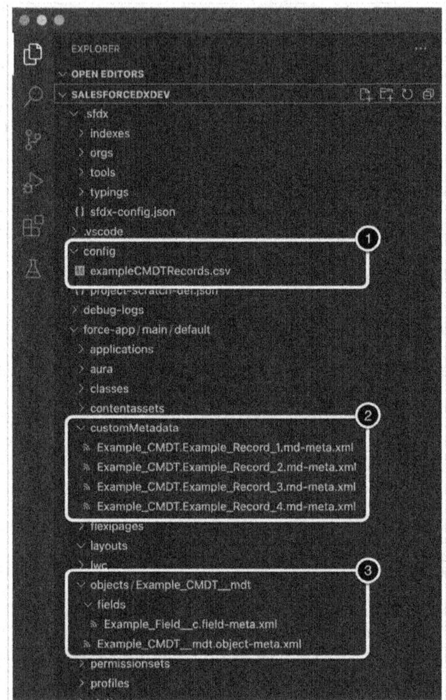

Figure 12-12. *Custom metadata type files*

Now push the files to the default org, which should be the one with the alias `MySO`, by executing the `force:source:push` command in the integrated terminal. To validate that the custom metadata type has been created in the org, open the org, and navigate to **Setup ➤ Custom Code ➤ Custom Metadata Types** where the new `Example_CMDT` custom metadata type can be seen.

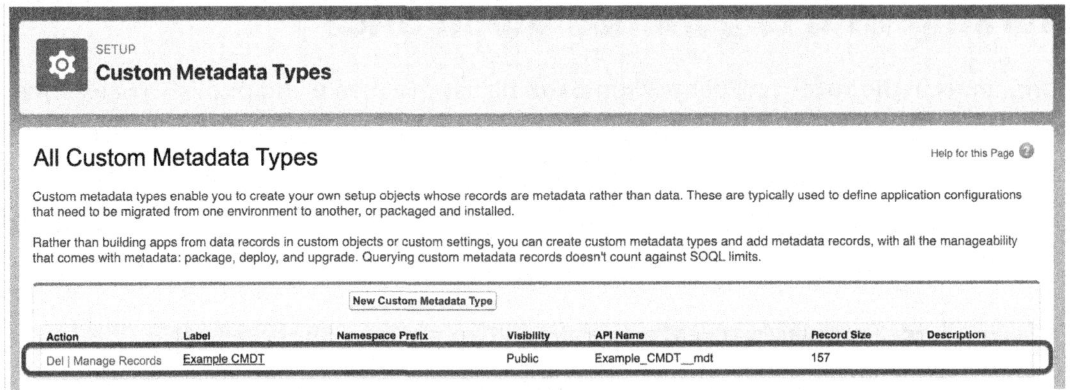

Figure 12-13. *New custom metadata type in Setup*

Click the **Manage Records** action to view the list of records for the custom metadata type.

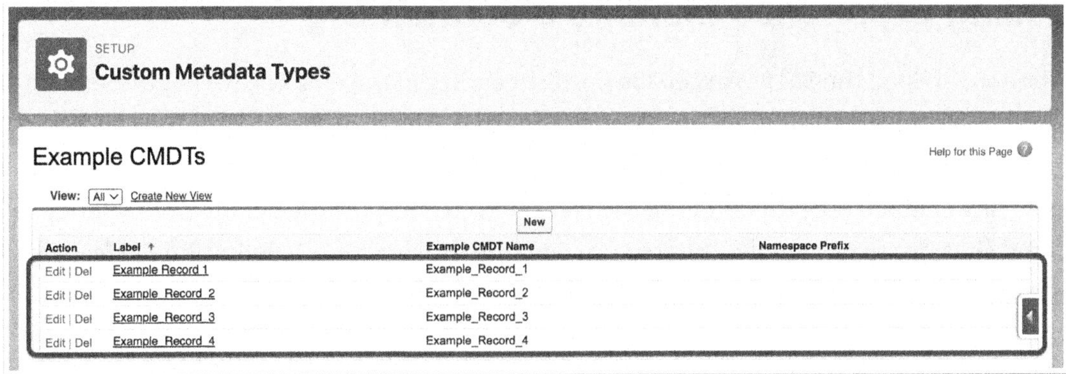

Figure 12-14. *New custom metadata type records in Setup*

We've just seen how to use the Salesforce CLI to create a custom metadata type from scratch. The next development subject that we will tackle is how to create and publish a Salesforce Experience Cloud site using CLI commands.

Working with Experience Cloud Sites

Commands in the `force:community` topic can be used to create and publish a Salesforce Experience Cloud site. We'll use the following commands to list available Experience Cloud templates in an org, create a site from one of the templates, and publish the site:

- **`force:community:template:list`**: Lists the Experience Cloud templates that are available in a target org
- **`force:community:create`**: Creates an Experience Cloud site from a template
- **`force:community:publish`**: Publishes an Experience Cloud site

Before working with the commands in the `force:community` topic, we will first create a fresh scratch org with Experience Cloud licenses included.

Adding Experience Cloud to a Scratch Org

When we created the `SalesforceDXDev` project earlier in the chapter, we left the scratch org definition file unmodified. Any scratch orgs that are created using this file will not support the creation of Experience Cloud sites unless the Digital Experiences feature is manually enabled in Setup after the org is created. To support the creation of Experience Cloud sites in a newly created scratch org, include the scratch org definition file features as in the following listing.

Listing 12-18. Scratch org definition file with Experience Cloud added

```
{
  "orgName": "ivanharris company",
  "edition": "Developer",
  "features": [
    "EnableSetPasswordInApi",
    "Communities"
  ],
  "settings": {
    "lightningExperienceSettings": {
      "enableS1DesktopEnabled": true
    },
```

```
    "mobileSettings": {
      "enableS1EncryptedStoragePref2": false
    },
    "communitiesSettings": {
      "enableNetworksEnabled": true
    }
  }
}
```

Note More information about scratch org definition files can be found in Chapter 7, "Orgs."

Create a new scratch org using the updated scratch org definition file, give it the alias `MySO-EC`, and set it as the org with the default username. Opening the org and navigating to **Setup ➤ Feature Settings ➤ Digital Experiences** will confirm that Digital Experiences have been enabled due to the presence of multiple menu items (when Digital Experiences have not been enabled, only the **Settings** menu item is available).

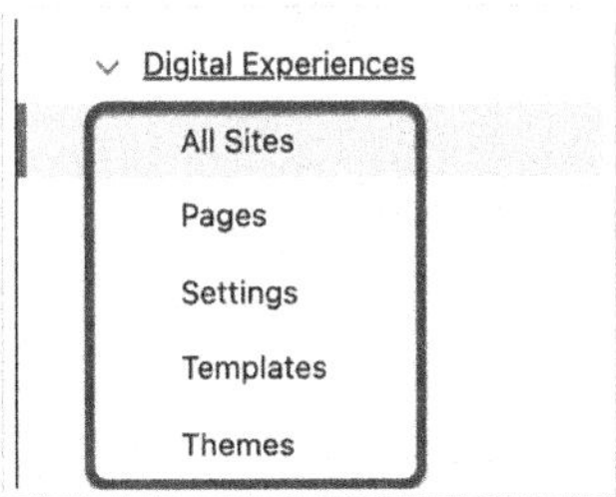

Figure 12-15. *Digital Experiences section in Setup*

Using this scratch org, we will next list the Experience Cloud site templates that it includes.

Listing Experience Cloud Site Templates

Salesforce Experience Cloud sites are created from templates. To list the templates in an org, perform these steps:

1. Launch Visual Studio Code if it's not already launched.
2. Open this chapter's `SalesforceDXDev` project.
3. Open the integrated terminal.

Then, execute the following Salesforce CLI command:

```
$ sfdx force:community:template:list
```

The parameters for the `force:community:template:list` command are as follows:

- `--targetusername|-u`: The username or alias of the org containing the Experience Cloud site templates to be listed. [Optional]
- `--apiversion, --json, --loglevel`: Please refer to the discussion on global parameters in the section "Command-Line Parameters and Arguments" in Chapter 4, "Salesforce CLI."

The command outputs the list of site templates in the org with the default username, which is `MySO-EC` in this example.

Listing 12-19. An org's available Experience Cloud site templates

```
=== Site list template result
 Template Name                  Publisher
 ─────────────────────────────  ─────────
 Build Your Own                 Salesforce
 Help Center                    Salesforce
 B2B Commerce                   Salesforce
 Microsite (LWR)                Salesforce
 Customer Account Portal        Salesforce
 Aloha                          Salesforce
 Partner Central                Salesforce
 Customer Service               Salesforce
 Build Your Own (LWR)           Salesforce
```

```
 B2C Commerce                  Salesforce
 Salesforce Tabs + Visualforce Salesforce

Total  11
```

We are now able to create an Experience Cloud site using one of the listed templates.

Creating an Experience Cloud Site

The Salesforce CLI provides the `force:community:create` command to spin up a new Salesforce Experience Cloud site in a target org from the command line. Note that unlike most of the other commands in this chapter, the `force:community:create` and `force:community:publish` commands do not create metadata files and boilerplate code in the local Salesforce DX project; rather, they create and publish sites directly in an org. Here's an example of the command that uses the `Customer Service` template that was listed when we executed the `force:community:template:list` command. The command is executed using the VS Code integrated terminal with the `SalesforceDXDev` project open.

```
$ sfdx force:community:create \
    --description 'My first SFDX created site!' \
    --name 'My SFDX Site' \
    --urlpathprefix 'service' \
    --templatename 'Customer Service'
```

Here are the parameters that can be used with the `force:community:create` command:

- `--description|-d`: A description of the site. [Optional]
- `--name|-n`: The name to be given to the created site. [Required]
- `--urlpathprefix|-p`: The URL to be appended to the org's digital experiences domain name. [Required]
- `--templatename|-t`: The name of the template to be used to create the site. Retrieve a list of templates using the `force:community:template:list` command. [Required]
- `--targetusername|-u`: The username or alias of the org where the Experience Cloud site will be created. [Optional]

- `--apiversion, --json, --loglevel`: Please refer to the discussion on global parameters in the section "Command-Line Parameters and Arguments" in Chapter 4, "Salesforce CLI."

The command outputs the following message, which includes instructions on how to open the page that lists the org's sites in the org where the site is being created. The `Action` column has been wrapped to aid readability.

Listing 12-20. Site creation command output message

```
=== Create Site Result
 Name          Message                        Action
 ───────────── ────────────────────────────── ──────────────────────────────────
 My SFDX Site Your Site is being created. We're creating your site. Run sfdx
                                           force:org:open -p
                                           _ui/networks/setup/
                                           SetupNetworksPage to view a
                                           list of your sites, and to
                                           confirm when this
                                           site is ready.
```

Executing this `force:org:open` command shows the created site in the org's **Setup ➤ Feature Settings ➤ Digital Experiences ➤ All Sites** page. Refresh occasionally if the site is not listed as it takes a few minutes to complete. The annotations in this screenshot show where the `force:community:create` command parameters are used.

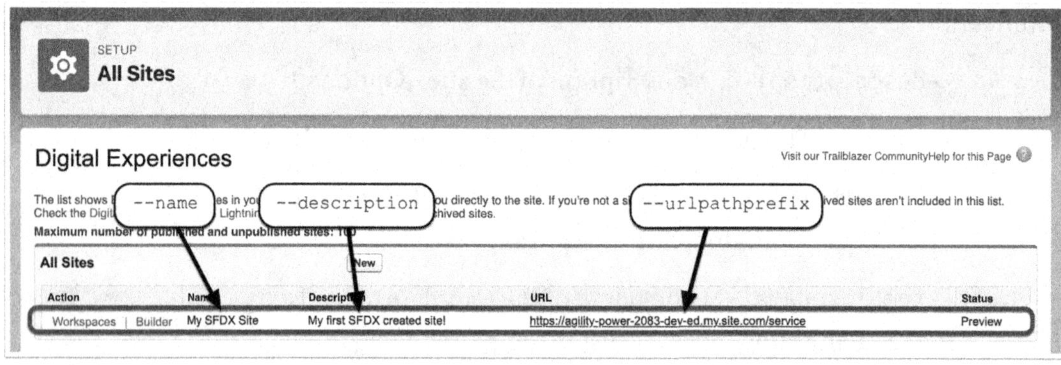

Figure 12-16. *New Experience Cloud site in Setup*

We'll now publish the site to make it accessible.

Publishing an Experience Cloud Site

To make an Experience Cloud site accessible to site members, and optionally to guest visitors if the appropriate setting is enabled, it needs to be published. Use the following command to publish the site that we have just created. As with the `force:community:create` command, it is executed from the VS Code integrated terminal with the `SalesforceDXDev` project open.

```
$ sfdx force:community:publish \
    --name 'My SFDX Site'
```

The parameters that can be used with the command are as follows:

- `--name|-n`: The name of the Experience Cloud site to publish. [Required]
- `--targetusername|-u`: The username or alias of the org where the Experience Cloud site will be published. [Optional]
- `--apiversion, --json, --loglevel`: Please refer to the discussion on global parameters in the section "Command-Line Parameters and Arguments" in Chapter 4, "Salesforce CLI."

The command outputs a message indicating that the site is being published. The `URL` column has been removed, and the `Message` column has been wrapped to aid readability.

Listing 12-21. Site publishing command output message

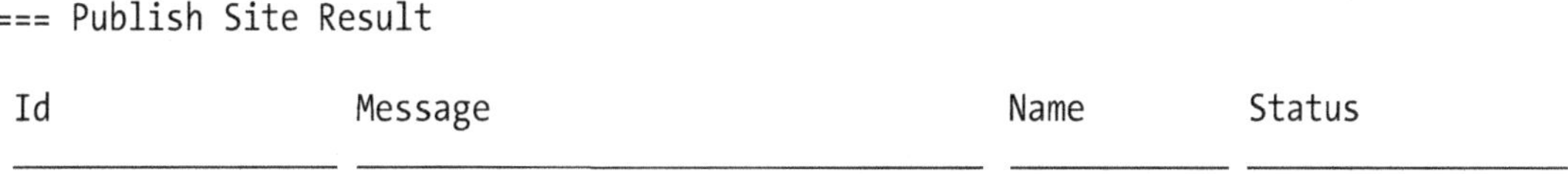

```
=== Publish Site Result

 Id                 Message                             Name         Status
 ────────────────── ─────────────────────────────────── ──────────── ──────────────────

 0DB2z0000004GAKGA2 We're publishing your changes now. My SFDX Site UnderConstruction
                    You'll receive an email confirmation
                    when your changes are live.
```

When you receive the email confirmation, return to your scratch org and navigate to **Setup ➤ Feature Settings ➤ Digital Experiences ➤ All Sites**, then click the URL for the site. The site will open in the browser, confirming that the site has been published.

Note You can view the site because the System Administrator profile is added to the site as a member automatically when the site is created.

That wraps up how to create and publish an Experience Cloud site using the Salesforce CLI. The next topic looks at creating Lightning web components.

Working with Lightning Web Components

The Salesforce CLI includes commands in the `force:lightning` topic to generate the metadata and boilerplate code for Lightning apps, components, unit tests, events, and interfaces. The commands support both Lightning Aura components and Lightning web components. Notwithstanding the fact that Lightning web components do not yet include all the functionality that Lightning Aura components do, they are set to supersede Aura components. The examples in this section will therefore focus on the following commands that can be used with Lightning web components:

- **`force:lightning:component:create`**: Create a Lightning web component bundle.
- **`force:lightning:lwc:test:setup`**: Install the Jest unit testing tools for testing Lightning web components.
- **`force:lightning:lwc:test:create`**: Create a Jest unit test file.
- **`force:lightning:lwc:test:run`**: Invoke a Jest unit test.

We won't describe the following Aura-specific commands that are part of the `force:lightning` topic:

- **`force:lightning:app:create`**: Creates a Lightning Aura app
- **`force:lightning:event:create`**: Creates a Lightning Aura app event or a Lightning Aura component event
- **`force:lightning:interface:create`**: Creates a Lightning interface that can be used by a Lightning Aura component
- **`force:lightning:test:create:`** Creates Lightning Test Service (LTS) unit tests for Lightning Aura components using frameworks such as Jasmine and Mocha

Note, if you have followed along with the examples in the previous section, "Working with Experience Cloud Sites," your default scratch org may no longer be MySO. If this is the case, make MySO the scratch org with the default username using the following command:

```
$ sfdx config:set defaultusername=MySO
```

We'll now see how to create a Lightning web component, after which we will investigate how to test it.

Creating a Lightning Web Component

To create the metadata files and boilerplate code for a Lightning web component bundle, execute the following command in the VS Code integrated terminal from the root directory of the SalesforceDXDev project:

```
$ sfdx force:lightning:component:create \
    --outputdir ./force-app/main/default/lwc \
    --componentname helloWorld \
    --type lwc
```

The command's available parameters are as follows:

- --outputdir|-d: The directory where the source format Lightning web component bundle files will be created. The parent folder must be called lwc. An absolute or relative path can be used. [Optional] [Default: Current working directory (.)]
- --componentname|-n: The Lightning web component name. [Required]
- --template|-t: The template to use for bootstrapping the Aura framework. Allowed values are default, analyticsDashboard, analyticsDashboardWithStep. As we are not exploring Lightning Aura components, we won't use this Aura-specific parameter. [Optional] [Default: default]
- --type: The type of Lightning component bundle to create. Allowed values are lwc or Aura. As we are focusing on Lightning web components, we will use the value lwc. [Optional] [Default: aura]

- `--apiversion, --json, --loglevel`: Please refer to the discussion on global parameters in the section "Command-Line Parameters and Arguments" in Chapter 4, "Salesforce CLI."

Note To create a Lightning web component bundle using the Visual Studio Code Command Palette, execute the command **SFDX: Create Lightning Web Component**. To create a Lightning web component using Visual Studio Code context menus, right-click the `lwc` directory and click the menu item **SFDX: Create Lightning Web Component**.

The command creates the bundle's HTML, JavaScript, and XML configuration files in a subdirectory of the `./force-app/main/default/lwc` directory with the same name as the component. A `__tests__` subdirectory containing a Jest test file is also created. We'll be working with Jest tests later in this section.

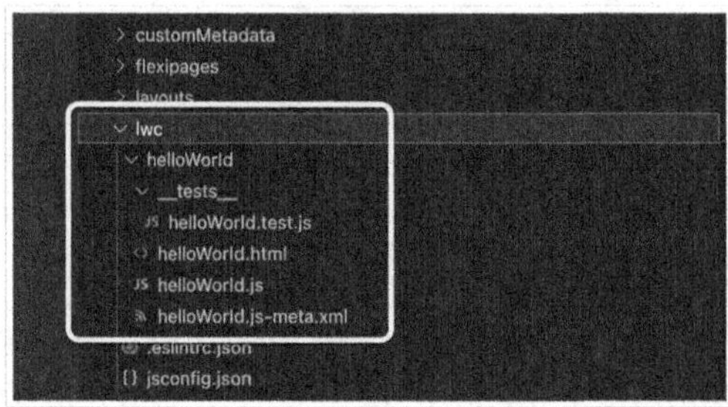

Figure 12-17. *New Lightning web component bundle files*

Before we push the files to our scratch org, change the HTML file and XML configuration file to the contents in the following two listings.

Listing 12-22. helloWorld.html

```
<template>
    <lightning-card title="Hello World" icon-name="utility:world">
        <div class="slds-m-around_medium">
            <p>Hello there!</p>
        </div>
    </lightning-card>
</template>
```

Listing 12-23. helloWorld.js-meta.xml

```
<?xml version="1.0" encoding="UTF-8"?>
<LightningComponentBundle xmlns="http://soap.sforce.com/2006/04/metadata">
    <apiVersion>52.0</apiVersion>
    <isExposed>true</isExposed>
    <targets>
        <target>lightning__HomePage</target>
    </targets>
</LightningComponentBundle>
```

Execute `force:source:push` to push the Lightning web component to the `MySO` scratch org. Open the scratch org, click the App Launcher (⁝⁝⁝) icon, and then click the **Sales** app. Next, click the cog (⚙) icon and then click **Edit Page**. This will open the Lightning App Builder for the Sales app's Home Page. In the list of components will be our new `helloWorld` custom component.

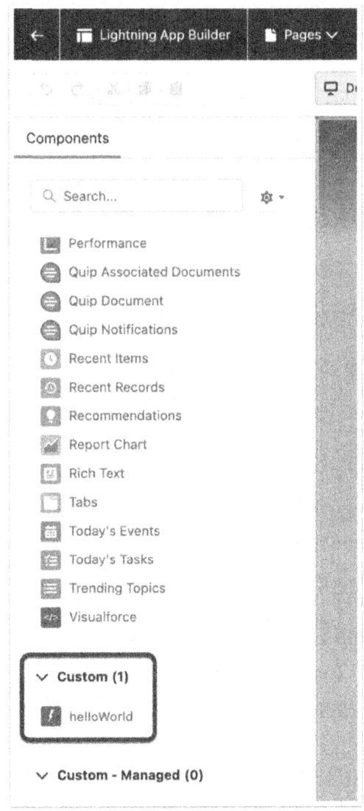

Figure 12-18. *The helloWorld LWC in Lightning App Builder*

We'll now see how to test our new Lightning web component.

Testing a Lightning Web Component

The Jest JavaScript testing framework is used by the Salesforce CLI to test Lightning web components. Testing using the Salesforce CLI consists of three steps with the following commands:

1. **force:lightning:lwc:test:setup**: Install Jest and its dependencies into a Salesforce DX project.
2. **force:lightning:lwc:test:create**: Create the boilerplate code for a Jest unit test.
3. **force:lightning:lwc:test:run**: Run the Jest unit test.

To install Jest, launch Visual Studio Code and run the following command in the integrated terminal from the SalesforceDXDev project's root folder:

```
$ sfdx force:lightning:lwc:test:setup
```

The only parameters available for this command are as follows:

- --json, --loglevel: Please refer to the discussion on global parameters in the section "Command-Line Parameters and Arguments" in Chapter 4, "Salesforce CLI."

The command installs the @salesforce/sfdx-lwc-jest node package and creates a jest.config.js file in the project's root directory.

The next step is usually to create the boilerplate code for a Jest unit test to test the helloWorld Lightning web component that we just created; however, when the Lightning web component was created, a __test__ subdirectory and a boilerplate Jest unit test file were automatically created for us. To illustrate how to create Jest unit test boilerplate code, delete the __test__ subdirectory and execute the following command:

```
$ sfdx force:lightning:lwc:test:create \
    --filepath ./force-app/main/default/lwc/helloWorld/helloWorld.js
```

The force:lightning:lwc:test:create command's parameters are as follows:

- --filepath|-f: The path to the Lightning web component bundle's root directory, below which the __tests__ subdirectory will be created. [Required]

- `--json`, `--loglevel`: Please refer to the discussion on global parameters in the section "Command-Line Parameters and Arguments" in Chapter 4, "Salesforce CLI."

Note To create a Lightning web component Jest unit test file using the Visual Studio Code Command Palette, execute the command **SFDX: Create Lightning Web Component Test**.

The command creates the Jest test file in a directory called `__tests__` as a subdirectory of the Lightning web component bundle's root directory.

Figure 12-19. *Jest unit test file*

Modify the Jest unit test file as follows to validate that the `Hello there!` greeting is displayed.

Listing 12-24. helloWorld.test.js Jest unit test file

```
import { createElement } from 'lwc';
import HelloWorld from 'c/helloWorld';

describe('c-hello-world', () => {
    afterEach(() => {
        // The jsdom instance is shared across test cases in a single file
           so reset
        // the DOM
        while (document.body.firstChild) {
            document.body.removeChild(document.body.firstChild);
        }
    });
```

```
    it('Displays a greeting', () => {
        const element = createElement('c-hello-world', {
            is: HelloWorld
        });
        document.body.appendChild(element);

        // Validate that the greeting is displayed.
        const div = element.shadowRoot.querySelector('div');
        expect(div.textContent).toBe('Hello there!');
    });
});
```

We're now ready to run the Jest unit test using the following command:

```
$ sfdx force:lightning:lwc:test:run
```

The parameters for this command are as follows:

- `--debug|-d`: Run the tests in debug mode. This parameter or the `--watch` parameter can be used, but not both. [Optional]
- `--watch`: Run the tests in watch mode. This parameter or the `--debug|-d` parameter can be used, but not both. [Optional]
- `--json, --loglevel`: Please refer to the discussion on global parameters in the section "Command-Line Parameters and Arguments" in Chapter 4, "Salesforce CLI."

Note To run Lightning web component Jest tests using the Visual Studio Code Command Palette, execute the command **SFDX: Run Current Lightning Web Component Test File** or **SFDX: Run All Lightning Web Component Tests**. To run Jest tests from the Visual Studio Code Editor, open a test file in the Editor and click **Run Test** above a test block.

The command executes all Lightning web component tests that it finds in `__tests__` directories and outputs the results.

Listing 12-25. helloWorld.test.js Jest unit test results

```
PASS  force-app/main/default/lwc/helloWorld/__tests__/helloWorld.test.js
  c-hello-world
    ✓ Displays a greeting (18 ms)

Test Suites: 1 passed, 1 total
Tests:       1 passed, 1 total
Snapshots:   0 total
Time:        1.055 s
Ran all test suites.
Test run complete. Exited with status code: 0
```

Running Jest tests in debug and watch mode is the subject of the next couple of sections.

Running Jest Tests in Debug Mode

Sometimes, you will find that your Jest unit tests are not executing as expected, especially when they become complex. Fortunately, it's possible to use Visual Studio Code's built-in debugger to set breakpoints, step through your test code, inspect variable values, and view the call stack.

To launch a Lightning web component Jest test in debug mode using the Salesforce CLI, we execute the `force:lightning:lwc:test:run` command with the `--debug|-d` parameter. Before this command will work though, we need to create a Visual Studio Code launch configuration so that the built-in VS Code debugger knows how to attach to the process running our Jest test. When a Salesforce DX project is created, a file called `launch.json` is added to the `.vscode` directory, which is a subdirectory of the project's root directory. The file includes the following launch configuration for the Apex Replay Debugger that ships with the Salesforce Extensions for Visual Studio Code.

Listing 12-26. Apex Replay Debugger launch configuration file

```
{
  // Use IntelliSense to learn about possible attributes.
  // Hover to view descriptions of existing attributes.
  // For more information, visit: https://go.microsoft.com/
     fwlink/?linkid=830387
```

```
  "version": "0.2.0",
  "configurations": [
    {
      "name": "Launch Apex Replay Debugger",
      "type": "apex-replay",
      "request": "launch",
      "logFile": "${command:AskForLogFileName}",
      "stopOnEntry": true,
      "trace": true
    }
  ]
}
```

If you are not going to use the Apex Replay Debugger, we can replace its launch configuration with the Jest test launch configuration; alternatively, you can add the Jest test launch configuration as an additional configuration. The following two listings show the Jest test launch configurations for Mac/Linux and Windows, respectively.

Listing 12-27. VS Code for Mac or Linux launch configuration file

```
{
  "version": "0.2.0",
  "configurations": [
    {
      "name": "Debug Jest Tests",
      "type": "node",
      "request": "launch",
      "runtimeArgs": [
        "--inspect-brk",
        "${workspaceRoot}/node_modules/.bin/jest",
        "--runInBand"
      ],
      "console": "integratedTerminal",
      "internalConsoleOptions": "neverOpen",
```

```
      "port": 9229
    }
  ]
}
```

Listing 12-28. VS Code for Windows launch configuration file

```
{
  "version": "0.2.0",
  "configurations": [
    {
      "name": "Debug Jest Tests",
      "type": "node",
      "request": "launch",
      "runtimeArgs": [
        "--inspect-brk",
        "${workspaceRoot}/node_modules/jest/bin/jest.js",
        "--runInBand"
      ],
      "console": "integratedTerminal",
      "internalConsoleOptions": "neverOpen",
      "port": 9229
    }
  ]
}
```

Note To learn more about VS Code launch configurations, refer to the VS Code documentation: `https://code.visualstudio.com/docs`. To learn more about Jest-specific launch configurations, refer to the Troubleshooting Guide in the Jest documentation: `https://jestjs.io/docs/troubleshooting`. The preceding configurations are copied from the Jest documentation.

This listing illustrates a launch configuration file for Mac/Linux that includes the Apex Replay Debugger configuration with the Jest test configuration added.

Listing 12-29. Updated launch configuration file

```
{
  // Use IntelliSense to learn about possible attributes.
  // Hover to view descriptions of existing attributes.
  // For more information, visit: https://go.microsoft.com/
     fwlink/?linkid=830387
  "version": "0.2.0",
  "configurations": [
    {
      "name": "Launch Apex Replay Debugger",
      "type": "apex-replay",
      "request": "launch",
      "logFile": "${command:AskForLogFileName}",
      "stopOnEntry": true,
      "trace": true
    },
    {
      "name": "Debug Jest Tests",
      "type": "node",
      "request": "launch",
      "runtimeArgs": [
        "--inspect-brk",
        "${workspaceRoot}/node_modules/.bin/jest",
        "--runInBand"
      ],
      "console": "integratedTerminal",
      "internalConsoleOptions": "neverOpen",
      "port": 9229
    }
  ]
}
```

To debug our Jest test, do the following. Note the references to "item" refer to the numbered items in the screenshot that follows these steps:

1. Open the Jest unit test file in the VS Code Editor (item 1).
2. Click the **Run and Debug** icon ( ) in the Activity Bar (item 2), which opens the Run and Debug view (item 3).
3. Select the **Debug Jest Tests** configuration in the Run and Debug view (item 4).
4. Execute the following command in the integrated terminal:
   `$ sfdx force:lightning:lwc:test:run --debug`
5. Set a breakpoint in the Jest unit test file by clicking next to line number 12, the line with the statement `it('Displays a greeting', () => {` (item 5).
6. Select **Run ➤ Start Debugging** from the VS Code menu.

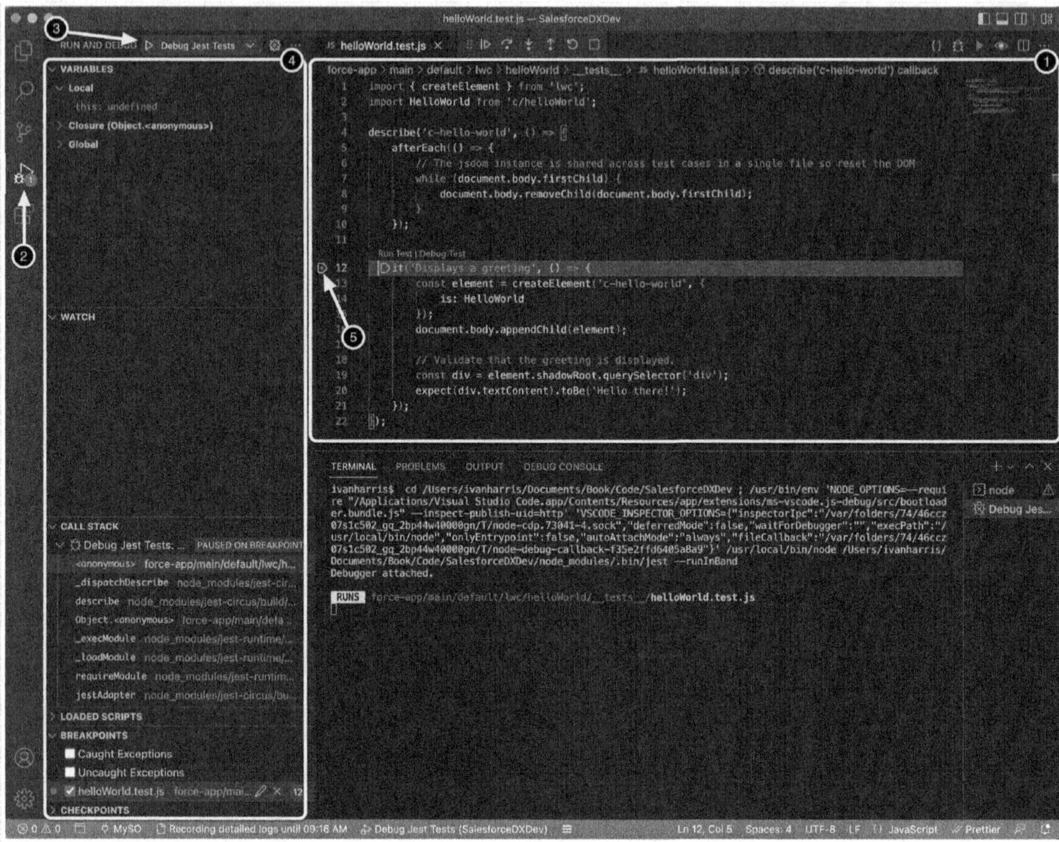

Figure 12-20. *Running Jest unit tests in debug mode*

The debugger runs to the first breakpoint and has stopped executing the test. In the Run and Debug view, the execution context is visible including variable values and the call stack.

Note To run Lightning web component Jest tests in debug mode using the Visual Studio Code Command Palette, execute the command **SFDX: Debug Current Lightning Web Component Test File**. To execute a Jest unit test in debug mode using the VS Code user interface, click **Debug Test** above the test block when the unit test file is open in the VS Code Editor. The advantage of using these methods is that it's a one-click execution, that is, you don't have to select the launch configuration in the Run and Debug view or click **Run ➤ Start Debugging** in the VS Code menu.

We'll now explore how to run Lightning web component Jest tests in watch mode.

Running Jest Tests in Watch Mode

Running Lightning web component Jest tests in watch mode continuously monitors JavaScript files for changes and re-runs tests when changes occur. Watch mode works in partnership with Git, which performs the file monitoring to detect changes; for that reason, ensure that Git is initialized in the `SalesforceDXDev` project by running the `git init` command in the project's root directory.

Note If you do not have Git installed on your computer, please refer to Chapter 9, "Version Control", for instructions.

To enter watch mode, enter the following command in the integrated terminal:

```
$ sfdx force:lightning:lwc:test:run --watch
```

If the command is executed from the project's root directory, all tests for all Lightning web components are initially run and then re-run if any Lightning web component files are changed. Alternatively, execute the command from a Lightning web component's root directory to monitor and run tests for just that component.

After executing the `force:lightning:lwc:test:run --watch` command, the following is output to the integrated terminal.

Listing 12-30. Watch mode initial test runs

```
PASS  force-app/main/default/lwc/helloWorld/__tests__/helloWorld.test.js
  c-hello-world
    ✓ Displays a greeting (19 ms)

Test Suites: 1 passed, 1 total
Tests:       1 passed, 1 total
Snapshots:   0 total
Time:        0.601 s, estimated 1 s
Ran all test suites related to changed files.

Watch Usage
 › Press a to run all tests.
 › Press f to run only failed tests.
 › Press p to filter by a filename regex pattern.
```

```
› Press t to filter by a test name regex pattern.
› Press q to quit watch mode.
› Press Enter to trigger a test run.
```

Note the `Watch Usage` options at the end of the listing that enable you to run tests or quit watch mode.

Now make a change to the `helloWorld.test.js` file that will cause the test to fail; for example, change the line

```
expect(div.textContent).toBe('Hello there!');
```

to

```
expect(div.textContent).toBe('Hi there!');
```

The Jest unit tests will automatically re-run and output the following in the integrated terminal.

Listing 12-31. Watch mode test re-run

```
FAIL  force-app/main/default/lwc/helloWorld/__tests__/helloWorld.test.js
  c-hello-world
    × Displays a greeting (21 ms)

  ● c-hello-world › Displays a greeting

    expect(received).toBe(expected) // Object.is equality

    Expected: "Hi there!"
    Received: "Hello there!"

      18 |         // Validate that the greeting is displayed.
      19 |         const div = element.shadowRoot.querySelector('div');
    > 20 |         expect(div.textContent).toBe('Hi there!');
         |                                 ^
      21 |     });
      22 | });

      at Object.toBe (force-app/main/default/lwc/helloWorld/__tests__/
      helloWorld.test.js:20:33)
```

```
Test Suites: 1 failed, 1 total
Tests:       1 failed, 1 total
Snapshots:   0 total
Time:        0.415 s, estimated 1 s
Ran all test suites related to changed files.

Watch Usage: Press w to show more.
```

Correct the error to automatically re-run the tests again. Running the Jest tests in watch mode allows you to work on your Lightning web components and very quickly discover if any changes cause unit tests to pass or fail.

The penultimate development area that we'll look at is how to work with static resources.

Working with Static Resources

A static resource is content uploaded to a Salesforce org that can be referenced in Visualforce pages. Content types include, but are not limited to, style sheets, images, and JavaScript. The `force:staticresource` topic includes a single command for creating static resources:

- **`force:staticresource:create:`** Create a static resource in a local Salesforce DX project.

Using the VS Code integrated terminal, execute the following command from the root directory of the `SalesforceDXDev` project to create the metadata and a placeholder file for a static resource:

```
$ sfdx force:staticresource:create \
    --outputdir \
      ./force-app/main/default/staticresources \
    --resourcename myStaticResource \
    --contenttype image/png
```

The set of parameters that can be used with the command are as follows:

- `--outputdir|-d`: The directory where the source format static resource files will be created. An absolute or relative path can be used. [Optional] [Default: Current working directory (`.`)]
- `--resourcename|-n`: The static resource API name. [Required]
- `--contenttype`: The static resource's MIME type. [Optional] [Default: `application/zip`]
- `--apiversion, --json, --loglevel`: Please refer to the discussion on global parameters in the section "Command-Line Parameters and Arguments" in Chapter 4, "Salesforce CLI."

Note For a list of valid MIME types that can be used with the `--contenttype` parameter, please refer to the Internet Assigned Numbers Authority website: `www.iana.org/assignments/media-types/media-types.xhtml`.

The command creates two files in the project's `./force-app/main/default/staticresources` directory.

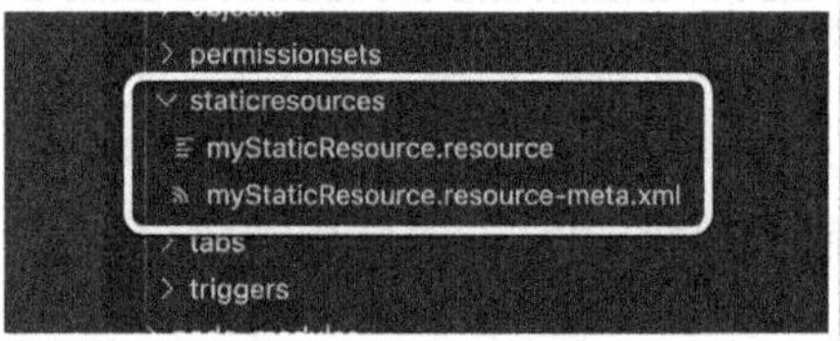

***Figure 12-21.** Created static resource files*

Note A static resource can be created in any directory. Creating it in the `./force-app/main/default/staticresources` directory as source format files allows the `force:source` push/pull and deploy/retrieve commands to synchronize the source format static resource metadata component between the local Salesforce DX project and an org. Furthermore, if the static resource has an archive MIME type, the commands will take care of compressing and decompressing the archive, which is a big benefit over working with static resources that are stored in metadata format in a project.

The `force:staticresource:create` command creates a `.resource-meta.xml` file that contains the static resource's metadata and the following `.resource` file that is a placeholder for the static resource's content.

Listing 12-32. Static resource placeholder content file

```
Replace this file with your static resource (i.e. an image)
The file name must be the same as your resource name but
the file extension can be changed.
```

As we have created a static resource with an `image/png` MIME type, we will replace the file with the following image file with a filename of `myStaticResource.png`.

Figure 12-22. *Static resource content image file*

The static resource files and content should look like the following in Visual Studio Code.

Figure 12-23. *Updated static resource content image file in VS Code*

Execute the `force:source:push` command to push the static resource to the default `MySO` scratch org. Open the scratch org and navigate to **Setup ➤ Custom Code ➤ Static Resources**, where the new static resource will be listed.

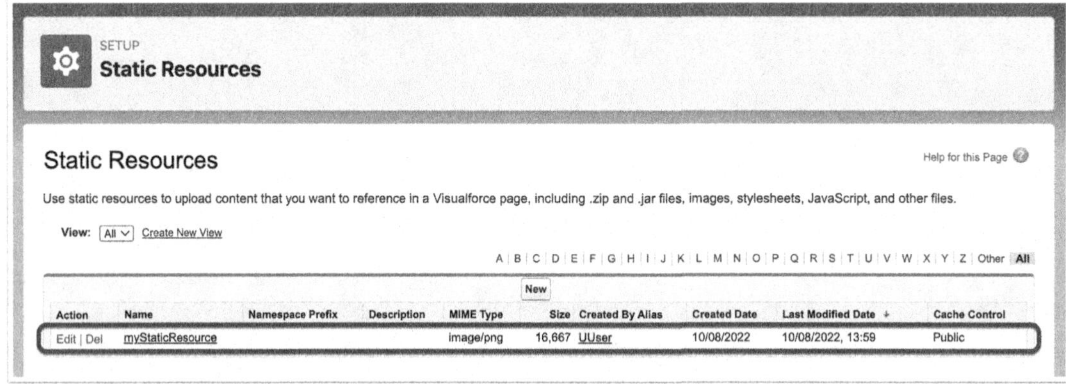

Figure 12-24. *The new static resource in the scratch org*

Click the **myStaticResource** name, then the **View File** link if you want to view the uploaded static resource's content.

We are now going to cover the final development topic in the chapter on how to work with Visualforce components and pages.

Working with Visualforce

The Salesforce CLI includes these commands for creating the metadata and boilerplate code for Visualforce components and pages:

- **`force:visualforce:component:create`**: Create the metadata and boilerplate code for a Visualforce component.
- **`force:visualforce:page:create`**: Create the metadata and boilerplate code for a Visualforce page.

Note Lightning web components, rather than Visualforce, is the preferred technology for creating user interfaces for Salesforce.

We'll cover each command in turn.

Creating a Visualforce Component

To create the metadata and boilerplate code for a Visualforce component, execute the following command from the VS Code integrated terminal. This command assumes that it's being executed from the `SalesforceDXDev` project's root directory:

```
$ sfdx force:visualforce:component:create \
    --outputdir ./force-app/main/default/components \
    --label 'My VF Component' \
    --componentname myVFComponent
```

The parameters that can be used with this command are as follows:

- `--outputdir|-d`: The directory where the source format Visualforce component files will be created. An absolute or relative path can be used. [Optional] [Default: Current working directory (`.`)]

- `--label | -l`: The Visualforce component's label. [Required]
- `--componentname | -n`: The Visualforce component's API name. [Required]
- `--template | -t`: The template to be used when creating the Visualforce component. The only allowable value is `DefaultVFComponent`. [Optional] [Default: `DefaultVFComponent`]
- `--apiversion, --json, --loglevel`: Please refer to the discussion on global parameters in the section "Command-Line Parameters and Arguments" in Chapter 4, "Salesforce CLI."

Note To create a Visualforce component using the Visual Studio Code Command Palette, execute the command **SFDX: Create Visualforce Component**. To create a Visualforce component using Visual Studio Code context menus, right-click the `components` directory and click the menu item **SFDX: Create Visualforce Component**.

When a new Salesforce DX project is created, the `components` subdirectory in the `./force-app/main/default` package directory does not exist. The command will create the subdirectory, which is the location that the Metadata API and the `force:source:push` and `force:source:pull` commands expect Visualforce components to be stored. The command also creates the metadata file and the boilerplate code file in the `components` directory.

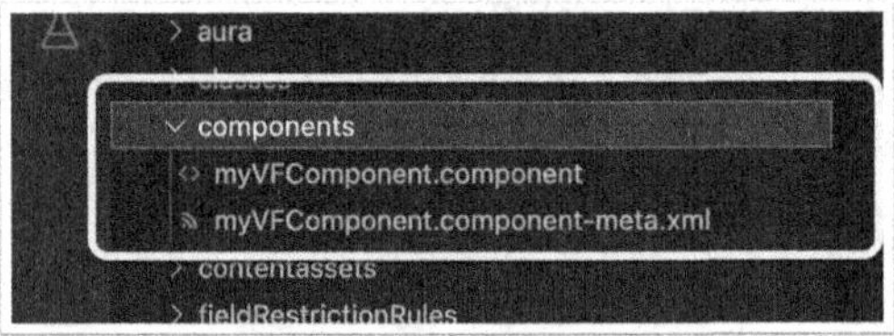

***Figure 12-25.** Visualforce component metadata file and boilerplate code file*

The following lists the boilerplate code that is created in the `myVFComponent.component` file.

Listing 12-33. Visualforce component boilerplate code

```
<apex:component>
<!-- Begin Default Content REMOVE THIS -->
<h1>Congratulations</h1>
This is your new Component
<!-- End Default Content REMOVE THIS -->
</apex:component>
```

Use the `force:source:push` command to push the Visualforce component to the `MySO` scratch org. Open the org and navigate to **Setup ➤ Custom Code ➤ Visualforce Components** to see the new Visualforce component listed.

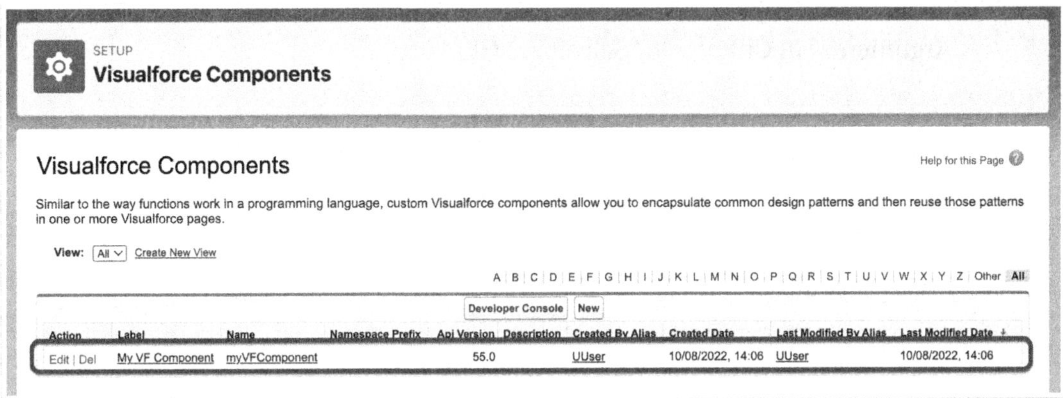

Figure 12-26. *The new Visualforce component in the scratch org*

The process for creating a Visualforce page is almost identical to creating a Visualforce component, which we will do next.

Creating a Visualforce Page

The metadata and boilerplate code for a Visualforce page are created by executing the following command in VS Code's integrated terminal from the root directory of the `SalesforceDXDev` project:

```
$ sfdx force:visualforce:page:create \
    --outputdir ./force-app/main/default/pages \
    --label 'My VF Page' \
    --pagename myVFPage
```

The command's parameters are as follows:

- `--outputdir|-d`: The directory where the source format Visualforce page files will be created. An absolute or relative path can be used. [Optional] [Default: Current working directory (`.`)]
- `--label|-l`: The Visualforce page's label. [Required]
- `--pagename|-n`: The Visualforce page's API name. [Required]
- `--template|-t`: The template to be used when creating the Visualforce page. The only allowable value is `DefaultVFPage`. [Optional] [Default: `DefaultVFPage`]
- `--apiversion, --json, --loglevel`: Please refer to the discussion on global parameters in the section "Command-Line Parameters and Arguments" in Chapter 4, "Salesforce CLI."

Note To create a Visualforce page using the Visual Studio Code Command Palette, execute the command **SFDX: Create Visualforce Page**. To create a Visualforce page using Visual Studio Code context menus, right-click the `pages` directory and click the menu item **SFDX: Create Visualforce Page**.

The `pages` subdirectory in the `./force-app/main/default` package directory does not exist when a new Salesforce DX project is created, but the `force:visualforce:page:create` command will create it for us.

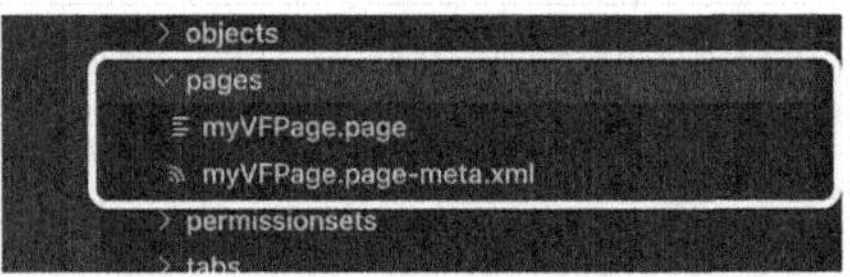

***Figure 12-27.** Visualforce page metadata file and boilerplate code file*

Here are the `myVFPage.page` boilerplate code file contents.

Listing 12-34. Visualforce page boilerplate code

```
<apex:page>
<!-- Begin Default Content REMOVE THIS -->
<h1>Congratulations</h1>
This is your new Page
<!-- End Default Content REMOVE THIS -->
</apex:page>
```

Push the new Visualforce page to the MySO scratch org using the `force:source:push` command. Then open the org and navigate to **Setup ➤ Custom Code ➤ Visualforce Pages** to see the new Visualforce page listed in the Visualforce Pages listing.

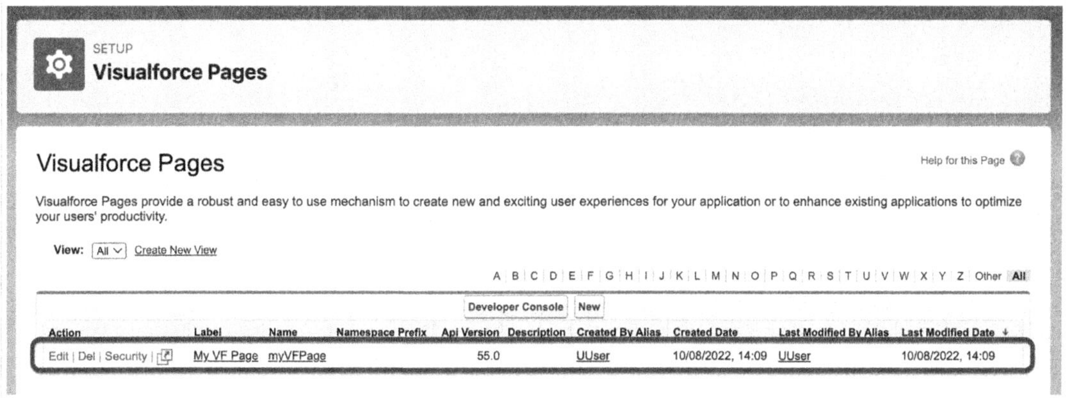

Figure 12-28. *The new Visualforce page in the scratch org*

Working with Visualforce is the last development topic in the chapter, so here is a summary of what we covered.

Chapter Summary

This chapter introduced a set of commands that bootstraps the development of metadata components by creating the metadata and boilerplate code to get you started. We looked at Apex, custom metadata types, Experience Cloud sites, Lightning web components, static resources, and Visualforce. We saw how to execute the commands using the Salesforce CLI and how to use the Visual Studio Code Command Palette and context menus when the commands are available via those methods.

Next is the final chapter of the book, where we will explore how to package metadata components into containers for deploying to production orgs.

CHAPTER 13

Package Development

Salesforce professionals developing applications and customizations for the Salesforce Platform operate in a very dynamic and demanding environment. In addition to keeping pace with new and changing business requirements, they must also leverage the additional features that are released three times a year by Salesforce to deliver better value to their stakeholders. When applications and customizations grow in number and complexity, and development teams expand, it becomes progressively harder to manage the development and release of the increasing volume of metadata components when they are unpackaged. When these unpackaged metadata components are deployed to a production org, it is known as "happy soup." Imagine for a moment, you have a bowl of alphabet soup in front of you with each letter representing a metadata component and a word represents a customization or application. It's hard to see the words, let alone which letters belong to each word. Similarly, in a production org's "happy soup," it's hard to see the applications and customizations and what components belong to each.

The solution to the "happy soup" challenge is packaging, where metadata components that are functionally related to the same application or customization are grouped into a container that can be deployed to an org as a single unit. With packages, not only can you see which metadata components belong to each customization or application, they bring other benefits that include the following:

- Each package can be developed and deployed separately, rather than waiting for all the changes, from all the teams, to be completed and added to the set of unpackaged metadata components.
- Smaller packages are easier to understand, less complex to comprehensively test, and quicker to deploy.
- An audit trail of application or customization changes is easier to maintain and follow.

I. Harris, *Beginning Salesforce DX*, https://doi.org/10.1007/978-1-4842-8114-7_13

- Postdeployment issues can be attributed to a specific application or customization for remediation.
- Common functionality can be packaged and reused. For example, a base package can contain functionality that is common to multiple extension packages.

These benefits contribute to a more agile, collaborative, and high-quality development lifecycle.

Prior to Salesforce DX, two deployment options that used packaging were supported: unmanaged packages and managed packages. The latter are now known as first-generation managed packages (1GP) as Salesforce DX introduced second-generation managed packages (2GP) along with unlocked packages as additional deployment options. Salesforce also supports three application development models that can be used to develop applications and customizations. In this chapter, we will explore how to develop unlocked packages and second-generation managed packages using the package development model.

Before we get stuck into the detail though, let's list the commands that will be covered in the chapter.

This Chapter's Commands

To develop unlocked packages and second-generation managed packages (2GP), we will gain experience using the following Salesforce CLI commands from the `force:package` topic:

- **`force:package:create`**: Create an unlocked package or a second-generation managed package.
- **`force:package:delete`**: Delete an unlocked package or a second-generation managed package.
- **`force:package:install`**: Install a version of an unlocked package, a first-generation managed package, or a second-generation managed package in a target org.

- **force:package:install:report**: Check the status of an unlocked package, a first-generation managed package, or a second-generation managed package installation that was initiated using the `force:package:install` command.
- **force:package:installed:list**: List the unlocked packages, first-generation managed packages, and second-generation managed packages that are installed in a target org.
- **force:package:list**: List the unlocked packages and second-generation managed packages that have been created by a Dev Hub.
- **force:package:uninstall**: Uninstall an unlocked package or a second-generation managed package version from a target org. First-generation managed packages must be uninstalled using an org's Setup user interface.
- **force:package:uninstall:report**: Check the status of an uninstall request that was initiated by the `force:package:uninstall` command.
- **force:package:update**: Update an unlocked package or second-generation managed package's details, such as the package name and description.
- **force:package:version:create**: Create a new version of an unlocked package or a second-generation managed package.
- **force:package:version:create:list**: List the requests that have been made to create new versions of unlocked packages and second-generation managed packages.
- **force:package:version:create:report**: Retrieve details about a request to create a new version of an unlocked package or a second-generation managed package that was initiated by the `force:package:version:create` command.
- **force:package:version:delete**: Delete an unlocked package or a second-generation managed package version.

- **`force:package:version:displayancestry`**: Display the ancestry tree for a specific second-generation managed package version or all versions of a second-generation managed package.
- **`force:package:version:list`**: List all of the unlocked package and second-generation managed package versions that have been created.
- **`force:package:version:promote`**: Promote an unlocked package or second-generation managed package version to released status.
- **`force:package:version:report`**: Retrieve details about an unlocked package or second-generation managed package version.
- **`force:package:version:update`**: Update an unlocked package or second-generation managed package version's details, such as version name, version description, or version tag.

Note As mentioned earlier, we won't include the development of first-generation managed packages using commands in the `force:package1` topic, as the Salesforce CLI support is more limited and the future clearly points to second-generation managed packages (2GP).

As with most of the previous chapters, and for the last time in the book, we'll next create a fresh project for the examples that follow.

This Chapter's Project

In the previous chapters, we've used snippets of code to illustrate how to use Salesforce CLI commands. As these snippets were small enough to show in listings, we would create a new Salesforce DX chapter for the project and then type in any required code.

For this chapter, we need something a little more substantial that can be deployed using multiple packages, so a sample app has been developed for you to use. The app can be found in the following GitHub public repository:

`https://github.com/IvanHarris-SalesforceDX-Book/SalesforceDXSampleApp.git`

We'll clone the repository as part of the project setup in a moment, but for those who have jumped straight to this chapter (I do it all the time!), let's ensure that the necessary prerequisites are set up.

Prerequisites

Before cloning the sample application's repository and performing some manual steps to complete the project setup, please ensure that the following is in place so that you can follow along with the rest of the chapter:

- **Salesforce DX Development Environment**: We've standardized on using Visual Studio Code with the Salesforce Extensions for Visual Studio Code throughout the book. To set up your development environment, please refer to Chapter 2, "Environment Setup," which walks through installing the Salesforce CLI, the Java Development Kit, Visual Studio Code, and the Salesforce Extensions for Visual Studio Code.
- **Authorized Dev Hub**: As we will be working with scratch orgs, packages, and package versions, an authorized Dev Hub org will be needed. Chapter 5, "Dev Hub," explains how to set one up. For the examples in this chapter, it is assumed that you have a Dev Hub org authorized with an alias of `MyDH`.
- **Git**: The sample application is hosted in a GitHub public repository. To be able to clone the repository, you need to install Git on your development computer. Chapter 9, "Version Control," shows how to install Git.

With these prerequisites in place, we can now create the Salesforce DX project by cloning the sample application's repository.

Creating the Salesforce DX Project

Rather than manually creating a Salesforce DX project for this chapter, we will clone the sample application's repository from GitHub, which already includes a project. Perform the following steps to create our project:

- Open a terminal application and change directory to where you would like to clone the sample application. Note that a subdirectory will be created in this directory during the cloning process that will have the same name as the repository (`SalesforceDXSampleApp`).
- Execute the following Git command to clone the repository (although the command is shown split across two lines, it should be entered on a single line):

```
git clone https://github.com/IvanHarris-↩
SalesforceDX-Book/SalesforceDXSampleApp.git
```

- Launch Visual Studio Code and open the `SalesforceDXSampleApp` directory using the **File ➤ Open Folder...** command.
- Open the integrated terminal and create a scratch org using the command:

```
sfdx force:org:create -s \
  -f ./config/project-scratch-def.json \
  -a MySO
```

- In the integrated terminal, push the sample app code to the scratch org:

```
sfdx force:source:push
```

- And then import the app's sample data:

```
sfdx force:data:tree:import \
  -f ./data/noplan-Account-Case.json
```

- [Optional] The sample app includes a Lightning web component and its Jest unit test. If you want to run the tests or create your own, execute the following command in the integrated terminal:

```
sfdx force:lightning:lwc:test:setup
```

- Open the scratch org:

```
sfdx force:org:open
```

- Click the App Launcher (⁝⁝⁝) and then open the **Sales** app.
- Click the **Accounts** tab, then the **Sample Account** account (note that you may have to change the list view to **All Accounts** to see the account).
- Click the **Setup** cog icon (⚙) and select **Edit Page** from the menu. This opens the App Builder.
- From the **Components** list, drag the **caseInfo** custom component onto the page.
- Click the **Save** button.
- In the Page Saved confirmation dialog, click the **Activate** button.
- In the Activation: Account Record Page dialog, click the **Assign as Org Default** button.
- Click the **Next** button in the Assign form factor dialog that appears.
- Click the **Save** button in the Review assignment dialog.
- Exit the Lightning App Builder by clicking the arrow button (←).

You should now be back on the Sample Account record page, where the sample app is on the page.

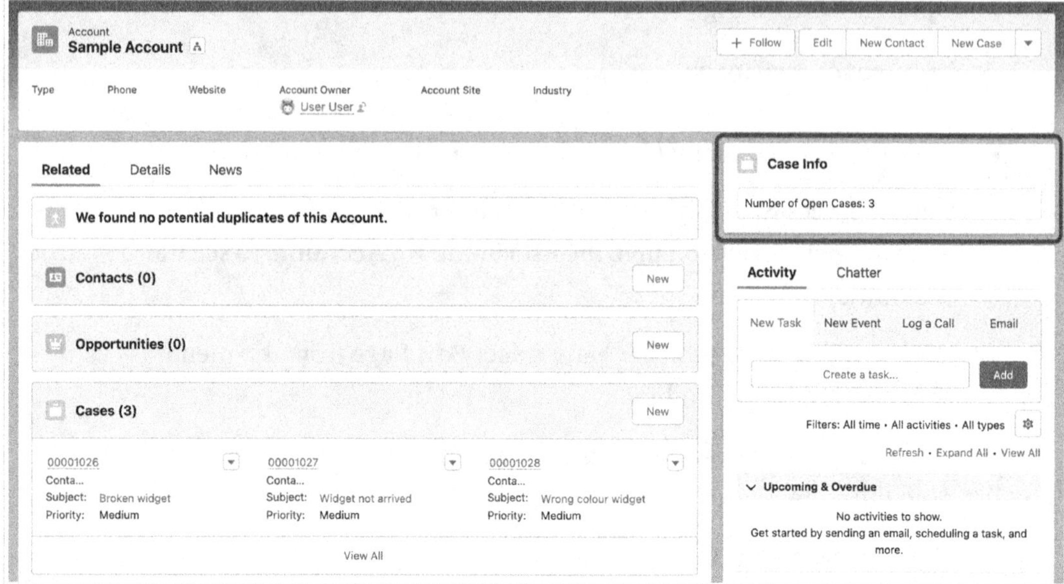

Figure 13-1. *Sample app on the Account record page*

The sample app is super simple and consists of

- A Lightning web component (LWC) that displays the number of open Case records related to an Account record. Although LWC test coverage is not enforced, a Jest unit test is included as best practice. The LWC files can be found in the Salesforce DX project directory:

  `./force-app/main/default/lwc/caseInfo`.

- An Apex class that queries for the number of open Case records that are related to an Account record. An Apex unit test is included to ensure that at least 75% of the class's code is tested, which is a requirement for deploying to a production org or when distributing an application via Salesforce's AppExchange enterprise marketplace. The Apex files can be found in the Salesforce DX project directory:

  `./force-app/main/default/classes`.

Our Salesforce DX project is now set up and ready for the chapter ahead.

We will now discuss namespaces, which are optional when creating unlocked packages and mandatory when creating second-generation managed packages.

Namespaces

Namespaces are identifiers consisting of 1–15 alphanumeric characters that are unique across all Salesforce orgs. When creating a namespaced unlocked package or a second-generation managed package (2GP), the namespace is added as a prefix to the package's API name and the API name of each component in the package. As namespaces are unique, this ensures that all API names associated with the package are also globally unique. This avoids any API name conflicts with other packages, packaged components, and unpackaged components in any Salesforce org. For example, if the following metadata components have been added to a production org:

- An unpackaged custom object called `ExampleObject__c`
- An unlocked package with the namespace `packageNS1`, which contains a custom object called `ExampleObject__c`
- A second-generation managed package with the namespace `packageNS2`, which contains a custom object called `ExampleObject__c`

The three objects can coexist in the org and are accessed using these API names, respectively:

- `ExampleObject__c`
- `packageNS1__ExampleObject__c`
- `packageNS2__ExampleObject__c`

When using scratch orgs as part of the development cycle for a namespaced unlocked package or a second-generation managed package, the Salesforce CLI asks the Dev Hub to create scratch orgs with an associated namespace. The Dev Hub can only create namespaced scratch orgs using a namespace that is registered in a namespace org that is linked to the Dev Hub. Multiple namespace orgs can be linked to a Dev Hub, and the Salesforce CLI asks the Dev Hub to create a new scratch org using one of those namespaces. The three steps to create and link a namespace org to a Dev Hub are as follows:

1. Create a namespace org.
2. Register a namespace in the namespace org.
3. Link the namespace org to the Dev Hub.

We'll start by creating a namespace org.

Creating a Namespace Org

A namespace org is a Developer Edition org with a registered namespace. If you don't have an org available, you can register for a free one at the following link:

- `https://developer.salesforce.com/signup`

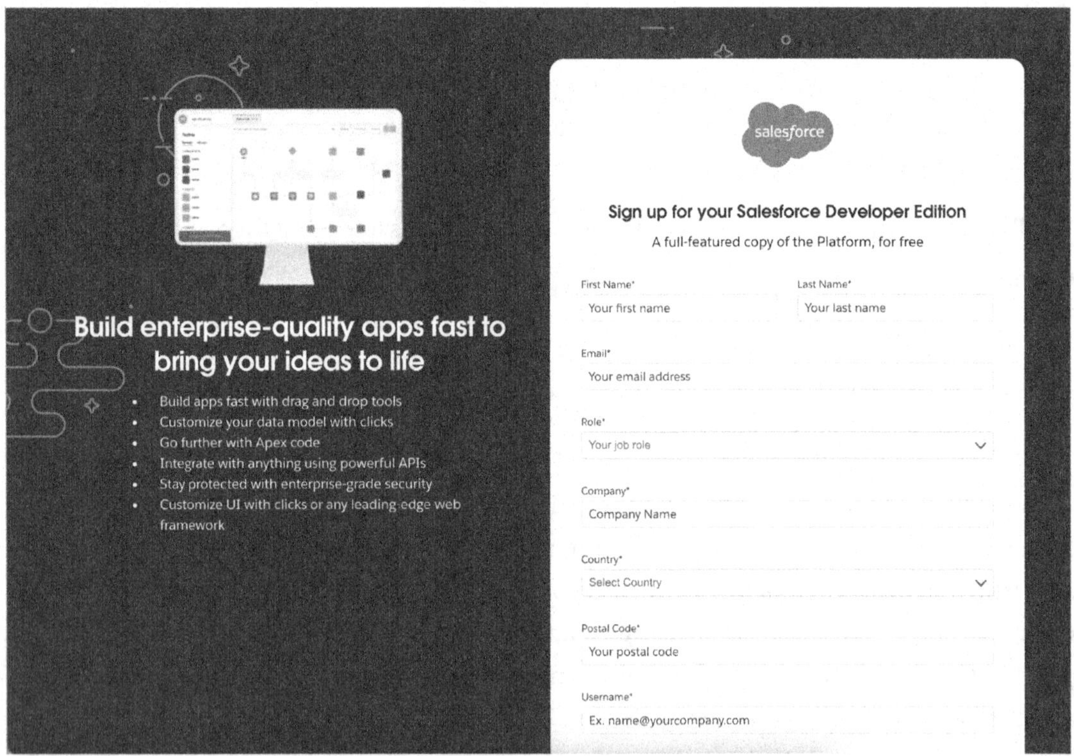

Figure 13-2. *Free Developer Edition org sign-up*

Enter your details in the form and click the **Sign me Up** button. Click the **Verify Account** button in the verification email that you will receive and enter your password. Make a note of the username in the verification email and the password that you choose, as you will need them later to (a) authorize the namespace org for use with Salesforce CLI and (b) when linking the namespace org to your Dev Hub.

Now that you have a new namespace org, the next step is to register a namespace in it.

Registering a Namespace

To simplify working with the namespace org that you created in the previous section, authorize the org with the Salesforce CLI and give it the alias `MyNS` by executing the following CLI command:

```
$ sfdx force:auth:web:login -a MyNS
```

When the Salesforce login screen appears, enter the username and password that you made a note of when registering the namespace org in the previous section. Next, click the **Allow** button to grant the CLI access to the org.

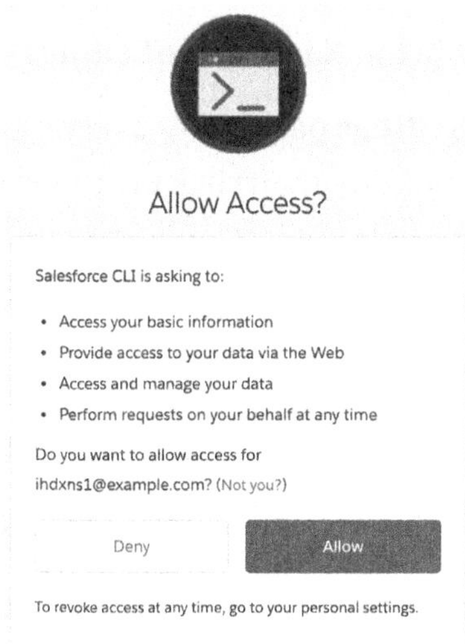

Figure 13-3. *Allow CLI access to the namespace org*

When opening any org for the first time, always click the **Allow** button in the Show notifications dialog that pops up as well.

Executing the `force:org:list` CLI command lists the authorized orgs, which should show the Dev Hub org, the namespace org, and the scratch org.

Listing 13-1. Authorized Dev Hub and namespace orgs

```
=== Orgs

     ALIAS   USERNAME              ORG ID             CONNECTED STATUS
───  ──────  ────────────────────  ─────────────────  ─────────────────
(D)  MyDH     ihdxdh@example.com   00D4K0000015OzMUAU Connected
     MyNS     ihdxns1@example.com  00D4K000000GJVfUAO Connected

     ALIAS   USERNAME                       ORG ID                EXPIRATION DATE
───  ──────  ─────────────────────────────  ──────────────────    ───────────────
(U)  MySO    test-5tdvz9nnngdx@example.com  00D0C0000000yPYUAY    2022-08-18
```

To register a namespace in the namespace org, follow these steps:

1. Open the namespace org, if it's not already open, by executing the CLI command: `force:org:open -u MyNS`.
2. Navigate to **Setup ➤ Apps ➤ Packaging ➤ Package Manager**.
3. Click the **Edit** button in the **Namespace Settings** section.
4. On the **Namespace Settings** page, enter a namespace name in the **Namespace** edit box and then click the **Check Availability** button. If the namespace is not available, try another one.
5. Click the **Review** button.
6. Click the **Save** button.

Note Once a namespace has been registered, it cannot be reused. Avoid registering a namespace that you might want to use later for production packages!

The Package Manager page will be displayed with the registered namespace included, like in the following screenshot.

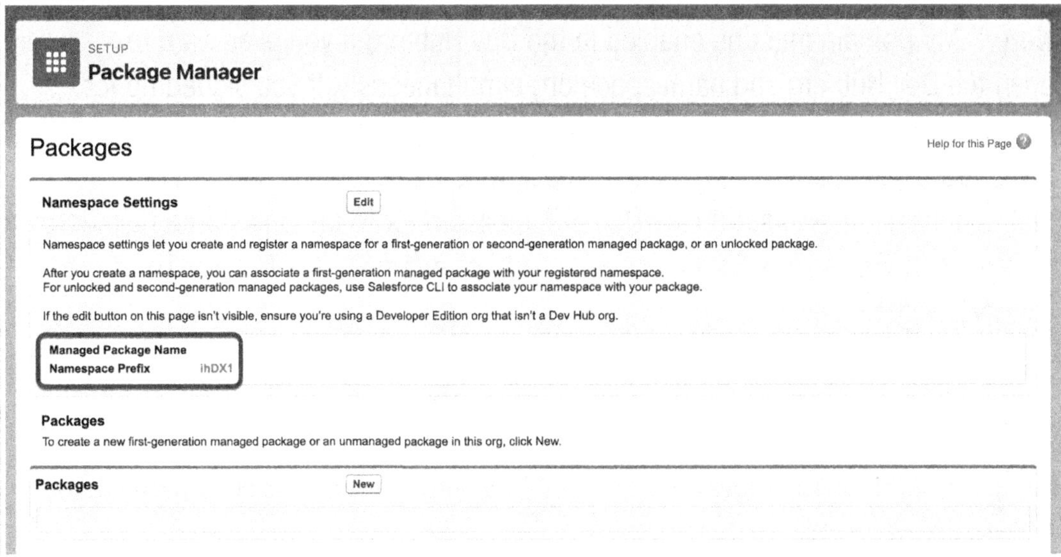

Figure 13-4. *Package Manager page with a registered namespace*

For the Salesforce CLI to use the registered namespace when creating scratch orgs, the namespace org needs to be linked to the Dev Hub; we will do this next.

Namespace Linking

By now, you know that the Salesforce CLI connects to a Dev Hub to create and manage scratch orgs on its behalf. For the Dev Hub to know what namespaces can be associated with scratch orgs, the namespace orgs where the namespaces are registered must be linked to the Dev Hub, which is performed in the Dev Hub org. The Salesforce CLI can then request the Dev Hub to create a scratch org with a registered namespace from one of the namespace orgs linked to the Dev Hub.

To link the namespace org to your Dev Hub, start by opening your Dev Hub org by executing the CLI command `force:org:open -u MyDH`.

Note My Domain must be enabled in the Dev Hub org if you ever want to open the Dev Hub org and namespace org simultaneously. If you signed up for a free 30-day Dev Hub trial org in Chapter 5, "Dev Hub," it is enabled by default. If you are using your own org, please check that My Domain is set up. For instructions on how to set up My Domain, please refer to the Salesforce help here: `https://help.salesforce.com/s/articleView?id=sf.domain_name_overview.htm`.

Navigate to **Setup ➤ Company Settings ➤ My Domain** and make a note of the domain name listed in the **My Domain Name** field of the **My Domain Details** section; you will need this to reauthorize the Dev Hub org with the Salesforce CLI so that it uses My Domain.

Click the App Launcher icon (⠿), then click the **View All** link and then the **Namespace Registries** link to open the Namespace Registries page. Click the **Link Namespace** button, as shown in the following, which will open a Salesforce login page where you log in to the namespace org that you want to link.

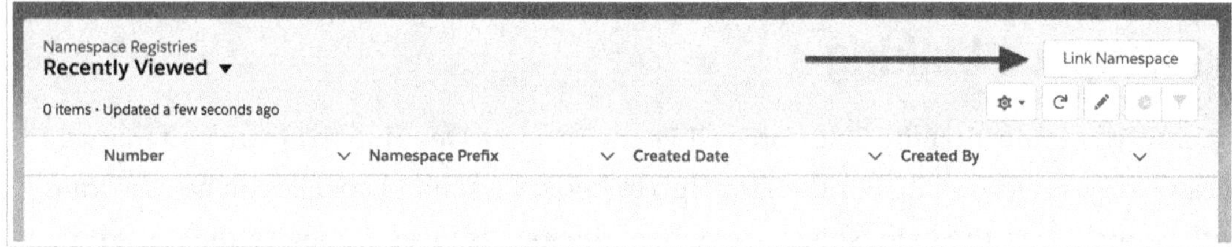

***Figure 13-5.** Namespace Registries page*

Note At the time of writing, there is a known issue where clicking the **Link Namespace** button opens a blank window in some Dev Hub orgs. If this issue affects you, then please follow the workaround notes described here: `https://success.salesforce.com/issues_view?id=a1p3A000000EFcgQAG`.

The steps are repeated here for your convenience:

1. Navigate to **Setup ➤ Apps ➤ App Manager**.
2. Click the **New Connected App** button and enter the following:

Name: `SalesforceDX Namespace Registry`

API Name: `DEVHUB_<some random string>`

Contact Email: `<your email>`

Enable OAuth Settings: `checked`

Callback URL: `https://<my-domain>.my.salesforce.com/environmenthub/soma-callback.apexp`

Selected OAuth Scopes: `Access and manage your data(api)` and `Access and manage your basic information(id, profile, email, address, phone)`

3. Click **Save**.

Where `<my-domain>` is the My Domain name of your Dev Hub org that you made a note of earlier.

Wait for two to ten minutes and then try to link namespace again; it should open a window prompting you to log in.

Enter the username and password for the namespace org that you created earlier in the login window that opens. In the Allow Access pop-up window that appears, click the **Allow** button to allow the Salesforce DX Namespace Registry access to the namespace org. The namespace registry is then listed in the Namespace Registries list view, as shown in the following. Note, you might have to select the **All Namespace Registries** list view.

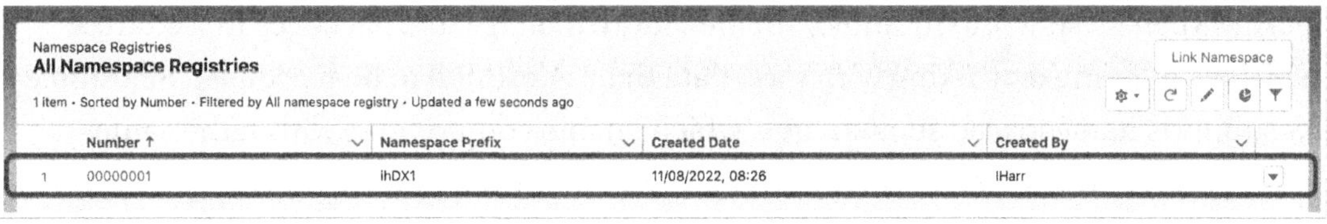

Figure 13-6. *Newly created namespace registry entry*

So that the CLI uses My Domain when logging in to the Dev Hub org, you now need to reauthorize the Dev Hub org using the following command, replacing <my-domain> with the Dev Hub org's **My Domain Name** that you made a note of earlier:

```
$ sfdx force:auth:web:login \
    --setalias MyDH \
    --setdefaultdevhubusername \
    --instanceurl https://<my-domain>.my.salesforce.com
```

Note that next time you open your Dev Hub org using the `force:org:open -u MyDH` CLI command, your My Domain can be seen in your browser's address bar.

With a namespace org linked to the Dev Hub, we can now use this setup to create a namespaced scratch org.

Namespaced Scratch Orgs

When developing a namespaced unlocked package or a second-generation managed package (2GP) using Salesforce DX, metadata components exist in unpackaged and packaged environments depending on which phase of the application development lifecycle you are in. For example, during the develop and test phases, metadata components are created or modified in a scratch org, which is an unpackaged environment. During the build, test, and release phases, the metadata is added to an unlocked package or second-generation managed package ready for integration testing, user acceptance testing, staging, and deployment as a single container. Occasionally, your code will need to reference metadata components using their fully qualified namespaced name when the component is packaged and without a namespace when unpackaged. Furthermore, unlocked packages and second-generation managed packages can be split into multiple, smaller, more manageable packages that share a namespace. To make working with metadata that is destined to be packaged, Salesforce DX supports namespaced scratch orgs, which enable components within the same namespace to be referenced consistently throughout the application development lifecycle, when the components are both unpackaged and packaged.

Note For those who have worked with namespaced first-generation managed packages for some time, this is a significant improvement. Before Salesforce DX and namespaced scratch orgs became available, special logic had to be written to access components in the managed package using its API name. If the component was running in a packaged environment, the namespace would be prefixed to the API name. If the component was running in a non-packaged environment, such as a Developer Edition org used for development and unit testing, the API name would be used for access without the namespace prefix.

To create a namespaced scratch org, the previously registered namespace must first be added to the Salesforce DX project's `sfdx-project.json` project configuration file by completing the following steps:

1. Launch Visual Studio Code if it's not already launched.
2. Open this chapter's `SalesforceDXSampleApp` project.
3. Open the project's `sfdx-project.json` project configuration file, which can be found in the project's root folder.
4. Update the `namespace` parameter's value to be the namespace that you registered earlier.
5. Save the file.

The project configuration file should resemble the following listing, where the updated namespace value is included; of course, the actual namespace will be the one that you registered in your namespace org earlier.

Listing 13-2. Adding a namespace to the project configuration file

```
{
  "packageDirectories": [
    {
      "path": "force-app",
      "default": true
    }
  ],
```

```
  "name": "SalesforceDXSampleApp",
  "namespace": "ihDX1",
  "sfdcLoginUrl": "https://login.salesforce.com",
  "sourceApiVersion": "53.0"
}
```

Any scratch orgs created using the Salesforce CLI from a command line within this project's directory hierarchy will have the `ihDX1` namespace associated with it. To see this in practice, and how the namespace is prefixed to metadata components, perform the following:

1. Open the `SalesforceDXSampleApp` project in VS Code.
2. Open the integrated terminal window using **Terminal ➤ New Terminal**.
3. If you created a scratch org with the alias `MySO` earlier in the project, delete it with the Salesforce CLI command `force:org:delete -u MySO`.
4. Create a new scratch org with an alias of `MySO` and set it as the org with the default username by executing the CLI command `force:org:create -a MySO -f ./config/project-scratch-def.json -s`.
5. Push the sample app metadata components to the scratch org using `force:source:push`.
6. Import the app's sample data with the command `force:data:tree:import \`

   `-f ./data/noplan-Account-Case.json`
7. Open the scratch org by executing the CLI command `force:org:open`.
8. Click **Allow** in the Show notifications window that appears the first time that you open the scratch org.
9. Navigate to **Setup ➤ Custom Code ➤ Apex Classes**.

The sample app's Apex class and unit test class can be seen as follows, where you will see that the namespace prefix is present. The Apex class name is now unique across all Salesforce orgs and can be accessed unambiguously.

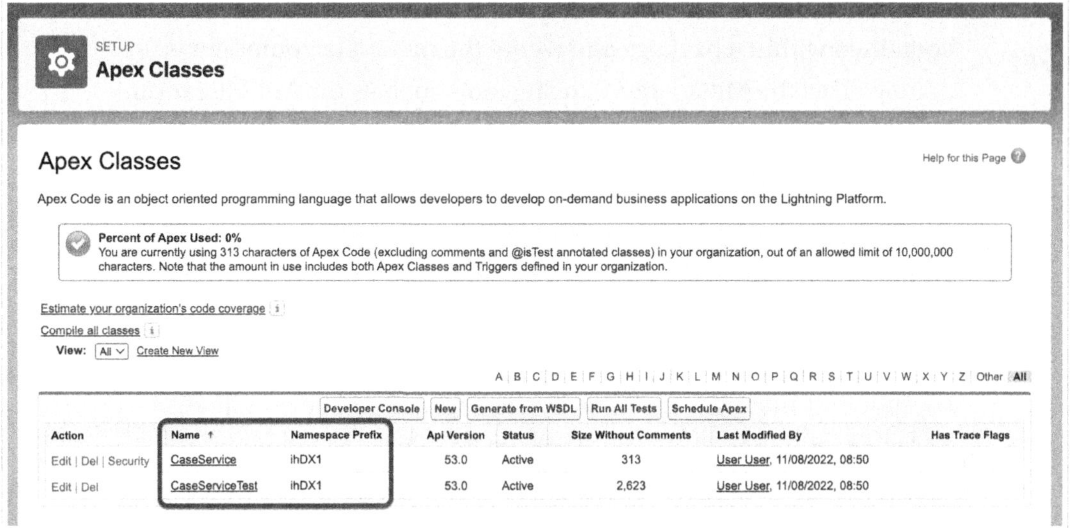

Figure 13-7. *Apex class namespace prefix*

Unlocked packages and second-generation managed packages are two of the six deployment options that are available. We'll explore all six in the next section to put the unlocked package and second-generation managed package deployment options into context.

Deployment Options

In Chapter 8, "Metadata," we learned how to use commands in the `force:source` and `force:mdapi` topics to synchronize metadata components between a local Salesforce DX project and a Salesforce org. We worked almost entirely with unpackaged metadata components, which is one of the six options available for deploying metadata components to a production org:

- **Change Sets**: Used to migrate metadata components between sandboxes and production orgs or between sandboxes that have been created from the same production org. Salesforce DX doesn't support change sets or the change set development model that will be discussed in the next section.

- **Unpackaged Metadata**: Metadata components that are not contained within a package and where the metadata components are deployed via the Metadata API using tools such as the Ant Migration Tool, Workbench, VS Code, and the Salesforce CLI. This deployment option is supported by Salesforce DX, as we discovered in Chapter 8, "Metadata."
- **Unmanaged Packages**: This package type was designed to distribute open source software or application templates to act as a starting point for a new application. Once installed in an org, any metadata components that were installed by the package can be modified; however, unmanaged packages cannot be upgraded as an older unmanaged package version must be uninstalled before installing a newer version, thereby losing any changes. This package type is not supported by Salesforce DX and should not be used to deploy metadata components to production orgs.
- **Unlocked Packages**: This package type is a compromise between unmanaged packages and managed packages. As with unmanaged packages, the metadata components that are added to a production org by installing an unlocked package can be modified. That said, like managed packages, unlocked packages support version upgrades, although any metadata components that have been changed will be overwritten when a later version of the unlocked package is installed. Leading practice is to add any changes to the unlocked package, rather than the org, and then perform an upgrade installation. Unlocked packages were introduced by Salesforce DX, and they are the recommended method to be used by internal development teams for deploying applications and customizations to a production org.
- **First-Generation Managed Packages (1GP)**: Used by Salesforce AppExchange partners when creating apps that are distributed via the Salesforce AppExchange enterprise marketplace. Managed packages act as a container for metadata components that can be deployed to a production org by installing the managed package. The metadata components can be removed from the production org by uninstalling the managed package. Managed packages are versioned,

meaning that you can upgrade an already installed package with a later version. The code is hidden to protect intellectual property, and some attributes cannot be changed to avoid breaking the app. Salesforce DX supports creating, viewing, and installing first-generation managed package versions; however, the package, from which a managed package version is created, cannot be created using the CLI - it must be created manually via the Setup area of a Packaging Org. A Packaging Org is a Developer Edition org with a managed package namespace configured.

- **Second-Generation Managed Packages (2GP)**: Introduced by Salesforce DX to take full advantage of the Salesforce CLI, source format metadata, scratch orgs, source tracking, and a version control system being the source of truth. Unlike first-generation managed packages, with second-generation managed packages, there is no need for Packaging Orgs. Multiple second-generation managed packages, with dependencies between them, can be mapped to separate package directories in a local Salesforce DX project, allowing metadata components to be partitioned into functionally related packages. The entire package development process can be executed from the Salesforce CLI and automated using scripting or continuous integration/continuous delivery.

Note Although Salesforce DX can bring benefits to the developers of first-generation managed packages, such as the use of source-tracked orgs for development and unit testing, we won't be covering them in this chapter as the development cycle is well established, and this package type cannot be developed end to end using the Salesforce CLI.

As mentioned in the introduction to this chapter, we will focus on developing unlocked packages and second-generation managed packages. As we will be using the package development model, we'll take a moment to describe all three application development models to understand how the package development model differs from the other two.

Application Development Models

Salesforce supports three different models for developing applications and customizations that are deployed to production orgs. Two of the models support the development of unpackaged metadata components, while the third supports the development of packaged metadata components. The three models are as follows:

- **Change Set Development Model**: Change sets are used by internal development teams to migrate unpackaged metadata components from a sandbox to a production org using outbound change sets, inbound change sets, and deployment connections. Change sets can also be used to move metadata components between two sandboxes that have been created from the same production org. With this development model, the production org is the source of truth. Development, unit testing, integration testing, QA, staging, UAT, and training sandboxes are all created directly from the production org, or indirectly via another sandbox created from the same production org, to mirror its shape. On the conclusion of the development lifecycle, the changes are released to the production org, which becomes the updated source of truth.
- **Org Development Model**: In this development model, a version control system, rather than the production org, becomes the source of truth. Tools such as the Ant Migration Tool, Workbench, VS Code, or the Salesforce CLI are used to move metadata components between the version control system and non-source-tracked orgs such as Developer Edition orgs, sandboxes (without source tracking enabled), and production orgs using the Metadata API. This model is typically used by internal development teams as an alternative to change sets and by developers of first-generation managed packages.
- **Package Development Model**: With this development model, the version control system remains the source of truth; however, in this instance, source-tracked orgs, including scratch orgs and Developer and Developer Pro sandboxes with source tracking enabled, are typically used when developing a package. This development model is used by internal development teams to create unlocked packages

and by teams creating second-generation managed packages (2GP) to distribute apps via the Salesforce AppExchange enterprise marketplace.

Note Although the org development model is described as typically using non-source-tracked orgs, and the package development model as typically using source-tracked orgs, it's not always as clear-cut as this. When designing your Salesforce DX–powered development lifecycle, you will discover the org types that work best for you and your specific needs.

We've set up our project, which includes a sample application. We've also looked at namespaces, deployment options, and application development models. We're now ready to get hands on and create unlocked packages and second-generation managed packages by walking through the development lifecycle.

Package Development Walk-Through

As we saw earlier in the "Deployment Options" and "Application Development Models" sections, the change set deployment option combined with the change set development model, or the unpackaged metadata deployment option combined with the org development model, is used to develop and deploy applications or customizations to a Salesforce org as unpackaged metadata components. To deploy metadata components in a versioned, upgradeable container of related components, the unlocked package deployment option or the second-generation managed package (2GP) deployment option combined with the package development model can be used.

Some benefits of working with unlocked packages or second-generation managed packages and the package development model include the following:

- The version control system is the source of truth, providing a repository of metadata components that teams of developers can collaborate on with an audit trail of all changes.
- Applications and customizations are organized into packages of related functionality. Grouping related functionality into highly cohesive containers that are loosely coupled to other containers is good practice to reduce complexity and improve agility.

- A team can focus on their own package's functionality by loading the metadata components from that package, and any packages that their package depends on, into an org and work without the distraction of unrelated metadata components.
- When inspecting packages that are installed in a production org, it's easy to view the contained metadata components. This association greatly simplifies root cause analysis if a package version introduces an issue when it is deployed.
- Unlocked packages and second-generation managed packages are versioned, which allows them to be upgraded by installing a later version of the package.

In this section, we're going to walk through a typical package development model lifecycle. The lifecycle is largely the same for both unlocked packages and second-generation packages, so when "package" is mentioned, it refers to both package types. If there are activities that are specific to one of the package types, it will be called out explicitly.

We're going to create two dependent packages, which uses the concept of package directories. The next section will illustrate how to restructure our Salesforce DX project to use multiple package directories.

Package Directories

Package directories make it easy to group related metadata components in a Salesforce DX project, where each package directory contains the source format files for the components to be bundled into a package. When a new Salesforce DX project is created, a single package directory called `force-app` is added. The sample application that was cloned in the section "Creating the Salesforce DX Project" earlier in the chapter uses the out-of-the-box `force-app` package directory for its source files, which can be seen by inspecting the `SalesforceDXSampleApp` project directories.

Listing 13-3. Default package directory structure

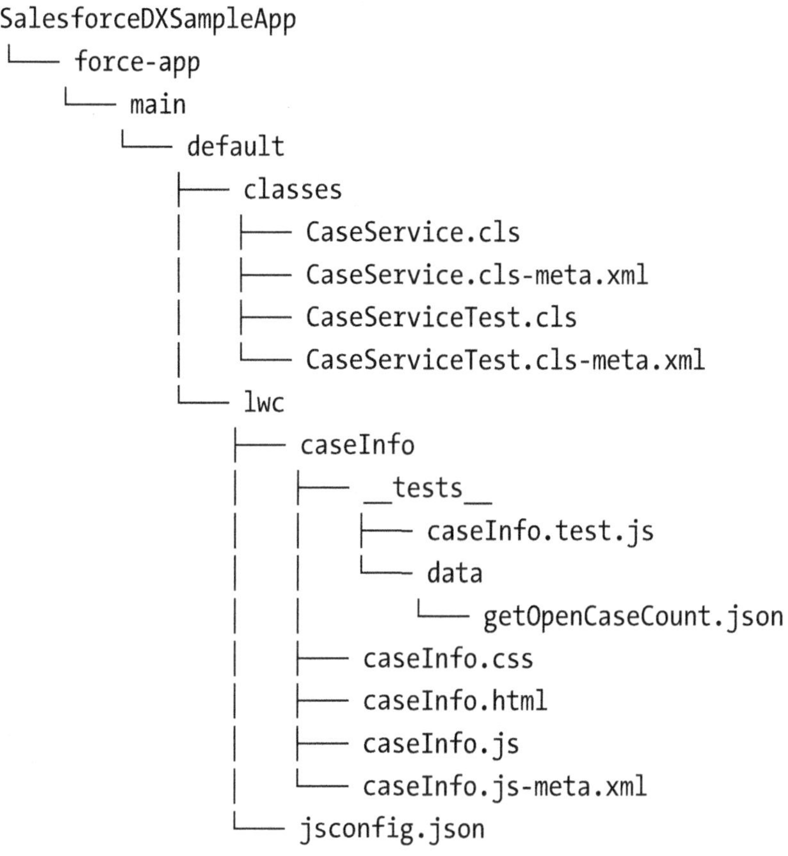

```
SalesforceDXSampleApp
└── force-app
    └── main
        └── default
            ├── classes
            │   ├── CaseService.cls
            │   ├── CaseService.cls-meta.xml
            │   ├── CaseServiceTest.cls
            │   └── CaseServiceTest.cls-meta.xml
            └── lwc
                ├── caseInfo
                │   ├── __tests__
                │   │   ├── caseInfo.test.js
                │   │   └── data
                │   │       └── getOpenCaseCount.json
                │   ├── caseInfo.css
                │   ├── caseInfo.html
                │   ├── caseInfo.js
                │   └── caseInfo.js-meta.xml
                └── jsconfig.json
```

The `lwc` directory contains the sample application's Lightning web component (LWC), and the `classes` directory contains an Apex class that the LWC uses to retrieve information about an account's Case records.

Note Please refer to the section "Creating the Salesforce DX Project" for a description of the sample application.

As we saw when working with source format files for metadata components in Chapter 8, "Metadata," synchronizing components between a local Salesforce DX project and a Salesforce org will use this package directory for local component storage. We could also use this single package directory structure to create a single unlocked package or a single second-generation managed package (2GP). Having said that, we're about to create two packages, one for the Lightning web component and one for the Apex class, to show how to create multiple packages with dependencies. In readiness, restructure the package directories in your `SalesforceDXSampleApp` Salesforce DX project into the following structure.

Listing 13-4. Multiple package directories

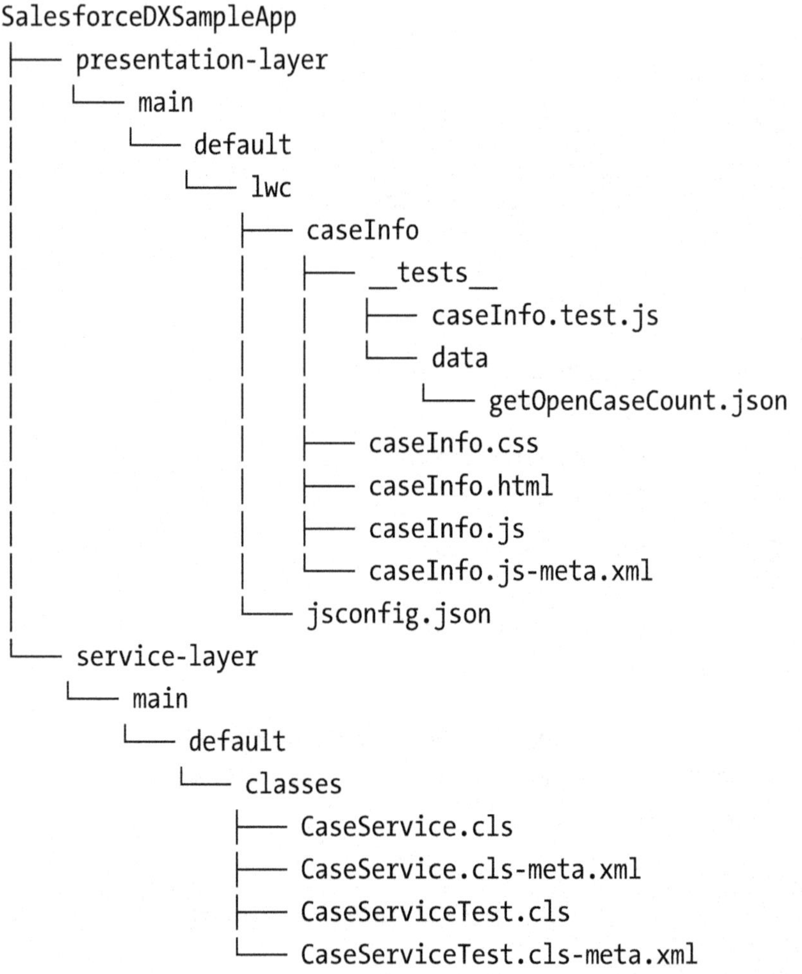

```
SalesforceDXSampleApp
├── presentation-layer
│   └── main
│       └── default
│           └── lwc
│               ├── caseInfo
│               │   ├── __tests__
│               │   │   ├── caseInfo.test.js
│               │   │   └── data
│               │   │       └── getOpenCaseCount.json
│               │   ├── caseInfo.css
│               │   ├── caseInfo.html
│               │   ├── caseInfo.js
│               │   └── caseInfo.js-meta.xml
│               └── jsconfig.json
└── service-layer
    └── main
        └── default
            └── classes
                ├── CaseService.cls
                ├── CaseService.cls-meta.xml
                ├── CaseServiceTest.cls
                └── CaseServiceTest.cls-meta.xml
```

The `force-app` package directory has been replaced by two package directories:

- **`service-layer`**: Which contains the Apex class
- **`presentation-layer`**: Which contains the Lightning web component

Below each package directory, the subdirectories must include `/main/default` in the path after the parent package directory and before the individual metadata component directories such as `classes` and `lwc`. This maintains the standard Salesforce DX directory structure.

After the package directories have been restructured, the `sfdx-project.json` project configuration file must be updated to reflect the new structure, as in the following.

Listing 13-5. Updated `sfdx-project.json` package directories

```
{
  "packageDirectories": [
    {
      "path": "service-layer",
      "default": true
    },
    {
      "path": "presentation-layer"
    }
  ],
  "name": "SalesforceDXSampleApp",
  "namespace": "ihDX1",
  "sfdcLoginUrl": "https://login.salesforce.com",
  "sourceApiVersion": "53.0"
}
```

Even when working with unpackaged components, package directories are a very useful method for organizing your components. With the preceding directory structure, changes to components in the Salesforce DX project are synchronized with a Salesforce org when using the `force:source:push` or `force:source:deploy` commands. Changes to components in a Salesforce org are synchronized with the source format files in the local package directories when the `force:source:pull` or `force:source:retrieve` commands are executed. Source format metadata files for new components that are created in a Salesforce org are always added to the default package directory when they are pulled or retrieved; however, the files can then be moved to the correct package directory where they will be synchronized thereafter.

With the package directories in place, we will create the two packages in the next section.

Creating Packages

In this section, we are going to create two packages:

- **CI - Svc**: This is the base package containing the Apex class from the `service-layer` package directory in the `SalesforceDXSampleApp` Salesforce DX project that we created earlier.
- **CI - Pres**: This package contains the Lightning web component from the `presentation-layer` package directory. It uses the Apex class in the base package.

To create the packages, open the `SalesforceDXSampleApp` project and execute the following two commands using the integrated terminal to create unlocked packages:

```
$ sfdx force:package:create \
    --name "CI - Svc" \
    --path service-layer \
    --packagetype Unlocked
```

```
$ sfdx force:package:create \
    --name "CI - Pres" \
    --path presentation-layer \
    --packagetype Unlocked
```

If you wanted to create second-generation managed packages instead, execute the following two commands:

```
$ sfdx force:package:create \
    --name "CI - Svc" \
    --path service-layer \
    --packagetype Managed
```

```
$ sfdx force:package:create \
    --name "CI - Pres" \
    --path presentation-layer \
    --packagetype Managed
```

The only difference between the two pairs of commands is the value passed to the `--packagetype|-t` parameter, which determines what type of package should be created.

The `force:package:create` command parameters are as follows:

- `--description|-d`: The package's description that is displayed when viewing installed packages in an org. [Optional]
- `--nonamespace|-e`: Only used for unlocked packages, not second-generation managed packages. Creates an unlocked package without a namespace, typically used when packaging existing metadata components. It's recommended that a namespace is used when packaging new metadata components. [Optional]
- `--name|-n`: The package's name, which must be unique in the namespace. [Required]
- `--errornotificationusername|-o`: The username of an active Dev Hub user who will receive email notifications when unhandled Apex exceptions occur or when issues happen when installing, upgrading, or uninstalling the package. [Optional]
- `--path|-r`: The path to the package directory containing the source format metadata component files that will be added to the package. The path is relative to the Salesforce DX project's root directory. [Required]
- `--packagetype|-t`: The type of package to create. [Required]
- Allowed values are as follows:
    - `Unlocked`: Creates an unlocked package
    - `Managed`: Creates a second-generation managed package (2GP)
- `--targetdevhubusername|-v`: The username or alias of the Dev Hub org that will create the package. [Optional]
- `--orgdependent`: Only used for unlocked packages, not second-generation managed packages. When creating unlocked packages, this parameter specifies that the packaged metadata components depend on unpackaged metadata components in the production org. Packaging the "happy soup" of unmanaged metadata components that exist in a mature production org is often done in phases, which means that until all components are packaged there will be dependencies on unpackaged components in the org. [Optional]

- `--apiversion, --json, --loglevel`: Please refer to the discussion on global parameters in the section "Command-Line Parameters and Arguments" in Chapter 4, "Salesforce CLI."

When each of the `force:package:create` commands completes, it outputs a successful package creation message.

Listing 13-6. Create package command outputs

```
sfdx-project.json has been updated.
Successfully created a package. 0Ho4K000000CarySAC
=== Ids
 Name         Value
 ──────────   ────────────────────
 Package Id  0Ho4K000000CarySAC

sfdx-project.json has been updated.
Successfully created a package. 0Ho4K000000Cas3SAC
=== Ids
 Name         Value
 ──────────   ────────────────────
 Package Id  0Ho4K000000Cas3SAC
```

Notice that the first line of the output states `sfdx-project.json has been updated.` Inspecting the project configuration file shows that it has been updated, as an be seen in the following listing.

Listing 13-7. Updated `sfdx-project.json` after creating packages

```
{
    "packageDirectories": [
        {
            "path": "service-layer",
            "default": true,
            "package": "CI - Svc",
            "versionName": "ver 0.1",
            "versionNumber": "0.1.0.NEXT"
        },
```

```
        {
            "path": "presentation-layer",
            "package": "CI - Pres",
            "versionName": "ver 0.1",
            "versionNumber": "0.1.0.NEXT",
            "default": false
        }
    ],
    "name": "SalesforceDXSampleApp",
    "namespace": "ihDX1",
    "sfdcLoginUrl": "https://login.salesforce.com",
    "sourceApiVersion": "53.0",
    "packageAliases": {
        "CI - Svc": "0Ho4K000000CarySAC",
        "CI - Pres": "0Ho4K000000Cas3SAC"
    }
}
```

The Salesforce CLI has added the following parameters to the packageDirectories elements:

- **package**: The name of the package that was specified using the force:package:create's --name|-n parameter.
- **versionName**: A friendly version name that will be used when creating a package version later. If a version name is not provided, the Salesforce CLI will use the version number as the version name.
- **versionNumber**: Version number in major.minor.patch.build format that will be used when creating a package version later. The NEXT keyword instructs the Salesforce CLI to automatically increment the build number when a new package version is created.

The CLI has also added a packageAliases object with name:value pairs providing friendly aliases for the Ids of the created packages. Either the alias, such as CI - Svc, or its Id, such as 0Ho4K000000CarySAC, can be passed to commands in the force:package topic that require a --package|-p parameter.

Note Search for "Project Configuration File for Packages" in the Salesforce DX Developer Guide to learn about all the configuration file parameters for creating unlocked and second-generation managed packages.

To view all of the packages that a Dev Hub has created, use the `force:package:list` command as described in the next section.

Listing Packages

After the packages have been created, execute the following command to view all the packages that the Dev Hub has created:

```
$ sfdx force:package:list
```

The command's parameters are as follows:

- `--targetdevhubusername|-v`: The username or alias of the Dev Hub org that has created the packages that we wish to list. [Optional]
- `--apiversion, --json, --loglevel, --verbose`: Please refer to the discussion on global parameters in the section "Command-Line Parameters and Arguments" in Chapter 4, "Salesforce CLI."

The command's output should resemble the following.

Listing 13-8. Listing a Dev Hub's created packages

```
=== Packages [2]
 Namespace Prefix Name       Id                   Alias      Description Type
 ──────────────── ────────── ──────────────────── ────────── ─────────── ─────────
 ihDX1            CI - Pres  0Ho4K000000Cas3SAC CI - Pres              Unlocked
 ihDX1            CI - Svc   0Ho4K000000CarySAC CI - Svc               Unlocked
```

In this instance, best practice hasn't been followed when creating metadata components as a description has not been provided, which we will fix now.

Updating Packages

After a package has been created, it's possible to change the package description, package name, and the user who will receive error messages by using the `force:package:update` command. For example, to add descriptions for the two packages, execute the following commands:

```
$ sfdx force:package:update \
    --description "Svc Layer" \
    --package "CI - Svc"
```

```
$ sfdx force:package:update \
    --description "Pres Layer" \
    --package "CI - Pres"
```

The `force:package:update` parameters are as follows:

- `--description|-d`: The new package description. [Optional]
- `--name|-n`: The new package name. [Optional]
- `--errornotificationusername|-o`: The new username of an active Dev Hub user who will receive error email notifications. [Optional]
- `--package|-p`: The alias or Id of the package to update. [Required]
- `--targetdevhubusername|-v`: The username or alias of the Dev Hub org that created the package to be updated. [Optional]
- `--apiversion, --json, --loglevel`: Please refer to the discussion on global parameters in the section "Command-Line Parameters and Arguments" in Chapter 4, "Salesforce CLI."

Running the `force:package:list` command again shows that the descriptions have been added.

Listing 13-9. Updated package descriptions

```
=== Packages [2]
 Namespace Prefix Name       Id                  Alias      Description Type
 ──────────────── ────────── ─────────────────── ────────── ─────────── ────────
 ihDX1            CI - Pres  0Ho4K000000Cas3SAC CI - Pres  Pres Layer  Unlocked
 ihDX1            CI - Svc   0Ho4K000000CarySAC CI - Svc   Svc Layer   Unlocked
```

Of course, we would normally provide more comprehensive descriptions; brief descriptions have been used to make the listing easier to read.

Before we create package versions for the two packages that we have created, we first need to define the dependency between the two packages.

Establishing Package Dependencies

Before we can create package versions for the two packages that we created in the previous section, we need to define the dependency between the two packages. The base package, called `CI - Svc`, contains an Apex class that is used by the extension package, called `CI - Pres`. After you create a base package version, you will receive an error when creating the extension package version as it doesn't know where to find the Apex class. To overcome this, the `sfdx-project.json` project configuration file must be updated to define the dependency. The required update is highlighted in this listing.

Listing 13-10. Project configuration file package dependencies

```
{
    "packageDirectories": [
        {
            "path": "service-layer",
            "default": true,
            "package": "CI - Svc",
            "versionName": "ver 0.1",
            "versionNumber": "0.1.0.NEXT"
        },
```

```
        {
            "path": "presentation-layer",
            "package": "CI - Pres",
            "versionName": "ver 0.1",
            "versionNumber": "0.1.0.NEXT",
            "default": false,
            "dependencies": [
                {
                    "package": "CI - Svc",
                    "versionNumber": "0.1.0.LATEST"
                }
            ]
        }
    ],
    "name": "SalesforceDXSampleApp",
    "namespace": "ihDX1",
    "sfdcLoginUrl": "https://login.salesforce.com",
    "sourceApiVersion": "53.0",
    "packageAliases": {
        "CI - Svc": "0Ho4K000000CarySAC",
        "CI - Pres": "0Ho4K000000Cas3SAC"
    }
}
```

The preceding dependencies parameter specifies that the CI - Pres package has a dependency on version number 0.1.0.LATEST of the package with the name CI - Svc. Package version numbers follow the format major.minor.patch.build, and using the LATEST keyword ensures that the dependency is on the latest build.

Note Rather than using the package name and version number in the dependencies parameter of the preceding listing, the package version alias can be used, such as "package": "CI - Svc@0.1.0-134"; however, we don't have any package versions yet.

Before we can create package versions for second-generation managed packages, there's an additional task that we need to take care of; namely, package ancestors need to be defined.

Defining Package Ancestry

The package ancestry feature is specific to second-generation managed packages and is not relevant for unlocked packages. Package ancestry determines the allowed upgrade paths that a subscriber can follow when installing package versions.

When creating second-generation managed package versions, it's mandatory that either the `ancestorVersion` parameter or the `ancestorId` parameter is included in the `sfdx-project.json` project configuration file to define a package version's ancestor.

By default, second-generation managed packages use linear package versioning, which is the same method used by first-generation managed packages. With linear versioning, each package version's ancestor is the highest package version that has been promoted to released status prior to the current package version being created.

Note We'll be covering how to promote beta package versions to released status later in the chapter.

The following figure illustrates that the ancestor for package versions Version 1.1 (Beta 1) and Version 1.1 (Beta 2) is Version 1.0 (Released) and that therefore a path exists for subscribers to upgrade from Version 1.0 (Released) to Version 1.1 (Released). The ancestor for package versions Version 1.2 (Beta 1), Version 1.2 (Beta 2), and Version 1.2 (Beta 3) is Version 1.1 (Released), and therefore there's an upgrade path from Version 1.1 (Released) to Version 1.2 (Released).

Figure 13-8. *Linear package versioning*

To maintain this default behavior, use the `HIGHEST` keyword for the `ancestorVersion` or `ancestorId` parameter's value in the `sfdx-project.json` project configuration file, as in the following listing. Using this keyword ensures that the package ancestor is always set to the highest released package version.

Listing 13-11. Project configuration file package ancestry

```
{
    "packageDirectories": [
        {
            "path": "service-layer",
            "default": true,
            "package": "CI - Svc",
            "versionName": "ver 0.1",
            "versionNumber": "0.1.0.NEXT",
            "ancestorVersion": "HIGHEST"
        },
        {
            "path": "presentation-layer",
            "package": "CI - Pres",
            "versionName": "ver 0.1",
```

```
            "versionNumber": "0.1.0.NEXT",
            "ancestorVersion": "HIGHEST",
            "default": false,
            "dependencies": [
                {
                    "package": "CI - Svc",
                    "versionNumber": "0.1.0.LATEST"
                }
            ]
        }
    ],
    "name": "SalesforceDXSampleApp",
    "namespace": "ihDX1",
    "sfdcLoginUrl": "https://login.salesforce.com",
    "sourceApiVersion": "53.0",
    "packageAliases": {
        "CI - Svc": "0Ho4K000000CarySAC",
        "CI - Pres": "0Ho4K000000Cas3SAC"
    }
}
```

Second-generation managed packages support nonlinear versioning, where a package version's ancestor doesn't have to be the highest released version. Consider the following scenario, where you discover that Version 1.1 (Released) contains unanticipated regression bugs when customers install the package version. In this situation, you don't want to use Version 1.1 (Released) as the ancestor for the package versions Version 1.2 (Beta 1), Version 1.2 (Beta 2), and Version 1.2 (Beta 3); rather, you want Version 1.0 (Released) to be the ancestor and for the upgrade path to be from Version 1.0 (Released) to Version 1.2 (Released).

Figure 13-9. *Nonlinear package versioning*

Note This is a simplistic example. Nonlinear package versioning allows you to branch package versions, rather than simply skipping linear versions. Refer to the Salesforce DX Developer Guide for branching examples: `https://developer.salesforce.com/docs/atlas.en-us.sfdx_dev.meta/sfdx_dev`.

To define an ancestor that is not the highest released version, use one of the following methods to set parameters in the `sfdx-project.json` project configuration file:

- Set the `ancestorVersion` parameter to a specific package version number, such as `"1.0.0"`.
- Set the `ancestorId` parameter to a specific package version Id, such as `"04t8d000000PzyjAAC"`.
- Set the `ancestorId` parameter to a specific package version alias, such as `"CI - Svc@0.1.0-1"`.

- Set the `ancestorVersion` parameter or the `ancestorId` parameter to the keyword `NONE`. Subscribers cannot upgrade to released package versions that do not have an ancestor defined, so only use this keyword for either beta packages or for released packages that can only be installed in a subscriber's org where a previous version does not exist.

When creating a package version, the Salesforce CLI assumes that the package ancestor is the highest released version. If any of the preceding methods are used to override the default linear versioning behavior, use the `force:package:version:create` command's `--skipancestorcheck` parameter.

Note Of course, until the first package version has been promoted to released status, there is no package ancestor available, in which case set the `ancestorVersion` parameter or the `ancestorId` parameter to `NONE`. There's no need to add the `--skipancestorcheck` parameter to the `force:package:version:create` command as there is no ancestry to check in this instance.

With our package dependencies defined and package ancestors specified for second-generation managed packages, we'll now see how to create a package version.

Creating Package Versions

To build the base package version, launch Visual Studio Code, open this chapter's `SalesforceDXSampleApp` Salesforce DX project, and enter the following command in the integrated terminal from the project's root folder:

```
$ sfdx force:package:version:create \
    --installationkey abc124 \
    --package "CI - Svc"
```

The full list of parameters that can be used with the `force:package:version:create` command is as follows:

- `--versionname|-a`: Overrides the package version name that is specified in the `sfdx-project.json` project configuration file's `versionName` parameter. [Optional]
- `--branch|-b`: When the package version's metadata components are associated with a version control system branch, you have the option to specify the branch name using this parameter. The branch name is then appended to the package version alias, such as "`CI - Svc @6.0.1.34-Utils`" to aid visibility. This parameter overrides the branch that is specified in the `sfdx-project.json` project configuration file's `branch` parameter. [Optional]
- `--codecoverage|-c`: Calculates the code coverage for the Apex classes included in the package version to be created. Package versions can only be promoted to released status if code coverage is calculated and the Apex tests meet or exceed the 75% coverage requirement. [Optional] [Default: No code coverage is calculated.]
- `--path|-d`: The path to the package directory containing the package's metadata components. Either the `--package|-p` parameter or the `--path|-d` parameter must be provided, but not both. [Optional]
- `--versiondescription|-e`: Overrides the package version description that is specified in the `sfdx-project.json` project configuration file's `versionDescription` parameter. [Optional]
- `--definitionfile|-f`: If the package version's metadata components depend on a target org's features and settings, provide a path to a configuration file, which is like a scratch org definition file, where the dependencies are defined. [Optional]
- `--installationkey|-k`: Provides a key that must be entered when installing the package. Either the `--installationkeybypass|-x` or the `--installationkey|-k` parameter must be provided, but not both. [Optional]
- `--versionnumber|-n`: Overrides the package version number that is specified in the `sfdx-project.json` project configuration file's `versionNumber` parameter. [Optional]

- `--package|-p`: The alias or Id of the package to create a package version for. Either the `--package|-p` parameter or the `--path|-d` must be provided, but not both. [Optional]
- `--tag|-t`: Tag package versions using the version control system's tag to provide traceability to the commit for the package's metadata components. [Optional]
- `--targetdevhubusername|-v`: The username or alias of the Dev Hub org where the package version will be created. [Optional]
- `--wait|-w`: The amount of time in minutes that the `force:package:version:create` command will wait for the org to be created before timing out. Use a value of `0` to cause the command to return immediately and then use the `force:package:version:create:report` command to check the creation status. [Optional] [Default: `0`]
- `--installationkeybypass|-x`: Bypasses the need to enter an installation key when installing the package, meaning that the package can be installed by anyone. Either the `--installationkeybypass|-x` or the `--installationkey|-k` parameter must be provided, but not both. [Optional]
- `--postinstallscript`: For second-generation managed packages only. The package's Apex class that is executed after the managed package is installed or upgraded. [Optional]
- `--postinstallurl`: URL for the package version's postinstall instructions. [Optional]
- `--releasenotesurl`: URL for the package version's release notes. [Optional]
- `--skipancestorcheck`: For second-generation managed packages only. When the ancestor for the package version that is being created is not the highest released package version, use this parameter. [Optional]

- `--skipvalidation`: Used to skip the validation of dependencies, package ancestors, and metadata to speed up the time it takes to create a version; that said, only validated package versions can be promoted to released status. The `--skipvalidation` or the `--codecoverage|-c` parameter can be specified, but not both. [Optional]
- `--uninstallscript`: For second-generation managed packages only. The package's Apex class that is executed after the managed package is uninstalled. [Optional]
- `--apiversion, --json, --loglevel`: Please refer to the discussion on global parameters in the section "Command-Line Parameters and Arguments" in Chapter 4, "Salesforce CLI."

Because the `--wait|-w` parameter was omitted, the default value of `0` minutes was used, causing the command to return control to the integrated terminal immediately while the command executes asynchronously. To execute the command synchronously and wait for it to complete, specify a larger value for the `--wait|-w` parameter. The output from the command looks like this.

Listing 13-12. Package version create output

```
Package version creation request status is 'Queued'. Run "sfdx force:packag
e:version:create:report -i 08c4K000000CbUFQA0" to query for status.
```

As instructed by the command output, use the `force:package:version:create:report` command to monitor when the package version has been created.

```
$ sfdx force:package:version:create:report \
    --packagecreaterequestid 08c4K000000CbUFQA0
```

This command can take the following parameters:

- `--packagecreaterequestid|-i`: The package version request Id that is returned by the `force:package:version:create` command. [Required]
- `--targetdevhubusername|-v`: The username or alias of the Dev Hub org where the package version is being created. [Optional]

- `--apiversion, --json, --loglevel`: Please refer to the discussion on global parameters in the section "Command-Line Parameters and Arguments" in Chapter 4, "Salesforce CLI."

The following list shows the command output after the package version has been created. It includes the `Subscriber Package Version Id` that is used to install the package.

Listing 13-13. Package version create request output

```
=== Package Version Create Request
 Name                          Value
 ───────────────────────────── ────────────────────────────────────────────
 ID                            08c4K000000CbUFQA0
 Status                        Success
 Package Id                    0Ho4K000000CarySAC
 Package Version Id            05i4K000000CayzQAC
 Subscriber Package Version Id 04t4K000002FUEGQA4
 Tag
 Branch
 Created Date                  2022-08-11 11:45
 Installation URL              ↩
  https://login.salesforce.com/packaging/installPackage.apexp?p0=04t4K00000
  2FUEGQA4
 Created By                    0054K000000iHmtQAE
```

The output includes the following information:

- **`ID`**: The package version create request Id that was returned by the `force:package:version:create` command and used by the `force:package:version:create:report` command to monitor the creation status
- **`Status`**: The package version creation status
- **`Package Id`**: The Id of the package that the package version was created for
- **`Package Version Id`**: The Id for the created package version

- **Subscriber Package Version Id**: The Id to be used for installing the package version in a Salesforce org
- **Tag/Branch**: The version control system tag and branch information that was provided to the package version create command
- **Created Date**: The date and time that the package version was created
- **Created By**: The Id of the Dev Hub user who created the package version

When the package version has been created, the Salesforce CLI updates the `sfdx-project.json` project configuration file with the project version's alias and Id.

Listing 13-14. Package version alias and Id updates

```
{
    "packageDirectories": [
        {
            "path": "service-layer",
            "default": true,
            "package": "CI - Svc",
            "versionName": "ver 0.1",
            "versionNumber": "0.1.0.NEXT"
        },
        {
            "path": "presentation-layer",
            "package": "CI - Pres",
            "versionName": "ver 0.1",
            "versionNumber": "0.1.0.NEXT",
            "default": false,
            "dependencies": [
                {
                    "package": "CI - Svc",
                    "versionNumber": "0.1.0.LATEST"
                }
            ]
```

```
        }
    ],
    "name": "SalesforceDXSampleApp",
    "namespace": "ihDX1",
    "sfdcLoginUrl": "https://login.salesforce.com",
    "sourceApiVersion": "53.0",
    "packageAliases": {
        "CI - Svc": "0Ho4K000000CarySAC",
        "CI - Pres": "0Ho4K000000Cas3SAC",
        "CI - Svc@0.1.0-1": "04t4K000002FUEGQA4"
    }
}
```

Note At the time of writing, executing the `force:package:version:create` command asynchronously followed by executing the `force:package:version:create:report` command does not automatically update the `sfdx-project.json` project configuration file; I therefore updated the file manually using the `Subscriber Package Version Id` returned by the `force:package:version:create:report` command.

To run the package version create command synchronously, execute the following command:

```
$ sfdx force:package:version:create \
    --installationkey abc124 \
    --package "CI - Svc" \
    --wait 10
```

Providing the `--wait 10` parameter causes the command to return control to the integrated terminal once the package version has been completed. The command displays updates and then displays the success status.

Listing 13-15. Synchronous package version create command output

```
Request in progress. Sleeping 30 seconds. Will wait a total of 600 more
seconds before timing out. Current Status='Queued'
Request in progress. Sleeping 30 seconds. Will wait a total of 570 more
seconds before timing out. Current Status='Verifying metadata'
sfdx-project.json has been updated.
Successfully created the package version [08c4K000000CbUKQA0]. Subscriber
Package Version Id: 04t4K000002FUELQA4
Package Installation URL: https://login.salesforce.com/packaging/
installPackage.apexp?p0=04t4K000002FUELQA4
As an alternative, you can use the "sfdx force:package:install" command.
```

To complete the creation of the package versions, create the extension package's first version using the following command:

```
$ sfdx force:package:version:create \
    --installationkey abc124 \
    --package "CI - Pres" \
    --wait 10
```

After the package version has been created, the Salesforce CLI updates the project configuration file again, which should now resemble the following, with all the package version aliases and their Ids included.

Listing 13-16. Initial package version aliases and Ids

```
{
    "packageDirectories": [
        {
            "path": "service-layer",
            "default": true,
            "package": "CI - Svc",
            "versionName": "ver 0.1",
            "versionNumber": "0.1.0.NEXT"
        },
```

```
        {
            "path": "presentation-layer",
            "package": "CI - Pres",
            "versionName": "ver 0.1",
            "versionNumber": "0.1.0.NEXT",
            "default": false,
            "dependencies": [
                {
                    "package": "CI - Svc",
                    "versionNumber": "0.1.0.LATEST"
                }
            ]
        }
    ],
    "name": "SalesforceDXSampleApp",
    "namespace": "ihDX1",
    "sfdcLoginUrl": "https://login.salesforce.com",
    "sourceApiVersion": "53.0",
    "packageAliases": {
        "CI - Svc": "0Ho4K000000CarySAC",
        "CI - Pres": "0Ho4K000000Cas3SAC",
        "CI - Svc@0.1.0-1": "04t4K000002FUEGQA4",
        "CI - Svc@0.1.0-2": "04t4K000002FUELQA4",
        "CI - Pres@0.1.0-1": "04t4K000002FUEQQA4"
    }
}
```

The package versions that have just been created have yet to be promoted to released status and are therefore beta package versions. We'll be looking at promoting package versions later.

We'll now see how to view all the package version creation requests that a Dev Hub has received.

Listing Package Version Creation Requests

To view all the package version creation requests that a Dev Hub has received, whether the creation request is queued, in progress, successful, or failed, and whether the package version has been deleted or not, we can use this command:

```
$ sfdx force:package:version:create:list
```

The command can take a few parameters:

- `--createdlastdays|-c`: Only lists the package version creation requests that have been made in the number of days passed as a data value, where `0` represents today and a day runs from `00:00:00`, that is, midnight. [Optional]
- `--status|-s`: Filters the package version creation requests by status. [Optional]
- Allowed values are
  - `Queued`
  - `InProgress`
  - `Success`
  - `Error`
- `--targetdevhubusername|-v`: The username or alias of the Dev Hub org that received the package version creation requests to be viewed. [Optional]
- `--apiversion, --json, --loglevel`: Please refer to the discussion on global parameters in the section "Command-Line Parameters and Arguments" in Chapter 4, "Salesforce CLI."

The output from the command is as follows, where only the first five columns are shown for readability.

Listing 13-17. Package version creation requests

```
=== Package Version  Create Requests  [3]
 Id                    Status  Package Id          Package Version Id Subscriber Pckg Ver Id
 ───────────────────── ─────── ─────────────────── ────────────────── ──────────────────────
 08c4K000000CbUFQA0    Success 0Ho4K000000CarySAC 05i4K000000CayzQAC 04t4K000002FUEGQA4
 08c4K000000CbUKQA0    Success 0Ho4K000000CarySAC 05i4K000000Caz4QAC 04t4K000002FUELQA4
 08c4K000000CbUPQA0    Success 0Ho4K000000Cas3SAC 05i4K000000Caz9QAC 04t4K000002FUEQQA4
```

We'll now see how to view all the package versions that a Dev Hub has created that are currently being tracked; that is, all package versions that have been successfully created and that have not been deleted.

Listing Package Versions

As the number of package versions increases, it's often useful to be able to view all the versions that have been created by a Dev Hub. This is easily achieved using the following command:

```
$ sfdx force:package:version:list \
    --concise
```

These are parameters for this command:

- `--createdlastdays` | `-c`: Only lists the package versions that have been created in the number of days passed as a data value, where `0` represents today and a day runs from `00:00:00`, that is, midnight. [Optional]
- `--modifiedlastdays` | `-m`: Only lists the package versions that have been modified in the number of days passed as a data value, where `0` represents today and a day runs from `00:00:00`, that is, midnight. [Optional]
- `--orderby` | `-o`: Orders the list by the fields on the `Package2Version` object. For example, the object includes the `MajorVersion`, `MinorVersion`, `PatchVersion`, and `BuildNumber` fields, among others. [Optional]

- `--packages` | `-p`: Only displays package versions for the comma-separated list of package aliases or Ids. [Optional]
- `--released` | `-r`: Only displays package versions that have been promoted to released status. [Optional]
- `--targetdevhubusername` | `-v`: The username or alias of the Dev Hub org that has created the package versions to be listed. [Optional]
- `--apiversion, --concise, --json, --loglevel, --verbose`: Please refer to the discussion on global parameters in the section "Command-Line Parameters and Arguments" in Chapter 4, "Salesforce CLI."

Note To discover all the `Package2Version` object's fields that can be passed to the command using the `--orderby` | `-o` parameter, search for the object in the Salesforce Tooling API documentation, which can be found here: `https://developer.salesforce.com/docs/atlas.en-us.api_tooling.meta/api_tooling`.

The output will resemble the following, which displays a subset of the available information due to the use of the `--concise` parameter to aid readability. Remove the `--concise` parameter to see more.

Listing 13-18. List of package versions

```
=== Package Versions [3]
 Package Id         Version Subscriber Package Version Id Released
 ────────────────── ─────── ───────────────────────────── ────────
 0Ho4K000000CarySAC 0.1.0.1 04t4K000002FUEGQA4            false
 0Ho4K000000CarySAC 0.1.0.2 04t4K000002FUELQA4            false
 0Ho4K000000Cas3SAC 0.1.0.1 04t4K000002FUEQQA4            false
```

To view details for a single package version, we can use the `force:package:version:report` command, which we will cover next.

Displaying Package Version Details

Listing package versions provides a good summary of all the versions that a Dev Hub has created. The Salesforce CLI also allows you to view more detail for an individual package version by running this command:

```
$ sfdx force:package:version:report \
    --package "CI - Pres@0.1.0-1"
```

The parameters that can be passed to this command are as follows:

- `--package|-p`: The alias or Id of the package version to display detailed information about. [Required]
- `--targetdevhubusername|-v`: The username or alias of the Dev Hub org that created the package version to display detailed information about. [Optional]
- `--apiversion, --json, --loglevel, --verbose`: Please refer to the discussion on global parameters in the section "Command-Line Parameters and Arguments" in Chapter 4, "Salesforce CLI."

The command's output is as follows.

Listing 13-19. Detailed package version information

```
=== Package Version
 Name                           Value
 ─────────────────────────────  ──────────────────
 Name                           ver 0.1
 Subscriber Package Version Id  04t4K000002FUEQQA4
 Package Id                     0Ho4K000000Cas3SAC
 Version                        0.1.0.1
 Description
 Branch
 Tag
 Released                       false
 Validation Skipped             false
 Ancestor                       N/A
 Ancestor Version               N/A
```

```
Code Coverage
Code Coverage Met                false
Org-Dependent Unlocked Package No
Release Version                  55.0
Build Duration in Seconds        66
Managed Metadata Removed         N/A
Created By                       0054K000000iHmtQAE
```

In the previous listing, we can see that a description for the package version was not provided, which is not good practice. We'll fix that now.

Updating Package Versions

As with packages, it's possible to update some package version information after the package version has been created. We'll update the package version descriptions by executing these commands:

```
$ sfdx force:package:version:update \
    --versiondescription \
        "Initial base package version" \
    --package "CI - Svc@0.1.0-2"

$ sfdx force:package:version:update \
    --versiondescription \
        "Initial extension package version" \
    --package "CI - Pres@0.1.0-1"
```

These are the parameters that can be used with this command:

- `--versionname`|`-a`: The new package version name. [Optional]
- `--branch`|`-b`: The new package version branch. [Optional]
- `--versiondescription`|`-e`: The new package version description. [Optional]
- `--installationkey`|`-k`: The new package version installation key. [Optional]
- `--package`|`-p`: The alias or Id of the package version to update information for. [Required]

- `--tag|-t`: The new package version tag. [Optional]
- `--targetdevhubusername|-v`: The username or alias of the Dev Hub org that created the package version that will have its information updated. [Optional]
- `--apiversion, --json, --loglevel`: Please refer to the discussion on global parameters in the section "Command-Line Parameters and Arguments" in Chapter 4, "Salesforce CLI."

Running the `force:package:version:report` command for the two package versions will show that the package version descriptions have been updated.

Listing 13-20. Base package version updated information

```
=== Package Version
 Name                              Value
 ──────────────────────────────── ─────────────────────────────────
 Name                              ver 0.1
 Subscriber Package Version Id     04t4K000002FUELQA4
 Package Id                        0Ho4K000000CarySAC
 Version                           0.1.0.2
 Description                       Initial base package version
 Branch
 Tag
 Released                          false
 Validation Skipped                false
 Ancestor                          N/A
 Ancestor Version                  N/A
 Code Coverage
 Code Coverage Met                 false
 Org-Dependent Unlocked Package    No
 Release Version                   55.0
 Build Duration in Seconds         59
 Managed Metadata Removed          N/A
 Created By                        0054K000000iHmtQAE
```

Listing 13-21. Extension package version updated information

```
=== Package Version
 Name                          Value
 ───────────────────────────── ─────────────────────────────────
 Name                          ver 0.1
 Subscriber Package Version Id 04t4K000002FUEQQA4
 Package Id                    0Ho4K000000Cas3SAC
 Version                       0.1.0.1
 Description                   Initial extension package version
 Branch
 Tag
 Released                      false
 Validation Skipped            false
 Ancestor                      N/A
 Ancestor Version              N/A
 Code Coverage
 Code Coverage Met             false
 Org-Dependent Unlocked Package No
 Release Version               55.0
 Build Duration in Seconds     66
 Managed Metadata Removed      N/A
 Created By                    0054K000000iHmtQAE
```

We're now ready to install the package versions, which we'll do in the next section.

Installing the Package Versions

If you have been following along with all the steps in this chapter, you now have two packages, a base package that contains an Apex class and an extension package with a Lightning web component that uses the Apex class that's in the base package. You have also created beta package versions that are ready to be installed into a scratch org, sandbox, or Developer Edition org.

Note Beta package versions, that is, those that have yet to be promoted to released status, cannot be installed in production orgs.

Earlier in the "This Chapter's Project" section, you created a scratch org with the alias MySO that was used to experience the sample application, which was deployed as unpackaged metadata components. We no longer need that scratch org so it can be deleted. Then, create a new scratch org and set it as the org having the default username of MySO.

Execute the following command to install the base package in the scratch org using the installation key that we provided when creating the package version:

```
$ sfdx force:package:install \
    --installationkey abc124 \
    --package "CI - Svc@0.1.0-2"
```

This command can take these parameters:

- --apexcompile | -a: For unlocked packages only. Determines whether just the Apex classes in the package should be compiled or all Apex classes in the target org. [Optional] [Default: All]
- Allowed values are as follows:
    - All: Compile all Apex classes in the target org.
    - Package: Only compile the Apex classes in the package.
- --publishwait | -b: The number of minutes that the command will wait for the package version to be available in the target org. If the wait period expires, the installation is terminated. Specifying 0 minutes causes the installation to be terminated immediately, unless the package version is already installed in the target org. [Optional] [Default: 0]
- --installationkey | -k: The installation key that was provided when creating the package version. [Optional] [Default: null]
- --package | -p: The alias or Id of the package version to install. [Required]
- --no-prompt | -r: Suppresses the confirmation prompt when using the --upgradetype delete parameter and when the package contains Remote Site Settings or CSP (Content Security Policy Trusted Site) settings. [Optional]

- `--securitytype|-s`: Specifies whether the installed package is accessible by administrators only or by all users. [Optional] [Default: `AdminsOnly`]
- Allowed values are as follows:
    - `AllUsers`: The installed package is accessible to all users.
    - `AdminsOnly`: The installed package is accessible to administrators only.
- `--upgradetype|-t`: For unlocked packages only. States what happens to metadata components in an older package version that is installed in the target org when components have been removed from the package version that is being installed. [Optional] [Default: `Mixed`]
- Allowed values are as follows:
    - `DeprecateOnly`: Mark removed metadata components as deprecated in the Salesforce user interface rather than deleting the components.
    - `Mixed`: Allow the system to determine which metadata components can be safely deleted and mark all others as deprecated.
    - `Delete`: Delete all removed metadata components that don't have any dependencies, except for custom objects and custom fields.
- `--targetusername|-u`: The username or alias of the org where the package version will be installed. [Optional]
- `--wait|-w`: Once the package version is available in the target org (see the `--publishwait|-b` parameter), this parameter specifies the number of minutes that the command will wait for installation to complete. The command will wait until the installation is complete or the wait period expires, whichever is the sooner, after which control will be returned to the integrated terminal. If the wait period expires before the installation is complete, use the `force:package:install:report` command to check the installation status. A value of `0` minutes causes the command to return control to the integrated terminal immediately. [Optional] [Default: `0`]

- `--apiversion, --json, --loglevel`: Please refer to the discussion on global parameters in the section "Command-Line Parameters and Arguments" in Chapter 4, "Salesforce CLI."

Because neither the `--publishwait|-b` nor the `--wait|-w` parameters are being used, the `force:package:install` command is executed asynchronously, and control is returned to the integrated terminal immediately, with the following output.

Listing 13-22. Package version asynchronous install command output

```
PackageInstallRequest is currently InProgress. You can continue to query
the status using
sfdx force:package:install:report -i 0Hf2z00000059dwCAA -u test-
ndblfeaweuhi@example.com
```

As instructed, to view the installation status, use the following command:

```
$ sfdx force:package:install:report \
    --requestid 0Hf2z00000059dwCAA
```

These are the parameters that can be used with this command:

- `--requestid|-i`: The package install request Id that is returned by the `force:package:install` command when the `--wait|-w` period expires and the command continues to execute asynchronously. [Required]
- `--targetusername|-u`: The username or alias of the org where the package version is being installed. [Optional]
- `--apiversion, --json, --loglevel`: Please refer to the discussion on global parameters in the section "Command-Line Parameters and Arguments" in Chapter 4, "Salesforce CLI."

If the package installation is in progress, the `force:package:install:report` command output will be the same as the output from the `force:package:install` command.

Listing 13-23. Package version asynchronous install progress

```
PackageInstallRequest is currently InProgress. You can continue to query
the status using sfdx force:package:install:report -i 0Hf2z00000059dwCAA -u
test-ndblfeaweuhi@example.com
```

Once installation is complete, the output will change to the following if the installation was successful.

Listing 13-24. Package version asynchronous install completion

```
Successfully installed package [04t4K000002FUELQA4]
```

To execute the same package installation command synchronously, use one or both of the `--publishwait|-b` and `--wait|-w` parameters as follows:

```
$ sfdx force:package:install \
    --publishwait 10 \
    --installationkey abc124 \
    --package "CI - Svc@0.1.0-2" \
    --wait 10
```

Please refer to the parameter descriptions earlier for the `force:package:install` command for more details on these extra parameters. The command executes synchronously, displaying a status update until it completes.

Listing 13-25. Package version synchronous install

```
Waiting for the package install request to complete. Status = IN_PROGRESS
Waiting for the package install request to complete. Status = IN_PROGRESS
Waiting for the package install request to complete. Status = IN_PROGRESS
Successfully installed package [04t4K000002FUELQA4]
```

To complete the installation of the package versions, perform the following installation command for the extension package:

```
$ sfdx force:package:install \
    --publishwait 10 \
    --installationkey abc124 \
    --package "CI - Pres@0.1.0-1" \
    --wait 10
```

To view the installed package versions in the scratch org, open the org and navigate to **Setup ➤ Apps ➤ Packaging ➤ Installed Packages**. The following shows installed beta unlocked packages.

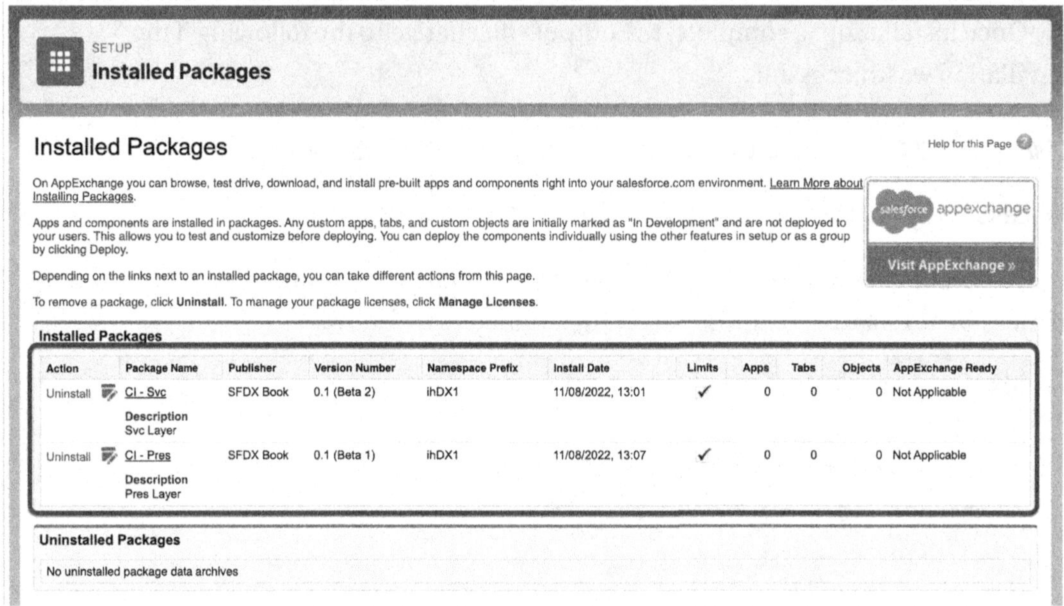

Figure 13-10. *Installed beta unlocked packages in a scratch org*

Note We've just installed the sample application as two packages. To see the app's Lightning web component in action, add it to the Account record page, create an Account, and create some open Case records for the account. For step-by-step instructions, please refer to the "Creating the Salesforce DX Project" section near the start of the project.

You may want to list packages that are installed in a target org from the command line, rather than via an org's Setup area.

Listing Installed Package Versions

The Salesforce CLI can also be used to list the packages installed in an org. Execute the following command to list the two packages that we just installed in the scratch org:

```
$ sfdx force:package:installed:list
```

The parameters that can be used with this command are as follows:

- `--targetusername|-u`: The username or alias of the org where the packages to be listed are installed. [Optional]
- `--apiversion, --json, --loglevel`: Please refer to the discussion on global parameters in the section "Command-Line Parameters and Arguments" in Chapter 4, "Salesforce CLI."

The command's output looks like the following, which has been wrapped across two blocks for readability.

Listing 13-26. Packages installed in an org

```
=== Installed Package Versions [2]
 ID                 Package ID           Package Name   Namespace Package Version ID
 ────────────────── ──────────────────── ────────────── ───────── ──────────────────
 0A32z000000AMHnCA0 0334K000000PxMAQA0   CI - Svc       ihDX1     04t4K000002FUELQA4
 0A32z000000AMI7CA0 0334K000000PxMFQA0   CI - Pres      ihDX1     04t4K000002FUEQQA4

Version Name Version
──────────── ───────
ver 0.1      0.1.0.2
ver 0.1      0.1.0.1
```

At this point, you would typically do some testing to prepare the app for deployment to a production org. Before you can deploy the app however, you need to promote the package versions to released status.

Promoting Package Versions

Beta package versions need to be promoted to released status before they can be installed in a production org. Attempting to install a beta package version in a production org using the Salesforce CLI will result in the following error message.

Listing 13-27. Installing a beta package version in a production org error message

```
Waiting for the package install request to complete. Status = IN_PROGRESS
ERROR:  Encountered errors installing the package!,Installation errors:
1) Package(0334K000000PxMA) Unable to install beta package, Details: The
package you attempted to install is a beta package, which you can only
install in sandbox or Developer Edition organizations.
ERROR running force:package:install:  Installation errors:
1) Package(0334K000000PxMA) Unable to install beta package, Details: The
package you attempted to install is a beta package, which you can only
install in sandbox or Developer Edition organizations.
```

Execute the following command to promote the base package from a beta package version to released status:

```
$ sfdx force:package:version:promote \
    --package "CI - Svc@0.1.0-2"
```

The parameters that are available for this command are as follows:

- `--noprompt|-n`: Suppress the prompt that requests confirmation to promote the package version to released status. [Optional]
- `--package|-p`: The alias or Id of the package version to promote to released status. [Required]
- `--targetdevhubusername|-v`: The username or alias of the Dev Hub org that created the package version that will be promoted to released status. [Optional]
- `--apiversion, --json, --loglevel`: Please refer to the discussion on global parameters in the section "Command-Line Parameters and Arguments" in Chapter 4, "Salesforce CLI."

When creating the package version, we didn't run code coverage using the `force:package:version:create` command's `--codecoverage|-c` parameter. This results in the following error when executing the preceding `force:package:version:promote` command.

Listing 13-28. No code coverage error when promoting a package version

```
ERROR running force:package:version:promote:  Code coverage has not been
run for this version.  Code coverage must be run during version creation
and meet the minimum coverage requirement to promote the version.
```

We'll remedy the situation by creating another package version and this time including the `--codecoverage|-c` parameter:

```
$ sfdx force:package:version:create \
    --codecoverage \
    --versiondescription \
      "Initial base package version" \
    --installationkey abc124 \
    --package "CI - Svc"
```

Executing the command `force:package:version:report -p "CI - Svc@0.1.0-3"` will display the new package version details, including the code coverage.

Listing 13-29. Package version with code coverage

```
=== Package Version
 Name                          Value
 ───────────────────────────── ──────────────────────────────
 Name                          ver 0.1
 Subscriber Package Version Id 04t4K000002FUEVQA4
 Package Id                    0Ho4K000000CarySAC
 Version                       0.1.0.3
 Description                   Initial base package version
 Branch
 Tag
 Released                      false
 Validation Skipped            false
```

```
Ancestor                       N/A
Ancestor Version               N/A
Code Coverage                  100%
Code Coverage Met              true
Org-Dependent Unlocked Package No
Release Version                55.0
Build Duration in Seconds      38
Managed Metadata Removed       N/A
Created By                     0054K000000iHmtQAE
```

Now we can successfully promote the package version to released status:

```
$ sfdx force:package:version:promote \
    --package "CI - Svc@0.1.0-3"
```

The success status that is output by the command is as follows.

Listing 13-30. Package version promotion success message

```
Successfully promoted the package version, ID: 04t4K000002FUEVQA4, to
released. Starting in Winter '21, only unlocked package versions that
have met the minimum 75% code coverage requirement can be promoted. Code
coverage minimums aren't enforced on org-dependent unlocked packages.
```

We'll now attempt to promote the extension package version to released status:

```
$ sfdx force:package:version:promote \
    --package "CI - Pres@0.1.0-1"
```

As with the base package, the promotion fails. Even though the extension package contains no Apex classes, the package version to be promoted must still include code coverage. Create a new extension package version and include code coverage:

```
$ sfdx force:package:version:create \
    --codecoverage \
    --versiondescription \
      "Initial extension package version" \
    --installationkey abc124 \
    --package "CI - Pres"
```

We can now successfully promote the extension package version:

```
$ sfdx force:package:version:promote \
    --package "CI - Pres@0.1.0-2"
```

To install the two package versions that have been promoted to released status in a production org, execute the following commands:

```
$ sfdx force:package:install \
    --publishwait 10 \
    --installationkey abc124 \
    --package "CI - Svc@0.1.0-3" \
    --targetusername MyProdOrg \
    --wait 10

$ sfdx force:package:install \
    --publishwait 10 \
    --installationkey abc124 \
    --package "CI - Pres@0.1.0-2" \
    --targetusername MyProdOrg \
    --wait 10
```

Note The preceding command assumes that a production org has been authorized using the `auth:web:login` command and has been assigned the alias `MyProdOrg`. Please refer to Chapter 7, "Orgs," for details on org authorization.

Opening the production org and navigating to **Setup ➤ Apps ➤ Packaging ➤ Installed Packages** shows the installed packages, which will either be unlocked packages or second-generation managed packages, depending on what you have chosen to create when following along.

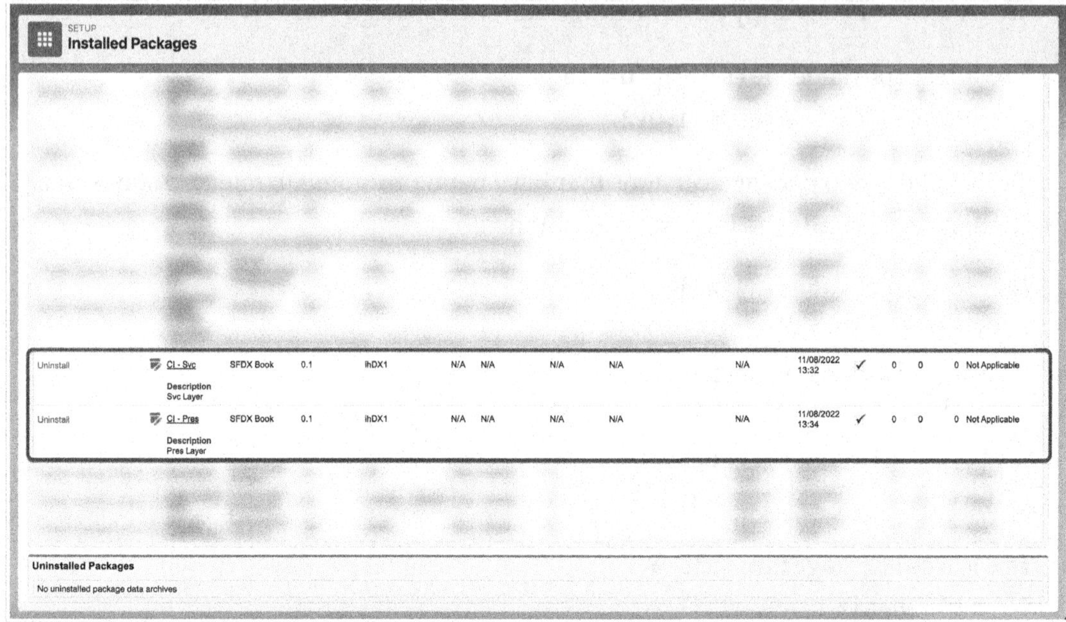

***Figure 13-11.** Installed released unlocked packages in a production org*

The next section will illustrate how beta and released package versions can also be uninstalled from an org using the Salesforce CLI.

Uninstalling Package Versions

So far, we have installed beta package versions of the sample application's base and extension packages in a scratch org and released package versions in a production org.

Note Before we can uninstall package versions, we must ensure that they are not being referenced in the target orgs. If you have added the sample application's Lightning web component to the Account object's record page in an org, remove the component before proceeding.

Uninstall the extension package version that is installed in the scratch org by using this command:

```
$ sfdx force:package:uninstall \
    --package "CI - Pres@0.1.0-1"
```

The command parameters are as follows:

- --package|-p: The alias or Id of the package version to uninstall. [Required]
- --targetusername|-u: The username or alias of the org to uninstall the package version from. [Optional]
- --wait|-w: The amount of time in minutes that the force:package:uninstall command will wait for the package version to be uninstalled before timing out. Use a value of 0 to cause the command to return immediately and then use the force:package:uninstall:report command to check the creation status. [Optional] [Default: 0]
- --apiversion, --json, --loglevel: Please refer to the discussion on global parameters in the section "Command-Line Parameters and Arguments" in Chapter 4, "Salesforce CLI."

We're using the default value of 0 for the --wait|-w parameter, which caused the command to execute asynchronously, return control to the integrated terminal immediately, and display the following message.

Listing 13-31. Package version asynchronous uninstall command output

```
PackageUninstallRequest is currently InProgress. You can continue to query
the status using
sfdx force:package:uninstall:report -i 06y2z0000000006AAA -u test-
ndblfeaweuhi@example.com
```

By following the instructions in the message, the package version uninstall request status can be queried using this rcport command:

```
$ sfdx force:package:uninstall:report \
    --requestid 06y2z0000000006AAA
```

The following parameters can be used with this command:

- --requestid|-i: The package uninstall request Id that is returned when running the force:package:uninstall command asynchronously. [Required]

- `--targetusername|-u`: The username or alias of the org where the package version is being uninstalled from. [Optional]
- `--apiversion, --json, --loglevel`: Please refer to the discussion on global parameters in the section "Command-Line Parameters and Arguments" in Chapter 4, "Salesforce CLI."

When the package version has been uninstalled, the report command will display the following output.

Listing 13-32. Package version asynchronous uninstall completion

```
Successfully uninstalled package [04t4K000002FUEQQA4]
```

To execute the `force:package:uninstall` command synchronously, specify a value greater than `0` for the `--wait|-w` parameter. This will cause the command to wait until either the wait period has expired or until the package version has been uninstalled, whichever occurs first. If the wait period expires before the package version has been uninstalled, the command returns control to the integrated terminal, and the command continues to execute asynchronously. Use the preceding `force:package:uninstall:report` command to query the command's asynchronous status.

The following command uninstalls the base package version from the scratch org synchronously:

```
$ sfdx force:package:uninstall \
    --package "CI - Svc@0.1.0-2" \
    --wait 10
```

While the command is executing, it displays a status update, and when the command completes, it displays a success message.

Listing 13-33. Package version asynchronous uninstall completion

```
Waiting for the package uninstall request to get processed. Status =
InProgress
Waiting for the package uninstall request to get processed. Status =
InProgress
Waiting for the package uninstall request to get processed. Status =
InProgress
Successfully uninstalled package [04t4K000002FUELQA4]
```

If you also installed the released package versions in a production org, uninstall those using the following commands:

```
$ sfdx force:package:uninstall \
    --package "CI - Pres@0.1.0-2" \
    --targetusername MyProdOrg \
    --wait 10

$ sfdx force:package:uninstall \
    --package "CI - Svc@0.1.0-3" \
    --targetusername MyProdOrg \
    --wait 10
```

We will now move on to deleting packages and package versions in the Dev Hub.

Deleting Packages and Package Versions

The Salesforce CLI supports deleting packages and package versions that are no longer required.

Note Beta package versions can be deleted for unlocked packages and second-generation managed packages. Package versions that have been promoted to released status can be deleted for unlocked packages but not for second-generation managed packages, that is, it's not possible to delete released package versions for second-generation managed packages.

Before a package can be deleted, all its package versions must be deleted first. Attempting to delete a package with existing package versions results in the following error message.

Listing 13-34. Deleting packages with associated package version error

```
ERROR running force:package:delete:  Can't delete the package. First delete
all associated package versions, then try to delete the package again.
```

To list all the package versions that the Dev Hub has created so far in this chapter, use the force:package:version:list command. The following output has been wrapped into three sections to make it easier to read.

Listing 13-35. All package versions created in the chapter

```
=== Package Versions [5]
Package Name  Namespace  Version Name  Version  Subscriber Package Version Id
────────────  ─────────  ────────────  ───────  ─────────────────────────────
CI - Svc      ihDX1      ver 0.1       0.1.0.1  04t4K000002FUEGQA4
CI - Svc      ihDX1      ver 0.1       0.1.0.2  04t4K000002FUELQA4
CI - Svc      ihDX1      ver 0.1       0.1.0.3  04t4K000002FUEVQA4
CI - Pres     ihDX1      ver 0.1       0.1.0.1  04t4K000002FUEQQA4
CI - Pres     ihDX1      ver 0.1       0.1.0.2  04t4K000002FUEaQAO

Alias                Installation Key  Released  Validation Skipped
──────────────────   ────────────────  ────────  ──────────────────
CI - Svc@0.1.0-1     true              false     false
CI - Svc@0.1.0-2     true              false     false
CI - Svc@0.1.0-3     true              true      false
CI - Pres@0.1.0-1    true              false     false
CI - Pres@0.1.0-2    true              true      false

Ancestor  Ancestor Version  Branch
────────  ────────────────  ──────
N/A       N/A
N/A       N/A
N/A       N/A
N/A       N/A
N/A       N/A
```

Start by deleting the extension package versions as they depend on the base package versions. Delete the first package version using this command:

```
$ sfdx force:package:version:delete \
    --package "CI - Pres@0.1.0-2"
```

The parameters that can be used with the command are as follows:

- --noprompt|-n: Deletes the package version without using the Deleted package versions can't be recovered. Do you want to continue? (y/n): confirmation prompt. [Optional]
- --package|-p: The alias or Id of the package version to delete. [Required]
- --targetdevhubusername|-v: The username or alias of the Dev Hub org that created the package version to be deleted. [Optional]
- --apiversion, --json, --loglevel: Please refer to the discussion on global parameters in the section "Command-Line Parameters and Arguments" in Chapter 4, "Salesforce CLI."

After answering "y" to the confirmation prompt, the command confirms that the package version has been deleted.

Listing 13-36. Deleted package version confirmation

```
Successfully deleted the package version. 04t4K000002FUEaQAO
```

Continue deleting the remaining extension package versions followed by the base package versions. Running the force:package:version:list command again should now output No results found indicating that there are no more package versions being tracked by the Dev Hub.

Now run the command force:package:list to list the packages that the Dev Hub has created.

Listing 13-37. All packages created in the chapter

```
=== Packages [2]
 Namespace Prefix Name      Id                  Alias     Description Type
 ──────────────── ──────── ─────────────────── ───────── ─────────── ────────
 ihDX1            CI - Pres 0Ho4K000000Cas3SAC CI - Pres Pres Layer  Unlocked
 ihDX1            CI - Svc  0Ho4K000000CarySAC CI - Svc  Svc Layer   Unlocked
```

To delete the extension package first, use this command:

```
$ sfdx force:package:delete \
    --package "CI - Pres"
```

This command's parameters are as follows:

- --noprompt|-n: Deletes the package without using the Deleted packages can't be recovered. Do you want to continue? (y/n): confirmation prompt. [Optional]
- --package|-p: The alias or Id of the package to delete. [Required]
- --targetdevhubusername|-v: The username or alias of the Dev Hub org that created the package to be deleted. [Optional]
- --apiversion, --json, --loglevel: Please refer to the discussion on global parameters in the section "Command-Line Parameters and Arguments" in Chapter 4, "Salesforce CLI."

As with deleting package versions, answering "y" to the confirmation prompt results in the command confirming that the package has been deleted.

Listing 13-38. Deleted package confirmation

```
Successfully deleted the package. 0Ho4K000000Cas3SAC
```

Delete the base package and confirm that the Dev Hub is no longer tracking any packages by using the force:package:list command, which should now output No results found.

Note Although the force:package:delete and the force:package:version:delete commands delete the packages and package versions, respectively, they do not remove the parameters from the sfdx-project.json project configuration file that were added when the packages and package versions were created. To remove the parameters from the project configuration file, they must be deleted manually.

We have now completed the package development model walk-through, where we created multiple dependent packages and their package versions and installed them in target orgs, all using the Salesforce CLI. We also explored several other commands that supported the lifecycle, such as listing, uninstalling, and deleting packages and package versions.

We'll finally wrap up the chapter.

Chapter Summary

In this chapter, we drew on all the lessons learned in the previous chapters and applied them to the package development model, where we developed unlocked packages and second-generation managed packages (2GP). We got up to speed with namespaces, summarized all the deployment options and the various application development models that are available to Salesforce developers, and then we walked through a typical package development model lifecycle. While walking through the lifecycle, we created packages and package versions, and we discovered how to install them in and uninstall them from target orgs and how to delete packages and package versions that a Dev Hub is tracking.

This is the last chapter in Part II of the book, where we explored the core concepts of Salesforce DX using hands-on examples. We'll close out the book next with an overall summary and some suggested areas to explore next.

Book Summary and Resources

Our journey through the 13 chapters of this book has taken the reader from a Salesforce DX novice through to a confident practitioner, although those with some prior knowledge can jump in and out of each chapter to brush up on or learn new skills. We started with how to set up your desktop development environment, followed by an overview of the key Salesforce DX concepts and the Salesforce command-line interface (CLI). We then got hands-on with Salesforce DX to work with Dev Hubs, projects, orgs, metadata, version control systems, test users, test data, and the CLI commands that bootstrap component development using boilerplate code templates. We finished with an end-to-end packaging workflow that added a simple Lightning web component to an unlocked package or a second-generation managed package (2GP).

Salesforce DX continues to evolve, and this book represents the tip of the iceberg. I covered the key concepts and a subset of the parameters that are available for each command; to cover everything would have tripled the length of the book. With the core knowledge that you now possess, it's possible to explore the commands that were omitted and the parameters that weren't included in the examples.

What follows is a list of areas that you might like to explore to take your skills to the next level. It's a mix of resources, Salesforce products and features related to Salesforce DX, and some Salesforce CLI commands that we didn't explore in the book. This information was correct at the time I completed writing the book in August 2022.

Trailblazer Community

I highly recommend immersing yourself in the free and fun Salesforce Trailblazer Community, which can be found here: `https://trailhead.salesforce.com/`.

The community includes Trailhead, an online environment for acquiring Salesforce skills. Once you have enrolled, search for "Build Apps Together with Package Development" and "Build Apps as an AppExchange Partner" to find a couple of trails to get started with. Then search for additional modules, trails, and projects that can help you grow your skillset.

I. Harris, *Beginning Salesforce DX*, https://doi.org/10.1007/978-1-4842-8114-7

Trailblazer Community Groups are great opportunities to meet like-minded professionals based on location (e.g., "London"), Salesforce product (e.g., "Sales Cloud"), and role (e.g., "Developer"). The group meetings can be virtual or in person.

Finally, there are credentials to evidence your acquired knowledge and enhance your resume, which include the following:

- **Superbadges**: Hands-on challenges that demonstrate that you can put your knowledge to practical use.
- **Super Sets**: Collections of Superbadges that show your expertise in a specific domain, such as "Admin" or "App Builder."
- **Certifications**: Boosts your resume and gives you a competitive edge by proving the Salesforce knowledge needed for a role, such as "Administrator" or "Developer." Note that a fee is needed to take the certification exam.

To be inspired and learn more about becoming a Trailblazer yourself, visit `www.salesforce.com/company/be-a-trailblazer/`, which mentions that "Salesforce Trailblazers deliver success in their careers, companies, and communities, fueling the entire Salesforce ecosystem."

Trailblazers are lifelong learners, and where better to learn about the latest Salesforce products and features than at a Salesforce event.

Salesforce Events

Salesforce runs multiple events around the world, where you can hear about the latest Salesforce product and feature innovations, learn how to leverage them to deliver stakeholder value, listen to many success stories, network with other Trailblazers, and have plenty of fun. Three events that focus on application or customization development, or have strong development tracks, that will be of interest to readers of this book are as follows:

- **Dreamforce**: A three-day event held in San Francisco every year, it's the world's largest software conference. Look out for the Dreamforce Bootcamp sessions to accelerate your path to certification. If you can't attend in person, register for free and watch the streamed sessions using Salesforce+ (`www.salesforce.com/plus/`). To find more information about Dreamforce, visit `www.salesforce.com/dreamforce/`.

- **World Tour**: A smaller version of Dreamforce hosted in several cities around the world. In 2022, for example, the host cities were Paris, Sydney, Washington DC, London, and New York City. As with Dreamforce, sessions are streamed via Salesforce+ for those who can't attend in person. Check out `www.salesforce.com/events/` to see upcoming World Tours once they have been announced.
- **TrailblazerDX**: An annual event held in San Francisco dedicated to application and customization development, which can be attended in person or watched via the Salesforce+ streaming service. Visit this site to learn more: `www.salesforce.com/trailblazerdx/`.

As you blaze your trail to becoming a Salesforce DX aficionado, there are ways to hear directly from the Salesforce DX product team and provide feedback to them.

Salesforce DX Product

Immersing yourself in the Trailblazer Community and attending Salesforce events will undoubtedly contribute to your professional development, provide opportunities to give back by helping others, and be a fundamental part of your Trailblazer journey. That said, if Salesforce DX is to become your go-to technology for building applications and customizations, how do you hear directly from the product team at Salesforce about the latest developments and what channels exist to provide feedback?

The best way to hear about new Salesforce DX features and bug fixes is by reviewing the release notes. A new, stable version of the `sfdx` application is released every Thursday. After updating the application on your computer, the release notes can be viewed using the following Salesforce CLI command:

```
$ sfdx info:releasenotes:display
```

Alternatively, all release notes can be viewed at this GitHub repository:

`https://github.com/forcedotcom/cli/tree/main/releasenotes/sfdx`

If you want to report a bug, or if you wish to make a feature request, you can do so via the following GitHub repository:

`https://github.com/forcedotcom/cli`

Make sure that you review the `README.md` file first, especially the part about checking if a bug has already been reported before you report it. Then click the **New Issue** button, where you can then report a bug, make a feature request, report a security vulnerability, or visit the known issues registry. If you report a bug and it gets fixed by the product team, you may even get a mention in a future release note!

Another good channel for hearing from the product team is the Salesforce Developers Blog. Past posts can be found here:

`https://developer.salesforce.com/blogs`

You can also sign up for updates to be delivered by email, Slack, or RSS feed.

As I mentioned at the start of this epilogue, not all Salesforce DX commands and parameters were discussed in the book. Some notable areas that are worth being aware of, and exploring at your leisure, are listed in the next section.

Noteworthy Developments

Some Salesforce DX commands and parameters were not covered in the book, either because they are considered more advanced, are not yet generally available (GA), became GA too late to squeeze in, or were omitted to conserve the page count. I've listed some of these products and features so that you can explore them yourself:

- **Code Builder**: After July 13, 2022, as part of the Summer '22 Salesforce release, Salesforce Code Builder became a Beta Service. In this book, we standardized on using Visual Studio Code with the Salesforce Extensions for Visual Studio Code as our desktop integrated development environment. Code Builder is a web-based development environment that comes preinstalled with the Salesforce Extensions for Visual Studio Code and the Salesforce CLI. Not only does it require no downloads, it enables users to develop from anywhere and is also very familiar to users of the desktop environment.
- **DevOps Center**: Also included in the Summer '22 Salesforce release, Salesforce DevOps Center became a Beta Service. DevOps Center uses DevOps practices and is an alternative to the change sets deployment model. Of particular interest to pro-code developers is that they can implement their DevOps Center work units using Salesforce DX, enabling them to collaborate on projects with no-code and low-code developers.

- **SOQL Builder**: Salesforce Extensions for Visual Studio Code includes SOQL Builder, a user interface for building, running, and saving SOQL queries.
- **Salesforce CLI Unification**: In addition to the `sfdx` application, Salesforce is working on an `sf` application with a vision to be the single CLI executable for all Salesforce products, such as MuleSoft, Commerce Cloud, and Heroku, to support cross-cloud application and customization development. Today, the `sf` application supports metadata and Salesforce Functions, although if the vision comes to fruition, the `sf` application will supersede the `sfdx` application. The `sf` release notes can be found here: `https://github.com/forcedotcom/cli/blob/main/releasenotes/sf`.
- **Debugging Extensions**: I mentioned this in Chapter 12, "Development," and I repeat it here for convenience. The Salesforce Extensions for Visual Studio Code includes three Apex code debuggers. (1) The Apex Replay Debugger requires no additional licenses. (2) The Apex Interactive Debugger requires Apex Debugger Sessions - Performance Edition and Unlimited Edition orgs come with a single Apex Debugger Session, and additional Apex Debugger Sessions can be purchased for those org editions and for Enterprise Edition orgs. (3) The ISV Customer Debugger comes with the Apex Interactive Debugger and allows ISVs to collaborate with customers to debug managed packages in customer sandboxes. We won't be covering these debuggers in this book; please refer to the Salesforce Extensions for Visual Studio Code documentation if you wish to explore further: `https://developer.salesforce.com/tools/vscode`.
- **CRM Analytics Extension**: If you develop for CRM Analytics (formerly Tableau CRM), the recommended method for pro-code development using Salesforce DX is to install the @salesforce/analytics plug-in for the Salesforce CLI, which we did not cover in the book. Search for "Salesforce Analytics CLI Plugin" to learn more.

- **Org Shapes**: On June 11, 2022, as part of the Summer '22 Salesforce release, this feature became generally available. It allows you to create scratch orgs with the correct features, settings, licenses, etc. Mimicking the "shape" of a production org can be a lengthy, error-prone experience. This Salesforce CLI feature allows you to create an Org Shape that mimics the production org shape, from which you can create multiple scratch orgs. This feature was omitted from the book.
- **Org Snapshots**: This Salesforce CLI feature is currently in an invitation-only pilot status and therefore not covered in the book. Org Snapshots capture the state of a scratch org, including its shape, installed metadata, installed packages, sample data, etc., so that other scratch orgs can be created from the Org Snapshot, rather than configuring each scratch org from scratch.
- **Alternative Org Authorizations**: Throughout the book, we used the `auth:web:login` command to authenticate our orgs, which uses the OAuth 2.0 web server flow. This type of OAuth 2.0 flow redirects a user to a login web page, which is not always convenient, such as when unattended DevOps pipelines are executing. There are other authorization types that were not explored, including an existing access token, a device code, a JSON Web Token (JWT), and an SFDX auth URL stored within a file.

That brings us to the end of the book; thank you for investing your time reading it! I've relished writing every one of the 13 chapters, and I've personally enriched my understanding of Salesforce DX on the way. I hope that if you are new to Salesforce DX, it has equipped you with the foundational skills and confidence to turbocharge your application or customization development. For seasoned practitioners, I trust that you have taken away a few nuggets of information to add to your existing knowledge.

Index

A

I. Harris, *Beginning Salesforce DX*, https://doi.org/10.1007/978-1-4842-8114-7

B

C

D

E

F

G

N

O

P, Q

R

S

T

Printed in the United States
by Baker & Taylor Publisher Services